CARSWELL

ONTARIO
EMPLOYMENT
STANDARDS
ACT

QUICK REFERENCE
2018 EDITION

Eric M. Roher, M.A., LL.B
and
Maciej Lipinski, Ph.D., J.D.

Borden Ladner Gervais LLP

THOMSON REUTERS®

A cataloguing record for this publication is available from Library and Archives Canada.

ISSN 1204-6736
ISBN 978-0-7798-7940-3 (2018 edition)

Printed in Canada by Thomson Reuters.

 THOMSON REUTERS®

TELL US HOW WE'RE DOING

Scan the QR code to the right with your smartphone to send your comments regarding our products and services.
Free QR Code Readers are available from your mobile device app store.
You can also email us at feedback.legaltaxcanada@tr.com

THOMSON REUTERS CANADA, A DIVISION OF THOMSON REUTERS CANADA

One Corporate Plaza	Customer Support
2075 Kennedy Road	1-416-609-3800 (Toronto & International)
Toronto, Ontario	1-800-387-5164 (Toll Free Canada & U.S.)
M1T 3V4	Fax 1-416-298-5082 (Toronto)
	Fax 1-877-750-9041 (Toll Free Canada Only)
	E-mail CustomerSupport.LegalTaxCanada@TR.com

DEDICATION

This edition is in memory of Melanie A. Warner, our former co-author, who we dearly miss.

ABOUT THE AUTHORS

Eric M. Roher, M.A., LL.B., is a partner with the law firm of Borden Ladner Gervais LLP and practices in the areas of employment law, labour relations and education law. He is the author of *Violence in the Workplace, Second Edition, A CLV Special Report*, released in 2004, author of *An Educator's Guide to Violence in Schools, Second Edition*, released in 2010 and co-author of *An Educator's Guide to the Role of the Principal, Second Edition*, released in 2008. Mr. Roher is an adjunct professor at the University of Toronto Faculty of Law. He advises employers on a range of labour relations and employment law issues including employment standards, termination of employment, unjust dismissal, employee discipline, human rights and workplace safety. Mr. Roher was admitted to the Ontario Bar in 1987.

Maciej Lipinski, Ph.D., J.D., is an associate with the law firm of Borden Ladner Gervais LLP and practices in the areas of employment law, labour relations and education law. Mr. Lipinski represents private and public sector employers and employees on all aspects of labour and employment law, including employee terminations, severance packages, employee discipline, employment policies and handbooks, employment standards, labour arbitrations, and human rights matters. He writes and advises on a wide range of issues, including employment standards, policies and contracts, wrongful dismissal claims, health and safety, and human rights issues. Mr. Lipinski is a graduate of Osgoode Hall Law School. He was admitted to the Ontario Bar in 2016.

SUMMARY TABLE OF CONTENTS

TABLE OF CONTENTS

Employment Standards Act, 2000
Part I — Definitions

Part II — Posting of Information Concerning Rights and Obligations

Part III — How this Act Applies

Part IV — Continuity of Employment

Part V — Payment of Wages

PART V.1— EMPLOYEE TIPS AND OTHER GRATUITIES

PART VI— RECORDS

PART VII — HOURS OF WORK AND EATING PERIODS

PART VIII — OVERTIME PAY

Part IX — Minimum Wage

Part X — Public Holidays

Part XI— Vacation with Pay

Part XXII — Complaints and Enforcement

Complaints

Enforcement under Collective Agreement

Enforcement by Employment Standards Officer

Settlements

Notices of Contravention

LIMITATION PERIOD

PART XXIII — REVIEWS BY THE BOARD
REVIEWS OF ORDERS

REFERRAL OF MATTER UNDER PART XIII

REVIEW OF NOTICE OF CONTRAVENTION

GENERAL PROVISIONS RESPECTING THE BOARD

PART XXIV — COLLECTION

COLLECTORS

PART XXV — OFFENCES AND PROSECUTIONS
OFFENCES

PART XXVI — MISCELLANEOUS EVIDENTIARY PROVISIONS

PART XXVII — REGULATIONS

PART XXVIII — TRANSITION, AMENDMENT, REPEALS, COMMENCEMENT AND SHORT TITLE

286/01 — Benefit Plans

287/01 — Building Services Providers

285/01 — Exemptions, Special Rules and Establishment of Minimum Wage

491/06 — TERMS AND CONDITIONS OF EMPLOYMENT IN DEFINED INDUSTRIES — AMBULANCE SERVICES

502/06 — TERMS AND CONDITIONS OF EMPLOYMENT IN DEFINED INDUSTRIES — AUTOMOBILE MANUFACTURING, AUTOMOBILE PARTS MANUFACTURING, AUTOMOBILE PARTS WAREHOUSING AND AUTOMOBILE MARSHALLING

160/05 — TERMS AND CONDITIONS OF EMPLOYMENT IN DEFINED INDUSTRIES — LIVE PERFORMANCES, TRADE SHOWS AND CONVENTIONS

159/05 — TERMS AND CONDITIONS OF EMPLOYMENT IN DEFINED INDUSTRIES — MINERAL EXPLORATION AND MINING

390/05 — TERMS AND CONDITIONS OF EMPLOYMENT IN DEFINED INDUSTRIES — PUBLIC TRANSIT SERVICES

RIGHTS AND RESPONSIBILITIES UNDER THE *EMPLOYMENT STANDARDS ACT, 2000*

Eric M. Roher and Maciej Lipinski, Borden Ladner Gervais LLP.

Introduction

The *Employment Standards Act, 2000* (*ESA, 2000*) is the primary piece of legislation governing Ontario's workplaces. It establishes minimum standards with respect to hours of work and overtime, vacation, public holidays, wages, specified leaves of absence, layoff, termination, severance, and other work related issues.

The Ontario Ministry of Labour administers the *ESA, 2000* and associated regulations by:

- promoting voluntary compliance;
- conducting proactive inspections of payroll records and workplace practices to ensure the *ESA, 2000* is being followed;
- investigating possible violations of the *ESA, 2000* and its regulations;
- resolving complaints; and
- enforcing the *ESA, 2000* and its regulations.

The most significant development in 2017 was the completion and publication of the *Final Report* of Ontario's "Changing Workplaces Review", and the subsequent passage of the *Fair Workplaces, Better Jobs Act, 2017* (also known as Bill 148).

Since its launch in February 2015, the Changing Workplaces Review involved a public consultation/engagement process regarding the changing nature of the modern workplace. Two special advisors with significant expertise and experience in the employment and labour law field were appointed and tasked with leading the Review: Michael Mitchell, formerly a lawyer at Sack Goldblatt Mitchell (now known as Goldblatt Partners LLP), and John Murray, a former justice of the Ontario Superior Court and prominent management-side labour lawyer. The Review examined workplace trends including: the rising prominence of the service sector, globalization and trade liberalization, accelerating technological change, greater workplace diversity, and the increase in non-standard working relationships such as temporary jobs, involuntary part-time work, and self-employment. The aim of the Review was to consider how the *ESA, 2000,* might be amended to best protect employees while also supporting businesses in a changing economy. A *Special Advisors' Interim Report* was prepared following the close of an initial round of submissions on September 18, 2015. In May 2017, the Government of Ontario received and then released the review's *Final Report,* which recommended instituting various changes to the *ESA, 2000,* including:

• Making personal emergency leave available to all employees in Ontario regardless of the number of workers employed by their workplace, and requiring employers to pay for any medical certificates required to verify employees' entitlement to this leave.

• Establishing measures to ensure that no employee is paid a lower rate than a comparable full-time employee of the same employer, except in certain circumstances where collective agreements or merit pay systems provide otherwise.

• Incorporating workers who are "dependent contractors" within the definition of "employee" under the *ESA, 2000,* thereby broadening the range of workers who are entitled to receive the employment standard minimums in the *ESA, 2000.*

• Increased fines for employers found to have violated the *ESA, 2000.*

On June 1, 2017, in response to the recommendations contained in the *Final Report*, Bill 148 was introduced and passed first reading in the Ontario Legislature. The bill was thereafter reviewed by the Standing Committee on Finance and Economic Affairs during the summer and fall of 2017. Bill 148 brings about various significant changes to Ontario's employment standards, including:

- An increase in the general minimum wage applicable to most employees to $14 per hour in 2018, and $15 per hour in 2019.
- New prohibitions against treating employees as non-employees (e.g., contractors).
- An increase in the minimum annual vacation time and vacation pay entitlement of employees who have worked with the same employer for five years or more.
- A broadened entitlement to various forms of job-protected leave, including personal emergency leave and family medical leave.
- New minimum entitlements for assignment employees employed by temporary help agencies, including provision of minimum notice or pay in lieu of notice where a long-term assignment is terminated earlier than previously estimated.
- New minimum entitlements for all employees subject to short-notice cancellation and shortening of scheduled shifts.

Bill 148 was passed by the Ontario Legislature on November 22, 2017 and received Royal Assent on November 27, 2017.

The Ontario Ministry of Labour also continued its proactive enforcement efforts in 2017, with the goal of ensuring that employers are complying with the *ESA, 2000* and educating employers about their obligations. The key sectors identified for provincial inspection blitzes (i.e., province-wide, sector-specific enforcement initiatives) in fiscal year 2017/2018 are: construction, transportation and warehousing, services to buildings and dwellings, and retail trade. Province-wide blitzes during this time period will have a special focus on employees' hours of work requirements. Smaller, regional inspection blitzes are also scheduled to take place in fiscal year 2017/2018 in the following sectors: independent grocery stores, shopping mall kiosks, professional services (e.g., dentists, law firms) and seasonal businesses. It would be prudent for employers in these sectors to review their policies, procedures and practices for compliance with the *ESA, 2000*, and correct any deficiencies, as soon as possible, to avoid any adverse consequences that might flow from an inspection.

This 2018 edition of the Ontario Employment Standards Act: Quick Reference will provide readers with an up-to-date guide to relevant legislation governing Ontario's workplaces including details on the significant amendments to the *ESA, 2000* arising from Bill 148.

No Contracting Out

The standards set out under the *ESA, 2000* are deemed to be minimum requirements only. These requirements are mandatory. In accordance with the *ESA, 2000*, no employer or employee may contract out of or waive an employment standard (for example, in an employment contract or policy), and any such attempt to contract out is null and void.

For example, in its 2017 decision in *Wood v. Fred Deeley Imports Ltd.*, 2017 CarswellOnt 2408, the Ontario Court of Appeal found that an employee's termination clause was void and unenforceable where the clause stated that "the Company shall not be obliged to make any payments to you other than those provided for in this paragraph", but did not include reference to *all* of an employee's termination-related entitlements under the *ESA, 2000*. As this case illustrates, Courts may take a strict approach to ensuring that terms in employment contracts do not open the door to employees receiving less than their minimum entitlements under the *ESA, 2000*. As such, careful drafting of employment contracts is essential, as even the inadvertent exclusion of a minimum entitlement may cause a contractual provision to be rendered void, unenforceable, or to be otherwise construed against an employer by a Court.

Greater Right or Benefit

Although the workplace parties are not allowed to waive the minimum employment standards in the *ESA, 2000*, they are certainly allowed to *exceed* these standards. Accordingly, where an employment contract or collective agreement provides for improved benefits (such as a higher salary than minimum wage, fewer hours of work, a longer vacation, higher percentage of vacation pay, increased termination or severance pay, etc.), these improved benefits will prevail.

It can sometimes be difficult to tell whether an employment contract or collective agreement actually provides for an improved benefit over the *ESA, 2000*. The Ministry of Labour takes the position that one should review the entire package related to the standard, including monetary and non-monetary aspects, as well as the stringency of any qualifying conditions (for example, see "Personal Emergency Leave").

An employer may not rely on a greater benefit in respect of one standard to offset a lesser benefit in respect of another standard. For example, an employer who provides longer vacations with pay than the *ESA, 2000* requires will not be permitted to off-set this benefit by paying less than minimum wage.

Who is Covered by the *ESA, 2000*

Most provincially regulated employers and employees conducting business in Ontario are covered by the *ESA, 2000*.

Section 3(1) of the legislation provides that it applies if: (a) the employee's work is to be performed in Ontario, or (b) the work is to be performed both in Ontario and outside Ontario but the work performed outside Ontario is a continuation of the work performed in Ontario. If the employee's work in Ontario is merely a continuation of the work performed in another jurisdiction, however, then the laws of the other jurisdiction may apply rather than the *ESA, 2000*. In some situations, there may also be dual jurisdiction for employment standards purposes. For example, an employee performing equal amounts of work in both Ontario and Newfoundland may be subject to both the *ESA, 2000* and Newfoundland's employment standards legislation.

The following factors are not relevant to whether the *ESA, 2000* applies:

- where the offer of employment was made or accepted;
- where the contract of employment was signed;
- where the employee resides;
- where the head office of the employer is located;
- where the wages are to be paid; or
- where the employer is incorporated.

Employees and employers who are specifically identified as not covered by the *ESA, 2000* at all include, *inter alia*, the following:

- employees and employers engaged in operations that fall within the federal jurisdiction, and are therefore governed (in respect of employment matters) by the *Canada Labour Code*. (This would include operations such as airlines, banks, the federal civil service, post offices, radio and television stations, and railways);

- secondary school students working in a work experience program authorized by their school board;

- college or university students, including students at private career colleges registered under the *Private Career Colleges Act, 2005*, working under a program approved by the institution;

- individuals performing community participation under the *Ontario Works Act, 1997*;

- police officers (except with respect to the provisions relating to lie detector tests);
- employees of embassies or consulates of foreign nations;
- inmates taking part in work programs, including those performing work pursuant to an order, sentence, or extra-judicial measure under the *Youth Criminal Justice Act*; and
- people who hold political, judicial, religious or trade union offices.

As of January 1, 2018, following changes made under Bill 148, all provisions of the *ESA, 2000* will apply to Crown employees, including the provisions dealing with equal pay for equal work, benefit plans, leaves of absence, termination and severance of employment, lie detectors, and building service providers.

The *ESA, 2000* does not apply between an independent contractor and the person who receives that contractor's services. As set out in the Supreme Court of Canada decision in *671122 Ontario Ltd. v. Sagaz Industries Canada Inc.*, the distinction between an employee and an independent contractor depends on various factors that go toward determining whether an individual is working on their own account or under the control and direction of an employer. Recognizing that the two categories of workers sometimes overlap, the Ontario Court of Appeal decision in *McKee v. Reid's Heritage Homes Ltd.* also recognized a third category of "dependent contractors" who are entitled to the benefit of reasonable notice under common law but not under the *ESA, 2000*.

The *Changing Workplaces Review* devoted close attention to the issue of workers being misclassified as contractors not entitled to the minimum standards under the *ESA, 2000* despite working under a level of control that could render them as employees by law. Out of concern that misclassification may be used by potential employers to avoid providing workers with entitlements under the *ESA, 2000*, the special advisors recommended increased proactive enforcement to identify cases of misclassification and introducing a "dependent contractor" category of worker to be covered by entitlements under the *ESA, 2000*. Bill 148 has made amendments that adopt only the former recommendation by enabling the Ministry of Labour to adopt a more proactive approach to identifying cases where employees' rights have been limited through their misclassification as contractors — but without including "dependent contractors" as a class of workers covered by the *ESA, 2000*. That is, as of 2018, a new Section 5.1 of the *ESA, 2000* makes it a contravention for an employer to treat a worker acting as an employee as if the worker was not an employee (i.e., treating an employee as an independent or dependent contractor). Where an employment standards officer in the course of an investigation or inspection raises this issue, an employer will have the burden of proving that its workers have been properly classified. Accordingly, beginning in 2018, employers who maintain a non-employee workforce will benefit from carefully documenting the basis for this classification, in the event that it is challenged by a Ministry inspector.

The *ESA, 2000*, in subsection 3(6), also deals with the concept of an employee who performs dual roles. Where an employee performs work that is excluded from the application of the *ESA, 2000*, as well as work to which the *ESA, 2000* applies, the *ESA, 2000* will apply to that individual and his or her employer to the extent of the included work.

Other categories of employees are subject to special rules or specific exemptions from some, but not all, of the *ESA, 2000* provisions. The *ESA, 2000*, Regulation 285/01 and other relevant regulations should be consulted in each case.

It is important to note that exemptions for teachers apply only to those employed "as a teacher as defined in the *Teaching Profession Act*". The *Teaching Profession Act* defines a "teacher" in section 1 as follows:

> "teacher" means a person who is a member of the Ontario College of Teachers and is employed by a board as a teacher

but does not include a supervisory officer, a principal, a vice-principal or an instructor in a teacher-training institution.

This definition means that teachers who teach at a private/independent school (which is not a "board") are not caught by the exemption. These teachers are therefore entitled to all of the protections of the *ESA, 2000*.

Agreements to Vary From Certain Employment Standards

The *ESA, 2000* permits employers and employees to make agreements to vary the statutory minimum standard in some instances. Areas where parties are permitted to do this include the following:

- to exceed the daily and/or weekly hours of work limits;
- to average hours of work for the purpose of determining overtime entitlements;
- to compensate an employee for overtime hours with paid time off rather than with overtime pay; and
- to take vacation time in increments of less than one week.

Employers and employees should be careful when drafting agreements to vary the above standards, in order to ensure that they are enforceable. Subsection 1(3) provides, for example, that the above-mentioned types of agreements must be in writing. In addition, one should consider the following guidelines regarding agreements to vary:

- Electronic agreements (i.e., through electronic mail correspondence) may be valid, provided the employee has done a positive act to demonstrate his or her agreement, such as replying to the electronic mail. It is not appropriate for an employer to send an electronic mail to the employee which provides, for example, "If you do not respond, you will be deemed to have agreed to this arrangement.": subsection 1(3.1)
- Generally speaking, an agreement will only be valid if it covers future arrangements. In rare circumstances, an agree-

ment may have retrospective effect, such as where the agreement does not purport to "undo" a violation of an employment standard, the agreement is not inconsistent with the intent of the legislation, or it is not possible to enter into the agreement before the relevant event.

• Written agreements should be signed by both parties as evidence that they both intended to enter into the agreement. However, if both parties have not signed the agreement, it may be possible to adduce other evidence that both parties consented to the arrangement, such as notes or drafts signed or sent by a party.

• Agreements should be clear and specific. Ambiguous agreements may not be enforceable. The following information should be included in all agreements:

(i) the names of the parties;

(ii) the date the agreement was entered into;

(iii) the effective date of the agreement;

(iv) the expiry date of the agreement;

(v) the employment standard that is being varied from;

(vi) the arrangement that is replacing the employment standard; and

(vii) the signatures of each party to the agreement.

• Certain types of agreements (such as excess hours of work agreements and agreements to average hours of work for the purpose of calculating overtime pay) may have specific statutory requirements. These are addressed under their respective subject headings herein.

• Both parties to the agreement must know and understand its contents and the consequences of entering into the agreement. This is known as "informed consent". The best way to make sure both parties have "informed consent" is to make the agreement clear and accurate. Employers can also help to ensure employees are fully informed by directing them to the Ministry of Labour or providing them with information published by the Ministry of Labour. Informed consent may not exist where:

(i) the employee did not read the agreement and was told he or she had to sign the agreement as a condition of the job;

(ii) the employee cannot read and the agreement was not read to the employee before he or she signed it;

(iii) the employee does not understand the language the agreement was drafted in, and the agreement was not translated or read to the employee in a language he or she can understand;

(iv) the employer simply informed the employee that he or she was bound by the terms contained in an employee handbook, without ensuring that the employee read and understood the provisions in the handbook; or

(v) an important term is not prominent or easily readable on the agreement.

• An agreement will not be valid if the employee was coerced or forced to sign it. This may occur where:

(i) the employer threatened to fire the employee;

(ii) the employer threatened to reduce the employee's hours or rate of pay; or

(iii) the employer penalized the employee's co-workers because they had refused to enter into the agreement, and the employee entered into the agreement to avoid being similarly penalized.

Payroll Administration

Section 11 of the *ESA, 2000* requires employers to establish a regular, recurring pay period and a regular, recurring pay day.

The regular pay day could be weekly, bi-weekly, semi-monthly, monthly, or any other specified period. An employer may establish recurring pay days for different employees, and/or for different components of the wage package (such as sales commissions, overtime pay, etc.).

The requirement to establish a recurring pay period and pay day does not prevent the employer from subsequently establishing a new and different pay period or pay day. (However, employers should always be mindful of the risk of constructive dismissal, if such change represents a substantial change to a fundamental term of the employment contract.)

Section 11 of the *ESA, 2000* also permits employers to choose between three different methods of paying wages to employees:

- by cash (provided the cash is given to the employee at the workplace or some other place agreeable to the employee);
- by cheque (provided the cheque is given to the employee at the workplace or some other place agreeable to the employee); or
- by direct deposit, provided:

(i) the account is in the employee's name;

(ii) no person other than the employee, or someone authorized by the employee, has access to the account; and

(iii) unless the employee agrees otherwise, an office or facility of the employee's financial institution is located within a reasonable distance from the workplace.

Under amendments made in Bill 148, additional methods of payment may be established through regulations by the Government of Ontario. No such additional methods have been prescribed at the time of this publication.

The Ministry of Labour takes the position that an employer may make having a suitable direct deposit account a condition of hire, and where an employee is subsequently directed to open an account and refuses, the employer may terminate his or her employment, since there is no right under the *ESA, 2000* not to open an account or to not be paid by direct deposit. (The employer would, however, be obliged to comply with the termination and severance provisions of the legislation.)

Protection of Tips

The *ESA, 2000* defines a "tip or other gratuity" provided to an employee in the course of employment as:

• a payment voluntarily made to or left for an employee by a customer of the employee's employer in such circumstances that a reasonable person would be likely to infer that the customer intended or assumed that the payment would be kept by the employee or shared by the employee with other employees;

• a payment voluntarily made to an employer by a customer in such circumstances that a reasonable person would be likely to infer that the customer intended or assumed that the payment would be redistributed to an employee or employees; and

• a payment of a service charge or similar charge imposed by an employer on a customer in such circumstances that a reasonable person would be likely to infer that the customer intended or assumed that the payment would be redistributed to an employee or employees.

Bill 12, *Protecting Employees' Tips Act, 2015*, came into force on June 10, 2016. As a result of this legislation, employers cannot withhold employee tips or require employees to give their tips to the employer unless there is an arrangement for the pooling and distribution of tips among employees. In general, an employer cannot receive any portion of the tips that are shared in such a pooling arrangement. However, an employer may receive part of a pool of tips if the employer also performs a "substantial degree of the same work" performed by their employees. As set out by the new provisions, tips include any amounts that "a reasonable person would likely infer" as being intended for redistribution to employees — which may include service charges imposed by the employer but does not include charges specifically for processing credit card payments.

Statement of Wages

There are strict rules in the *ESA, 2000* regarding the provision of a statement of wages to employees. Section 12 provides that, on or before each pay day, the employer must provide employees with a written statement setting out the following:

• the pay period for which the wages are being paid;

• the wage rate, if there is one;

• the gross amount of wages, and how that amount was calculated (unless the manner of calculation has been communicated to the employee in some other fashion);

• the amount and purpose of each deduction from wages;

• any amount with respect to the provision of room and board by an employer that is deemed to have been paid to the employee pursuant to the *ESA, 2000*; and

• the net amount of wages.

Subsection 12(3) of the *ESA, 2000* permits an employer to provide the employee with a statement of wages by electronic mail rather than in paper copy, as long as the employee has access to a means of making a paper copy.

Statement of Wages on Termination

Employers must provide employees with a statement of wages when their employment ends: section 12.1.

The statement of wages must be provided to employees by the later of:

• seven days after the employment ends; and

• the day that would have been the employee's next regular pay day.

The statement of wages must include the following information:

• the gross amount of any termination pay and severance pay being provided to the employee and (unless this information is provided in some other way) how this amount is calculated;

• the gross amount of any vacation pay being paid to the employee and (unless this information is provided in some other way), how this amount is calculated;

• the pay period for which any wages (other than termination pay, severance pay and vacation pay) are being paid;

• the wage rate, if there is one;

• the gross amount of any wages (other than termination pay, severance pay and vacation pay) being paid to the employee and (unless this information is provided in some other way) how this amount is calculated;

• the amount and purpose of each deduction from wages;

• any amount with respect to room or board that is deemed to have been paid to the employee; and

• the net amount of any wages being paid to the employee.

Deductions from Wages

Section 13 of the *ESA, 2000* provides that there are only three circumstances in which an employer can deduct from, withhold, or require the return of wages:

• pursuant to a federal or Ontario statute or court order;

• where the employee has provided written authorization to do so, *provided*:

(i) the employee's authorization refers to a specific amount or a specific formula for calculating an amount;

(ii) the employee's wages are not being deducted from, or withheld, or required to be returned:

1. because of faulty work or

2. because the employer had a cash shortage, lost property, or had property stolen, and someone other than the employee had access to the cash or property; and

15

• the employee is required to return wages, and an order has been made for the return of those wages under the *ESA, 2000*.

The most common statutory deductions from wages are income tax, Canada Pension Plan contributions and Employment Insurance premiums.

With respect to deductions taken for failure to return the employer's property, the Ontario Court of Appeal has affirmed that contractual language requiring an employee to return the employer's property will not suffice to allow the employer to make such a deduction from wages. As set out in *Gill v. CPNI Inc.*, 2015 CarswellOnt 18118, the employer may only make such a deduction where the employment contract specifically provides for a deduction from wages where the employer's property is not returned.

Notwithstanding the above, it would appear from the case law that employers may deduct wages paid in error in the past from an employee's subsequent pay cheque. The reasoning is that when an employee is overpaid, he or she was never entitled to that amount in the first place, so it cannot be regarded as "wages".

Priority of Claims

Subsection 14(1) of the *ESA, 2000* provides that the amount of an employee's entitlement to wages, in preference to other unsecured creditors, is $10,000, subject to any federal legislation respecting bankruptcy or insolvency. As determined by the 2017 Ontario Labour Relations Board decision in *Tire To Go Inc. v. Fatehbasharzad*, 2017 CarswellOnt 6397 (Ont. L.R.B.), wages protected under subsection 14(1) are considered as being separate and apart from any outstanding loans that may have been made by an employee to their employer.

Record Keeping

The *ESA, 2000* requires employers to collect and keep certain records pertaining to employees. Section 15 of the *ESA,*

2000 provides that an employer must record the following specific types of information:

- the employee's name and address;
- if the employee is a student under the age of 18, the employee's date of birth;
- the date on which the employee began his or her employment;
- the number of hours worked each day and each week;
- the information contained in each statement of wages, statement of wages provided on termination, and statement of vacation pay (if the employee is paid vacation pay as it accrues, and a statement of vacation pay is provided separately from the statement of wages, in accordance with subsection 36(3)(b); and
- all vacation time earned and taken by the employee, in accordance with Section 15.1.

Under Bill 148, the following additional types of information will also be required to be kept by employers as of January 1, 2018:

- The dates and times that the employee worked.
- If the employee has two or more regular rates of pay for work performed for the employer and, in a work week, the employee performed work for the employer in excess of the overtime threshold, the dates and times that the employee worked in excess of the overtime threshold at each rate of pay.

Bill 148 will also require employees to keep records of the following as of January 1, 2019:

- The dates and times that the employee was scheduled to work or to be on call for work, and any changes made to the on call schedule.
- Cancellations of a scheduled day of work or scheduled on call period of the employee and the date and time of the cancellation.

The employer need not include information about the number of hours worked by the employee in each day and each week or, following Bill 148, the dates and times that the employee worked if the employee is paid a salary and:

• the employer records any hours in excess of those in the employee's regular work week; and

(i) the employer records the number of hours in excess of eight that the employee worked in each day; or

(ii) the employer records the number of hours in excess of the number of hours in the employee's regular work day, if the regular work day is in excess of eight hours; or

• the employee is exempt from the hours of work and overtime provisions of the *ESA, 2000*.

Under subsection 15(5) of the *ESA, 2000*, information pertaining to employees must generally be kept for three years, as follows:

• the employee's name, address and start date must be kept for three years after the employee ceases to be employed;

• if the employee is a student and under the age of 18, the employee's date of birth must be kept until the earlier of:

(i) three years after the employee's 18th birthday; and

(ii) three years after the employee ceases to be employed;

• the number of hours worked in each day and week (if the employee is paid on an hourly basis), or the number of excess hours worked in each day and week (if the employee receives a salary and is not exempt from the hours of work and overtime provisions of the *ESA, 2000*), as well as the additional information required under Bill 148 concerning the dates and times when work was completed or cancelled, must be kept for three years after the day or week to which the information relates;

• the employee's statements of wages and any statements of vacation pay must be kept for three years after the information was given to the employee; and

• a record of the amount of vacation time taken and earned by the employee must be kept for three years after that record was made. Bill 148 extends this period to 5 years as of January 1, 2018.

Employers are also required, by subsection 15(7) of the *ESA, 2000*, to retain or cause to be retained by a third party, all documents relating to an employee's statutory leave of absence under the *ESA, 2000* for three years after the day on which the leave expired.

The employer must ensure that all of the records and documents that the employer is required to retain are readily available for inspection, if necessary, by an employment standards officer, even if the employer has arranged for a third party to retain the records: section 16.

If any of these records are maintained in electronic form, then, in accordance with the *Electronic Commerce Act, 2000*, such electronic documents must be organized in substantially the same way as the paper documents they replace, and must be accessible and capable of being printed and retained by their intended recipient. These recipients may include employees to whom the documents pertain, or an employment standards officer investigating an employer's compliance with the *ESA, 2000*.

Equal Pay for Equal Work

Following from amendments made under Bill 148 that take effect as of April 1, 2018, Sections 42, 42.1, and 42.2 of the *ESA, 2000* will require employers to ensure equal rates of pay to employees who:

• are performing substantially the same kind of work in the same establishment, which need not be identical work;

• perform work that requires substantially the same skill, effort and responsibility; and

• perform this work under similar working conditions.

Where the above conditions are met, the amended *ESA, 2000* prohibits paying differing rates of pay to such employees where the difference is based on (i) the respective sex of the employees; (ii) the respective "employment status" of the employees (as defined below), or (iii) the fact that one employee is employed by a temporary help agency and the other is employed directly by the agency's client.

As of April 1, 2018, the *ESA, 2000* will include the following definition of "employment status":

(a) a difference in the number of hours regularly worked by the employees (e.g., part-time or full-time); or

(b) a difference in the term of their employment, including a difference in permanent, temporary, seasonal or casual status;

Accordingly, under the amendments made by Bill 148, employers must pay equal rates to employees performing substantially the same work, regardless of whether employees' status is part-time, full-time, permanent, temporary, seasonal or otherwise distinguishable on the basis of "employment status" as defined above. There is one exception to this requirement, which applies to pay differences based on employment status that are provided for in a collective agreement made or renewed prior to April 1, 2018. Where such collective agreement terms have been entered into, an employer will not be required to ensure equal pay for equal work based on the employment status of the affected employees until a new collective agreement is entered into with those employees.

Where a difference in rates of pay is contrary to the *ESA, 2000*, employers are prohibited from remedying the difference through a reduction in any employee's rate of pay. In other words, remedying a contravention of equal pay for equal work provisions under the *ESA, 2000* requires increasing the rate of pay of the employee receiving the lower rate of pay.

An employer is, however, permitted under subsections 42(2), and 42,1(2) of the *ESA, 2000* to provide different rates of pay to employees of different sex or employment status when the difference results from:

- a seniority system;
- a merit system;
- a system that measures earnings by quantity or quality of production; or
- any factor other than sex or employment status.

With respect to temporary help agencies, such agencies must ensure that their employees receive equal pay relative to employees of the client who perform substantially the same work under similar working conditions. According to subsections 42(3), 42.1(3), and 42.2(3) of the *ESA, 2000*, as legislated under Bill 148, an employer temporary help agency and clients of temporary help agencies are prohibited from reducing the wages of their employee in order to comply with their obligations to provide equal pay for equal work.

A temporary help agency is permitted, under subsection 42.2(2) of the *ESA, 2000*, to differentiate between employees of the agency and employees of the client where such difference is based on a factor other than an employee's sex, employment status or status as an assignment employee.

As of April 1, 2018, following from amendments to the *ESA, 2000* made under Bill 148, employees who believe that their rate of pay does not comply with the above requirements may request a review of their rate of pay by their employer, including an employer temporary help agency. In response to such a request, an employer is required carry out a review that results in either (i) adjustment of the requesting employee's rate of pay to accord with the *ESA, 2000* (i.e., raise the rate paid to the employee to ensure equal pay with another employee performing substantially the same work); or (ii) providing the employee written reasons concerning why the employer disagrees with the employee.

Where an employment standards officer finds that any employer, including a temporary help agency, has violated the equal pay for equal work provisions of the *ESA, 2000*, the officer has the power to find that an employee is owed unpaid wages corresponding to the difference between the amount of remuneration paid and the amount required to be compliant with the *ESA, 2000*.

Benefit Plans

Part XIII of the *ESA, 2000* prohibits employers from treating certain enumerated groups of employees differently because of age, sex, or marital status, in respect of benefit plans.

Ontario Regulation 286/01 sets out exceptions, for which some level of differentiation is permissible. Permissible differentiation is allowed, in certain circumstances, under pension plans, life insurance plans, disability benefit plans, health benefit plans and during certain leaves of absence.

Posting of Information Concerning Rights and Obligations

Section 2 of the *ESA, 2000* requires that the employer post certain prescribed information in the workplace. Such information shall be prepared by the Ministry, and may describe the rights of employees and obligations of employers, and other details about the *ESA, 2000*.

According to subsection 2(3) of the *ESA, 2000*, if the majority language of a workplace is not English, the employer must contact the Ministry to enquire whether the Ministry has prepared a translation of the prescribed information into the applicable language. If the Ministry has prepared such a translation, the employer is required to post both the English version and the translation in the workplace.

Ontario Regulation 316/04 (Posting of Information Concerning Rights and Obligations) provides that the materials that must be posted consist of a single poster prepared by the Ministry of Labour entitled "What You Should Know About The Ontario Employment Standards Act".

The poster must be printed out on legal-size paper (8.5 x 14 inches). It can be printed in colour or black and white. It is available on the Ministry of Labour website, through ServiceOntario Publications, or at ServiceOntario Centres.

In May 2015, the Ministry of Labour published an updated version (version 6.0) of the "What You Should Know About The Ontario Employment Standards Act" poster. Employers should remove any earlier versions of this poster and replace them with version 6.0. If the majority language of a workplace is a language other than English, and the Ministry has published a version of the poster in that language, then the employer is required to post a copy of the translated version of the poster next to the English version of the poster. Currently, version 6.0 of the poster is available in the following languages: English, French, Arabic, Chinese (Simplified or Traditional), Hindi, Portuguese, Punjabi, Spanish, Tagalog, Thai, and Urdu.

As of May 20, 2015, every employer must provide each of its employees with a copy of the most recent poster. The poster must be provided to new employees within 30 days after their start date. Employees who were hired before May 20, 2015 should have been provided with the poster by June 19, 2015.

Sale of Business and Continuity of Employment

Subsection 9(1) of the *ESA, 2000* provides for continuity of employment when there is a sale of a business and the purchaser employs an employee of the seller. In particular, the employee is deemed not to have had his or her employment terminated for the purposes of the *ESA, 2000*, and his or her length of employment with the seller is included in any subsequent calculation of length of employment with the purchaser. This is significant when calculating entitlements to vacation (employees may be entitled to two or three weeks' vacation with pay, depending on their length of service after completing each 12-month vacation entitlement year); certain types of leave, notice of termination or pay in lieu thereof, and severance pay.

Subsection 9(1) will not apply if there is a gap of more than 13 weeks between the employee's last day with the seller or the date of sale (whichever is earlier) and the employee's first day with the purchaser.

Although not expressly stated in the *ESA, 2000*, the Ministry of Labour has taken the position that the effect of section 9 is to transfer any liability for employees' accrued but unused vacation pay from the seller to the purchaser at the time of sale.

Note that Section 9 of the *ESA, 2000* does not require a purchaser to hire employees of the seller. The purchaser can elect to hire some, all, or none of the seller's employees. Where the purchaser does hire an employee of the seller, the offer of employment may be made on whatever terms and conditions the purchaser chooses, subject to these provisions of the *ESA, 2000*.

Associated or Related Businesses

Section 4 of the *ESA, 2000* provides that an employer and an entity that carries on an associated or related activity or business will be treated as a single employer. As of January 2018, following amendments under Bill 148, this treatment would apply to such entities *regardless* of whether the intent or effect of them carrying on an activity/business separately directly or indirectly defeats the intent or purpose of the *ESA, 2000*. In other words, separate entities need only carry on "associated or related activities" in order to be considered common employers under the *ESA, 2000*. Crown employer entities, however, are exempt from this provision.

In determining whether the "associated or related" test is met, the following criteria will be considered (in descending order of significance):

- common management;
- common financial control;
- common ownership;
- existence of common trade name or logo;

- movement of employees between two or more entities;
- use of the same assets by two or more entities, or transfer of assets between them; and
- common market or customers served by the two or more entities.

This list is not exhaustive; there may be other relevant factors in the context of a particular case. It should also be noted that it is not necessary for all of the factors to be present in order for a finding of relatedness or association to be made.

It is important to note that the activities need not be carried on at the same time. Corporation A and Corporation B may be treated as one employer even if Corporation B did not start carrying on business until such time as Corporation A ceased to do so.

Some examples of situations where this issue arises include the following:

- A growing business is carried on through a number of small corporations, in an attempt to avoid the $2.5 million payroll threshold giving rise to severance pay obligations;
- A corporation closes down its business in an attempt to avoid the claims of its creditors, and re-starts under a second corporation. The first corporation still legally exists, but is dormant. The second corporation has the same management and ownership, and performs the same or similar operations as the first corporation using funds diverted from the old corporation;
- A corporation becomes insolvent and its employees are dismissed. Its parent corporation, which controls its operations, is not insolvent;
- An employee works for one corporation for several years, and then transfers to its sister corporation. The employee is terminated shortly thereafter; and

Employees regularly move between two corporations owned by the same shareholder, which perform similar activities. Employees work several hours per week at one corporation, and several hours per week at the other corporation. Cumulatively, the employee's hours exceed 44 hours in a week.

In each of the above examples, the two corporations may be treated as one employer, such that either or both will be responsible for satisfying *ESA, 2000* obligations to employees.

In a 2011 case decided by the OLRB, *Repower Automotive Services Inc.* (Dec. 21, 2011) Doc. 70056891-6[2011] O.E.S.A.D. No. 1676 (Ont. L.R.B.), this concept of associated or related businesses was explored. The employee began working for a company called Reman in 2007. That same year, Reman started to experience serious financial difficulties. The owner's spouse started a new company called Repower, which supplied many of the same products as Reman, operated out of the same address, and shared the same equipment. Moreover, employees of Reman allegedly worked for Repower, and the two companies had common banking arrangements for a period of time. One day, the employee advised Reman that he was unable to report for work because his son was sick. Reman told him to report for work immediately. The employee refused and was dismissed. He sought termination pay from Reman, but because Reman was insolvent by this point, his only avenue for obtaining compensation was from Repower, if it could be found that they were associated or related businesses.

The OLRB found that Reman and Repower were associated or related businesses. They were under common management, had the same directing mind, common financial control, common employees, shared premises and the same customer base. The OLRB concluded that the employee "was nominally employed by Reman but that Repower had the benefit of [his] labour".

Retail Business Establishments

Part XVII of the *ESA, 2000* contains special rules pertaining to most retail establishments. A retail establishment is a business that sells goods or services to the public, but does not include those whose primary retail business is to:

• sell prepared meals (i.e., restaurants, cafeterias, cafés);

• rent living accommodations (i.e., hotels, tourist resorts, camps, inns);

• provide educational, recreational or amusement services to the public (i.e., museums, art galleries, sports stadiums); and

• sell goods and services that are incidental to the businesses described above and are located on the same premises (i.e., museum gift shops, souvenir shops in sports stadiums).

The rules in this section focus on when an employee in a retail business establishment can refuse to work. Specifically, section 73 of the *ESA, 2000* provides that such employees may refuse to work:

• on a public holiday (as defined in the *ESA, 2000*);

• on a day declared to be a holiday under the *Retail Business Holidays Act*; and

• on a Sunday.

Special Public Holiday Rules

Retail workers covered by this section have the right to refuse to work on public holidays. Where the public holiday falls on a day that would ordinarily be a working day, retail workers qualify for the public holiday off work, and for public holiday pay. Where the public holiday falls on a day that would ordinarily not be a working day, or the employee is on vacation, retail workers qualify for a substitute day off and public holiday pay.

If a retail worker agrees to work on a public holiday, he or she may subsequently decline to work on that day, provided he or she gives the employer at least 48 hours notice in advance of when the employee was scheduled to commence work: subsection 73(3).

Special Sunday Work Rules — Employees Hired Before September 4, 2001

Retail workers hired before September 4, 2001, have the right to refuse to work on Sundays. If the employee previously agreed to work on Sundays, either at the time of commencing work or thereafter, the employee may subsequently decline to work Sundays upon giving the employer at least 48 hours notice in advance of when the employee was scheduled to commence work: subsection 73(3).

Special Sunday Work Rules — Employees Hired After September 4, 2001

Retail workers hired after September 4, 2001, have a more limited right to refuse to work on Sundays than retail workers hired before September 4, 2001.

Retail workers who did not agree in writing at the time of being hired (on or after September 4, 2001) may refuse to work on Sundays. If the employee agrees to work on a Sunday and later changes his or her mind, he or she must provide the employer with 48 hours' advance notice.

However, retail workers who did agree in writing at the time of being hired (on or after September 4, 2001) to work on Sundays may not subsequently refuse to work on Sundays, unless the refusal is for reasons of religious belief or religious observance: Ontario Regulation 285/01, section 10.

Employers should pay careful attention to the interaction of these provisions and the Ontario *Human Rights Code* (the "*Code*"). Ontario Regulation 285/01 forbids employers from making work on Sundays a condition of employment, if such a condition would violate section 11 of the *Code*, which provides:

A right of a person under Part I is infringed where a requirement, qualification or factor exists that is not discrimination on a prohibited ground but that results in

28

the exclusion, restriction or preference of a group of persons who are identified by a prohibited ground of discrimination and of whom the person is a member, except where,

(a) the requirement, qualification or factor is reasonable and *bona fide* in the circumstances; or

(b) it is declared in this Act, other than in section 17, that to discriminate because of such ground is not an infringement of a right.

In other words, employers are prohibited from requiring all employees to work on Sundays if this adversely affects employees of certain religious backgrounds and *unless* the requirement to work Sunday is an essential requirement of the job. Employers and employees are encouraged to consult the *Code* and the Ontario Human Rights Commission for further information about these obligations.

Employees of a retail business establishment do not, as a rule, have to explain why they choose not to work on a public holiday or a Sunday.

Hours of Work

The general rule under the *ESA, 2000* is that employers may not require or permit hours of work exceeding eight hours in a day (or the number of hours in an established regular work day that is longer than eight hours), and 48 hours in a work week: section 17(1).

There are however, exceptions to these basic hours of work rules.
The exceptions are as follows:

• **Excess Daily Hours:** An employee can work up to a specified number of hours in excess of the daily maximum if he or she agrees in writing to do so: section 17(2). The agreement is not valid unless the employer has, before the agreement is made, given the employee a copy of a document prepared by the Director of Employment Standards that describes the rights of employees and obligations of employers under the hours of work and overtime pay provisions: section 17(5). The agreement can be revoked by the employee with two weeks' written notice and by the employer with reasonable notice: sections 17(6) and (7). Agreements to work excess daily hours can specify the exact number of hours that the employee is agreeing to work, the exact number of hours over and above the daily limit, or an upper limit (such as "up to 10 hours in a day"). In addition, the parties may enter into either single-occasion agreements (where the employee agrees to work excess daily hours on one occasion, such as during the Christmas season), or as-required agreements (where the employee agrees to work a specified number of excess daily hours whenever required by the employer).

• **Excess Weekly Hours:** An employee can work up to a specified number of hours in excess of the weekly 48 hours maximum if he or she agrees in writing to do so and the employer has applied for and been issued an approval by the Director of Employment Standards: section 17(3). The agreement can be revoked by the employee with two weeks' written notice and by the employer with reasonable notice: sections 17(6) and (7). The employee's agreement is not valid unless the employer has, before the agreement is made, given the employee a copy of a document prepared by the Director of Employment Standards that describes the rights of employees and obligations of employers under the hours of work and overtime pay provisions: section 17(5). If an employer has applied for an approval but has not yet received either an approval or a refusal from the Director within 30 days, an employee can begin working more than 48 hours in a work week, up to the lesser of 60 hours, the number of hours specified in the agreement, and the number of hours specified in the application, if certain conditions are met: section 17(4). Agreements to work excess weekly hours can specify the exact number of hours that the employee is agreeing to work, the exact number of hours over and above the daily limit, or an upper limit (such as "up to 60 hours in a week"). In addition, the parties may enter into either single-occasion agreements (where the employee agrees to work excess weekly hours for a specified period, such as during the Christmas season), or as-required agreements (where the employee agrees to work a specified number of excess weekly hours whenever required by the employer).

An employee who was hired on or after September 4, 2001, and who agreed in writing at the time of hiring to work hours in excess of the daily maximum cannot unilaterally withdraw from that agreement, even with two weeks' notice, if the Director of Employment Standards approved the agreement: Ontario Regulation 285/01, section 32. Employees who are parties to such approved agreements cannot be required to work more than 10 hours in a day, except in "exceptional circumstances" [see below]: section 141(9).

An employee who was hired prior to September 4, 2001, and who entered into an arrangement at or before the time of hiring that provided that he or she would work excess hours upon request cannot unilaterally withdraw from that arrangement, even with two weeks' notice, if the employer had received a "gold" permit under section 18 of the former *ESA*, and so long as the employee is not required to work more than 10 hours in a day: Ontario Regulation 285/01, section 32.1.

As indicated above, an employer may revoke an excess hours agreement on "reasonable notice". This term is not defined in the legislation. What is reasonable depends upon each employee's individual circumstances.

It is very important to note that an excess hours agreement is not valid unless the employee specifically consents to the arrangement in writing. If the employee does not agree in writing to work extra hours, the employer cannot force him or her to do so, unless the employee is otherwise exempt from the hours of work provisions or the *ESA, 2000*.

An excess hours agreement should be specific. The agreement should state that the employee is agreeing to work in excess of eight hours in a day and/or 48 hours in a week. The agreement should also specify the exact or maximum number of hours that the employee is agreeing to work.

In addition, excess hours agreements should avoid the use of the word "overtime", because hours of work and overtime pay are different and distinct concepts (e.g., the standard hours of work threshold is eight hours in a day and 48 hours in a week, whereas the standards overtime pay threshold is 44 hours in a week). An employee could agree to work "overtime", for example, without agreeing to work in excess of the maximum hours of work.

Excess hours of work permits are valid for a maximum of three years (or for a maximum of one year if the hours of work are to exceed 60 in a week).

The Director of Employment Standards will consider such factors as the employer's compliance history and employee health and safety in determining whether to grant a permit.

Scheduling and the "three-hour rule"

Bill 148 has made numerous changes — to become effective as of January 1, 2019 — impacting on the payment of employees who complete shift-work.

In accordance with the recommendations of the *Changing Workplaces Review*, Bill 148 introduced a "three-hour rule" requiring payment equivalent to at least an employee's "regular rate" for three hours' work in the following circumstances:

• Where an employee is required to present themselves for work for less than three hours despite being available to work longer and the employee nevertheless "regularly works" more than three hours per day. This rule is meant to apply in circumstances where an employer exercises discretion to shorten the usual length of an employee's shift, and would not apply in circumstances where employees' shifts are shortened due to circumstances outside of the employer's control - such as fire, a storm or a power failure: Section 21.3.

• In every 24-hour period where an employee is on-call and either (i) not required to work; or (ii) required to work for less than three hours despite being available to work longer. This applies regardless whether the circumstances giving rise to these outcomes were within the employer's control. However, this does not apply where the employee is on call to ensure continued delivery of essential public services and is not required to work: Section 21.4

• Where the employer cancels an employee's scheduled day of work or scheduled on-call period within 48 hours of when the employee was scheduled to begin work or the on-call period in question. This applies only where the applicable shift or on-call period is cancelled rather than shortened or lengthened. This rule does not apply in circumstances where employees' shifts are shortened due to circumstances outside of the employer's control — such as fire, a storm or a power failure: Section 21.6

The calculation of employees' "regular rate" depends on whether or not employees are paid by the hour. For those who are paid by the hour, the "regular rate" is the amount earned per hour in a regular work week, not counting overtime. For employees who are not paid by the hour, the "regular rate" is the amount earned in a work week divided by the number of non-overtime hours worked in that week.

When requiring employees to work a scheduled shift or to be on-call, employers are also required to provide 96 hours' (i.e., 4 days) notice. If such notice is not provided, then a new Section 21.5 would give employees the right to refuse the employer's request or demand. The *ESA, 2000* requires employees to provide their employers with notice of such refusal as soon as possible. As this does not provide a specific timeline for when such notice must be received by an employer, a valid refusal may be made even shortly before a scheduled shift where sufficient advance notice of that shift has not been provided by the employer. However, the changes in Bill 148 nevertheless provide that such refusals cannot be made in circumstances where the required work is intended to (i) deal with an emergency; or (ii) address a threat to public safety.

Notably, as each of the above provisions have been introduced under a new part of the *ESA, 2000*, these obligations may extend to various professions otherwise exempted from other parts of the *ESA, 2000* through Regulation 285/01. These professions include but are not limited to managerial employees, information technology professionals, teachers under the *Teaching Profession Act*, various medical practitioners, and students in training for these professions. As these new proposed entitlements will not come into effect until January 2019, however, it remains to be seen whether further measures will be taken to exclude members of certain professions.

Employee Requests for Changes in Scheduling and Location

A further change to taking effect as of January 1, 2019 provides all employees of three months' tenure or more with the right to request that their employer change their work schedule or location. Such a request must be made in writing and an employer who receives the request will be required to provide due process in response. Such due process *must* include:

- Discussing the request with the employee;
- Making a decision to accept or decline the request within a reasonable period of time;
- Notifying the employee of the employer's decision. If the employer accepts the request, such notification must specify the date when the requested changes will take effect. If the employer declines the request, such notification must state the reasons for refusal.

The provisions of the *ESA, 2000* setting out employees' rights to request a change to their scheduling or work location do not specify what period of time is "reasonable" for an employer's response, or what level of detail is required in the reasons provided for a denial. In keeping with the general principles set out by the Supreme Court of Canada in *Baker v. Canada*, such obligations to provide due process are likely to be met by adopting processes that are proportionate to the legitimate expectations of a requesting employee, among other factors.

This new entitlement has been introduced under a new part of the *ESA, 2000*, and may therefore extend to various professions otherwise exempted from other parts of the *ESA, 2000* through Regulation 285/01. These professions include but are not limited to managerial employees, information technology professionals, teachers under the *Teaching Profession Act*, various medical practitioners, and students in training for these professions. As this new proposed entitlement would not come into effect until January of 2019, however, it remains to be seen whether further measures will be taken to exclude members of certain professions.

Overtime

Subsection 22(1) of the *ESA, 2000* provides that most employees are entitled to overtime pay at the rate of one and one-half times their regular rate of pay after working 44 hours in a week. Where an employee has more than one regular rate corresponding to work with the same employer (i.e., for different types of work), proposed changes under Bill 148 provide that the employee will be entitled to overtime pay at a rate that corresponds to the type of work performed during hours worked in excess of 44 hours per week.

Overtime Averaging

Employers and employees may enter into written agreements to average hours of work over a specified period of two or more weeks, for the purposes of determining entitlement to overtime pay. In an averaging scenario, overtime pay would not be payable to the employee unless the average work week exceeds 44 hours.

However, the employer must apply for and obtain approval from the Director of Employment Standards to engage in averaging: section 22(2) and 22.1.

If the employer has applied for an overtime averaging approval and the Director of Employment Standards has not yet made a decision on the application, the employer may begin averaging, using averaging periods of up to two weeks, 30 days after the application is made, if certain conditions are met: section 22(2.1).

In deciding whether to grant overtime averaging approval, the Director of Employment Standards may consider such factors as he or she considers relevant, including an employer's compliance history and employee health and safety: section 22.1(7).

With respect to the employer's compliance history, the director may consider whether the employer has previously been found to be in contravention of the *ESA, 2000*, and if so, the number of contraventions, the extent of the contraventions (e.g., the number of employees affected by the contraventions), the monetary amounts involved, and the provisions of the legislation to which the contraventions relate. With respect to the health and safety of employees, the Director may consider the past health and safety record of the employer, and whether the health and safety of employees covered by the application may be put at risk. Other factors the Director may consider include:

- whether information provided by the employer during the application process was false, inaccurate or misleading;
- whether the employer cooperated with the Ministry of Labour's request for further information during the application/approval process;
- whether the employer has also filed an application for approval for excess weekly hours, and if so, does it appear that employees will work a large number of excess hours without ever receiving overtime pay;

- whether there are any benefits to the employees that accompany the proposed work schedule and hours of work scheme; and
- whether the employer's reason for requesting overtime averaging is limited to a brief time frame.

Overtime averaging agreements must contain an expiry date. An averaging agreement cannot be revoked before its expiry date unless the employer and employee both agree in writing: section 22(6).

The Ministry of Labour suggests that employers include in any averaging agreement a statement notifying the employee that the averaging agreement may affect the employee's entitlement to overtime pay. The inclusion of such a statement could protect the employer at a later date, should the employee argue that he or she did not provide fully informed consent to the arrangement.

Although the *Changing Workplaces Review* has proposed that further measures be taken to limit the use of overtime averaging agreements, including a hard cap on the number of weeks that such arrangements can apply to, these recommendations were not subsequently adopted by the Ontario Government in Bill 148.

Time Off in Lieu of Overtime Pay

Subsection 22(7) of the *ESA, 2000* provides that an employee, if the employer agrees, may take paid time off in lieu of being provided with overtime pay. The employee would be entitled to one and one-half hours of paid time off for each hour of overtime worked. The employee is required to take the paid time off work within three months of the work week in which the overtime was earned or, with the employee's agreement, within 12 months of that work week. If the employee's employment happens to end before he or she has an opportunity to take the time off in lieu of overtime, the employer must provide the employee with overtime pay: section 22(8).

Meal Breaks and Rest Periods

Under the *ESA, 2000*, employers must ensure that employees work no more than five consecutive hours without a 30-minute meal break. The meal break can begin at the five-hour mark. However, the *ESA, 2000* provides that, if the employer and employee agree (not necessarily in writing), this 30-minute meal break may be divided into two shorter meal breaks, so long as the total length of the breaks equals at least 30 minutes within (not after) each consecutive five-hour period: section 20.

If the 30-minute meal break is divided into two shorter meal breaks, these shorter meal breaks need not be 15-minutes each. In fact, they can be open-ended, with the employer and employee agreeing that the two shorter periods will be of unspecified lengths that together total 30 minutes, as may be necessary to address business needs. For example, if a salesperson has a 20-minute uninterrupted period before a customer comes in, there will be compliance with the *ESA, 2000* so long as the employee subsequently has a 10-minute uninterrupted period within the requisite five-hour period.

The Ministry of Labour takes the position that employers may require employees to take their meal breaks in a designated place (such as on the employer's premises) and to be "on call" (available to return to work) while on the meal break. Unless the employee is actually required to work during the meal break, the employee will be considered to have received the meal break entitlement. If the employee does not receive an uninterrupted 30-minute meal break (or two shorter uninterrupted meal breaks), then he or she is not considered to have received his or her full entitlement, and a new uninterrupted meal break must be given during the requisite period.

There is no obligation on employers to provide any additional breaks, such as coffee breaks, in addition to this meal break requirement.

There is no provision in the *ESA, 2000* allowing the employer and employee to agree to take the meal break in more than two instalments, to eliminate meal breaks altogether, or to extend the time in which a meal break must be given (e.g., six or seven hours).

Section 21 of the *ESA, 2000,* provides that an employer is not required to pay an employee for a meal break in which work is not being performed, unless the employee's contract of employment requires such payment. As determined by the 2017 Ontario Labour Relations Board in *1786237 Ontario Inc. v. Bougria*, 2017 CarswellOnt 5945 (Ont. L.R.B.), this provision also extends to exclude time allotted for statutory meal breaks from the calculation of employees' entitlements to overtime pay.

Under amendments arising from Bill 148, payment will also be required — as of January 2019 — where an employee is required to be on-call during a meal break that occurs in the course of a shift that is less than 3 hours in length.

In addition to meal breaks, the *ESA, 2000* introduces further rest periods. For example, pursuant to section 18 of the legislation, employees are entitled to:

- 11 hours free from work in each day, *unless*:

(i) the employee is on call; and

(ii) the employee is called in during a period in which they would not normally be expected to work;

- eight hours free from work between shifts, *unless*:

(i) the total time worked on successive shifts does not exceed 13 hours; or

(ii) the employer and employee agree otherwise; and

- 24 consecutive hours free from work in each work week *or* 48 consecutive hours free from work in each period of two consecutive work weeks.

Special Rules and Notable Exemptions

The *ESA, 2000* exempts particular classes of employees from certain minimum entitlements Notably, under amendments made by Bill 148, employees in the categories discussed below will not be exempt from the new three-hour rule and the entitlement to request a scheduling and location change following 3 months' service with their employer.

Supervisory/Managerial Employees

Under the *ESA, 2000*, employees whose *only* role was supervisory or managerial in *character* were exempt from hours of work and overtime provisions. This definition led to considerable confusion about who qualified as a supervisor or manager for purposes of the legislation. For example, certain cases held that a person was not a supervisor or manager, and therefore not exempt from certain sections of the Act, if he or she performed *any* non-supervisory or non-managerial work at all. Not surprisingly, many employers were frustrated by this result, and by the fact that their "managers" could be subject to the hours of work and overtime provisions.

Ontario Regulation 285/01 under the *ESA, 2000* clarifies this exemption by broadening the "supervisory or managerial" definition. Sections 4 and 8 of the Regulation provide that a person will be excluded from the hours of work, eating periods and overtime provisions of the *ESA, 2000*, even though he or she performs non-supervisory or non-managerial tasks, provided those tasks are performed only on "an irregular or exceptional basis". Certainly, the amount of time devoted to supervisory and/or managerial tasks will be considered in relation to the employee's other duties in determining whether the person falls within this exemption.

The Ministry of Labour has provided some clarification around the meaning of "supervisory or managerial". In its view, work that is "supervisory or managerial" generally refers to the supervision of employees rather than the supervision of machines.

However, employees can be considered managerial even though they do not supervise other employees. Some examples of managerial functions include: hiring and firing of employees, responsibility for making substantial purchases, financial control and budgeting, publicly representing the employer, and production planning. Other management functions would include the regular exercise of discretion and independent judgment in management affairs.

Just because a contract of employment or collective agreement states that a person is a manager or supervisor does not mean that the exemption will automatically apply. The actual functions of the person must be assessed.

The term "exceptional" suggests that non-supervisory or non-managerial duties may be performed so long as they are being performed outside of the ordinary course of the employee's duties. For example, if, as a result of a severe snowstorm, the manager were to assist a staff member to clear snow from the entrance to the employer's establishment (ordinarily the responsibility of the staff member), the performance of this non-supervisory duty would be considered "exceptional".

The term "irregular" implies that although the performance of non-supervisory or non-managerial duties is not unusual or unexpected, their performance is unscheduled or sporadic, and does not occur at a regular or set time. For example, if a manager is expected to cover staff duties because a non-supervisory employee has called in sick or there is an unexpected rush of customers, these duties would be considered "irregular". However, the exemption will not apply if a pattern develops, for example if the manager is called upon to cover staff duties every day when the staff member is on a lunch break. It is also important to consider the frequency of non-supervisory or non-managerial duties. For example, if a manager at a fast food restaurant spends an hour or more of each shift assisting at the cash or in food preparation, these duties will likely be considered a "regular" part of his or her job, even though they are not scheduled or performed at a set time every day. Finally, it is also important to consider that similar tasks may take on a managerial or supervisory character when performed in the context of an employee's other managerial or supervisory responsibilities. For instance, whereas both a senior director and administrative personnel may spend a significant portion of their work day responding to telephone calls, this task is likely to take on a managerial character when performed in the context of the position of senior director, but not in the context of the position of administrative personnel.

Hours of Work in Emergency Situations

Another noteworthy exemption is found in section 19 of the *ESA, 2000*, which provides that employees can be required to work in excess of the maximum hours of work, or to work during otherwise mandatory rest periods, in certain exceptional circumstances. Specifically, employers can require employees to work "only so far as is necessary to avoid serious interference with the ordinary working of the employer's establishment or operations" in four situations:

- to deal with an emergency;

- to ensure the continued delivery of essential public services, regardless of who delivers those services, if something unforeseen occurs;

- to ensure that continuous processes or seasonal operations are not interrupted, if something unforeseen occurs; and

- to carry out urgent repair work to the employer's plant or equipment.

Information Technology Professionals

Another important exemption relates to "information technology professionals". The term "information technology professional" is defined in Ontario Regulation 285/01 as "an employee who is primarily engaged in the investigation, analysis, design, development, implementation, operation or management of information systems based on computer and related technologies through the objective application of specialized knowledge and professional judgment." This class of employees is exempt from the hours of work, eating period and overtime provisions of the *ESA, 2000*, pursuant to sections 4 and 8 of Ontario Regulation 285/01.

The scope of this exemption is narrower than one might think. Formal education is not a determining factor. Also, the mere fact that an employee works for a software company or other information technology business does not mean the exemption will apply. The term "information technology professional" also does not involve the following: "trouble-shooting", repairing home computers sold by the employer, the mere use of hardware or software products developed and maintained by information technology professionals (such as by computer animators), development or operation of "high tech" equipment such as TVs, DVDs or stereos, sale of information technology products, and/or routine, unsophisticated tasks.

Dual Role Employees

Section 22(9) provides that where an employee performs one type of work that qualifies him or her for overtime pay, and another type of work that is exempt from the overtime pay provisions, the employee is entitled to overtime pay or time off in lieu of overtime pay for *all* work, unless the non-exempt work is less than half of the total work of the employee.

The principles in section 22(9) were applied in the case of *Sanago v. Glendale Golf and Country Club*, 2010 OLRB 4265 (CanLII). In that case, Mr. Sanago was employed as Executive Chef by the golf club. He was responsible for supervising all aspects of the kitchen operation, had his own budget, and was responsible for interviewing, hiring, training, scheduling and managing line cooks. He was also expected to assist line cooks during peak hours. Shortly after Mr. Sanago was hired, he lost five kitchen staff (approximately one-half of his total staff). In the ensuing two months, as he tried to fill the numerous staff vacancies, Mr. Sanago typically worked seven days a week, 12-16 hours a day. The majority of these hours (at least 55%) involved Mr. Sanago performing the non-supervisory/non-managerial duties of line cooking.

The OLRB held that the Executive Chef position was managerial/supervisory in character. The OLRB then went on to assess whether Mr. Sanago was performing non-supervisory or non-managerial tasks on "an irregular or exceptional basis". It determined that during the two-month crisis period, Mr. Sanago came to perform non-managerial/non-supervisory duties on a regular basis. However, it also held that the events giving rise to the crisis were "out of the ordinary" and "exceptional". Accordingly, the OLRB found that the overtime exemption applied to Mr. Sanago.

The OLRB then went on to consider section 22(9) of the *ESA, 2000*, noting that during the crisis period, Mr. Sanago was expected to perform two kinds of work: Executive Chef duties, and line cook duties. In a number of those weeks, he performed line cook duties more than half the time. The OLRB held that during those weeks, Mr. Sanago was entitled to overtime pay in respect of all hours worked over 44 hours each week.

Commissioned Salespersons

Salespersons, other than route salespersons, who earn commissions on the sale of goods or services where such sales are normally made away from the employer's place of business, are exempt from the hours of work, eating periods, overtime pay, minimum wage, public holidays, and vacation provisions of the *ESA, 2000*. The salesperson does not have to earn *all* of his/her remuneration as commissions; it is sufficient if a part of their remuneration consists of commissions.

Route salespersons are not subject to the exemption. The question of what is a "route salesperson" has frequently been considered by the OLRB. These cases have held that the degree of control exercised by the employee (as opposed to the employer) is a significant factor in determining whether the work in issue was "route" sales, though the issue does not turn on the degree of control alone. For example, children selling chocolates door-to-door on streets determined by the employer were considered route salespersons. Similarly, where the employer provides the employee with a list of individuals to solicit on particular streets within an assigned neighbourhood (for example, for the purpose of selling newspaper subscriptions door-to-door), and the employee cannot increase his or her ability to earn more by working at a time or in neighbourhoods not assigned to him or her by the employer, the employee will be considered a route salesperson.

Volunteers

The *ESA, 2000* does not apply to volunteers, who do not fall within the definition of "employee" in subsection 1(1) of the legislation.

However, one must determine whether a person is a true volunteer. The fact that no wages are paid is not necessarily determinative of volunteer status, nor is the fact that some form of payment is made necessarily determinative of employee status (for example, where the person receives an honorarium or stipend as opposed to wages). A key factor in determining whether the person is a volunteer is the extent to which the person providing the services views the arrangement as being in pursuit of a livelihood. Other factors to consider are how the arrangement was initiated, and whether an economic imbalance between the two parties was a factor in structuring the arrangement.

Trainees/Students/Interns

There are very few circumstances in which a student who performs services for another person or company will be exempt from minimum wage protections. These exceptions are very limited and would become more limited following the coming into force of applicable amendments under Bill 148 in January 2018. The fact that someone is called a "student" or "intern" or "trainee" is irrelevant. The exceptions are as follows:

1. — True Interns

The *ESA, 2000* aims to prevent employers from using unpaid interns in the place of paid workers. An employer who provides an intern with training in skills that are normally used by the employer's employees will be considered an employee (and will be entitled to all of the *ESA, 2000* protections including payment of at least the minimum wage). Previously, the *ESA, 2000* provides an exemption for workers who receive the benefit of training similar to that provided in a vocational school and the employer derives limited benefit from the activities of the intern. However, following Bill 148, these exemptions no longer apply as of January 2018. Accordingly, as of January 2018, true interns who are *not* working in the capacity of students registered in a school program would be entitled to receive the minimum entitlements set out in the *ESA, 2000*.

Industries employing unpaid interns have been the subject of Ministry enforcement blitzes in both 2016 and 2017, and will likely continue to be subject to close scrutiny by the Ministry.

2. — Secondary School, College and University Programs

The *ESA, 2000* nevertheless encourages employers to provide necessary practical experience to students, to complement their classroom learning. So, for example, the *ESA, 2000* provides in subsection 3(5) that it does not apply to:

(i) a secondary school student who performs work under a work experience program authorized by the school board where the student is enrolled in a school; or

(ii) an individual who performs work under a program approved by a college of applied arts and technology, a university or a private career college registered under the *Private Career Colleges Act, 2005.*

3. — Students in Training to Become Certain Professionals

Pursuant to subsection 2(1) of Ontario Regulation 285/01 under the *ESA, 2000*, students of certain professions, including architecture, law, professional engineering, public accounting, surveying, veterinary science, chiropody, chiropractic, dentistry, massage therapy, medicine, optometry, pharmacy, physiotherapy, psychology, naturopathy (and other drugless practitioners), as well as teaching as defined in the *Teaching Profession Act*, are exempt from the minimum wage, hours of work, overtime pay, paid vacations and public holiday provisions of the *ESA, 2000*.

Most of these professions have some type of work experience or apprenticeship requirement that must be completed before a person can qualify to practise in the profession, and such work experience is often mandated by the profession's governing statute.

This particular exemption will not apply merely because a student who is studying a particular professional subject area at a university or college is seeking employment.

Minimum Wage

Wages are defined as any monetary payment to an employee under an oral or written agreement, and any room or board allowances as are prescribed by regulation. Tips or other gratuities are not considered wages, nor are any sums paid at the employer's discretion, such as gifts or bonuses that are not related to hours, production or efficiency. Also not included in the definition of wages are travelling allowances or expenses, or contributions by an employer to a fund, plan or arrangement for the benefit of employees, which come within the provisions of the *ESA, 2000*.

The major industries employing minimum wage earners are accommodation and food, retail trade, and agriculture.

Following from changes under Bill 148, minimum wage will be kept updated based on changes to the Consumer Price Index as of October 1 of each year starting in 2019. Prior to that date, increases in minimum wage will be made on January 1, 2018 and January 1, 2019 in accordance with amounts prescribed in Bill 148. Minimum wage amounts coming into effect on each date are set out in the chart below:

Type of Employee	Minimum Wage Rate as of January 1, 2018	Minimum Wage Rate as of January 1, 2019
General minimum wage (applicable to *most* employees)	$14.00 per hour	$15.00 per hour
Students under the age of 18, employed for a maximum of 28 hours per week (or employed during a school holiday)	$13.15 per hour	$14.10 per hour
Liquor server in licenced premises	$12.20 per hour	$13.05 per hour
Hunting or fishing guide	$70.00 for less than 5 consecutive hours in a day; $140 for 5 or more hours in a day (whether or not those hours are consecutive)	$75.00 for less than 5 consecutive hours in a day; $150 for 5 or more hours in a day (whether or not those hours are consecutive)
Homeworker (employees who do paid work in their own homes)	$15.40 per hour	$16.50 per hour

Under Bill 148, students who are homeworkers will be entitled to receive the homeworker minimum wage.

Calculating Hours of Work, Overtime and Minimum Wage — Special Considerations

For the purposes of determining compliance with hours of work, overtime and minimum wage standards, employers should keep the following considerations in mind.

Room and Board (meal) Allowances

Subsection 5(4) of Ontario Regulation 285/01 provides that the following amounts shall be deemed to have been paid as wages to an employee who provides room or board to an employee, for the purpose of determining whether the prescribed minimum wage has been paid:

Room, Board (meal) or Both	Deemed Payment (for Minimum Wage Calculation Purposes)
Private Room Only	$31.70 per week
Non-Private Room Only	$15.85 per week
Non-Private Room Only — *Domestic Workers*	$0.00 per week
Board (Meals)	$2.55 per meal; weekly maximum of $53.55
Private Room and Board (Meals)	$85.25 per week
Non-Private Room and Board (Meals)	$69.40 per week
Non-Private Room and Board (Meals) — *Domestic Workers*	$53.55 per week

It should be noted that special rules and figures apply with respect to room, board and housing accommodation to domestic workers and fruit, vegetable and tobacco harvesters. These provisions are located in Ontario Regulation 285/01, which should be specifically consulted if you are an employer or employee in these occupations.

Call-In Pay and Minimum Wage

Subsection 5(7) of Ontario Regulation 285/01 currently provides that, for the purpose of determining whether an employee has been paid his or her minimum wage entitlements, the employee will be deemed to have worked for three hours if he or she:

1. regularly works more than three hours in a day;

2. is required to present themselves to work (i.e., are "called in"); and

3. works less than three hours.

As of January 1, 2019, this requirement will be replaced by the "three-hour rule"; which provides for employees to receive payment for three hours of work *at their regular rate* in the circumstances set out above.

Work Deemed to be Performed

Ontario Regulation 285/01 describes certain situations in which work will be *deemed* to be performed by an employee, even though the employee may not in fact be performing work. The reason for "deeming" work to be performed in certain instances is to ensure that employees are appropriately compensated.

Work is deemed to be performed in the following circumstances, according to subsection 6(1) of Ontario Regulation 285/01:

• where work is:

(i) permitted or suffered (i.e., not expressly authorized, but not expressly prohibited) to be done, by an employer; or

(ii) performed by an employee *even though* the employee's employment contract expressly forbids or limits the employee's hours of work or requires the employer to authorize hours of work in advance.

These provisions, though they are found in Ontario Regulation 285/01 rather than the *ESA, 2000*, are extremely

50

important. Employers should take careful note of the fact that, even where unauthorized overtime is expressly forbidden, the employer will be required to provide overtime pay to an employee who nevertheless proceeds, without the employer's permission, to work more than 44 hours in a week. Although this may seem harsh, it is likely an effective deterrent to those employers who might otherwise turn a blind eye to employees who violate overtime rules.

On-Call and Meal/Rest Periods

According to subsection 6(1) of Ontario Regulation 285/01, work will be *deemed* to be performed if the employee is required to remain at the place of work, and is not actually performing work, but is:

(i) waiting or ready for a call to work; or

(ii) on a rest or break time other than a meal period.

According to subsection 6(2) of Ontario Regulation 285/01, work will *not* be deemed to be performed:

(i) during the time that the employee is entitled to:

(a) take time off work for a meal period; or

(b) take at least six hours, or a longer established period, for sleeping, and the employer provides sleeping facilities; or

(c) take time off work in order to engage in the employee's own private affairs or pursuits, as established by custom, contract or practice; or

(ii) is not at the place of employment and is waiting or holding himself or herself ready for call to work.

It is clear from these provisions that on-call employees who are waiting off-site are not entitled to be paid, while on-call employees who are waiting on-site are entitled to be paid. In addition, employees are not entitled to be paid for statutory meal breaks, but are entitled to be paid for other rest periods and breaks if they are required to remain on-site. Under changes arising from Bill 148 and coming into effect on January 1, 2019,

51

on-call employees will be entitled to receive at least three hours' pay for each 24-hour period in which they are required to remain on-call, regardless of whether the employee attends the place of work during this period. In other words, an employee waiting or holding themselves available for work will be entitled to receive at least 3 hours' pay at their regular rate for each 24-hour period of such waiting — regardless of whether any portion of that period is spent at the workplace.

Travel Time

The Ministry of Labour takes the position that any time a person spends travelling (irrespective of the mode of transportation) for the purpose of getting to or from somewhere where work will be or was performed, with the exception of commuting time, must be counted as hours of work. Commuting time means the time required for an employee to travel to their usual workplace from home and vice versa, with the following exceptions:

- If the employee takes a work vehicle home in the evening for the convenience of the employer, the hours of work begin when the employee leaves home in the morning and end when he or she arrives home in the evening; and
- If the employee is required to transport other staff or supplies to or from the workplace or work site, this time must be counted as hours of work.

Training Time

The Ministry of Labour takes the position that time spent in training that is made mandatory by the employer or by law will be considered hours of work for the purposes of the *ESA, 2000*. Mandatory employer training would include any training that the employer requires the employee to take as a condition of employment or continued employment. Other mandatory training would include training that the employee is obliged to take pursuant to a statute or regulation in order to perform the duties and functions of the position held by the employee.

Training that is taken at the option of the employee is not considered hours of work. This includes training that is required in order for an employee to meet the necessary qualifications of a promotion with her or her current employer (for example, a course and certificate in project management for a position as a manager). Such training would not be considered hours of work if the job offer is contingent upon the employee having the necessary qualifications (and training) to perform the job.

Leaves of Absence

The *ESA, 2000* provides for the following unpaid, job-protected leaves of absence:

1. pregnancy leave
2. parental leave
3. personal emergency leave
4. declared emergency leave
5. family medical leave
6. reservist leave
7. organ donor leave
8. family caregiver leave
9. critical illness leave
10. child death leave and crime-related child disappearance leave (formerly crime-related child death or disappearance leave)

Some employers offer *paid* plans for some or all of these leaves of absence. However, employers are not *required* under the *ESA, 2000* to pay employees during any leave of absence.

Each of these leaves of absence is described in more detail below.

Pregnancy Leave

A pregnant employee must have started employment with her employer at least 13 weeks before her due date in order to qualify for a 17-week job-protected pregnancy leave without pay: section 47, *ESA, 2000*.

Subsection 46(2) of the *ESA, 2000* provides that an employee may begin her pregnancy leave no earlier than the earlier of:

• the day that is 17 weeks before her due date; and

• the day on which she gives birth.

Accordingly, pregnancy leave may begin earlier than 17 weeks before the employee's due date if the employee gives birth before that time.

An employee may begin her pregnancy leave no *later* than the earlier of:

• her due date; and

• the day on which she gives birth.

Accordingly, a woman whose child is "overdue" is required to commence her pregnancy leave on her due date, notwithstanding that she has not yet given birth.

The *ESA, 2000* contains a written notice requirement in order to begin pregnancy leave. Section 46(4) of the *ESA, 2000* provides that a pregnant employee must provide a medical certificate stating the due date *if the employer requests it*. Under changes arising from Bill 148, such a certificate can be provided by various professionals including a physician, midwife, or a registered nurse.

In addition, the employee must give two weeks' written notice of the date that the leave is to begin: subsection 46(4) of the *ESA, 2000*.

Parental Leave

Under the *ESA, 2000*, as of December 3, 2017, a parent is entitled to take up to 61 weeks' unpaid parental leave if the employee also took pregnancy leave, and 63 weeks of unpaid parental leave if the employee did not take pregnancy leave: section 49.

The term "parent" is defined in the *ESA, 2000* as including "a person with whom a child is placed for adoption and a person who is in a relationship of some permanence with a parent of a child and who intends to treat the child as his or her own". The Ministry specifically considers the following individuals to be parents:

• Birth parents — All birth parents are parents and are entitled to parental leave. Birth parents who put a child up for adoption continue to be parents within the *ESA, 2000* definition and are entitled to parental leave. Surrogate mothers, whether genetically related to the child or not, are also entitled to pregnancy leave. However, where a court declares that birth parents are no longer a child's parents (i.e., by way of an adoption order) prior to the commencement of a parental leave, the employee is not entitled to parental leave.

• Adoptive parents — Parents include those with whom a child is placed for adoption. It is not necessary that adoption proceedings have been finalized; it is sufficient if they have been commenced. (Note, however, that the definition of "parent" does not include foster parents who have not commenced adoption proceedings.)

• Person in a relationship of some permanence with a parent and who intends to treat the child as his or her own—This part of the "parent" definition was intended to cover a person who is in a spousal-like relationship with a parent. The words "some permanence" require that the relationship not be temporary or occasional. In assessing whether the person intends to treat the child as his or her own, employers should consider whether the person plans to assume a significant degree of responsibility for raising the child, including participating in the support, guidance, education and discipline of the child.

• Other parents — The Ministry recognizes that other categories of people may also be entitled to parental leave in some cases. For example, in some cases, individuals who are granted legal custody of children, play a significant role in their care and upbringing, and demonstrate an intention to permanently treat the child as their own, may be entitled to parental leave.

For employees who take pregnancy leave, the parental leave must begin immediately after the pregnancy leave period ends: subsection 48(3). For other parents, parental leave must begin no later than 78 weeks after the child was born or came into their care: subsection 48(2).

For example, if the child has significant medical problems that necessitate a lengthy hospital stay following birth, the date that the child was actually released from hospital into his or her parents' care should be regarded as the date that the child came into their care for the first time.

The *ESA, 2000* also contains a "resignation" notice requirement. Employees who take pregnancy or parental leave are not permitted to terminate their employment prior to the expiry of the leave, or upon its expiry, unless they provide they employer with at least four weeks' written notice of the termination, pursuant to subsections 47(4) and 49(4) of the *ESA, 2000*. This requirement does not apply if the employer constructively dismisses the employee (subsections 47(5) and 49(5)).

Personal Emergency Leave

The *ESA, 2000* allows for a job-protected leave called personal emergency leave. As of January 2018, following from amendments under Bill 148, all employees who have worked with an employer for more than one week will be entitled to receive two days of paid leave, plus a further eight days of unpaid leave in relation to various circumstances constituting personal emergencies. Where an employee who has worked with the employer for more than one week opts to take this form of leave, the *ESA, 2000* would require that the first two days of leave taken in a given year constitute paid days of leave. Employees who have worked with the employer for less than one week may use only unpaid days of personal emergency leave that will count against their annual allotment.

According to subsection 50(1) of the *ESA, 2000*, an employee who is entitled to personal emergency leave may take up to two days' paid leave and an additional eight days' unpaid leave of absence each calendar year due to the following:

• personal illness, injury or medical emergency;

• the death, illness, injury or medical emergency of certain individuals; or

• an urgent matter concerning certain individuals.

The "individuals" in respect of whom a personal emergency leave can be taken by an employee are set out in subsection 50(2), as follows:

• the employee's spouse;

• a parent, step-parent or foster parent of the employee, or the employee's spouse;

• a child, step-child or foster child of the employee or the employee's spouse;

• a grandparent, step-grandparent, grandchild or step-grand-child of the employee or of the employee's spouse;

• the spouse of a child of the employee;

• the employee's brother or sister; and

• a relative of the employee who is dependent on the employee for care or assistance.

The *ESA, 2000* does not define the term "relative". Absent a definition in the legislation, the term "relative" should be interpreted in accordance with its plain, ordinary grammatical sense and commonly understood meaning. A relative should be related through blood or through a legally recognized affinity, such as marriage, adoption or partnerships between people of the same or opposite sex who are not married.

The *ESA, 2000* also does not define the term "dependent". However, generally speaking, the term "dependent" refers to any relative who relies on the employee to some degree for care or assistance in meeting their basic living needs. The relative does not have to be completely reliant on the employee for all of their needs, and does not have to live with the employee. Furthermore, the event for which an employee requests personal emergency leave does not have to relate to the particular type of dependence the relative has on the employee.

The Ministry of Labour has suggested that the word "illness" includes all surgeries — both pre-planned and elective — if they are performed to address or prevent a medical condition. An illness, injury or medical emergency caused by the employee's own actions will also entitle the employee to personal emergency leave. However, medically unnecessary cosmetic surgery unrelated to any illness or injury, is not covered.

The Ministry of Labour has suggested that the word "urgent matter", as it relates to certain individuals other than the employee, must:
- be unplanned or out of the employee's control; and
- involve the possibility of serious negative consequences, including emotional harm, if it is not attended to.

The test of an "urgent matter" is whether a reasonable person in the employee's circumstances would feel that the matter is an urgent one. The Ministry of Labour lists the following examples of events that would constitute "urgent matters":
- The employee's babysitter calls in sick.

• The house of the employee's elderly parent is broken into, and the parent is very upset and needs the employee's help to deal with the situation.

• The employee has an appointment to meet with his or her child's counsellor to discuss behavioural problems at school. The appointment could not be rescheduled outside the employee's working hours.

The Ministry of Labour has also indicated that the following events would not qualify as an "urgent matter":

• An employee wants to leave work early to watch his daughter's track meet.

• An employee wants the day off in order to attend her sister's wedding as a bridesmaid.

The employer may require an employee to provide proof that he or she is eligible for a personal emergency leave of absence. Specifically, the employer may request "evidence reasonable in the circumstances" that the employee is entitled to personal emergency leave: subsection 50(7). Such evidence may take many forms, including confirmation of medical appointments, employee attestations, death certificates, notes from a school or day care facility, or receipts. Employers are prohibited by the *Regulated Health Professions Act, 1991* from speaking directly with an employee's doctor, unless the employee provides written consent. As of January 2018, under proposed changes arising from Bill 148, employers will no longer be permitted to request a medical certificate from employees who receive personal emergency leave under the terms of the *ESA, 2000*. However, this restriction may not apply where the employer provides leave that constitutes a greater benefit than what is provided for under the *ESA, 2000*, as further discussed below.

Evidence that is "reasonable in the circumstances" will depend on all of the facts in any given situation. The following factors and principles will be relevant:

Evidence With Respect to Medical Matters

- the duration of the leave;
- whether there is a pattern of absenteeism;
- whether it is possible to obtain the evidence after the fact;
- the cost of the evidence; and
- whether there is a contract of employment or workplace policy regarding the circumstances under which employees have to provide proof of the reason for their absence.

Evidence With Respect to Non-Medical Matters

- Many of the points listed above with respect to medical matters are also relevant when determining what evidence is "reasonable in the circumstances" in a non-medical matter.

- It should be remembered that third parties to whom the leave relates cannot be compelled by the employer to provide evidence. If the third party refuses to provide evidence, it is not "reasonable in the circumstances" for the employer to require that the employee provide it.

Where the emergency leave is in respect of the illness, injury or medical emergency of an employee's relative, an employer cannot require a medical certificate in respect of that person. All that an employer can require is that the employee disclose the name of the person, their relationship to that person, and a statement that the absence is required because of an illness, injury or medical emergency in respect of that person.

The ten days of personal emergency leave each year need not be taken consecutively. However, personal emergency leave is counted in full days. Therefore, if an employee takes only part of a day off for personal emergency leave, the employer can count it as a full day of leave.

The ten-day leave entitlement cannot be pro-rated. In other words, an employee who commences employment part way through the calendar year is entitled to the full ten days' leave, including a full two days' paid leave. Similarly, part-time employees are entitled to the full ten days leave, including two days' paid leave.

Unused personal emergency leave days, whether paid or unpaid, may not be carried over from one calendar year to the next.

The terms of an employment contract or collective agreement will prevail over the emergency leave provisions in the *ESA, 2000*, if such terms represent a greater right or benefit to the employee. Unfortunately, it can be a very difficult exercise to determine whether the terms of an employment contract or collective agreement truly represent a greater right or benefit to the employee. This can be especially complicated with personal emergency leave because of the numerous events that might be involved (i.e., illness, injury, medical emergency, urgent matter), the number of features of the employment standard (i.e., reinstatement entitlement, prohibition against reprisal), and the virtually limitless variation in contractual schemes. Generally speaking, one must examine whether the relevant contractual provisions, taken in their entirety, give the employee a better deal than the corresponding employment standard, taken in its entirety.

To assist, the Ministry of Labour has provided the following list of criteria relevant to determining whether, *on balance*, the employment contract/collective agreement or *ESA, 2000* provides a "better deal" for the employee. The criteria are not all of equal significance. They are listed below in the order of *most important to least important*.

• *Qualifying Events* — If the employment contract/collective agreement does not cover all of the different types of leave mentioned in the *ESA, 2000* (i.e., illness, injury, medical emergency, urgent matter, involving self or dependent relative), this is a very strong indication that it does not provide a greater right or benefit than the *ESA, 2000*. It is not, however, conclusive.

• *Number of Days of Leave* — If the employment contract/ collective agreement provides for less than ten days' leave, this suggests that it does *not* provide a greater right or benefit than the *ESA, 2000*.

• *Paid or Unpaid Leave* — If the employment contract/ collective agreement provides for more than two days' paid leave, this suggests that it provides a greater right or benefit than the *ESA, 2000* (remember that only two days' emergency leave under the *ESA, 2000* is paid following amendments under Bill 148).

• *Reinstatement Right* — If the employment contract/collective agreement does not provide that the employee is entitled to be reinstated to the original position (if it still exists) or a comparable position (if the original position no longer exists), this suggests that it does not provide a greater right or benefit than the *ESA, 2000*.

• *Negative Consequences* — If the employee may be adversely affected because he or she takes a leave under the employment contract/collective agreement (i.e., demotion, loss of seniority, denial of bonus, denial of pay increase, interruption in benefit coverage, forfeiture of contractual vacation entitlement), this suggests that it does not provide a greater right or benefit than the *ESA, 2000*.

• *Eligible Relationships* — If the employment contract/ collective agreement covers a narrower range of relatives than the *ESA, 2000* (i.e., an employee may take leave to attend the funeral of his or her mother, but not his or her spouse's mother), this suggests that it does *not* provide a greater right or benefit than the *ESA, 2000*.

• *Other Criteria* — Other minor criteria could have some impact on the overall analysis in a "close case". These criteria include:

> • what sort of evidence the employer requires to support the leave (the *ESA, 2000* requires "evidence reasonable in the circumstances" and, under amendments in Bill 148,

prohibits employers from requesting medical certificates in relation to personal emergency leave);

• whether the employment contract/collective agreement right is based on the calendar year or the employee's anniversary date (the *ESA, 2000* is based on the former); and

• whether the employment contract/collective agreement allows the employer to deduct a part day of leave from the employee's entitlement as if it were a whole day (the *ESA, 2000* allows the employer to do this, but the employment contract/collective agreement may be more favourable to the employee).

It is important to note that if the employment contract/collective agreement does not entitle the employee to return to work following the leave, the employment contract/collective agreement will not be considered to be a greater right or benefit. This is because the reinstatement entitlement is inherent to the concept of a leave under the *ESA, 2000*.

Employers should note that the personal emergency leave provisions do not detract from employers' separate and distinct human rights obligations. Pursuant to the Ontario *Human Rights Code*, the employer is required to accommodate persons with "handicaps". This statutory requirement may require the employer to provide more than the ten days' total personal emergency leave provided for in the *ESA, 2000*.

An employee must inform the employer, in advance, of his or her intention to take a personal emergency leave. However, if the matter is so urgent that an employee does not have time to inform the employer before commencing the leave, he or she has an obligation to advise the employer as soon as possible after starting the leave: subsections 50(3) and (4). The *ESA, 2000* does not specify any particular method by which the employee must advise the employer that he or she intends to take personal emergency leave. Accordingly, it would seem that an employee may advise the employer by telephone, leave a note on the manager's desk, or ask a colleague to inform the employer on his or her behalf.

As of January 2018, following from amendments under Bill 148, personal emergency leave will no longer only be available to employees who work for companies that *regularly* employ at least 50 employees (with the exception of employees working in automobile manufacturing, automobile parts manufacturing, automobile parts warehousing and automobile marshalling industries). In other words, as of 2018, an employee who works for a company that regularly employs less than 50 employees will also be entitled to 10 days' personal emergency leave, including 2 paid days' leave, where they previously had no such entitlement. Beginning in 2018, many smaller employers will be required to ensure that their policies providing for leave in the event of an employee having a personal emergency are consistent with satisfying these minimum requirements provided for under the *ESA, 2000.* Prior to January 1, 2018, this requirement only applied to employers who regularly employ at leave 50 employees, as determined based on the following principles:

• The "Quirk" Principle — An employer may have employed an unusually high or low number of employees for a temporary period. Employers may also revert to their "normal" number of employees after such a period. For example, if an employer had 30 employees for three years in a row, then increased the workforce to 60 employees for seven months of the previous calendar year, and has plans to return the workforce to 30 employees for more than six months of the coming year, it would be justifiable to conclude that the employer does not meet the 50-employee threshold. This principle also works in reverse: If the employer has an unusually low number of employees for a portion of one year, the Ministry of Labour may find that it meets the 50-employee threshold.

• The "Sea Change" Principle — Employers may experience a dramatic and lasting increase or decrease in employee complement. For example, an employer may lose a significant customer toward the end of the calendar year, and be forced to reduce its regular workforce of 65 employees to 30 employees. In such a case, the Ministry may conclude that the employer does not meet the 50-employee threshold. Like the "Quirk" Principle, this also works in reverse: If an employer experiences a dramatic growth in the latter part the year, and increases its regular workforce of 30 to 65, the Ministry of Labour may conclude that the employer meets the 50-employee threshold.

Pursuant to Ontario Regulation 285/01, personal emergency leave is not available to the following professional employees, if taking a leave would constitute an act of professional misconduct or a dereliction of professional duty:

• a practitioner or student in training of:

    (i) architecture;

    (ii) law;

    (iii) professional engineering;

    (iv) public accounting;

    (v) surveying;

    (vi) veterinary science;

• a practitioner or student in training under the *Drugless Practitioners Act*;

• a teacher, as defined in the *Teaching Profession Act*, or a student in training for such occupation; and

• a practitioner of a health profession set out in Schedule 1 to the *Regulated Health Professions Act, 1991*, including chiropody, chiropractic, dentistry, massage therapy, medicine, optometry, pharmacy, physiotherapy and psychology, and students training for such occupations.

As of January 1, 2017, following amendments made to Ontario Regulation 502/06, employees who perform essential activities in the automobile manufacturing, automobile parts manufacturing, automobile parts warehousing and automobile marshalling industries are limited to an entitlement of only seven days' leave in relation to personal emergencies. For these workers, such leave also may not be taken in relation the *death* of individuals listed under Section 50 of the *ESA, 2000*, or in relation to incidents involving sexual or domestic violence or the threat thereof.

Questions have arisen as to whether an employee who is absent from work for one of the reasons listed in this section *must* utilize one of the 10 days of personal emergency leave, whether paid or unpaid. The Ministry of Labour takes the position that it is the *employee*, and not the *employer*, who may decide whether to designate an absence as a personal emergency leave day. In other words, an employee may be entitled to personal emergency leave and be absent from work due to one of the reasons listed in this section, and decide not to claim the absence as a personal emergency leave day. However, if the employee does not wish to claim the absence as a personal emergency leave day, and the absence cannot be considered an authorized absence on some other ground (such as approved vacation), then the absence would be considered unauthorized and the employee would have no protection in respect of it (such as protection against reprisal by the employer). Effectively and for practical purposes, then, the employee may feel forced into designating the day as a personal emergency leave day.

The Ministry of Labour also takes the position that, if an employer offers a benefit plan for sick days, bereavement days, paid personal days, or the like, and the employee opts to claim benefits under that plan, then the employee has *in effect* designated the absence as a personal emergency leave day. The same approach applies with respect to workplace injuries, so that if an absent employee claims benefits under the *Workplace Safety and Insurance Act, 1997*, the employee is effectively designating the absences as personal emergency leave.

Declared Emergency Leave

Declared emergency leave gives employees the right to a leave without pay if the employee will not be performing the duties of his or her position because of an emergency declared under the *Emergency Management and Civil Protection Act* (the "*EMCPA*"), and if one of certain other eligibility criteria are met, namely:

1. an order has been issued that applies to the employee under the *EMCPA* or the *Health Protection and Promotion Act* (under the latter legislation, orders can be made by a medical officer of health or a public health inspector requiring a person to take or refrain from taking any action in respect of a health hazard, including the performance of specified work); or

2. the employee is needed to provide care of assistance to specified close or dependent relatives (i.e., employee's spouse; parent, step-parent, or foster parent of the employee or his/her spouse; child, step-child or foster child of the employee or his/her spouse; grandparent, step-grandparent, grandchild or step-grandchild of the employee or his/her spouse; spouse of a child of the employee; employee's brother or sister; and other relatives dependent on the employee for care or assistance).

As with personal emergency leave, an employee who wishes to take declared emergency leave must advise the employer in advance, or if that is not possible, as soon as possible after starting the leave. In addition, an employer may require that the employee provide "evidence reasonable in the circumstances at a time that is reasonable in the circumstances" that the employee is entitled to the leave.

Generally speaking, a declared emergency ends after 14 days, unless it is terminated earlier. However, a declared emergency can be extended beyond 14 days in certain circumstances. Declared emergency leave lasts for as long as the employee is not performing the duties of his or her position because of an emergency declared under the *EMCPA* and one or more of the qualifying conditions exists.

All employees are entitled to declared emergency leave, whether they are full-time, part-time, permanent or on contract, whether they work for small or large companies, and whether they work for private or public companies. Unlike personal emergency leave, there is no requirement for an employer to regularly employ 50 or more employees before an employee becomes entitled to declared emergency leave.

Family Medical Leave

Family medical leave allows employees to take up to eight weeks' leave of absence without pay to provide care or support to specified family members who are terminally ill. Under amendments to the *ESA, 2000* under Bill 148, this entitlement increases to 28 weeks as of January 1, 2018.

Originally, the *ESA, 2000* listed only the following specific family members in respect of whom family medical leave could be taken:

- the employee's spouse
- a parent, step-parent or foster parent of the employee; and
- a child, step-child or foster child of the employee or the employee's spouse.

However, as of the passage of Bill 148 the list also includes the following additional people:

- siblings
- grandparents and grandchildren of the employee or the employee's spouse
- certain in-laws (parents, children, siblings, step-siblings)
- aunts and uncles of the employee or the employee's spouse

- nieces and nephews of the employee or the employee's spouse
- certain step-relationships; and
- "a person who considers the employee to be like a family member".

In order for an employee to qualify for family medical leave, the individual in question must have a serious medical condition with a significant risk of dying within a period of 52 weeks as of January 1, 2018. The serious medical condition and risk of death within 26 weeks must be confirmed in a certificate issued by a qualified health practitioner. Following from changes arising under Bill 148, such practitioners include physicians, registered nurses and other prescribed classes of practitioners.

In addition, those employees who wish to take family medical leave in respect of a person who is "like a family member" must complete a "Compassionate Care Benefits Attestation" form, which was developed by the federal government as a requirement to apply for employment insurance compassionate care leave benefits. The form must be signed by the gravely ill person or his or her legal representative, confirming that the caregiver is "like a family member".

An employer may request the above documents from an employee who is taking family medical leave, to confirm the employee's eligibility to do so, regardless of whether the employee is also applying for the employment insurance compassionate care leave benefits.

Family medical leave is available to all employees covered by the *ESA, 2000*, including full-time, part-time, permanent and contract employees. Employees do not have to work for a specified length of time in order to qualify for the leave. Family medical leave is in addition to emergency leave entitlements. If two or more employees qualify to take family medical leave in respect of the same family member, the leave of absence allotment must be shared between them.

The employee must inform the employer in writing that he or she will be taking family medical leave before the leave begins, or as soon as possible thereafter. Family medical leave must be taken in periods of entire weeks. If less than one week of leave is actually taken, the *ESA, 2000* deems the employee to have used an entire week. If the employee's family member dies before the full allotment of family medical leave is taken, the family medical leave will end on the last day of the week in which the family member dies. If the family member is still critically ill at the end of the 52-week period starting on the first day of the week referred to in the medical certificate corresponding to this leave, the employee is entitled to another 28 weeks of job-protected leave, provided that a new medical certificate is obtained.

During family medical leave, employees earn seniority and credit for length of service and length of employment, just as if they had stayed at work. While the employee is on family medical leave, the employer must continue to pay its share of the premiums for any benefit plans that were offered before the leave.

Reservist Leave

This is a job-protected leave for military reservists serving on domestic operations (such as search and rescue operations or national disasters like flood relief or ice storms) or international deployments.

The term "reservist" is defined in the *ESA, 2000* to mean a member of the reserve force of the Canadian Forces. All employers covered by the *ESA, 2000*, regardless of size, are required to provide this leave to eligible employees. Reservists who have worked for their employer for at least six (6) consecutive months are entitled to an unpaid leave of indefinite length, if the employee will not be performing the duties of his or her position due to a domestic or international deployment. The duration of the leave will depend on the operation to which the reservist is deployed, and, in the case of international operations, may include participation in both pre- and post-deployment activities. The leave is only available if the deployment begins on or after December 3, 2007.

Reservists are required to provide "reasonable notice" in writing before beginning or ending the leave, unless an alternate period of notice is prescribed by regulation, and may be required to provide proof of military service if requested by the employer.

Reservists' seniority and length of service credits continue to accumulate during the leave. Upon return from reservist leave, the employee is entitled to be reinstated to the same position if it still exists, or to a comparable position if it does not. Unlike other types of leave, reinstatement may be postponed until the later of one (1) pay period or two (2) weeks after the end of the reservist leave. Also unlike other types of leave, employers are not required to continue any pension or benefit plan contributions during the reservist leave (although they can if they like). However, if the reservist's reinstatement is postponed for one (1) pay period or two (2) weeks as described above, the employer is obligated to resume all payments during the postponement period.

Organ Donor Leave

This is an unpaid, job-protected leave for employees who donate certain organs to another individual. Currently, this job-protected leave applies to persons who are donating all or part of the following organs: kidney, liver, lung, pancreas and small bowel.

Donors must be employed by the same employer for at least 13 weeks in order to be entitled to the leave. Employers may require that an employee who takes organ donor leave provide a medical certificate confirming that the employee has undergone or will undergo surgery for the purpose of organ donation. Employees are required to provide at least two weeks' written notice to the employer in advance of taking the leave, if possible.

The leave may last up to 13 weeks, but can be extended by up to 13 additional weeks if a medical practitioner issues a certificate stating that the employee is not yet able to perform the duties of his or her position because of the organ donation and will not be able to so for a specified time. The organ donor may commence organ donor leave on the date that he or she undergoes surgery for the purpose of organ donation, or on an earlier date that may be specified by his or her medical practitioner.

Organ donor leave attracts the same general protections afforded to other *ESA, 2000* leaves.

Family Caregiver Leave

Family caregiver leave came into effect on October 29, 2014.

Employees are entitled to take up to eight weeks' leave of absence without pay, in each calendar year, in order to provide care or support to any/each of the following specified family members with a serious medical condition:

• the employee's spouse;

• a parent, step-parent or foster parent of the employee or the employee's spouse;

• a child, step-child or foster child of the employee or the employee's spouse;

• a grandparent, step-grandparent, grandchild or step-grandchild of the employee or the employee's spouse;

• the spouse of a child of the employee;

• the employee's brother or sister; or

• a relative of the employee who is dependent on the employee for care or assistance.

This is identical to the list of individuals with respect to whom personal emergency leave may be taken.

The legislation does not require that family caregiver leave be taken in complete weeks, nor does it require that the weeks be taken consecutively. However, it is Ministry of Labour policy that there are eight weeks *in which* the employee may take family caregiver leave, and thus where an employee takes any time off during a week for family caregiver leave — even as little as one day — he or she is deemed to have used up one week of his or her eight weeks of entitlement. Under amendments in Bill 148, an employer would have discretion to deem an employee to have taken a full week of leave where the employee takes part of the week off work on family caregiver leave.

The employee is only entitled to be on family caregiver leave when the employee is actually providing care or support to one of the listed family members. If the employee ceases to provide care or support to the family member before a full week passes, the employee is required to return to work. Similarly, the employer cannot require the employee to take an entire week of leave, and cannot prevent the employee from returning to work as soon as the employee ceases to provide care or support to the family member.

There is no upper limit on the number of family caregiver leaves an employee may take in a calendar year. For example, if an employee provides care or support to two different family members during the year, the employee is entitled to two family caregiver leaves, of up to eight weeks each. The eight-week entitlement is not pro-rated for 2014, or if the employee commences or leaves employment with the employer part-way through the calendar year.

The employee must be providing "care or support" to the family member with a "serious medical condition". According to the Ministry of Labour, "care or support" includes providing psychological or emotional support, practical support (such as housekeeping, laundry, or shopping), arranging for care by a third party, assisting the family member to get their affairs in order, or directly providing or participating in the personal care of the family member. The employer is entitled to require that the employee produce a certificate from a qualified health practitioner indicating that the family member has a "serious medical condition", which could be chronic or episodic. The employer is not entitled to know *what* the medical condition is;

only that it is serious. The Ministry of Labour takes the position that a medical condition will be considered serious if the individual could die or is expected to die (e.g., if the certificate indicates that the condition is life-threatening or the family member is terminally ill), although other medical conditions could also be considered serious.

Employees who wish to take family caregiver leave must tell their employers in writing, ahead of time, that they intend to do so. If they must start the leave before advising the employer, they must tell the employer as soon as possible after beginning the leave.

Critical Illness Leave

Critically ill child care leave came into effect on October 29, 2014. Bill 148 amended this to Critical Illness Leave as of December 3, 2017, adding new provisions extending this leave to time taken to care for critically ill adults.

Employees are entitled to take up to 37 weeks of critically ill child care leave in order to provide care or support to a critically ill child (defined as a child, step-child, foster child or child who is under guardianship, and who is under 18 years of age). Such care or support could include psychological or emotional support, or providing or participating in the child's personal care.

As of December 3, 2017, following from amendments made under Bill 148, employees will also be entitled to take up to 17 weeks' leave to care for an adult family member who is 18 years or older. Family members include children and step-children, siblings and step-siblings, grandparents, grandchildren, certain in-laws, and nephews and nieces.

The weeks of leave need not be taken consecutively, and need not be taken in periods of entire weeks. The employer cannot require the employee to take an entire week of leave at a time, and cannot prevent the employee from returning to work as soon as he or she is no longer providing care or support to the child or family member.

In order to qualify for this leave, employees must have been employed for at least six consecutive months prior to the first day of the leave.

Employees must inform the employer in writing that they intend to take this leave, and must provide a written plan that indicates the weeks in which they intend to take the leave. Where employees will be taking some of the leave in single days, the written plan must indicate the weeks in which the leave will be taken; it need not indicate which days in those weeks it will be taken. If the employee cannot advise the employer before beginning the leave, he or she must do so as soon as possible after beginning the leave. An employee can change his or her plan by providing "reasonable" written notice to the employer, or by seeking and obtaining written permission from the employer. What is "reasonable" will depend on the circumstances of both the employer and the employee.

The employee must provide the employer with a certificate from a qualified health practitioner indicating that the child or family member is critically ill and requires the care or support of one or more parent, and setting out the period during which the child or family member requires the care or support. Following changes arising under Bill 148, such practitioners include a physician, nurse, psychologist or other prescribed practitioners. The certificate need not specify what the illness or injury is; it need only state that it is "critical". An illness or injury may be deemed to be "critical", even if that word is not used in the certificate, if it contains words that suggest a child's or family member's life is at risk. The certificate should describe the period during which care or support is required; typically, this would include a start date and end date. However, it may not always be possible to specify an end date, and therefore a certificate which indicates that the care or support will be required indefinitely or to the end of the child's or family member's life will be acceptable.

If the certificate indicates that the child or family member will require care or support for 52 weeks or longer, the employee's leave ends no later than the last day of the 52-week period that begins on the earlier of:

(a) the first day of the week in which the certificate was issued; and

(b) the first day of the week in which the child or family member became critically ill.

However, if the child or family member remains critically ill after this 52-week period, the employee is entitled to take another critical illness leave of up to 37 weeks or 17 weeks, as applicable. There is no upper limit on the number of additional critical illness leaves an employee is entitled to. After each 52-week period elapses, an employee whose child or family member remains critically ill may qualify for a fresh critical illness leave again, if all of the above requirements are met.

Employees who are entitled to critical illness leave may be eligible to receive corresponding Employment Insurance benefits from the federal government.

Domestic or Sexual Violence Leave

Bill 148 established a new form of unpaid leave, domestic or sexual violence leave, to come into effect as of January 1, 2018. Under this form of leave, employees who have worked for an employer for at least 13 consecutive weeks, are entitled to both 10 days' leave and 15 weeks' leave — not necessarily to be taken consecutively — in any calendar year in relation to any of the following purposes:

• To seek medical attention for the employee or the child of the employee, including a step-child, foster child, or child under the employee's guardianship, in respect of a physical or psychological injury or disability caused by the domestic or sexual violence.

• To obtain services from a victim services organization for the employee or the child of the employee.

• To obtain psychological or other professional counselling for the employee or the child of the employee.

• To relocate temporarily or permanently.

• To seek legal or law enforcement assistance, including preparing for or participating in any civil or criminal legal proceeding related to or resulting from the domestic or sexual violence.

To ensure financial support to individuals in the above circumstances, the first five days of such leave are required to be paid. Such payment is to include either (i) the wages the employee would have earned if they had not taken the leave; or (ii) if the employee receives performance-based pay, the greater of the employee's hourly rate and the applicable minimum wage. However, employees who take this leave would not be entitled to overtime pay or shift premiums that could have been earned on those days when the employee takes leave.

Employees are required to inform employers as soon as possible before or after having taken domestic or sexual violence leave. In relation to employees who take this form of leave, employers have discretion to (i) request evidence that is reasonable in the circumstances to support an employee's entitlement to the leave; (ii) deem an employee who has taken part of a week of leave as having used a full week of their leave entitlement; and (iii) deem an employee who has taken part of a day of leave as having used a full day of their leave entitlement. Employers are required to ensure mechanisms are in place for maintaining the confidentiality of such information and records connected with this leave.

Importantly, an employee will have no entitlement to take this leave where the employee has committed the domestic or sexual violence giving rise to the leave.

Child Death Leave and Crime-Related Child Disappearance Leave (formerly Crime-Related Child Death or Disappearance Leave)

Crime-related child death or disappearance leave came into effect as a single form of job-protected leave on October 29, 2014. Following amendments that come into force in January 2018 under Bill 148, this formerly single form of leave will compose two distinct forms of leave: Child Death Leave and Crime-Related Child Disappearance Leave.

Employees who have been employed by their employer for at least six months will be entitled to an unpaid, job-protected Child Death Leave if their child has died. Similarly, employees who have been employed by their employer for at least six months would be entitled to an unpaid, job-protected Crime-Related Child Disappearance Leave where a child of the employee disappears and it is probable, considering the circumstances, that the child disappeared as a result of a crime Both types of leave may last for up to 104 weeks, and must be taken within 105 weeks after the week in which the child dies or disappears, as applicable. Either form of leave may be taken *only* in a single period (ie., the duration of the leave, however long, must be taken all at once).

For the purposes of both types of leave, a "child" includes the employee's own child, step-child, foster child or child who is under legal guardianship of the employee, and who is under 18 years of age.

Employees who wish to take either of these forms of leave must inform their employer in writing and provide a written plan indicating the weeks in which they intend to take the leave. If they cannot inform the employer before beginning the leave, then they must do so as soon as possible thereafter. An employee may later change his or her plan if either (i) the employee seeks and obtains written permission for the change from their employer; or (ii) the employee provides the employer with four weeks' advance notice of the change. In other words, changes to the plan cannot be made on short notice except with an employer's permission.

Employers are entitled to request "evidence reasonable in the circumstances" from employees to verify entitlement to either of these forms of leave.

Employees are *not* entitled to these leaves if they are charged with a crime in relation to the death or disappearance of the child *or* if it is probable that the child was a party to the crime that caused his or her own death or disappearance. "Crime" is defined in the *ESA, 2000* as a *Criminal Code* offence (other than offences described in Regulations under the *Canada Labour Code*). An employee's entitlement to Crime-Related Child Disappearance Leave will also end where there is a change in circumstances that renders it no longer probable that the child disappeared as a result of a crime.

In particular, if an employee's child is found after the employee has taken Crime-Related Child Disappearance Leave, then the following rules apply with respect to the employee's return to work:

- If the child is found alive, the employee is entitled to remain on leave under this section for 14 days after the child is found.
- If the child is found dead, the employee's entitlement to be on Crime-Related Child Disappearance Leave ends at the end of the week in which the child is found. However, the employee will remain entitled to commence a separate Child Death Leave of up to 104 weeks.

Child Death Leave and Crime-Related Child Disappearance Leave each attract the same general protections afforded to other *ESA, 2000* leaves.

Rights During A Leave of Absence

Employers are not required to pay wages to employees on a job-protected leave. However, employees on leave continue to accrue seniority and earn credit for service and length of employment while on leave, just as if they had remained at work. The only exception to the rule that employees will continue to accrue service and seniority during a leave is the case of probationary employees: for these individuals, any time spent on leave will not be included in calculating the probationary period: subsection 52(2).

Except for reservist leave, the employer must continue to pay its share of the premiums for certain benefit plans, such as pension plans, life insurance, accidental death insurance, extended health insurance plans and dental plans, that were offered before the leave, while the employee is on leave: subsection 51(3). The employer will only be relieved of its obligation to continue making contributions to applicable benefits plans if the employee elects, in writing, not to continue his or her participation in a particular benefit plan or to discontinue employee contributions to such plans.

Employees are also entitled to be reinstated to their previous position with the employer following the leave period, if it exists, or to a comparable position if it does not, unless the employee's employment is ended for reasons *solely* unrelated to the leave: section 53.

Employers have argued that an employee's previous position no longer exists because another person is now filling it. However, the Ministry of Labour does not view this as a valid reason for failing to reinstate the employee to the previous position. If the job is still there, and the same work is being done, then the employee has a right to be reinstated.

Where the employee's job has been modified to an extent that it can no longer be considered the same position (although it is comparable), and the employee would otherwise have been moved into this position, then the employer will be obliged to reinstate the employee to this position. In order to determine whether the position is comparable, one should consider the following factors (in comparison to the previous position):

- the location of the job;
- the hours of work;
- the quality of the working environment;
- the degree of responsibility;
- job security and the possibility of advancement; and
- prestige and prerequisites.

One question that sometimes arises following a leave of absence is whether the employer is obligated to provide an employee with a part-time position, rather than his or her previous full-time position, at the employee's request. It is clear, however, that there is no such obligation under the *ESA, 2000*.

There is no positive obligation on the employer to create a comparable position in circumstances where the employee has been terminated for reasons completely unrelated to the leave of absence and the previous position. In this way, the right of reinstatement is not absolute. The leave provisions are meant to ensure that an employee who goes on leave is in the same position that he or she would have been in had they not taken the leave. The provisions are not meant to give a greater right or benefit to employees on leave. In determining whether termination is legitimate, the test is: "Would this employee have lost his or her job if he or she had not gone on leave?"

Subsection 53(3) of the *ESA, 2000* provides that once the employee returns to work, he or she is entitled to be paid his or her most recent wage rate, or the wage rate that would have been earned had the employee continued to work throughout the leave. This means that the employee will be entitled to receive the benefit of any salary increases that may have been granted in his or her absence, if the salary increase would have been received had they remained at work during that period.

Interaction Between Leave and Vacation Entitlements

Many employers and employees are concerned about whether an employee's vacation pay and vacation time entitlements continue to accrue while the employee is on a job-protected leave.

As indicated above, section 52 of the *ESA, 2000* provides that an employee's leave shall be included in calculating the employee's length of employment, length of service and seniority (except for the purposes of determining whether an employee has completed a probationary period). In addition, both active and non-active employment shall be included in determining whether an employee has been "employed" for 12 months, thereby qualifying for a two-week paid vacation: subsection 33(2).

In light of the above provisions, an employee does continue to accrue both vacation pay and vacation time entitlements while on leave. Specifically, an employee who is on leave accrues vacation pay equal to 4% or 6%, based on the employee's length of service, of any wages earned, and vacation time of two weeks, for each twelve-month period. If the employee does not earn any wages during the period of leave, he or she may not have any vacation pay entitlement in respect of that period (i.e., 4% or 6% of nothing equals nothing); however, he or she would still be entitled to take vacation time.

As with all minimum employment standards in the *ESA, 2000*, if the employer has promised the employee a greater right or benefit, that greater right or benefit will prevail, and will be enforced by an employment standards officer in the event of a complaint. It is noteworthy, however, that the Ministry of Labour now takes the position that employees earn credit for *length of service*, but not *service per se*, or *active service*, when they are on leave. In other words, employees are not treated for all purposes as if they were actively at work during the leave. The Ministry offers two examples of scenarios where these concepts are relevant:

- Vacation time earned through service and vacation pay earned as a percentage of wages — An employment contract provides that employees are entitled to four weeks of vacation for every year of service and accrue vacation pay at the rate of eight per cent of gross wages. An employee who is on leave for the entire vacation entitlement year will not accrue any vacation time under this employment contract (because the employee is not credited with *active service*; only *length of service*). Since that is less than what the *ESA, 2000* provides, the employment contract will not prevail, and the employment standard will apply to provide the employee with two or three weeks of vacation time, as applicable. The employee will not accrue any vacation pay under the employment contract, because vacation pay is a percentage of wages, and she has no wages for the year.

• Vacation time and vacation pay earned through service — An employment contract provides that employees are entitled to 1.5 paid vacation days for each month of active service during the year. An employee who is on leave for the entire vacation entitlement year will not accrue any vacation time under this employment contract (because the employee is not credited with *active service*, only *length of service*). Since that is less than what the *ESA, 2000* provides, the employment contract will not prevail, and the employment standard will apply to provide the employee with two weeks of vacation time. The employee will not accrue any vacation pay under the employment contract, because she did not have any active service during the year.

In keeping with the Ministry's position that employees will earn credit for *length of service* during a leave, increases in vacation entitlements that are based on *length of service* will continue to accrue. For example, an employment contract provides that employees are entitled to two weeks of paid vacation in each of the first three years of employment, and three weeks of paid vacation thereafter. The increase is based on *length of service*. An employee's period of time spent on leave will therefore be included in determining whether she has met the three-year threshold to get to three weeks of paid vacation.

Section 51.1 of the *ESA, 2000* addresses the additional problem of when and how an employee may utilize accrued vacation time, after returning from a leave. Specifically, subsection 51.1(1) provides that if an employee's contract does not allow the employee to defer taking vacation or restricts the employee from doing so, *and as a result*, the employee would have to forfeit vacation time or vacation pay or take less than his or her full leave entitlement in order to exercise his or her right to a leave, *then* the employee may defer taking vacation until the leave expires, or a later date if the employer and employee agree.

Similarly, subsection 51.1(2) of the *ESA, 2000* provides that if an employee is on leave on the day by which his or her vacation must be completed (i.e., within ten months after the 12-month period for which it is given — section 34), the employee shall take his or her vacation immediately after the leave expires, or at a later date if the employer and employee agree.

In both of the above situations, the *ESA, 2000*, in subsection 51.1.(3), allows an employee to elect to forego taking vacation, and receive vacation pay, if the employer agrees and the Director of Employment Standards approves the arrangement.

Interaction Between Leave and Public Holiday Entitlements

As indicated below in the Public Holiday section, a public holiday may fall during an employee's absence on a job-protected leave. Should this occur, the employee is entitled to public holiday pay for the day.

Interaction Between Leave and Bonus Entitlements

The Ministry of Labour has provided some guidance with respect to the interaction between leaves and perfect attendance bonuses. Where an employer awards a bonus to employees for perfect attendance, employees on leave should not be disqualified from the bonus, as this could be seen as a penalty for having taken the leave. However, it would seem absurd to count the time off on leave as "perfect attendance". The Ministry has proposed two ways of dealing with such bonuses:

(i) The employer could give the employee a prorated amount for the portion of the year that he or she was at work, both before and after the leave.

(ii) The employer could extend the period of time considered when determining whether an employee is eligible for a bonus. For example, if an employee was on leave for six months of the year, the employer would extend the assessment period for six months after her return from leave. Note, however, that where the assessment period is extended in this way, the next eligibility period will have to commence on the date it would ordinarily have commenced, notwithstanding the extension.

Interaction Between Leave Entitlements and Attendance Management Programs

The Ministry of Labour has also provided some guidance with respect to the interaction between leaves and attendance management programs. An attendance management program that counts any of the statutory leaves of absence towards the threshold to enter into the next stage would be problematic in most cases. To bring such employees in for an interview, for example, to discuss their attendance, could very well be seen as a reprisal for having taken the leave. The Ministry notes that there are two ways of dealing with such absences:

(i) The first, and less problematic, option is to not include any absences due to a statutory leave of absence towards the threshold to reach the next step in an attendance management program.

(ii) Alternatively, an employer could count any absences due to a statutory leave of absence toward the threshold to meet the next step in an attendance management program. However, the Ministry emphasizes that "extreme care would have to be taken to ensure that the steps in the program are set out in such a way that an employee is not penalized, threatened, or disadvantaged for having taken" a statutory leave of absence. At a minimum, interviews with the employee should be conducted in a non-threatening, non-disciplinary manner.

Public Holidays

Eligible employees are entitled to take the following public holidays off work each year, and receive public holiday pay for that day as listed in section 1 of the *ESA, 2000*:

- New Year's Day
- Good Friday
- Victoria Day
- Canada Day
- Labour Day
- Thanksgiving Day
- Christmas Day
- December 26 (Boxing Day)
- Family Day (3rd Monday in February)

Qualifying Conditions

Eligible employees will forfeit the right to a paid public holiday or a substitute day off if:

- they fail to work all of their regularly scheduled shift before or after the public holiday without reasonable cause; or
- they previously agreed, or were required, to work on a public holiday and failed to do so without reasonable cause; orthey previously agreed, or were required, to work on a public holiday and failed to work all of their regularly scheduled shift before or after the public holiday without reasonable cause. (In this last scenario, the employee is entitled only to premium pay for each hour worked on the public holiday.)

A person who resigns or whose employment is terminated immediately *after* a public holiday (i.e., before the commencement of what would have been his or her first regularly scheduled day of work after the holiday) is not considered to have failed to work the "first regularly scheduled day of work after the public holiday", since the individual was no longer employed on that day, and work could not have been scheduled for him or her on that day.

The Ministry of Labour takes the view that an employee who has been suspended by the employer on a day that would otherwise have been the last regularly scheduled day before a public holiday or the first regularly scheduled day after a public holiday is not considered to have failed to work the requisite qualifying days. Since the employee was on suspension, work could not have been scheduled for him or her on that day.

These employees will still be entitled to receive at least one and one-half times their regular wages for each hour actually worked on a public holiday.

Public Holiday Falls on a Regular Working Day

If a public holiday falls on a day that would ordinarily be a working day for an eligible employee, and the employee is not on vacation that day, the employer is required to give the employee the day off work and pay him or her public holiday pay for that day: subsection 26(1).

The *ESA, 2000* also provides for the situation where an employer's operations remain open and an employee agrees to work on a public holiday. Under the *ESA, 2000*, an employee may *elect* (but generally cannot be *required*, unless the employer operates an essential service, hospitality business or continuous operation, and the employee is not on vacation) to work on a public holiday that falls on a regular working day: section 27.

Section 27 of the *ESA, 2000* provides that an employee who works on a public holiday can either:

• receive regular wages for the day plus a substitute day off with holiday pay within three months (or within 12 months, if both parties agree); or

• if the employer agrees, receive public holiday pay for the day plus premium pay (defined in the legislation as 1 1/2 times regular wages).

As of January 1, 2018, where a substitute day off is provided to an employee who works on a public holiday, employers will be required to provide the employee with a written record, prior to the public holiday, setting out:

• the public holiday on which the employee will work;

• the date of the day that is substituted for a public holiday; and

• the date on which the statement is provided to the employee.

Significantly, if an employee receives premium pay for working on a public holiday, the hours worked are not taken into consideration in calculating overtime pay to which the employee may be entitled: section 31, *ESA, 2000*.

Public Holiday Falls on a Non-Working Day

Section 29 of the *ESA, 2000* provides that if a public holiday falls on a non-working day, an employee may either:

• take a substitute day off within three months with public holiday pay (or within 12 months, if both parties agree); or

• if the employer agrees, receive public holiday pay for the public holiday.

As of January 1, 2018, where a substitute day off is provided to an employee who works on a public holiday, employers will be required to provide the employee with a written record, prior to the public holiday, setting out:

• the public holiday that is being substituted;

• the date of the day that is substituted for a public holiday; and

• the date on which the statement is provided to the employee.

Calculation of Public Holiday Pay

As of January 2018, amendments under Bill 148 will alter the calculation of public holiday pay under the *ESA, 2000* with the purpose of simplifying the calculation process. Following these amendments, public holiday pay will be determined by dividing employees' total wages in the pay period prior to the holiday by the number or days worked in that period. For employees who did not work for the employer during the entirety of the pay period preceding the holiday, payment of holiday pay will be determined by dividing the amount of regular wages in the pay period including the holiday by the number of days worked by the employee during that period. Periods where the employee is on vacation or personal emergency leave in the pay period preceding the holiday are not counted for the purpose of making this calculation: section 24(1).

Public Holiday Falls During an Employee's Vacation

A public holiday may fall during an employee's vacation. If the employee otherwise qualifies for a public holiday benefit, he or she remains on vacation, and in addition is entitled to one of the following:

• a substitute day off work with public holiday pay, taken within three months of the public holiday or, if the employer and employee agree in writing, within 12 months of the public holiday; or

• if the employer and employee agree in writing, payment of public holiday pay for the public holiday, without a substitute day off work.

Public Holiday Falls During Employee's Leave of Absence or Lay-Off

As indicated above in the Leaves of Absence section, a public holiday may fall during an employee's absence on pregnancy leave, parental leave, personal or declared emergency leave, family medical leave, or lay-off. Should this occur, the employee is entitled to public holiday pay for the day.

Vacation

Vacation Entitlement Periods

The basic rule regarding vacations for employees whose period of employment is less than five years is as follows: Employees must receive two weeks of vacation, with pay, after each 12-month period of employment. As of January 2018, amendments to the *ESA, 2000* under Bill 148 will provide employees with a period of employment that is greater than five years with a minimum entitlement of three weeks' vacation, with pay, after each 12-month period of employment.

Questions arise, however, regarding the "12-month period of employment". What is it? When does it start? When does it end? Is it the same for all employees? The best place to start is with the following key definitions:

• *Vacation Entitlement Year* — The 12-month period during which the employee earns vacation time with pay is referred to as the "vacation entitlement year".

• *Standard Vacation Entitlement Year* — The "standard vacation entitlement year" starts on the day the employee is hired and lasts for 12 consecutive months. For example, an employee may start on June 1. The "standard vacation entitlement year" is June 1 to May 31.

• *Alternative Vacation Entitlement Year* — The "alternative vacation entitlement year" starts on a date set by the employer and lasts for 12 consecutive months. For example, an employee may start on June 1, but the employer has established an "alternative vacation entitlement year" that begins each year on January 1. The "alternative vacation entitlement year" is January 1 to December 31.

• *Stub Period* — The "stub period" is the period of time between the employee's first day of work and the start of the next "alternative vacation entitlement year" or, under amendments arising from Bill 148, the period between the fifth anniversary of the employee's start date and the start of the next "alternative vacation entitlement year". Using the above example, the period between June 1 (the employee's start date) and January 1 (the start of the next "alternative vacation entitlement year") is the "stub period".

• In addition, should the employer switch from using a "standard vacation entitlement year" to using an "alternative vacation entitlement year", the period of time between them, the end of the last "standard vacation entitlement year" and the first "alternative vacation entitlement year", is a "stub period".

Vacation With Pay

The vacation entitlements in the *ESA, 2000* embody two separate and distinct concepts:

1. *vacation time*: time off work; and

2. *vacation pay*: payment during or in respect of such time off work.

With respect to vacation time, employees having less than five years' tenure with an employer are entitled to two weeks' time off work after each "standard vacation entitlement year" or "alternative vacation entitlement year", whichever the employer is using. Employees are also entitled to a pro-rated amount of time off work after a "stub period" (a formula for determining this pro-rated amount is set out in section 34(1) of the *ESA, 2000*). Following changes under Bill 148, employees having a tenure of more than five years with an employer will be entitled to three weeks' vacation time after each "standard vacation entitlement year" or "alternative vacation entitlement year". Where the fifth anniversary of an employee's start date falls within an "alternative vacation entitlement year", the employer must provide the following total vacation time entitlement during the following vacation entitlement year:

(3 weeks x (months worked following fifth anniversary/12 months))

+

(2 weeks x (months worked prior to fifth anniversary/12 months))

With respect to *vacation pay*, employees having less than five years' tenure with an employer are entitled to at least four percent of the gross wages earned during each "standard vacation entitlement year", "alternative vacation entitlement year", or "stub period". Following changes under Bill 148, employees having a tenure of more than five years' with an employer will be entitled to 6% vacation time after each "standard vacation entitlement year" or "alternative vacation entitlement year". Where the fifth anniversary of an employee's start date falls within an "alternative vacation entitlement year", the employer must provide the following total vacation time entitlement during the following vacation entitlement year:

(6% weeks x (months worked following fifth anniversary/12 months))

+

(4% weeks x (months worked prior to fifth anniversary/12 months))

The distinction between *vacation time* and *vacation pay* is critical because they do not necessarily go hand-in-hand.

For example, if an employee is terminated before he or she has taken vacation, he or she is not entitled to vacation *time*. However, he or she is still entitled to vacation *pay*, equal to the applicable percentage of all wages earned to the date of termination. Even if an employee works for only one hour, he or she is entitled to the applicable percentage of the hour's wages as vacation pay. (This paragraph assumes that there is no employment contract granting the employee a greater benefit. In fact, many employers offer more than the minimum statutory vacation benefits, such as vacation pay of 8% of wages or allowing employees to take vacation *time* before completing twelve months of employment.) This amount must be paid no later than seven days after the employment ended or on what would have been the employee's next pay day, whichever is later.

When Vacation Shall Be Taken

• *Vacation With Pay Earned During "Standard Vacation Entitlement Year"* — The employee must receive his or her vacation with pay within ten months after the end of the "standard vacation entitlement year".

• *Vacation With Pay Earned During "Alternative Vacation Entitlement Year"* — The employee must receive his or her vacation with pay within ten months after the end of the "alternative vacation entitlement year".

• *Vacation With Pay Earned During "Stub Period"* — The employee must receive his or her vacation with pay within ten months after the start of the first "alternative vacation entitlement year".

Subject to these rules, the employer is entitled to determine when the employee may receive his or her vacation with pay.

Length of Vacation Periods

The general rule is that an employee must take vacation in one, two, or three week blocks, as applicable. However, if the employee makes a written request, and the employer agrees in writing, vacation may be scheduled in shorter periods, including periods as short as one day: section 35.

For vacation time earned during "stub periods", if the amount of vacation time earned is between *two* and *five* days, the vacation days must be taken in a row, unless the employee requests in writing and the employer agrees in writing to shorter periods: section 35.1. If the amount of vacation time earned is *more than five days*, the first five days must be taken in a row and any additional days may be taken together with the first five days or in one separate period. However, the employee may request in writing, and the employer may agree in writing, to shorter periods.

An employee can elect not to take vacation, provided the employer agrees and the Director of Employment Standards approves. However, even if the employee does not take vacation, he or she must still be paid vacation pay earned with respect to that vacation.

Timing and Manner of Providing Vacation Pay

The general rule is that an employee must receive his or her vacation pay in a lump sum before taking a vacation.

There are four exceptions to the general rule:

1. If the employer pays the employee his or her wages by direct deposit into an employee's account at a financial institution, the vacation pay must be paid on or before the pay day for the pay period in which the vacation falls.

2. When the vacation time is being taken in periods of less than one week, the vacation pay may be paid on or before the pay day for the period in which the vacation falls.

3. The vacation pay earned in each pay period may be paid on the pay day for that pay period if the employee has agreed in writing that his or her vacation pay will be paid on each paycheque as it is earned.

4. If the employee agrees in writing, the employer can pay the vacation pay at any time agreed to by the employee.

Vacation Records

Employers must keep detailed records with respect to each employee's entitlement to vacation time and vacation pay.

The vacation records must include the following information:

• the amount of vacation time, if any, that the employee had earned since the start of employment, but had not taken before the start of the vacation entitlement year;

• the amount of vacation time that the employee earned during the vacation entitlement year;

• the amount of vacation time, if any, taken by the employee during the vacation entitlement year;

• the amount of vacation time, if any, that the employee had earned since the start of employment but had not taken as of the end of the vacation entitlement year;

• the amount of vacation pay paid to the employee during the vacation entitlement year (unless vacation pay is paid as it accrues);

• the amount of wages on which the vacation pay paid to the employee during the vacation entitlement year was calculated, and the period of time to which those wages relate (unless vacation pay is paid as it accrues); and

• *in respect of a stub period, if there is one:*

    • the amount of vacation time that the employee earned during the stub period;

    • the amount of vacation time, if any, that the employee took during the stub period;

    • the amount of vacation time, if any, earned but not taken by the employee during the stub period;

    • the amount of vacation pay paid to the employee during the stub period (unless vacation pay is paid as it accrues); and

    • the amount of wages on which the vacation pay paid to the employee during the stub period was calculated, and the period of time to which those wages relate (unless vacation pay is paid as it accrues).

The vacation records must be prepared not later than the later of:

- seven days after the start of the next vacation entitlement year or the first vacation entitlement year, as the case may be; and

- the first pay day of the next vacation entitlement year or the first vacation entitlement year, as the case may be.

Provision of Vacation Statements to Employees

Employers must provide a vacation statement (containing the same information as a vacation record, described above) to employees only once with respect to a stub period or vacation entitlement year, and only if the employee makes a written request.

The vacation statement must be provided to the employee not later than the later of:

- seven days after the employee makes his or her request; and

- the first pay day after the employee makes his or her request.

However, if the request is made *during* the stub period or vacation entitlement year to which the request relates, the vacation statement must be provided to the employee not later than the later of:

- seven days after the start of the next vacation entitlement year; and

- the first pay day of the next vacation entitlement year.

Significantly, employees who receive vacation pay as it accrues are *not* entitled to receive these annual vacation statements. Instead, the employer must report the vacation pay on each wage statement, or provide a separate statement (at the same time) setting out the vacation pay that it being paid.

Temporary Lay-Offs

Under the *ESA, 2000*, an employer may impose a temporary lay-off without providing notice of termination (or pay in lieu thereof) or severance pay, and without specifying a date on which the employee will be recalled to work.

For termination pay purposes, a temporary lay-off is defined as:

(a) a lay-off of not more than 13 weeks in any period of 20 consecutive weeks;

(b) a lay-off of more than 13 weeks in any period of 20 consecutive weeks, if the lay-off is less than 35 weeks in any period of 52 consecutive weeks *and* one of the following conditions exists:

(i) the employee continues to receive substantial payments from the employer,

(ii) the employer continues to make benefit plan contributions for the employee,

(iii) the employee receives supplementary unemployment benefits from the employer,

(iv) the employee works elsewhere during the lay-off and would otherwise be entitled to receive supplementary unemployment benefits from the employer,

(v) the employer recalls the employee within the time approved by the Director of Employment Standards, or

(vi) in the case of a non-unionized employee, the employer recalls the employee within the time frame set out in an agreement between the employer and the employee; or

(c) in the case of a unionized employee, a lay-off longer than 35 weeks in any period of 52 consecutive weeks, if the employer recalls the employee within the time set out in the collective agreement.

For termination pay purposes, an employee is considered to be laid off if he or she is earning less than one-half the amount he or she would normally earn in a week, and the week is not an excluded week (i.e., for one or more days, the employee is not able to work, is not available for work, is subject to a disciplinary suspension, or cannot work due to a strike or lockout). However, an excluded week *is* counted towards the 20 or 52 consecutive weeks period, as the case may be.

If a lay-off lasts longer than the period of a temporary lay-off, it is treated as a termination, and the employee is entitled to notice of termination or pay in lieu thereof. For the purpose of calculating these entitlements, the person's employment is deemed to be terminated on the first day of the lay-off.

For severance pay purposes, a temporary lay-off is defined as a lay-off of less than 35 weeks in any period of 52 consecutive weeks. Also for severance pay purposes, an employee is considered to be laid off if he or she is earning less than one-quarter the amount he or she would normally earn in a week, and the week is not an excluded week (i.e., for one or more days, the employee is not able to work, is not available for work, is subject to a disciplinary suspension, or cannot work due to a strike or lockout). However, an excluded week *is* counted towards the 52 consecutive weeks period.

Employers should be aware that just because the *ESA, 2000* allows for temporary lay-offs does not mean that the common law does. In most cases, absent an express provision in the employment contract or collective agreement allowing an employer to implement temporary lay-offs, courts will treat temporary lay-offs as a constructive dismissal. This is because employees expect to work in exchange for an established salary, and this expectation forms a vital component of the employment contract. If the contract does not contemplate temporary lay-offs, the employer's unilateral decision to withhold work and pay for a temporary period could be perceived as a fundamental breach entitling the employee to treat himself or herself as having been dismissed without just cause.

Please refer to the section on Temporary Help Agencies for special lay-off rules that apply to such entities and their employees.

Termination and Severance of Employment

Termination

Subsection 56(1) of the *ESA, 2000* provides that a termination occurs in the following circumstances:

- when an employer dismisses an employee or otherwise refuses or is unable to continue employing him or her;
- when an employer constructively dismisses an employee and the employee resigns in response to the constructive dismissal within a reasonable period; and
- when the employer lays the employee off for a period longer than a temporary lay-off.

While an employer is not required to give an employee a reason why his or her employment is being terminated, it cannot terminate an employee's employment if any part of the reason for the termination is based on the employee exercising his or her rights under the *ESA, 2000*.

Generally, notice of termination must be in writing and given to the employee either:

- personally, by leaving a copy of the document with the employee;
- by verifiable mail to the employee's last known address;
- by fax or email if the employee is able to receive it that way;
- by a courier service; or
- leaving it in a sealed envelope addressed to the employee, with a person who appears to be at least 16 years of age, at the employee's last known address.

The decision of the Ontario Labour Relations Board in *McClelland v. King Coating Roofing Inc.*, 2016 CarswellOnt 12017, also indicates that notice of termination may be provided via text message. However, courts require that such a message clearly and unequivocally state that the employee is terminated.

The Board found that an expression of frustration with the employee does not suffice for this purpose.

If notice of termination is served to the employee either personally or in a sealed envelope to an individual who appears to be at least 16 years of age at the employee's last known address, notice is effective on the day it was given. If notice is served by fax or email it is effective on the day it was sent unless the notice was sent after 5:00 pm, on a Saturday, Sunday, or public holiday, in which case it would be effective on the next business day. If notice is served by verifiable mail it is effective five days after the document is mailed. If notice is served by a courier it is considered effective two days after the courier takes the document. Except in cases of personal service, if the person establishes that the service was not effective due to an absence, accident, illness or cause beyond the person's control, the above timelines will not apply.

Section 61 of the *ESA, 2000* expressly provides that an employer may terminate an employee using notice of termination, termination pay, or a combination of both, provided:

• the employee is given a lump sum payment equal to the amount he or she would have received had they been given notice of termination; and

• the employer continues to make benefit plan contributions for the period of notice.

Thus, if the employee does not get the required notice of termination, he or she will be entitled to the difference as pay in lieu thereof.

Employees who are entitled to notice of termination or termination pay shall receive the following:

Length of Employment	Minimum Notice of Termination or Termination Pay or Combination of Both
less than three months	nil
more than three months but less than one year	at least one week

one year or more but less than three years	at least two weeks
three years or more but less than four years	at least three weeks
four years or more but less than five years	at least four weeks
five years or more but less than six years	at least five weeks
six years or more but less than seven years	at least six weeks
seven years or more but less than eight years	at least seven weeks
eight years or more	at least eight weeks

Accordingly, the maximum amount of termination notice/pay required to be provided under the *ESA, 2000* is eight weeks. However, if the employment contract provides a greater right or benefit — as many do by failing to reference the *ESA, 2000* requirement or another formula specifically — the employer may very well be required to provide more than eight weeks.

During the statutory notice period (whether the employee is given notice of termination, termination pay, or a combination of both), the employer must:

• not reduce the employee's wage rate or alter any other term or condition of employment;

• continue to pay the employee the wages to which he or she is entitled to receive, which can be no less than his or her regular wages for a regular work week; and

• continue to maintain the employee's benefit plans.

Termination pay is a lump sum payment equal to the regular wages for a regular work week that an employee would otherwise be entitled to during the written notice period. Under amendments in Bill 148, as of January 2018, the calculation of regular wages will include tips and gratuities received by the employee. For the purposes of the *ESA, 2000*, however, overtime pay, vacation pay, public holiday pay, premium pay, termination pay and severance pay are not considered "regular wages". Amendments under Bill 148 also provide that personal emergency leave pay, termination of assignment pay (for assignment employees) will not be considered as "regular wages" for the purposes of the *ESA, 2000*. For an employee who usually works the same number of hours every week, a regular work week is a week of that many hours, not including overtime hours. If the employee does not have a regular work week or is paid on a basis other than time, the amount the employer must pay the employee is equal to the average amount of regular wages earned by the employee per week for the weeks in which the employee worked in the 12-week period immediately preceding the day of termination.

The question arises as to how to calculate the weekly entitlement for the notice period if the employee did not work any of the weeks within the 12-week period immediately preceding the day of termination. The *ESA, 2000* does not address this situation. Ministry policy therefore provides that the employer must continue to look back in blocks of 12 weeks, until a 12-week period can be found in which the employee has weeks worked, and then average the wages earned over that 12-week period.

Employers often ask whether they are required to pay the employee his/her bonus during the termination period. This question was addressed in a 2012 case by the Ontario Superior Court of Justice. In *Sandhu v. Solutions 2 go Inc.*, 2012 CarswellOnt 4115 (Ont. S.C.J.), the employer paid a profit-sharing bonus each year to employees who had worked for the full fiscal year. According to the employee, this bonus "became an integral part of her compensation package". The employee was dismissed, and in accordance with the *ESA, 2000*, she was provided with four weeks' pay in lieu of notice. Approximately one month later, the employer paid out its 2010 fiscal year profit sharing bonus. Despite having worked the entire fiscal year, this employee did not receive a profit sharing bonus.

The employer alleged that the profit sharing bonus was discretionary and subject to the condition that the employee be actively employed when the bonus was paid out after the fiscal year concluded. The Court disagreed, referring to that section of the *ESA, 2000* which provides that an employer "shall not reduce the employee's wage rate or alter any other term or condition of employment" during the termination period. Because the Court held that the bonus was not discretionary — as there was no evidence that performance or any other criteria was used to differentiate between qualifying employees — the employee was deemed to be an active employee during the notice period and was therefore found to be entitled to receive the 2010 fiscal year profit sharing bonus.

The Ontario Court of Appeal addressed this subject further in its 2016 decision in *Paquette v. TeraGo Networks Inc.*, 2016 CarswellOnt 12633 (Ont. C.A.). In that matter, an employer argued that a dismissed employee was not entitled to receive a bonus payment during his notice period because the employer's bonus policy expressly required active employment as a condition for bonus eligibility. The Court of Appeal determined that, as the employee's bonus made up an integral part of his compensation package, it could not be denied to him during the notice period on only the ground that the employer's policy required active employment as a condition of bonus eligibility. According to the Court of Appeal, an employer may only deny bonus payments during the notice period through clear policy language that expressly removes an employee's common law entitlement to receive the bonus during the notice period. Accordingly, the employee was awarded an amount to compensate for his bonus entitlement during the notice period.

If the employee was employed by the employer for two different periods, separated by a break of at least 13 weeks, only the last period of employment is used in calculating whether the employee is entitled to termination notice/pay, and how much.

The *ESA, 2000* contemplates that there will be times when an employer wishes to postpone an employee's termination date after having provided notice of termination. Ontario Regulation 288/01 provides that an employer may provide temporary work to an employee who has received a notice of termination for up to 13 weeks after the original termination date. The provision of such temporary work does not affect the employee's entitlement to notice of termination (or pay in lieu), and the employer is not required to provide any further notice when the employee's employment eventually does end. According to the Ministry, the main purpose of this section is to allow employers in a plant closure situation, for example, to continue to employ some of the employees on a temporary basis past their original termination dates to assist in winding up operations, without the employer having to provide further notice of termination.

A recent case of the Ontario Court of Appeal considered whether Ontario Regulation 288/01 contemplates a single period of temporary work for up to 13 weeks following the original termination date, or whether employers may extend employment for multiple, serialized periods of less than 13 weeks. In *Di Tomaso v. Crown Metal Packaging Canada LP*, 2011 CarswellOnt 5356, Crown Metal provided Mr. Di Tomaso with five separate written notices of termination, with four different termination dates, as follows:

- September 9, 2009, with a termination date of November 6, 2009;
- November 4, 2009, with a termination date of December 18, 2009;
- December 15, 2009, with a termination date of February 19, 2010;
- February 18, 2010, with a termination date of February 26, 2010; and
- February 24, 2010, confirming the termination date of February 26, 2010.

The Court of Appeal held that Regulation 288/01 contemplates a single period of temporary work after the termination date, which is not to exceed 13 weeks. If the temporary work exceeds that duration, then fresh notice of termination (or pay in lieu thereof) is required. To allow employers to extend employment for multiple, serialized periods of less than 13 weeks "would be inconsistent with the *ESA*'s status as remedial, benefit-conferring legislation designed to protect the interests of employees". The cumulative effect of multiple extensions would create uncertainty as to when one's employment will end.

An arbitrator has recently considered whether employers are obligated to provide employees who are on sick leave (and therefore unable to work) with termination pay under the *ESA, 2000*: see *Quality Meat Packers Limited and United Food and Commercial Workers Canada, Local 175 (Jaiteh Grievance)* [2013] O.L.A.A. No. 1 (Arbitrator Randy Levinson). The union argued that the employees were entitled to receive the wages they would have received had they not been on sick leave during the notice period. The employer argued that it was only required to pay employees those wages they were entitled to receive under the collective agreement. In this case, the collective agreement did not provide for the payment of any wages while an employee was not at work; it only required that the employer maintain benefits and seniority. Arbitrator Levinson concluded that the *ESA, 2000* only requires employers to pay the wages the employers are entitled to under the collective agreement during the statutory notice period, which may be zero if the employee is not at work, plus any benefits the employee is entitled to receive while on such leave of absence.

Mass Termination

Ontario Regulation 288/01 sets out an employer's notice obligations in situations of "mass termination" where 50 or more employees are terminated within a prescribed period.

Special rules apply where 50 or more employees receive notice of termination at an employer's establishment within a four-week period (otherwise known as a "mass termination"). In particular, the following notice periods are prescribed by section 3 of Ontario Regulation 288/01:

Number of Employees Affected	Minimum Notice of Termination or Termination Pay or Combination of Both
50 or more but fewer than 200	at least eight weeks
200 or more but fewer than 500	at least 12 weeks
500 or more	at least 16 weeks

When a mass termination occurs, the employer is required to provide the Director of Employment Standards with certain prescribed information, and the notice of termination is not effective unless the employer submits it in the prescribed form prior to giving notice to the affected employees.

The mass termination rules do not apply if:

• the number of employees whose employment is terminated at the establishment is not more than 10 per cent of the number of employees who have been employed there for at least three months; and

• the terminations were not caused by the permanent discontinuance of part of the employer's business at the establishment.

Termination Pay Exemptions

Ontario Regulation 288/01 also lists those employees who are not entitled to notice of termination or termination pay under the *ESA, 2000*. These employees include:

• employees who have been hired for a definite term or a specific task, *unless*:

(i) the employment terminates before the end of the term or completion of the task;

(ii) the term expires or the task is not yet completed more than 12 months after the employment commences; or

(iii) the employment continues for three months or more after the expiry of the term or completion of the task;

• an employee on temporary lay-off;

• an employee who has been guilty of wilful misconduct, disobedience or wilful neglect of duty that is not trivial and has not been condoned by the employer;

• an employee whose contract of employment has become impossible to perform or has been frustrated by a fortuitous or unforeseeable event or circumstance, unless the impossibility or frustration is the result of an illness or injury suffered by the employee;

• an employee whose employment is terminated after refusing an offer of reasonable alternative employment with the employer;

• an employee whose employment is terminated after refusing alternative employment made available through a seniority system;

• an employee who is on a temporary lay-off and who does not return to work within a reasonable time after having been requested by his or her employer to do so;

• an employee whose employment is terminated during or as a result of a strike or lockout at the place of employment;

• a construction employee;

• an employee whose employment is terminated when he or she reaches the age of retirement in accordance with the employer's established practice, but only if the termination would not contravene the Ontario *Human Rights Code*;

• an employee:

(i) whose employer is engaged in building, altering or repairing ships or vessels over ten gross tonnes designed for and used in commercial navigation;

(ii) to whom a legitimate supplementary unemployment benefit plan applies; and

(iii) who agrees to the application of this exemption.

The scope of the above exemption for construction employees was elaborated in the OLRB decision in *1703171*

Ontario Inc. operating as The Construction Group and Bath Solutions v. Rosa Russo-Janzen, 2016 CarswellOnt 2564 [*Russo-Janzen*]. In that matter, an off-site office manager for a construction company was found to fall outside of the scope of the exception, and was therefore entitled to termination pay. Arbitrator Turtle's decision clarified that the exemption for construction employees does not apply to employees who work off-site and whose work is not sufficiently connected to the work of on-site employees.

With respect to the exclusion of employees who are "guilty of wilful misconduct, disobedience or wilful neglect," the OLRB decision in *Rosario Sacco v. MMCC Solutions Canada Company (Teleperformance Canada)*, 2015 CarswellOnt 18966 [*Sacco*], found that the employer must prove that such breaches were "not trivial" and were "not condoned" by the employer. Accordingly, employers may be required to provide evidence and applicable metrics in cases where a decision to deny termination pay on this basis is challenged by a worker.

Severance Pay

Severance pay is designed to compensate an employee for the loss of seniority and job-related benefits as well as to recognize his or her long service.

Severance of employment occurs where:

• the employer dismisses the employee or refuses to continue employing the employee or is unable to continue employing the employee;

• the employer constructively dismisses the employee and the employee resigns from his or her employment in response within a reasonable period of time;

• the employer lays the employee off for a period longer than a temporary lay-off;

• the employer lays the employee off because of a permanent discontinuance of all of the employer's business at an establishment; or

• the employer gives the employee notice of termination, the employee then gives the employer written notice at least two weeks before resigning, and the employee's notice of resignation is to take effect during the statutory notice period.

In order to qualify for severance pay, an employee must have been employed by the employer for five years or more when his or her employment is severed and:

• the employer's payroll must be at least $2.5 million annually; or

• the severance occurs as a result of a permanent discontinuance of all or part of the employer's business and the employee is one of at least 50 employees who have had their employment relationship severed within a six-month period.

In determining whether an employee has been employed by the employer for five or more years, one must include *all* time spent by the employee in the employment of the employer, whether continuous or not (e.g., due to resignation, termination for any reason, or otherwise), and whether active or not.

Employers will be considered to have an annual payroll of $2.5 million or more if either:

• the total wages earned by all employees in the four weeks immediately prior to the employee's dismissal, multiplied by 13, totals $2.5 million or more; or

• the total wages earned by all employees in the last or second-last fiscal year of the employer prior to the employee's dismissal was $2.5 million or more.

There is some question as to whether the $2.5 million annual payroll threshold refers to *Ontario* payroll only, or to company-wide payroll. The Ministry of Labour takes the position that only *Ontario* payroll should be considered. However, a recent decision of the Ontario Superior Court of Justice has called such position into question. In *Paquette v. Quadraspec Inc.*, 2014 ONSC 2431 (CanLII) (*"Paquette"*), the employer's annual payroll for Ontario employees was well below the $2.5 million threshold. However, its annual payroll for all employees (it had employees in both Ontario and Quebec) was well over the $2.5 million threshold. In contrast to a 2011 decision of the Ontario Superior Court (*Altman v. Steve's Music Store Inc.*, 2011 CarswellOnt 1703 (Ont. S.C.J.) at para. 36, additional reasons 2011 CarswellOnt 6609 (Ont. S.C.J.) (*"Altman"*), the Court in *Paquette* held that the $2.5 million threshold must refer to the total wages earned by *all* of the employer's employees, and not only those situated in Ontario. The Court reasoned that if the legislature had intended to include only Ontario payroll, it would have done so clearly and explicitly. It remains to be seen whether future decision-makers will follow Ministry of Labour policy and the *Altman* decision and include only Ontario payroll, or whether they will follow the decision in *Paquette* and include all of an employer's payroll, for the purposes of determining whether the $2.5 million payroll threshold has been met.

Section 9 of Ontario Regulation 288/01 sets out the circumstances in which employees are not entitled to receive severance pay. The exemptions from the obligation to pay severance pay are as follows:

- an employee whose employment is severed due to a permanent discontinuance of all or part of a business, if the employer shows that such discontinuance was caused by the economic consequences of a strike;
- an employee whose contract of employment has become impossible to perform or has been frustrated, *unless* the impossibility or frustration is the result of:

(i) a permanent discontinuance of all or part of the employer's business because of a fortuitous or unforeseen event; or

(ii) the employer's death; or

(iii) the employee's death, if the employee received a notice of termination before his death; or

(iv) an illness or injury suffered by the employee,

• an employee who, having had his or her employment severed, retires and receives an actuarially unreduced pension that reflects any service credits which the employee would have been expected to earn in the normal course of events for the purposes of the pension plan;

• an employee whose employment is severed after refusing an offer of reasonable alternative employment with the employer;

• an employee whose employment is severed after refusing reasonable alternative employment made available through a seniority system;

• an employee who has been guilty of wilful misconduct, disobedience, or wilful neglect of duty that is not trivial and has not been condoned by the employer;

• a construction employee; and

• an employee engaged in the on-site maintenance of buildings; structures, roads, sewers, pipelines, mains, tunnels or other works.

As with termination pay, the above exemption respecting construction employees will not apply to off-site employees whose work is not sufficiently connected to the work of on-site employees (See discussion of *Russo-Janzen* under "Termination Pay Exemptions" above).

The exemption for employees who, upon having their employment severed, retire and receive an actuarially unreduced pension that reflects any service credits the employee would have expected to earn in the normal course, has been considered by the Ontario Divisional Court in *National Automobile, Aerospace, Transportation and General Workers' Union of Canada (CAW-Canada), Local 1451 v. Kitchener Frame Ltd.*, 2010 CarswellOnt 5199. Kitchener Frame was a manufacturer of automobile parts that went out of business in April 2009. Employees of Kitchener Frame belonged to a defined benefit pension plan that provided for immediate retirement in the event of a plant closure, with supplementary pension payments to the age of 65, and/or a special early retirement allowance payable until the age of 60. A supplemental agreement between the union and the employer also included an income security program that provided for various pension benefits upon plant closure.

Arbitrator Knopf concluded that in determining whether employees were entitled to severance pay, she should consider whether the total pension benefits they received compensated them for the loss of service credits they could have earned in the normal course if the plant had not closed. She decided that this required including the additional benefits in the valuation of the actual pension benefit received. She also utilized commuted values to compare the actual pension benefits employees would receive on plant closure to what they would have received in the "normal course". Ultimately, the arbitrator concluded that the affected employees were receiving pension benefits equal to or greater than what they would have received had the plant not been closed. As such, they were not entitled to severance pay. The decision was upheld by the Ontario Divisional Court.

Section 66 of the *ESA, 2000*, provides that an employer and employee may agree to pay severance pay in instalments, provided the instalment payments do not exceed a period of three years.

For employees with a regular work week, severance pay is calculated by multiplying the employee's regular wages for a regular work week by the sum of: (a) the number of years of employment the employee has completed; and (b) the number of additional months of employment the employee has completed, divided by 12. For employees without a regular work week, the same formula is used, however the employee's "regular wages for a regular work week" are deemed to be the average of wages earned in the 12-week period preceding the date on which the employee was severed.

As with termination pay, the question arises as to how to calculate the weekly entitlement for the severance period if the employee did not work any of the weeks within the 12-week period preceding the day of severance. The *ESA, 2000* does not address this situation. Ministry policy therefore provides that the employer must continue to look back in blocks of 12 weeks, until a 12-week period can be found in which the employee has weeks worked, and then average the wages earned over that 12-week period.

The maximum amount of severance pay required to be paid under the *ESA, 2000* is 26 weeks. However, if the employment contract provides a greater right or benefit — as many do, by not specifically referencing the *ESA, 2000* requirement or another formula — the employer may be required to pay more than 26 weeks.

Subsection 65(2.1) of the *ESA, 2000* clarifies how severance pay is to be calculated when an employee is already in receipt of a pension at the time of termination. Specifically, new subsection 65(2.1) of the *ESA, 2000* provides that if an employee in receipt of an actuarially unreduced pension benefit has his or her employment severed on or after November 6, 2009, time spent in the employer's employ for which the employee received service credits in calculating the pension benefit is not to be included in determining whether that employee is eligible for severance pay, and/or in calculating severance pay. (This is relevant only if the pension benefit was provided under a defined benefit pension plan, where the benefit is calculated according to a formula involving years of employment and earnings.) An "actuarially unreduced pension benefit" is a *full* pension, that is, the pension benefit produced by the formula is not reduced to reflect the fact that the employee is retiring before the normal age of retirement under the pension plan.

What happens when an employee is provided with an extended period of working notice that greatly exceeds his or her entitlement to notice of termination? Is the employer still required to pay the full amount of severance pay? The answer is "yes". This issue was addressed in the 2011 Ontario Small Claims Court decision in *Mattiassi v. Hathro Management Partnership*, 2011 CarswellOnt 11431. The employee in that matter worked at a law firm for 28 years. He was dismissed without cause and given 54 weeks of working notice. The employer also offered the employee a two-month gratuitous payment at the end of the working notice period. The employee rejected the gratuitous payment and filed a claim for severance pay under the *ESA, 2000*. The employer disputed the employee's claim, arguing that the employee had already been adequately compensated by the lengthy working notice period (which exceeded her *ESA, 2000* termination notice/pay entitlement by 46 weeks) and the gratuitous payment.

The Court in *Mattiassi* ruled that the employee was entitled to his full severance pay entitlement, noting subsection 67(7) of the *ESA, 2000* which provides that "Subject to subsection (8), severance pay under this section is in addition to any other amount to which an employee is entitled under this Act or his or her employment contract." The Court also noted that termination notice/pay and severance pay may not be set off against each other: they are two distinct entitlements under the *ESA, 2000* which serve different purposes. Accordingly, regardless of the length of an employee's working notice period, he or she will still be entitled to full severance pay (assuming all qualifying conditions are met).

Similarly, in *Garreton v. Complete Innovations Inc.*, 2016 CarswellOnt 2500, the Ontario Superior Court concluded that notice provisions in an employment contract will be rendered void where those provisions operate to deny severance entitlements under the ESA, 2000. However, the 2017 Ontario Superior Court in *Nemeth v. Hatch Ltd.*, 2017 CarswellOnt 3782 (Ont. S.C.J.) nevertheless concluded that an employment contract did not serve to deny an employee's severance entitlements where the contract was simply silent with respect to these entitlements (ie., the contract did not expressly mention the entitlement).

"Wilful misconduct, disobedience, or wilful neglect of duty that is not trivial and has not been condoned by the employer"

As indicated above, employers are not required to provide notice of termination (or pay in lieu) or severance pay to employees who are guilty of wilful misconduct, disobedience, or wilful neglect of duty that is not trivial and has not been condoned by the employer (See reference to the OLRB decision in *Sacco* under "Termination Pay Exemptions" above). This exemption is often referred to as the "just cause" exemption, but it should not be confused with the common law test for just cause. A March 14, 2011 decision of the Ontario Superior Court of Justice made clear that proving just cause at common law may not be sufficient to satisfy this exemption under the *ESA, 2000*.

In *Oosterbosch v. FAG Aerospace Inc.*, 2011 CarswellOnt 1702, a 17-year employee was dismissed at the age of 53 as a result of five incidents that occurred in a span of approximately seven months. The employer was a manufacturer of bearings for the aerospace industry. The incidents included production of 30 faulty parts, falling asleep in his truck resulting in lateness, five additional occurrences of lateness, the production of 77 non-conforming parts, failure to recognize incorrectly drilled parts and the falsification of records. The employee was given multiple verbal warnings, written warnings, and a suspension before he was dismissed. The Superior Court held that the employee's sustained course of casual and careless conduct was inconsistent with his continued employment and, in the face of progressive discipline, amounted to a repudiation of the employment contract. Accordingly, his dismissal for just cause at common law was warranted.

However, despite finding that the employee was dismissed for just cause at common law, the Court held that he was nevertheless entitled to statutory termination pay and severance pay. Although the employee's conduct was persistently careless, the Court did not believe that it was intentional, wilful, or even reckless. As such, it did not meet the threshold of "wilful misconduct" required by Ontario Regulation 288/01.

This distinction was also addressed in a November 18, 2010 decision of the OLRB in *Singh v. Rea International Inc. (Atlas Fluid Systems)*, 2010 CarswellOnt 18590. In that case, the employee was incarcerated for non-work related misconduct. As a result, he was unable to attend work for six days. He was also unable to notify the employer promptly. The employer terminated his employment, relying on a company rule stating that employees who are absent and fail to call in after three consecutive working days will be deemed to have resigned. The OLRB held that it had no authority to engage in a common law just cause analysis, and found that the employee was entitled to termination pay and severance pay under the *ESA, 2000*, stating:

> "Does ... Mr. Singh's breach of this rule constitute wilful misconduct or disobedience such as would disentitle him to termination and severance pay under the Act? As described in greater detail above, this requires that the employer establish two things: that the employee's failure to comply with the rule seriously interferes with either the performance of the employee's job duties or those of his or her co-workers; and that the employee purposefully breached the rule knowing that doing so was serious misconduct, neglect of duty or was disobedient, and deliberately and consciously disobeyed the authority of the employer. In my view, the employer in this case has failed to establish either of these things."

Similarly, a 2012 OLRB decision noted that there is a general presumption in favour of termination notice/pay and severance pay, and that any exceptions to that presumption must be strictly construed. In *Tracks & Wheels Equipment Brokers Inc. v. Craig Craftchick and Director of Employment Standards*, 2012 CarswellOnt 6832, the employee worked as a mechanic and acting supervisor for a company that rents, sells and services heavy equipment. The employee had a history of being difficult to work with, including incidents of swearing at other employees.

The employer directed the employee to make a service call and dispatch a mechanic to fix a customer's forklift. However, when the employee called the customer, the customer indicated that it was too busy for the forklift to be taken out of service. The employer discovered that no mechanic had been dispatched, and confronted the employee, alleging that the malfunction could have been a safety concern. The employee stated three times in the course of a heated discussion: "I did what I did! What are you going to do about it?". The employer dismissed the employee for insubordination and did not provide termination notice or pay.

The OLRB determined that although the employee's behaviour may have been insolent, it was not disobedient, as there was no instance of deliberate disregard for a specific instruction. The employee's decision not to dispatch a mechanic was an exercise in good judgment, given that the customer specifically asked that no mechanic be dispatched. The OLRB stated that it therefore could not "find that [the employee's] conduct rose to the level contemplated by the [*ESA, 2000*] that would deprive an employee of his minimum notice and/or severance pay".

These decisions emphasize that "wilful misconduct, disobedience or wilful neglect of duty" generally require some deliberate or intentional act by the employee. Careless, thoughtless, heedless, insolent, or inadvertent conduct, no matter how serious, does not meet the standard.

Another 2012 OLRB case considered the meaning and significance of an employer's "condonation" of employee misconduct. In *The Dollco Corporation v. Steve Frobel and Director of Employment Standards*, 2012 CarswellOnt 11713 [*Dollco*], a 13-year employee worked for a large printing business. It was the company's written policy that employees were required to "clock in" and "clock out" when entering or leaving the premises and during breaks. The written policy also stated that breaks must be taken at designated times and could not be accumulated. The employee was aware of these policies. A supervisor detected the employee exiting and re-entering the building many times during his shift, and outside of scheduled break times. The employer started an investigation, and in the meantime the employee worked another shift. The employer dismissed the employee during this second shift, citing a pattern of "unsafe behaviour, poor performance, and poor attitude". The employee alleged that the employer had condoned his behaviour by allowing him to work a further shift following the incidents. The OLRB held that there was no condonation, indicating "that a lapse of time is only one factor to consider in determining the issue of condonation. What mattered more was what the employer did in that period". It could not be inferred that the employee's behaviour was condoned because the time between the incidents and the dismissal was used to investigate the incidents.

Regarding the "wilful misconduct" standard, the OLRB indicated that: "The employer must show that the employee purposefully engaged in conduct that he or she knew to be serious misconduct. It is, to put it colloquially, being bad on purpose" and found that the employee in *Dollco* had indeed engaged in such behaviour.

Constructive Dismissal

As indicated above, a termination or severance will occur when the employer constructively dismisses the employee and the employee resigns in response to the constructive dismissal within a reasonable period of time.

So what is a "constructive dismissal"? A constructive dismissal occurs when an employer makes a significant change to a fundamental term or condition of employment without the employee's consent, and the employee resigns within a reasonable time after learning of the change. A constructive dismissal may occur, for example, when an employer significantly reduces an employee's salary or changes, in a fundamental way, the employee's job duties, work location, hours of work, reporting structure, authority or position. Constructive dismissal may also

118

occur when an employer harasses or abuses an employee, or gives an employee an ultimatum to "quit or be fired".

A 2011 class action certification decision expanded on the meaning of constructive dismissal, and in particular emphasized that each case must be examined on its own facts to determine whether constructive dismissal has occurred. In the case of *Kafka v. Allstate Insurance Company of Canada*, 2011 ONSC 2305, 2011 CarswellOnt 3118, a group of employees claimed that they were constructively dismissed when their employer introduced a revised product distribution model and compensation system. The employees sought termination and severance pay under the *ESA, 2000*. In assessing whether to certify the employees' claims as a class action, the Ontario Superior Court held that "the law of constructive dismissal requires an individual inquiry to determine if an employee's claim should succeed" and "whether a constructive dismissal has occurred, is a question of fact." Employment changes occurred in three areas: changes to the business model, changes in job description, and changes to compensation. However, the impact on individual employees was likely to vary significantly. Determining the degree of change in each employee's employment contract involved a "contextual, relative and individual assessment", and therefore it was not appropriate to certify the lawsuit as a class action. The decision was upheld by the Ontario Divisional Court on appeal.

As affirmed in the Ontario Superior Court's decision in *Lawrence v. Norwood*, 2016 CarswellOnt 14939 [*Lawrence*], constructive dismissal occurs where "*a reasonable person* in the same situation as the employee would have felt that the essential terms of the employment contract were being substantially changed" [emphasis added]. In other words, a claim of constructive dismissal must be based on the objective, observable conduct of an employer and not just the perceptions of an employee. In *Lawrence*, the Superior Court found that an employee's perception that she had been singled out and unfairly treated by her employer did not suffice to amount to a constructive dismissal, particularly as the employee in question had not taken any steps to address her concerns with her employer.

Quit Versus Fired

An issue that sometimes arises is whether the employee was dismissed, or voluntarily resigned. According to the Ministry of Labour, two things must be established in order to demonstrate that an employee has resigned:

1. a statement by the employee informing the employer of an intention to quit (or, in the absence of any statement, some act from which it may be inferred that the employee intended to quit); and

2. some action on the part of the employee to carry out that intention.

The following conduct has been found to be inconsistent with quitting:

• where the employee says "I quit" in the heat of the moment and quickly withdraws the remark or returns to work;

• where the employee says "I quit" without saying when he or she will leave and continues to work; and

• where the employer advises the employee that unless he or she quits, he or she will be fired, and the employee resigns as a result.

On the other hand, the following conduct is consistent with a resignation:

• where the employee says "I quit" and then requests his or her Record of Employment; and

• where an employee says "I quit", returns work equipment, and does not present himself or herself for subsequent shifts, but later attempts to withdraw the remark;

• where an employee signs a resignation letter but attempts to withdraw his or her resignation weeks later; and

• where the employee fails to return to work after announcing an intention to quit, coupled with cleaning out his or her desk and leaving keys behind.

Timing of Payments Due on Termination/Severance

The *ESA, 2000* provides that if an employee's employment ends, the employer must pay any wages owing to the employee no later than the later of:

• seven days after the employment ends; and

• the day that would have been the employee's next regular pay day.

Similarly, termination pay and severance pay must be paid to an employee by the later of seven days after the employee's employment is terminated or the employee's next regular pay day. However, unlike termination pay, an employer may pay severance pay in instalments with the written agreement of the employee or the approval of the Director of Employment Standards over a period not exceeding three years. Where an employer fails to make a severance pay instalment payment, all severance pay not yet paid will immediately become payable.

Building Services Providers

Section 10 and Part XIX of the *ESA, 2000*, as well as Ontario Regulation 287/01, deal with the special category of employment known as building services. In general, these provisions are applicable in a situation where a building services provider for a building is replaced by a new provider. The provisions of the statute and Regulation specify the respective obligations of the replaced and new building services providers for, among other things, termination and severance pay and accrued vacation pay.

The term "building services" is defined in section 1 of the *ESA, 2000* as "services for a building with respect to food, security and cleaning and any prescribed services for a building".

Ontario Regulation 287/01 contains the following list of the additional "prescribed" services which fall under the definition of "building services":

- services that are intended to relate only to the building, its occupants and visitors with respect to:

    (i) a parking garage or parking lot; and

    (ii) a concession stand; and

- property management services that are intended to relate only to the building.

The term "building services provider" is defined in section 1 of the *ESA, 2000* as "a person who provides building services for a premises and includes the owner or manager of a premises if the owner or manager provides building services for premises the person owns or manages".

Section 10 of the *ESA, 2000* provides that where a building services provider for a building is replaced by a new building services provider, and the new building services provider continues to employ an employee of the replaced building services provider, then:

- the employment of the employee shall be deemed *not* to have been terminated or severed; and

- the employee's length or period of employment with the new building services provider will be deemed to include his or her length or period of employment with the replaced building services provider.

According to section 75 of the *ESA, 2000*, a new building services provider must comply with the termination and severance provisions of the *ESA, 2000* with respect to every employee of the replaced building services provider whom the new building services provider does not continue to employ. Furthermore, the new provider must recognize such employees' prior years of service in calculating the employees' entitlement to termination and severance pay under the *ESA, 2000*.

Subsection 75(4) stipulates that the new building services provider is not required to comply with the termination and severance provisions of the *ESA, 2000* in respect of any employees whom the replaced building services provider retains, or in respect of any "prescribed" employees. A list of "prescribed" employees is included in section 2 of Ontario Regulation 287/01. Specifically, the new building services provider will not be responsible for providing termination or severance pay to the following individuals:

• an employee whose work, before the changeover, included providing buildings services at the premises, but who did not perform his or her job duties primarily at those premises during the 13 weeks prior to the changeover date;

• an employee whose work included providing building services at the premises, but who:

(i) was not actively at work immediately before the changeover date; and

(ii) did not perform his or her job duties during the most recent 13 weeks of active employment;

• an employee who did not perform his or her job duties at the premises for at least 13 weeks during the 26-week period before the changeover date (not including any period during which the employee was on a pregnancy, parental or emergency leave of absence under the *ESA, 2000*); and

• an employee who refuses an offer of employment with the new provider that is reasonable in the circumstances.

Section 76 of the *ESA, 2000* provides that the replaced building services provider, who ceases to provide services at a premises and ceases to employ an employee, must pay to the employee any accrued vacation pay. The accrued vacation pay must be paid to the employee by the later of:

• seven days after the employee's employment with the replaced building services provider ceases; and

• the date that would have been the employee's next regular pay day.

Section 77 of the *ESA, 2000* requires that a building services provider furnish certain information where a person is seeking to be the new provider of building services, if requested to do so. Ontario Regulation 287/01, in section 3, sets out the specific information, in respect of each employee, that must be provided to the prospective building services provider, including:

• the employee's job classification or job description;

• the wage rate actually paid to the employee;

• a description of the employee's benefits, including their cost;

• the number of hours that the employee works in a regular work day and week;

• the date on which the building services provider hired the employee;

• any period of employment attributed to the building services provider under section 10 of the *ESA, 2000* (i.e., employment with a replaced building services provider);

• the number of weeks that the employee worked at the premises during the 26 weeks before the request for information was made; and

• a statement indicating whether:

> (i) the employee did not perform his or her duties primarily at the premises during the 13 weeks before the request for information was made; and

> (ii) the employee was not actively at work immediately before the request for information was made, and did not perform his or her duties primarily at the premises during the most recent 13 weeks of active employment.

Temporary Help Agencies

As of January 2018, Bill 148 brings about important changes to the *ESA, 2000* regarding temporary help agencies and the individuals they hire. These amendments follow previous amendments made in 2009 that provided greater rights to temporary help agency employees (or "assignment employees", as they are defined in the *ESA, 2000*) and removed some of the barriers to permanent employment.

The 2009 amendments to the *ESA, 2000* clarified that a temporary help agency is the employer of those individuals it places on assignment with a client business. However, the client business also has certain responsibilities to the employee. For example, a client business cannot punish the employee in any way for making enquiries about, or attempting to enforce, his or her employment standards rights.

In 2014, the *Stronger Workplaces for a Stronger Economy Act, 2014*, established important changes in the relationship and respective responsibilities of temporary help agencies and their clients. For example, since November 20, 2015, both the temporary help agency and its clients have been required to record the number of hours in each day and each week that an employee works, and retain the required records for three years. In addition, these changes have made the temporary help agency primarily responsible for employee wages. However, the temporary help agency and its client may be held jointly and severally liable for wages, including regular wages, overtime pay, public holiday pay, and premium pay. Furthermore, a client of the temporary help agency is deemed to be an employer of the temporary help agency's employee for enforcement purposes under the *ESA, 2000*.

The 2018 amendments arising from Bill 148 provide new protections to assignment employees. In particular, those who are assigned to perform work with an estimated term of three months or more, but have such an assignment cut short will be entitled to receive one week's written notice from their employer temporary help agency. This notice may be provided alongside a working notice period or payment in lieu of notice — which must be equal to the pay that the assignment employee would have received if one week's working notice had been provided. Under new provisions arising from Bill 148, employer temporary help agencies would also be required to maintain written records of notice provided to employees under this provision. To satisfy this new notice requirement, a temporary help agency may also provide the assignment employee a different assignment of one week or more with the same client or with a different client; so long as such a work assignment is "reasonable" in the circumstances. As recognized by Justice Michael Moldaver in *Stelco Inc., Hilton Works v. U.S.W.A., Local 1005*, 1994 CarswellOnt 831 (Ont. Div. Ct.), to be "reasonable", a decision by an employer should be free from bad faith, discrimination, or arbitrariness.

Importantly, assignment employees will not be entitled this new one-week notice where the early termination of their assignment results from any one of the following:

• Where the assignment employee is guilty of wilful misconduct, disobedience or wilful neglect of duty that is not trivial and has not been condoned by the employer;

• Where the assignment has become impossible to perform or has been frustrated by a fortuitous or unforeseeable event or circumstance; or

• Where the assignment is terminated during or as a result of a strike or lock-out at the location of the assignment.

As discussed above, following from the OLRB decision in *Sacco*, where assignment employees are alleged to be "guilty of wilful misconduct, disobedience or wilful neglect," the employer may be required to prove that such breaches were "not trivial" and were "not condoned" by the temporary help agency or client if their decision is challenged.

The *ESA, 2000* expressly prohibits clients of temporary help agencies from reprising against assignment employees — through intimidation, refusal to have the assignment employee perform work, termination or other penalties — in response to various actions by the employee. Such actions include the assignment employee's filing a complaint with the Ministry of Labour, making inquiries about their rights under the *ESA, 2000*, and attempting to exercise such rights. As of April 1, 2018, under amendments contained in Bill 148, these protected employee actions would also include circumstances where an assignment employee discloses their rate of pay to another employee, or inquires about another employee's rate of pay for the purpose of ensuring that the temporary help agency is complying with its duties to provide equal pay for equal work under the *ESA, 2000* (See "Equal Pay for Equal Work"). Where a client is accused of carrying out a reprisal against an assignment employee in contravention of these prohibitions, the client will have the burden of proving that such reprisal did not occur. A client who violates these provisions may be ordered to provide compensation accordingly.

A temporary help agency cannot prevent a client business from hiring one of its employees, if the client business wants to do so. The temporary help agency may charge the client business a fee for hiring one of its employees, but only during the six-month period beginning on the day when the employee first began working for the client business. Temporary help agencies also cannot prevent the client business from giving employees a reference letter if an employee asks for one. As of January 2018, following from amendments to the *ESA, 2000* made under Bill 148, a temporary help agency found to have imposed such restrictions in violation of the *ESA, 2000* could be ordered to (i) pay compensation directly to the employee; or (ii) pay compensation to the Director in trust, alongside an administration fee.

If the client business wants to hire one of the temporary help agency employees, the agency cannot tell the employee not to take the job, and the agency cannot charge the employee a fee. Temporary help agencies are also prohibited from charging employees fees associated with the following:

- becoming an assignment employee;
- assigning work for the employee or attempting to find an assignment for the employee; or
- assistance with preparing a resume or preparing for job interviews.

Where an employment standards officer finds that a temporary help agency charged a fee in connection with any of the above services or outcomes, the officer may arrange for the amount to be repaid to the employee or, otherwise, order payment to the employee or the Director in trust.

Temporary help agencies are required to provide their employees, in writing, with the agency's legal name (and operating or business name, if that is different than the legal name) and contact information. They must also provide employees with an information sheet prepared by the Ministry of Labour outlining the employee's rights pursuant to the *ESA, 2000*. When the agency offers an employee an assignment with one of its client businesses, the agency must provide the employee with the following information in writing:

- the client's legal name (and operating or business name, if that is different than the legal name) and contact information;
- the wage rate and benefits;
- the hours of work;
- the estimated term of the assignment (if known); and
- the pay period and pay day.

Temporary help agency employees are entitled to the same rights to public holidays as other employees in Ontario. Generally speaking, if the employee is on an assignment and the public holiday falls on a day when the employee would ordinarily be working, the employee has a right to take the public holiday off work and be paid public holiday pay for that day. The formula for public holiday pay in these circumstances is as follows:

the employee's regular wages earned + vacation pay payable in the four weeks before the week in which the holiday falls (*regardless* of the number of assignments the employee may have been on within that four week period), divided by 20.

If the public holiday falls on a day when the employee is not on an assignment, the employee may be entitled to public holiday pay only.

Temporary help agency employees are entitled to notice of termination (or pay in lieu thereof) and severance pay (if applicable) upon termination by the temporary help agency, in the same way that other employees are. These entitlements are distinct and separate from the entitlement to one week's notice arising where an assignment employee's long-term assignment with a client is cancelled (see above). For the purposes of determining assignment employees' notice and severance entitlement on termination, the employee's length of service refers to the period of time that the employee has been employed by the temporary help agency (including time prior to November 6, 2009), not the length of time working on assignments at clients of the agency. For the purposes of calculating termination and severance pay, the employee's weekly wage is determined by averaging the employee's wages over the 12-week period ending on the last day on which the employee performed work for a client business of the temporary help agency.

Standard mass termination rules under the *ESA, 2000* do not apply to temporary help agencies and their employees. Instead, temporary help agencies need only provide standard amounts of mass termination notice (based on the number of terminations; as set out under "Mass Terminations", above) if the assignments of 50 or more temporary help agency employees *at a single client's establishment* are ended and, as a result, the agency terminates the employment of 50 or more such employees within a four-week period.

In addition, the temporary lay-off provisions of the *ESA, 2000* apply to temporary help agency employees, albeit with some modifications. For example:

- A week of lay-off is defined as a week where the employee is not assigned any work (whereas most employees are considered to be on lay-off during a week in which they earn less than 50% of wages for the purposes of termination and less than 25% of wages for the purposes of severance);
- In the event that a temporary lay-off becomes permanent, termination and severance pay will be calculated by averaging the employee's wages over the 12-week period immediately preceding the first day of the lay-off; and
- Weeks of lay-off, as well as the periods of 20 or 52 consecutive weeks (within which weeks of lay-off are counted) are to be counted from November 6, 2009 forward for the purposes of triggering termination and severance entitlements.

Employee Discounts

Discounts are not covered by the *ESA, 2000*. The employer is responsible for deciding whether employees are entitled to discounts on products the employer makes or sells, or on services the employer provides. The employer is also entitled to determine the amount of any discount.

Dress Codes

The employer is responsible for making decisions about dress codes, uniforms and other clothing requirements, and about who pays for them. However, a dress code cannot violate (i) a collective agreement at the workplace; (ii) human rights requirements; or (iii) health and safety requirements. With respect to the second requirement, the Ontario Human Rights Commission has published policies stressing the importance of offering employees a variety of uniform options and avoiding uniforms that cause employees to appear sexualized or gender-stereotypical. More information on these policies can be found at www.ohrc.on.ca.

An employer may make a deduction from wages to cover the cost of a uniform or other clothing requirements, but only if it has a signed, specific written authorization from the employee permitting the deduction and setting out the amount of the deduction.

Enforcement

Complaint Procedure

Subsection 96(1) of the *ESA, 2000* permits an employee, other than an employee represented by a trade union, to file a complaint with the Ministry of Labour in a form approved by the Director of Employment Standards if he or she believes there has been a contravention of the legislation. (However, the Director has the discretion to permit the filing of a complaint by an employee who is represented by a trade union, in appropriate circumstances, pursuant to subsection 99(3).) A complaint that is not in the approved form shall be deemed not to have been filed: subsection 96(2). Amendments under Bill 148 scheduled to come into effect in January 2018 would have the effect of repealing the processes for filing employment standards claims that was previously established under the *Open for Business Act, 2010*. Following these amendments, employees will be able to submit complaints to the Ministry of Labour without being required to strictly follow the steps previously required by the Ministry. In other words, employees will no longer be required to first attempt to contact an employer or former employer to resolve a matter, and to gather all relevant documents prior to completing a Claim Form. Rather, employees may proceed to make a written complaint directly to the Ministry of Labour and have it investigated without having taken further additional steps beforehand.

To make a complaint with the Ministry, employees must complete and file a Claim Form, which requires details about:

- contact information for the employee;
- contact information for the employer;
- whether the employer is still operating;
- whether the employer conducts business at other locations or operates using any other names;
- the employee's work history with the employer;
- which minimum standards were allegedly violated;
- when it happened;
- what is being claimed (including dollar amounts, if applicable); and
- what supporting documents are available.

It is recommended that employees file their Claim Form online, although Claim Forms may also be filed in person, by mail, or by fax.

Once a Claim Form is filed, it is reviewed to ensure that it includes all of the required information. If it does, it is assigned to an employment standards officer for investigation. If it does not, then the employee will be contacted and asked to provide the missing information within a stated period of time. The matter will not be assigned to an employment standards officer for investigation unless the required information is provided within the stated time period.

As a result of amendments arising from the *Open for Business Act, 2010*, employment standards officers and labour relations officers are also specifically authorized to attempt to settle complaints. If the employer and employee agree to a settlement, then the settlement is binding, the complaint is deemed to have been withdrawn, the investigation is terminated. Following this, any proceeding regarding the allegations, other than a prosecution, is terminated.

Section 102 of the *ESA, 2000* provides that an employment standards officer may, upon providing 15 days' written notice, require the employer (or a director or employee thereof, if the employer is a corporation) and/or the employee to attend a fact-finding meeting and to bring relevant documents. Where a person who is required to attend the meeting fails to attend, or fails to provide evidence as required, the employment standards officer will proceed to make a decision on the basis of the available evidence.

Employment standards officers have the authority to enter and inspect any place (except a dwelling) without a warrant to investigate an alleged contravention of the *ESA, 2000*: section 91. In addition, the officer may:

- examine relevant records or things that the officer thinks may be relevant;
- require the production of relevant records or things that the officer thinks may be relevant;
- remove records or things that the officer thinks may be relevant for review and copying;
- order the production of a record in readable form; and
- question any person on matters that the officer thinks may be relevant to the investigation or inspection.

The *ESA, 2000* requires employment standards officers to follow any policies established by the Director of Employment Standards: subsection 89(2). Section 88 of the *ESA, 2000* allows the Director to establish policies respecting the interpretation, administration and enforcement of the *ESA, 2000*.

Even in the absence of a complaint, an employment standards officer may require parties to attend a fact-finding meeting where the officer:

- while inspecting a place in the course of an investigation, has reasonable grounds to believe that an employer has contravened the *ESA, 2000* or the regulations;
- acquires information that suggests the possibility of a contravention of the legislation; or

- wishes to determine whether the employer of an employee who resides in the employer's residence is complying with the legislation.

Order to Pay Wages

If the employment standards officer finds that wages are owing to an employee, the officer may order that the employer pay wages either directly to the employee or to the Director of Employment Standards in trust: section 103 of the *ESA, 2000.*

An order to pay must set out the amount that an employer is required to pay. If the order requires payment to be made to the Director in trust, then the order will also include an administration fee. The administration fee is equal to the greater of $100 or 10% of the wages owing: subsection 103(2).

The employer must comply with the order according to its terms, or appeal the order within 30 days of the date the order is served. Where an employer is ordered to pay wages directly to an employee who cannot be located despite the employer's reasonable efforts, then the employer will be required to pay the wages in question, alongside the applicable administration fee, to the Director in trust.

The order to pay wages is probably the most common enforcement tool used by employment standards officers.

There is no limit on the amount of wages that an employment standards officer can order to be paid.

Order for Compensation or Reinstatement

An employment standards officer may also, pursuant to section 104 of the *ESA, 2000*, order that an employer compensate an employee for any losses and/or reinstate the employee if the employer has breached the statutory provisions pertaining to leaves of absence, lie detectors, retail business establishments, and reprisals. The compensation may be ordered to be paid to the Director of Employment Standards in trust along with an administration fee, or to be paid directly to the employee without an administration fee applied: subsection 104(3) of the *ESA, 2000*.

Any applicable administration fee must be paid to the Director of Employment Standards in trust, and is equal to the greater of $100 and 10% of the amount of compensation ordered: subsection 104(3).

Compensation orders can include a variety of types of damages. These can be summarized as follows:

• *Direct Earnings Loss* — This head of damages includes any actual loss of earnings (including wages and other types of earnings such as top-up benefits) suffered by the employee.

• *Pre-Reinstatement Compensation* — This head of damages applies only where there is an order for reinstatement. In conjunction with the order for reinstatement, the employer may be required to provide the employee with any earnings that would have been earned between the date the employee should have been reinstated and the date the order for reinstatement is made.

• *Time Required to Find a New Job and Termination Notice or Pay* — This head of damages applies only where there has been a termination and no reinstatement order has been issued. The amount awarded under this head of damages is the greater of:

   • an amount equal to the employee's weekly earnings, multiplied by the number of weeks it took or should have taken (whichever is less) for the employee to find a new job; and

   • the employee's termination pay entitlement under the *ESA, 2000* (with vacation pay).

• *Expenses Incurred in Seeking New Employment* — This head of damages applies if the employee's employment was terminated and no reinstatement order was issued. Expenses incurred in seeking new employment include transportation costs associated with travelling to job interviews, costs of preparing a resume, and other reasonable expenses. Employees should keep receipts to prove such expenses.

• *Loss of Employee's Reasonable Expectation of Continued Employment with the Former Employer* — This head of damages compensates the employee for the loss of the job itself. The employee's length of service, the nature of his or her employment, economic conditions, and mitigation (i.e., whether the employee found new employment, and the nature of the new employment) should be taken into account in making this assessment.

• *Emotional "Pain and Suffering"* — This head of damages refers to any emotional pain and suffering (and consequential physical suffering) caused by the loss of a job. The employee should provide evidence of such damages, i.e., a medical report.

• *Severance Pay* — An employer may be ordered to pay severance pay if the employee's employment has been severed and the employee would otherwise qualify for severance pay under the *ESA, 2000.*

• *Benefit Plan Entitlements* — The employer may be liable for any expenses incurred as a result of the loss of benefit coverage.

• *Reasonable Foreseeable Damages* —The above categories of damages are not exhaustive. Any damages that flow directly from a violation of the *ESA, 2000* may be awarded, provided they are reasonable and foreseeable.

An employee has an obligation to mitigate his or her losses, for example, by accepting reinstatement offers (provided that would represent a reasonable course of action for the employee, such as where the employer acted inadvertently and the workplace is not poisoned) and/or searching for a new job. Where the employee fails to mitigate, the amount of a compensation order should be reduced.

There is no limit on the amount of a compensation order. An order for reinstatement should be considered in light of the likelihood of its purpose being achieved (i.e., as a disincentive for employers to terminate employees). Therefore, the Ministry of Labour takes the position that if the employer is adamantly opposed to reinstatement, careful consideration should be given to the circumstances before reinstatement is ordered, since its purpose will be defeated over the long term. Furthermore, an employer may subsequently terminate an employee for unrelated reasons (such as performance).

Orders for reinstatement will generally require the employer to reinstate the employee to the position that he or she most recently held. If that position no longer exists, the Ministry of Labour has suggested that the employee should be reinstated to a comparable position.

Third Party Demands

Amendments resulting from Bill 85, *Strengthening and Improving Government Act, 2015*, came into effect on December 3, 2015. Prior to these amendments, Section 125 of the *ESA, 2000* gave the Director of Employment Standards the power to demand all or part of any money that was owed by the employer to the employee where that money was being held by a third-person. Following the amendments in Bill 85, the Director of Employment Standards may now make such demands of a third-party where the Director suspects that the third-party is holding money owed to the employee or *will be* holding such monies within the next 365 days. Money collected under this procedure will be held in trust by the Director of Employment Standards.

Third parties who may be subject to these provisions include but are not limited to temporary help agencies and clients who enter into a three-party relationship with employees.

Compliance Orders

An employment standards officer may issue a compliance order, requiring a person to perform, or cease performing, certain actions.

Specifically, pursuant to section 108 of the *ESA, 2000*, if the employment standards officer finds that a person has contravened a provision of the *ESA, 2000* or its regulations, the officer may:

- order that the person cease contravening the provision;
- specify what action the person shall take or refrain from taking, in order to comply with the provision; and
- specify a date by which the person must do so.

A compliance order cannot require the payment of wages or compensation to an employee, according to subsection 108(2) of the *ESA, 2000*. However, a compliance order can be issued in conjunction with an order or orders for the payment of wages (section 103), payment of compensation (section 104), reinstatement (section 104) or against the directors of a corporation (sections 106 and 107).

Obviously, the compliance order is designed to remedy non-monetary violations of the *ESA, 2000*, such as permitting or requiring employees to work in excess of the maximum hours of work, or failing to make and keep accurate records. It is also clear that the legislature meant for such compliance orders and their enforcement to be treated seriously: the *ESA, 2000* provides that, at the instance of the Director of Employment Standards, the contravention of a compliance order may be restrained upon an application to a judge of the Ontario Superior Court of Justice, *made without notice to the offending party*: subsection 108(5).

Notice of Contravention

According to section 113 of the *ESA, 2000*, where an employment standards officer *believes* that a person has contravened the *ESA, 2000*, the officer may issue a notice of contravention, setting out the following:

• the officer's belief; and

• the amount of the penalty for that contravention, as set out according to regulations. Where regulations prescribe a range of penalties in relation to a particular contravention, the officer will determine the amount of the penalty by applying any criteria prescribed by regulation.

The notice of contravention must also contain, or be accompanied by, information describing the nature of the contravention, pursuant to subsection 113(2) of the *ESA, 2000*.

The notice of contravention must be served in accordance with certain methods outlined in subsection 113(3) of the *ESA, 2000*.

Subsection 113(5) of the *ESA, 2000* provides that a person (usually an employer) who is served with a notice of contravention will be *deemed*, without a hearing, to have contravened the provision set out in the notice of contravention *if*:

• the person fails, *within 30 days after the date of service of the notice* (or within an appropriate, extended period specified by the OLRB), to apply to the OLRB for a review of the notice; or

• the person applies to the OLRB for a review of the notice and is found to have contravened the provision set out in the notice.

As of January 2018, under amendments contained in Bill 148, the details of such deemed contravention would be subject to publication by the Director, including online publication. The information contained in such publication could include (i) the name of the contravening party; (ii) a description of the contravention; (iii) the date of the contravention; and (iv) the penalty arising from the contravention.

A party may dispute a notice of contravention issued under section 113 of the *ESA, 2000* by making a written application to the OLRB pursuant to section 122 of the *ESA, 2000*. As indicated above, the application must be made within 30 days after the date of service of the notice of contravention or any appropriate extension of such period specified by the OLRB. On an application under this section, the OLRB will hold a hearing for the purposes of reviewing the notice of contravention. At the hearing, the onus is on the Director of Employment Standards, who is a party to the proceeding, to establish, on a balance of probabilities, that the person against whom the notice of contravention was issued contravened the specified provision of the *ESA, 2000*.

Ontario Regulation 289/01 currently prescribes the following penalties for a notice of contravention:

Contravention	Penalty
Contravention of section 2 (posting), 15 (record-keeping) or 16 (availability of records) of the *ESA, 2000*	$250
Second contravention of section 2, 15 or 16 of the *ESA, 2000* in a three-year period	$500
Third or subsequent contravention of section 2, 15 or 16 of the *ESA, 2000* in a three-year period	$1,000
Contravention of a provision of the *ESA, 2000* other than section 2, 15 or 16	$250
Second contravention of a provision of the *ESA, 2000* other than section 2, 15 or 16 in a three-year period	$500
Third or subsequent contravention of a provision of the *ESA, 2000* other than section 2, 15 or 16 in a three-year period	$1,000
Contravention of a provision of the *ESA, 2000* other than section 2, 15 or 16, where the contravention affects more than one employee	$250, multiplied by the number of employees affected
Second contravention of a provision of the *ESA, 2000* other than section 2, 15 or 16, in a three-year period, where the contravention affects more than one employee	$500, multiplied by the number of employees affected

Contravention	Penalty
Third or subsequent contravention of a provision of the *ESA, 2000* other than section 2, 15 or 16, in a three-year period, where the contravention affects more than one employee	$1,000, multiplied by the number of employees affected

As of January 2018, the Government of Ontario will have new powers to issue regulations establishing penalty *ranges* and related criteria for determining penalty amounts to be applied to contraventions such as the above. Accordingly, the above figures will likely be revised in 2018 to reflect ranges of penalty amounts, with the exact amount of a penalty for a particular contravention left to the determination of employment standards officers exercising reasonable discretion and applying any criteria set out in the regulation.

It is important to note that a notice of contravention may not be issued in respect of an employee who is represented by a union: subsection 113(8). Furthermore, an arbitrator does not have the authority to issue such a notice: section 100.

The penalty amount specified in a notice of contravention must be paid to the Ministry of Finance, along with any collector's fees and disbursements that have been added: subsection 113(6). The amount must be paid within 30 days after the day the notice of contravention was served or, if the notice of contravention is appealed, within 30 days after the OLRB finds that there was a contravention: subsection 113(6.1).

Ticketing

Employment standards officers who have been appointed as provincial offences officers may issue tickets under the Ontario *Provincial Offences Act* for certain violations of the *ESA, 2000*. Regulation 950 of the *Provincial Offences Act* allows for such ticketing.

All tickets allow for a set fine of $295 plus applicable costs and victim fine surcharge. Money collected from the fines will go to the municipality in which the offence took place, while the victim fine surcharge will go to the provincial Victims' Justice Fund. Tickets will be issued to the employer responsible for the offence.

Generally speaking, tickets may be issued for less serious violations of the *ESA, 2000*, being those that do not raise complex factual or legal issues. Ticketable offences fall into three broad categories:

- administration and enforcement (e.g., failure to retain records, post materials, prepare vacation statements, provide wage statement, etc.);
- wage-based entitlements (e.g., failure to pay overtime pay, minimum wage, vacation pay, termination/severance pay, etc.); and
- other entitlements (e.g., requiring employee to exceed maximum hours of work, failure to provide eating period, failure to provide public holiday, etc.)

The precise offences for which tickets may be issued are set out in three Schedules to Regulation 950 of the *Provincial Offences Act*: Schedules 4.2, 4.3 and 4.4.

Tickets may be issued as a result of proactive inspections or after investigation of an employee complaint. If issued a ticket, an employer has three options:

- plead guilty by signing the guilty plea on the ticket and paying the set fine at the court office specified on the ticket;
- plead guilty and make submissions respecting the fine by appearing before a provincial judge or justice of the peace (who may impose the set fine or reduce it); or
- plead not guilty by giving notice of intention to appear in court and requesting a trial.

The issuance of a ticket against an employer does not preclude the Ministry of Labour from also taking other action against the employer in order to ensure compliance with the *ESA,*

2000, such as requesting voluntary compliance, issuing a notice of contravention, or issuing an order to comply, pay wages, compensate or reinstate.

Effective as of May 2015, the *Stronger Workplaces for a Stronger Economy Act, 2014* established a new enforcement mechanism: the mandatory employer "self-audit". Under this mechanism, an employment standards officer may, by giving written notice, require an employer to conduct an examination of its records, practices or both to determine whether the employer is in compliance with one or more provisions of the *ESA, 2000*. The employment standards officer's notice must indicate the period of time to be covered by the examination, the provision(s) of the *ESA, 2000* to be covered by the examination, and the deadline by which the employer must provide a report of the results of the examination to the employment standards officer. The notice may specify the method to be used in carrying out the examination, the format of the report, and/or the information that must be included in the employer's response. If an employer's report concludes that the employer owes wages to one or more of its employees, then the employment standards officer may issue an order to pay or take such other enforcement steps as are considered appropriate.

Security, Warrants and Liens

As of January 2018, amendments to the *ESA, 2000* arising from Bill 148 extend new powers to the Director of Employment Standards to ensure payment of orders by parties who have contravened the *ESA, 2000*. These powers include:

- accepting security for payment in any form, as determined by the Director;
- issuing a warrant — having the same effect as a writ of execution — in any area where the contravening party has property, for enforcement of the amount of any order to pay money, and costs associated with the enforcement of the warrant; and

• registering a lien against the real property or personal property of the contravening party, for the amount of the order in addition to any accumulated interest on that amount. Such a lien will stand in priority over subsequent registered security interests other than money security interests in collateral or its proceeds.

Employer Recognition

In addition to providing for new enforcement mechanisms for contravention of the *ESA, 2000,* amendments under Bill 148 also provide for recognition of employers who have met their employment standards obligations. Under a new Section 88.2, an employer may apply for recognition to the Director of Employment standards, or their delegate, who will then exercise discretion to determine whether the employer meets the criteria for recognition. As part of such an application, an employer may be required to provide any information, records, or accounts requested by the Director or their delegate. Where an employer meets the applicable criteria for recognition, the employer may have their recognition published or otherwise made publicly available at the discretion of the Director of Employment Standards, for a period of time determined by the Director or until the recognition is revoked.

However, employers will not be able to apply for and receive such recognition until applicable criteria are passed and published by the Ontario Legislature.

Liability of Directors

Although a corporate employer is primarily responsible for paying employee wages, the directors of the corporation are jointly and severally liable for wages if:

• the corporation is insolvent, the employee has filed a claim for unpaid wages with the receiver or trustee in bankruptcy, and the claim has not been paid;

• an employment standards officer has made an order that the corporation is liable for wages, the corporation has not applied for a review, and the order remains unpaid;

• an employment standards officer has made an order that a director is liable for wages, the director has not applied for a review, and the order remains unpaid; or

• the OLRB has made an order that a corporation or director is liable for wages, and the order remains unpaid.

Directors are not liable for termination or severance pay. However, they are liable for the following types of payments:

• wages;

• vacation pay;

• holiday pay;

• overtime.

The *maximum* liability of the directors of an employer corporation is:

(i) six months' wages that become payable while they are directors of the corporation; plus

(ii) vacation pay accrued for up to 12 months while they are directors of the corporation.

Limitations on Recovery

Time Limits

In 2014, the *Stronger Workplaces for a Stronger Economy Act, 2014* amended rules with respect to deadlines for filing a complaint under the *ESA, 2000*. Prior to this legislation's coming into force, an employee could not recover wages that had been outstanding for more than six months at the time of filing the complaint. Now, the deadline has been extended such that an employee cannot recover wages or compensation in respect of a contravention that occurred more than two years before the filing of the complaint.

Although the time limits on recovering wages and filing a claim set out in the *ESA, 2000* are mandatory, it may be possible to make a claim that would be outside the applicable time limit if:

• An employee has been misled as to his or her entitlements under the *ESA, 2000* by his or her employer and for that reason delayed in filing a claim; and

• The employee took prompt steps to file a claim after learning that what the employer said about the *ESA, 2000* entitlement was inaccurate.

The Ontario Court of Appeal in *Halloran v. Crown Cork & Seal Canada Inc.*, (2002) 217 D.L.R. (4th) 327, held that the equitable doctrine of "fraudulent concealment" can provide relief against statutory time limits and caps on damages, where the employer is responsible for the employee's delay in filing a claim. In that case, the Plaintiff was dismissed, after 31 years of employment, due to a corporate re-organization. He was provided with a termination letter that gave him two compensation options. Option A permitted him to retire on an unreduced early pension. Option B provided a special retirement package. The termination letter indicated that both options exceeded Mr. Halloran's entitlements under provincial law. Mr. Halloran elected Option A, but discovered, nearly four years later, that he was also entitled to severance pay under the employment standards legislation as it existed at that time. A referee determined that Mr. Halloran's claim was statute-barred due to a two-year limitation period and a two-year cap on damages. The Divisional Court disagreed, applying the doctrine of fraudulent concealment. Upholding the Divisional Court's decision, the Court of Appeal stated:

"In my view, it was not in accordance with what is right or reasonable for the company to make an unqualified statement containing a misrepresentation which caused its employee to act to his detriment. The company was in a position to ascertain the state of the law at the time and provide accurate information to Mr. Halloran. There is nothing in the record to suggest otherwise. I believe that it was unconscionable for the company to invoke the limitation period ... in order to deny Mr. Halloran's claim when it was responsible for his delay in filing the claim. Mr. Halloran is, in the circumstances, a completely innocent party who did no more than take the word of his employer of 31 years to his detriment. To put it another way, I believe that Crown Cork breached its obligation of good faith and fair dealing to Mr. Halloran and thereby acted unconscionably." [at paragraph 33]

While it remains questionable whether a decision-maker deriving its authority solely from statute (such as an employment standards officer) has authority to use equitable doctrines (such as the doctrine of fraudulent concealment) to relieve against clear statutory restrictions on its authority, employment standards officers nevertheless continue to apply the reasoning in *Halloran* when they perceive there would be an injustice otherwise.

Monetary Limits

The *Stronger Workplaces for a Stronger Economy Act, 2014* established new rules with respect to the amount of money an employee can recover from the employer in the event of a contravention of the *ESA, 2000*. Prior to these amendments, the maximum amount that an employment standards officer could order an employer to pay an employee in respect of wages was $10,000.00. Now, there is no limit on the amount of wages that an employment standards officer can order an employer to pay an employee. As of February 20, 2017, transitional provisions in the *ESA, 2000* referring to the previous $10,000 monetary limit have been repealed.

Concurrent Proceedings

Section 97 of the *ESA, 2000* addresses the situation where an employee first files a complaint under the *ESA, 2000*, and then starts a civil proceeding. It provides that an employee may not commence a civil proceeding alleging entitlement to wages, benefits or payments after filing a complaint under the *ESA, 2000* with respect to these matters. However, it should be noted that section 97 does not prevent a complaint from nevertheless being investigated under these circumstances. It may be that, in light of section 97, a court would not allow the civil proceeding to continue, but that is a matter for the court to decide. There is also a "cooling off period": subsection 97(4) of the *ESA, 2000* permits an employee who has filed a complaint to commence a civil proceeding thereafter, *provided* the employee withdraws the complaint within two weeks after it is filed.

Section 98 addresses the situation where an employee first starts a civil proceeding, and then files a complaint under the *ESA, 2000*. It provides that an employee who commences a civil proceeding alleging entitlement to wages, benefits or payments and then files a complaint under the *ESA, 2000* with respect to these matters may not have such a complaint investigated.

Settlements

An employer and employee may agree to a settlement respecting a contravention, or alleged contravention of the *ESA, 2000*. The settlement will be binding on the parties, and any complaint filed by the employee respecting the contravention or alleged contravention is deemed to have been withdrawn, provided:

- the parties inform the employment standards officer, in writing, of the terms of the settlement; and
- the employer and employer actually do what they have agreed to do under the settlement: subsection 112(1).

In addition, any order made in respect of the contravention is void, and any proceeding *other than a prosecution*, respecting the contravention is terminated.

It is recommended that employers and employees, when informing an employment standards officer of a settlement, ensure that the information provided to the officer discloses all of the terms of the settlement and not merely the fact of settlement. The parties may wish to consider preparing a joint statement to the officer outlining the terms of the settlement, and requesting that the officer acknowledge receipt of the statement to the parties in writing.

There are two major restrictions imposed on settlements under the *ESA, 2000*. First, the *ESA, 2000* prohibits any person from entering into a settlement where the terms of the settlement would permit or require that person or any other person to engage in future contraventions of the *ESA, 2000*: subsection 112(7). Second, where, upon application to the OLRB, the employee demonstrates that he or she entered into the settlement as a result of fraud or coercion, the settlement is void and the complaint is deemed never to have been withdrawn. In addition, any order previously made in respect of the contravention is reinstated and any proceedings respecting the contravention that were terminated shall be resumed: subsection 112(8). As set out in the OLRB decision in *Watkins v. Public Services Health & Safety Assn.*, 2015 CarswellOnt 16579, allegations of such fraud or coercion must be based upon evidence that an individual was forced into making a settlement — and bald allegations against the other party will not suffice.

Interestingly, if the parties reach a settlement concerning an employment standards officer's order to pay wages, the Director may require that the administrative surcharge be *pro rated* in relation to the amount of wages the employee actually received under the settlement and, following amendments under Bill 148, in relation to collector's fees and disbursements added to the amount of the order according to the same proportion: subsection 112(6). As an example, if the employee and employment standards officer took the position that the employee was owed six months' wages, and the employee subsequently settled for four months' wages, the Director would claim an administrative surcharge equal to 10% of four months' wages, rather than 10% of six months' wages, along with collector's fees and disbursements thus making the agreement more acceptable from the employer's perspective. This provision may be an added incentive for parties to settle their disputes, given that previously, parties were required to pay administrative charges at the level initially assessed.

Application for Review

Sections 116 and 122 of the *ESA, 2000* provide that an employee, employer, or director of a company may apply to the OLRB for a review of certain employment standards officers' decisions, including (a) an order to pay wages; (b) a reinstatement order; (c) an order to pay compensation; (d) a compliance order; (e) a refusal to make an order; and (f) a notice of contravention.

The OLRB is a quasi-judicial administrative tribunal, and its decisions are independent of the Ministry of Labour.

An employer who has been ordered to pay wages under section 103 of the *ESA, 2000*, and wishes to make an application for review, must first pay the amount owing under the order to the Director of Employment Standards, in trust, or provide the Director with an irrevocable letter of credit acceptable to the Director in that amount: subsection 116(1)(b).

An employer who has been ordered to pay compensation under section 104 of the *ESA, 2000*, and wishes make an application for review, must first pay the amount ordered or $10,000 (whichever is less) to the Director of Employment Standards, in trust, or provide the Director with an irrevocable letter of credit acceptable to the Director in that amount: subsection 116(1)(c).

An application for review must be made within 30 days after the day on which the order, letter advising of the order, letter advising of the refusal to issue an order, or notice of contravention was served: subsections 116(4) and 122(1). (Previously, under the *ESA*, the time limit for seeking a review was 45 days.) The OLRB may extend the time for applying if it considers it appropriate to do so in the circumstances: subsections 116(5) and 122(1).

An application for review form can be obtained from any Ministry of Labour office or the OLRB. The application for review should set out the facts and reasons for the application, and, once completed, should be sent to: The Registrar, OLRB, 505 University Avenue, 2nd Floor, Toronto, Ontario, M5G 2P1.

If a party wants the OLRB to consider its application for review despite its having been filed past the 30-day time limit, the party's application should include all of the reasons why it believes an extension of time is warranted.

Where the application for review is filed in a timely manner, the applicant is entitled to a hearing before the OLRB: subsections 116(6) and 122(2). However, (except where the application for review is in respect of a notice of contravention) the OLRB may assign a labour relations officer to attempt to mediate a settlement between the parties before proceeding with a hearing: section 120. The Information Bulletin published by the OLRB indicates that the role of the labour relations officer is to assist the parties in reaching an agreement to settle the application and therefore avoid the need for a hearing. The labour relations officer may explain the case law relevant to the issues in dispute, but will not provide legal advice. The mediation usually takes place in the regional centre closest to the workplace, but may also occur by telephone.

If a settlement is reached at mediation, and the Director has been holding money in trust in the interim period in respect of the matter, the Director shall distribute the amount held in trust in accordance with the settlement, and shall retain an administrative fee that is proportionate to the amount of money distributed to the employee, along with applicable collector's fees and disbursements, under the settlement (rather than the administrative fee originally imposed by the employment standards officer): subsection 120(6).

In the event that the matter cannot be resolved at mediation, and in all cases where the application for review is in respect of a notice of contravention, a hearing will be held in the regional centre closest to the workplace.

At the conclusion of a hearing, if the matter involves an order to pay wages, a reinstatement order, an order to pay compensation, a compliance order, or a refusal to make an order, then the OLRB may substitute its own decision for that of the employment standards officer: subsection 119(6). If the matter involves a notice of contravention, then the OLRB may rescind the notice, affirm the notice, or amend the notice to reduce the penalty: subsection 122(5).

According to subsection 119(13) of the *ESA, 2000*, the OLRB's decision is final and binding on the parties. There is no appeal from the OLRB's decision; however, the parties may apply to the Ontario Superior Court of Justice, Divisional Court, for a judicial review of the OLRB's decision. In most cases, the applicant on judicial review must demonstrate that the OLRB's decision was "unreasonable": subsection 119(14). Because a decision can be incorrect but nevertheless reasonable at the same time, succeeding in a judicial review may prove difficult.

Offences and Penalties

Section 132 of the *ESA, 2000* provides that it is an offence to contravene the *ESA, 2000* or the regulations, or to fail to comply with an order, direction or other requirement under the *ESA, 2000* or the regulations.

To obtain a conviction for an offence, the Crown has to prove its case beyond a reasonable doubt, which is the standard of proof in criminal and quasi-criminal cases.

On conviction, the following penalties apply:

Party	Penalty
Individual	Fine of not more than $50,000 and/or imprisonment of not more than 12 months
Corporation, first conviction	Fine of not more than $100,000
Corporation, second conviction	Fine of not more than $250,000
Corporation, third or subsequent conviction	Fine of not more than $500,000

Apart from general offences, the *ESA, 2000* prescribes specific offences. It is a specific offence, under subsection 131(1), to make, keep or produce false records or documents that are required to be kept under the *ESA, 2000*, or to participate or acquiesce in the making, keeping or production of false records or other documents. It is also a specific offence, under subsection 131(2), for any person to provide false or misleading information in relation to obligations arising from the *ESA, 2000*.

Section 135 of the *ESA, 2000* provides that, if an employer is convicted of an offence involving a contravention of a provision other than the reprisal provisions of the *ESA, 2000*, then the court *shall*, in addition to any fine or term if imprisonment that may be imposed, assess any amount owing to the employee and order the employer to pay the amount to the Director of Employment Standards. This is a mandatory direction to the court.

Reprisals

Part XVIII of the *ESA, 2000* deals with reprisals by employers against employees for exercising their rights or otherwise attempting to enforce their rights under the *ESA, 2000*.

Pursuant to section 74(1) of the *ESA, 2000*, employers are prohibited from intimidating, dismissing or otherwise penalizing an employee, or threatening to do so, because the employee has:

- asked the employer to comply with the *ESA, 2000* and the regulations;
- made inquiries about his or her rights under the *ESA, 2000*;
- filed a complaint with the Ministry of Labour under the *ESA, 2000*;
- exercised or attempted to exercise a right under the *ESA, 2000*;
- provided information to an employment standards officer;
- inquired about another worker's rate of pay or disclosed their rate of pay to another employee for the purpose of determining or assisting another person with determining

whether the employer is complying with its duties to provide equal pay for equal work provisions of the *ESA, 2000* (as of April 1, 2018 under amendments contained in Bill 148; See "Equal Pay for Equal Work");

• testified, is required to testify, participates, or is going to participate in a proceeding under the *ESA, 2000*;

• participated in proceedings under section 4 of the *Retail Business Holidays Act*; or

• taken, or plans to take, or will become eligible to take pregnancy, parental or emergency leave.

An employer is also prohibited from penalizing an employee in any way due to the fact that the employer has to pay to a third party monies owed by the employee as a result of a court order or garnishment.

The *ESA, 2000* specifically provides in subsection 74(2) that if an employee alleges that he or she has been subjected to a reprisal, then the onus is on the employer to prove that the employer's impugned actions were not a reprisal. There is an exception to this reverse onus in cases where the employer has applied for a review of a notice of contravention. Under these circumstances, the onus of proof is on the Director to establish, on a balance of probabilities, that the person against whom the notice of contravention was issued contravened the provision of the *ESA, 2000* indicated in the notice: subsection 122(4).

The Ministry of Labour uses a four-step test to determine whether an employer has engaged in a reprisal, as follows:

1. Is the person who is alleged to have committed a reprisal the employee's employer or a person acting on behalf of the employee's employer?

2. Did the employer or person acting on behalf of the employer intimidate, dismiss or otherwise penalize or threaten to intimidate, dismiss or otherwise penalize the employee?

3. Did the employee engage in any of the protected activities in subsection 74(1)?

4. Did the employer or person acting on behalf of the employer intimidate, dismiss or otherwise penalize or threaten to intimidate, dismiss or otherwise penalize the employee because the employee engaged in any of the protected activities in subsection 74(1)?

If all four questions are answered in the affirmative, a reprisal is established.

The OLRB decision in *Weihua (Marie) Shi v. Holcim (Canada) Inc. and Director of Employment Standards*, [2011] O.E.S.A.D. No. 1128, demonstrates the importance of not penalizing employees for attempting to exercise or enforce their rights under the *ESA, 2000*. In that matter, the OLRB considered whether an employee's dismissal was motivated in whole or in part by her refusal to work overtime. The employee was an accountant. She had previously expressed concerns about, and resisted, the employer's demands to work overtime. During the holiday season, the employer sent an email to employees indicating that it expected those in the tax department to work overtime, and prohibited them from taking days off during the first two weeks of January. The employer also insisted that all work must be performed on site, and could not be done at home. The employee responded that she could not guarantee attendance on weekends and may work from home. The employer responded that she must work "whatever hours it takes to get all [the work] done". The employee responded that she would do her best, but could not guarantee that she would be available for overtime. The employee proceeded to work overtime over the holidays, and worked for twelve consecutive days. Immediately after the holidays, the employer terminated her employment. The employee filed an employment standards claim seeking overtime pay and compensation for reprisal.

The OLRB found that the employee's termination was motivated "at least in part, by her unwillingness to accept [the employer's] demanding work schedule for the completion of year-end work." The OLRB held that the employer could not lawfully require the employee to work an unlimited number of hours or consecutive work days, and that the employee was entitled to overtime pay for each hour worked in excess of 44 in a work week. The OLRB further found that, by refusing to guarantee that she would be able to adhere to the employer's scheduling demands during the holiday season and the first two weeks of January, the employee was effectively exercising her rights under the *ESA, 2000*. Accordingly, the employer was found to have engaged in a reprisal.

Two 2017 OLRB decisions demonstrate a similar outcome where employees were dismissed in relation to taking leaves of absence to which they were entitled under the *ESA, 2000*.

In *Tempest Global Telecom Inc. v. Maddison*, 2017 CarswellOnt 9512 (Ont. L.R.B.), varied 2017 CarswellOnt 10956 (Ont. L.R.B.), an employee was terminated for cause shortly after she had taken maternity leave in accordance with her entitlements under the *ESA, 2000*. The employer alleged that grounds for termination arose from the discovery, after the employee had taken leave, of numerous significant errors made by the employee prior to her leave. In its decision, the OLRB took issue with the employer's failure to contact the employee in order to seek an explanation of these errors prior to issuing a notice of termination. The OLRB disagreed with the employer's claim that the employee should not be contacted during her maternity leave. In view of the employer's failure to provide due process, combined with the fact that the employee was on maternity leave and the employer failed to meet the burden of proving that her dismissal was not a reprisal, the OLRB found that the employer had violated section 74(1) and awarded damages accordingly.

In *Shaikh v. Temperenceco Inc.*, 2017 CarswellOnt 2967 (Ont. L.R.B.), varied 2017 CarswellOnt 9409 (Ont. L.R.B.), the OLRB similarly determined that a reprisal contrary to the *ESA, 2000* had occurred where an employer failed to reinstate an employee following the completion of his parental leave. According to the OLRB, such failure to reinstate constituted a dismissal. Because the employer was unable to offer any valid reason for its failure to reinstate given that the employee's position continued to exist, the OLRB found that the *only possible conclusion* was a determination that the employer had reprised against the employee as a direct result of his having taken a lawful leave of absence.

Enforcement by Employment Standards Officer

Section 104 of the *ESA, 2000* provides that an employment standards officer has the authority, if he or she finds that an employee has been the subject of a reprisal, to do the following:

- order that the employee be compensated for any loss incurred as a result of the contravention;
- order that the employee be reinstated; or
- order that the employee be both compensated for any loss *and* be reinstated.

Where the employer is ordered to pay compensation to an employee under the reprisal provisions, the employer may pay the amount of the compensation to the Director of Employment Standards, in trust, together with an administrative fee equal to the greater of $100 and 10% of the amount of the compensation. Under amendments arising from Bill 148, the employer may also pay the amount of compensation directly to the employee, if possible, without being required to pay an administrative fee: subsection 104(3). There is no maximum recovery amount under the reprisal provisions.

Remedies and Penalties Upon Conviction

Section 133 of the *ESA, 2000* provides that, if an employer is convicted of an offence involving a contravention of the reprisal provisions of the *ESA, 2000* (section 74), the court shall also order that the employer take specific action, or refrain from taking specific action, to remedy the contravention. This is a mandatory direction to the court. The order by the court may also require that an employee be paid wages owing, or that the employee be reinstated or compensated for any loss incurred as a result of the contravention, or a combination of reinstatement and compensation. If the contravention was in relation to Part XVI (Lie Detectors) of the *ESA, 2000*, and the contravention affected an applicant for employment, or an applicant to be a police officer, the court may order the employer to hire or compensate the applicant: subsection 133(2).

Additional Penalties for Failure to Comply with Court Order

An employer who has been convicted of an offence involving a contravention of the reprisal provisions, and who fails to comply with an order issued as a result of the contravention and conviction, is guilty of an offence and upon conviction is liable:

- if the employer is an individual, to a fine of not more than $2,000 for each day during which the failure to comply continues or to imprisonment for a term of not more than six months or to both; and

- if the employer is a corporation, to a fine of not more than $4,000 for each day during which the failure to comply continues.

These penalties are in addition to the penalties prescribed for a conviction involving a contravention of the reprisal provisions in the first instance.

Conclusion

This 2018 edition of the *Ontario Employment Standards Act: Quick Reference* has been updated to review various changes to the legislation in 2017, particularly the significant changes made under the *Fair Workplaces, Better Jobs Act, 2017* (Bill 148) that followed from the recommendations contained in the *Final Report* of the *Changing Workplaces Review*. The changes brought about under Bill 148 will have a significant impact on employers throughout Ontario. The most notable changes arising from Bill 148 include provisions for significant increases to the general minimum wage for most Ontario employees: from $11.40 per hour in 2017 to $14.00 in 2018 and $15.00 per hour in 2019. In addition to increases to the minimum wage, Bill 148 provides for other new minimum entitlements for employees in Ontario, including (i) two paid days of personal emergency leave; (ii) payment of wages equal to at least three hours at the employee's regular rate for all completed regular shifts; and (iii) increased vacation pay and vacation time entitlements for employees who have at least five years' tenure with the same employer.

Where employers are found to have acted in contravention of the standards set out in the *ESA, 2000*, amended enforcement provisions arising from Bill 148 will give Employment Standards Officers new discretion to impose a range of monetary penalty amounts, and will enable the issuing of warrants and registration of liens against employers who fail to pay penalties arising from contraventions. These significant changes to the entitlements and enforcement powers under the *ESA, 2000* will likely translate into a need for employers in Ontario to carefully review their employment policies, procedures and agreements to ensure compliance prior to the coming into effect of Bill 148's various provisions throughout 2018 and 2019.

Temporary Help Agencies constituted one of the focal points of the *Changing Workplaces Review*, and this focus translated into numerous significant changes under Bill 148. These changes include provision for one weeks' notice — or pay in lieu — to be provided when assignments of three months or more end earlier than initially estimated. Importantly, this notice requirement is separate from the notice and severance entitlements that apply to employees of temporary help agencies. Under other amendments, assignment employees will also receive new entitlements to (i) make a written request to their employer temporary help agency asking for a change in scheduling or work location following the completion of 3 months' continuous employment; (ii) receive equal pay in comparison to employees of the client who complete substantially the same work under similar conditions; and (iii) receive a minimum of three hours' pay where a scheduled shift is cancelled on short notice. Accordingly, both temporary help agencies and client organizations are well-advised to take careful note of changes to the *ESA, 2000* and to review their policies and practices accordingly.

We hope that this latest edition of our book will provide you with an accurate, up-to-date and useful tool for understanding the *Employment Standards Act, 2000*, including the significant amendments made under Bill 148.

EMPLOYMENT STANDARDS ACT, 2000

S.O. 2000, c. 41, as am. S.O. 2001, c. 9, Sched. I, s. 1; 2002, c. 18, Sched. J, s. 3; 2004, c. 15; 2004, c. 21; 2005, c. 5, s. 23; 2006, c. 13, s. 3; 2006, c. 19, Sched. D, s. 7, Sched. M, s. 1; 2006, c. 21, Sched. F, s. 136(1), Table 1; 2006, c. 34, Sched. C, s. 23; 2006, c. 35, Sched. C, s. 33; 2007, c. 16, Sched. A; 2008, c. 15, s. 85; 2009, c. 9, ss. 1-23, 24(1), (2) (Fr.), 25-29; 2009, c. 16; 2009, c. 32, s. 51; 2009, c. 33, Sched. 20, s. 1; 2010, c. 15, s. 224 [Not in force at date of publication.]; 2010, c. 16, Sched. 9, s. 1; 2011, c. 1, Sched. 7, s. 1; 2013, c. 13, Sched. 1, s. 12; 2014, c. 5, s. 48; 2014, c. 6, ss. 1, 2(1) (Fr.), (2), 3-5; 2014, c. 10, Sched. 2, ss. 1(1) (Fr.), (2), 2-10; 2015, c. 27, Sched. 4, s. 1; 2015, c. 32; 2016, c. 23, s. 46 (Fr.); 2016, c. 30, s. 36; 2017, c. 22, ss. 1-69 [ss. 1(2), 25-29, 41, 45 to come into force April 1, 2018.] [ss. 2(3), 8(2), (6), 11, 12, 69(3) to come into force January 1, 2019.]

Her Majesty, by and with the advice and consent of the Legislative Assembly of the Province of Ontario, enacts as follows:

PART I — DEFINITIONS

1. (1) Definitions — In this Act,

"agent" includes a trade union that represents an employee in collective bargaining;

"alternative vacation entitlement year" means, with respect to an employee, a recurring 12-month period that begins on a date chosen by the employer, other than the first day of the employee's employment;

"arbitrator" includes,

(a) a board of arbitration, and

(b) the Board, when it is acting under section 133 of the *Labour Relations Act, 1995*;

"assignment employee" means an employee employed by a temporary help agency for the purpose of being assigned to perform work on a temporary basis for clients of the agency;

"benefit plan" means a benefit plan provided for an employee by or through his or her employer;

"Board" means the Ontario Labour Relations Board;

"building services" means services for a building with respect to food, security and cleaning and any prescribed services for a building;

"building services provider" or **"provider"** means a person who provides building services for a premises and includes the owner or manager of a premises if the owner or manager provides building services for premises the person owns or manages;

"business" includes an activity, trade or undertaking;

"client", in relation to a temporary help agency, means a person or entity that enters into an arrangement with the agency under which the agency agrees to assign or attempt to assign one or more of its assignment employees to perform work for the person or entity on a temporary basis;

"collector" means a person, other than an employment standards officer, who is authorized by the Director to collect an amount owing under this Act;

"continuous operation" means an operation or that part of an operation that normally continues 24 hours a day without cessation in each seven-day period until it is concluded for that period;

Proposed Addition - 1(1) "difference in employment status"

"difference in employment status", in respect of one or more employees, means,

    (a) a difference in the number of hours regularly worked by the employees; or

(b) a difference in the term of their employment, including a difference in permanent, temporary, seasonal or casual status;

2017, c. 22, Sched. 1, s. 1(2) [To come into force April 1, 2018.]

"Director" means the Director of Employment Standards;

"domestic or sexual violence leave pay" means pay for any paid days of leave taken under section 49.7;

"employee" includes,

(a) a person, including an officer of a corporation, who performs work for an employer for wages,

(b) a person who supplies services to an employer for wages,

(c) a person who receives training from a person who is an employer, if the skill in which the person is being trained is a skill used by the employer's employees, or

(d) a person who is a homeworker,

and includes a person who was an employee;

"employer" includes,

(a) an owner, proprietor, manager, superintendent, overseer, receiver or trustee of an activity, business, work, trade, occupation, profession, project or undertaking who has control or direction of, or is directly or indirectly responsible for, the employment of a person in it, and

(b) any persons treated as one employer under section 4, and includes a person who was an employer;

"employment contract" includes a collective agreement;

"employment standard" means a requirement or prohibition under this Act that applies to an employer for the benefit of an employee;

"establishment", with respect to an employer, means a location at which the employer carries on business but, if the employer carries on business at more than one location, separate locations constitute one establishment if,

(a) the separate locations are located within the same municipality, or

(b) one or more employees at a location have seniority rights that extend to the other location under a written employment contract whereby the employee or employees may displace another employee of the same employer;

"homeworker" means an individual who performs work for compensation in premises occupied by the individual primarily as residential quarters but does not include an independent contractor;

"hospital" means a hospital as defined in the *Hospital Labour Disputes Arbitration Act*;

"labour relations officer" means a labour relations officer appointed under the *Labour Relations Act, 1995*;

"Minister" means the Minister of Labour;

"Ministry" means the Ministry of Labour;

"overtime hour", with respect to an employee, means,

(a) if one or more provisions in the employee's employment contract or in another Act that applies to the employee's employment provides a greater benefit for overtime than Part VIII (Overtime Pay), an hour of work in excess of the overtime threshold set out in that provision, and

(b) otherwise, an hour of work in excess of the overtime threshold under this Act that applies to the employee's employment;

"person" includes a trade union;

"personal emergency leave pay" means pay for any paid days of leave taken under section 50;

"premium pay" means an employee's entitlement for working on a public holiday as described in subsection 24(2);

"prescribed" means prescribed by the regulations;

"public holiday" means any of the following:

    1. New Year's Day.

    1.1 Family Day, being the third Monday in February.

    2. Good Friday.

    3. Victoria Day.

    4. Canada Day.

    5. Labour Day.

    6. Thanksgiving Day.

    7. Christmas Day.

    8. December 26.

    9. Any day prescribed as a public holiday;

"public holiday pay" means an employee's entitlement with respect to a public holiday as determined under subsection 24(1);

"regular rate" means, subject to any regulation made under paragraph 10 of subsection 141(1),

    (a) for an employee who is paid by the hour, the amount earned for an hour of work in the employee's usual work week, not counting overtime hours,

    (b) otherwise, the amount earned in a given work week divided by the number of non-overtime hours actually worked in that week;

"regular wages" means wages other than overtime pay, public holiday pay, premium pay, vacation pay, domestic or sexual violence leave pay, personal emergency leave pay, termination pay, severance pay and termination of assignment pay and entitlements under a provision of an employee's contract of employment that under subsection 5 (2) prevail over Part VIII, Part X, Part XI, section 49.7, section 50, Part XV or section 74.10.1;

"regular work day", with respect to an employee who usually works the same number of hours each day, means a day of that many hours;

"regular work week", with respect to an employee who usually works the same number of hours each week, means a week of that many hours but not including overtime hours;

"regulations" means the regulations made under this Act;

"reservist" means a member of the reserve force of the Canadian Forces referred to in subsection 15(3) of the *National Defence Act* (Canada);

"standard vacation entitlement year" means, with respect to an employee, a recurring 12-month period that begins on the first day of the employee's employment;

"statutory notice period" means,

(a) the period of notice of termination required to be given by an employer under Part XV, or

(b) where the employer provides a greater amount of notice than is required under Part XV, that part of the notice period ending with the termination date specified in the notice which equals the period of notice required under Part XV;

"stub period" means, with respect to an employee for whom the employer establishes an alternative vacation entitlement year comes into force,

(a) if the employee's first alternative vacation entitlement year begins before the completion of his or her first 12 months of employment, the period that begins on the first day of employment and ends on the day before the start of the alternative vacation entitlement year,

(b) if the employee's first alternative vacation entitlement year begins after the completion of his or her first 12 months of employment, the period that begins on the day after the day on which his or her most recent standard vacation entitlement year ended and ends on the day before the start of the alternative vacation entitlement year;

"temporary help agency" means an employer that employs persons for the purpose of assigning them to perform work on a temporary basis for clients of the employer;

"termination of assignment pay" means pay provided to an assignment employee when the employee's assignment is terminated before the end of its estimated term under section 74.10.1;

"tip or other gratuity" means,

(a) a payment voluntarily made to or left for an employee by a customer of the employee's employer in such circumstances that a reasonable person would be likely to infer that the customer intended or assumed that the payment would be kept by the employee or shared by the employee with other employees,

(b) a payment voluntarily made to an employer by a customer in such circumstances that a reasonable person would be likely to infer that the customer intended or assumed that the payment would be redistributed to an employee or employees,

(c) a payment of a service charge or similar charge imposed by an employer on a customer in such circumstances that a reasonable person would be likely to infer that the customer intended or assumed that the payment would be redistributed to an employee or employees, and

(d) such other payments as may be prescribed,

but does not include,

(e) such payments as may be prescribed, and

(f) such charges as may be prescribed relating to the method of payment used, or a prescribed portion of those charges;

"trade union" means an organization that represents employees in collective bargaining under any of the following:

1. The *Labour Relations Act, 1995.*

2. The *Crown Employees Collective Bargaining Act, 1993.*

3. The *School Boards Collective Bargaining Act, 2014.*

4. Part IX of the *Fire Protection and Prevention Act, 1997.*

5. The *Colleges Collective Bargaining Act, 2008.*

6. Any prescribed Acts or provisions of Acts;

"vacation entitlement year" means an alternative vacation entitlement year or a standard vacation entitlement year;

"wages" means,

(a) monetary remuneration payable by an employer to an employee under the terms of an employment contract, oral or written, express or implied,

(b) any payment required to be made by an employer to an employee under this Act, and

(c) any allowances for room or board under an employment contract or prescribed allowances,

but does not include,

(d) tips or other gratuities,

(e) any sums paid as gifts or bonuses that are dependent on the discretion of the employer and that are not related to hours, production or efficiency,

(f) expenses and travelling allowances, or

(g) subject to subsections 60(3) or 62(2), employer contributions to a benefit plan and payments to which an employee is entitled from a benefit plan;

"work week" means,

(a) a recurring period of seven consecutive days selected by the employer for the purpose of scheduling work, or

(b) if the employer has not selected such a period, a recurring period of seven consecutive days beginning on Sunday and ending on Saturday.

(2) Assignment to perform work includes training — For greater certainty, being assigned to perform work for a client of a temporary help agency includes being assigned to the client to receive training for the purpose of performing work for the client.

(3) Agreements in writing — Unless otherwise provided, a reference in this Act to an agreement between an employer and an employee or to an employer and an employee agreeing to something shall be deemed to be a reference to an agreement in writing or to their agreeing in writing to do something.

(3.1) Electronic form — The requirement in subsection (3) for an agreement to be in writing is satisfied if the agreement is in electronic form.

(4) Exception — Nothing in subsection (3) requires an employment contract that is not a collective agreement to be in writing.

2001, c. 9, Sched. I, s. 1(1); 2002, c. 18, Sched. J, s. 3(1), (2); 2007, c. 16, Sched. A, s. 1; 2008, c. 15, s. 85; 2014, c. 5, s. 48; 2017, c. 22, Sched. 1, s. 1(1), (3)-(12)

PART II — POSTING OF INFORMATION CONCERNING RIGHTS AND OBLIGATIONS

2. (1) Minister to prepare poster — The Minister shall prepare and publish a poster providing such information about this Act and the regulations as the Minister considers appropriate.

(2) If poster not up to date — If the Minister believes that the poster prepared under subsection (1) has become out of date, he or she shall prepare and publish a new poster.

(3) Material to be posted — Every employer shall post and keep posted in at least one conspicuous place in every workplace of the employer where it is likely to come to the attention of employees in that workplace a copy of the most recent poster published by the Minister under this section.

(4) Where majority language not English — If the majority language of a workplace of an employer is a language other than English, the employer shall make enquiries as to whether the Minister has prepared a translation of the poster into that language, and if the Minister has done so, the employer shall post and keep posted a copy of the translation next to the copy of the poster.

(5) Copy of poster to be provided — Every employer shall provide each of his or her employees with a copy of the most recent poster published by the Minister under this section.

(6) Same — translation — If an employee requests a translation of the poster into a language other than English, the employer shall make enquiries as to whether the Minister has prepared a translation of the poster into that language, and if the Minister has done so, the employer shall provide the employee with a copy of the translation.

(7) When copy of poster to be provided — An employer shall provide an employee with a copy of the poster within 30 days of the day the employee becomes an employee of the employer.

(8) Same — transition — If an employer has one or more employees on the day section 1 of Schedule 2 to the *Stronger Workplaces for a Stronger Economy Act, 2014* comes into force, the employer shall provide his or her employees with a copy of the poster within 30 days of that day.

2004, c. 21, s. 1; 2014, c. 10, Sched. 2, s. 1(2)

PART III — HOW THIS ACT APPLIES

3. (1) Who Act applies to — Subject to subsections (2) to (5), the employment standards set out in this Act apply with respect to an employee and his or her employer if,

(a) the employee's work is to be performed in Ontario; or

(b) the employee's work is to be performed in Ontario and outside Ontario but the work performed outside Ontario is a continuation of work performed in Ontario.

(2) Exception, federal jurisdiction — This Act does not apply with respect to an employee and his or her employer if their employment relationship is within the legislative jurisdiction of the Parliament of Canada.

(3) Exception, diplomatic personnel — This Act does not apply with respect to an employee of an embassy or consulate of a foreign nation and his or her employer.

(4) [Repealed 2017, c. 22, Sched. 1, s. 2(1).]

(5) Other exceptions — This Act does not apply with respect to the following individuals and any person for whom such an individual performs work or from whom such an individual receives compensation:

1. A secondary school student who performs work under a work experience program authorized by the school board that operates the school in which the student is enrolled.

2. An individual who performs work under a program approved by a college of applied arts and technology or a university.

2.1 An individual who performs work under a program that is approved by a private career college registered under the *Private Career Colleges Act, 2005* and that meets such criteria as may be prescribed.

3. A participant in community participation under the *Ontario Works Act, 1997*.

4. An individual who is an inmate of a correctional institution within the meaning of the *Ministry of Correctional Services Act*, is an inmate of a penitentiary, is being held in a detention facility within the meaning of the *Police Services Act* or is being held in a place of temporary detention or youth custody facility under the *Youth Criminal Justice Act* (Canada), if the individual participates inside or outside the institution, penitentiary, place or facility in a work project or rehabilitation program.

5. An individual who performs work under an order or sentence of a court or as part of an extrajudicial measure under the *Youth Criminal Justice Act* (Canada).

6. An individual who performs work in a simulated job or working environment if the primary purpose in placing the individual in the job or environment is his or her rehabilitation.

Proposed Repeal — 3(5) para. 6

6. [Repealed 2017, c. 22, Sched. 1, s. 2(3).]

2017, c. 22, Sched. 1, s. 2(3) [To come into force January 1, 2019.]

7. A holder of political, religious or judicial office.

8. A member of a quasi-judicial tribunal.

9. A holder of elected office in an organization, including a trade union.

10. A police officer, except as provided in Part XVI (Lie Detectors).

11. A director of a corporation, except as provided in Part XX (Liability of Directors), Part XXI (Who Enforces this Act and What They Can Do), Part XXII (Complaints and Enforcement), Part XXIII (Reviews by the Board), Part XXIV (Collection), Part XXV (Offences and Prosecutions), Part XXVI (Miscellaneous Evidentiary Provisions), Part XXVII (Regulations) and Part XXVIII (Transition, Amendment, Repeals, Commencement and Short Title).

12. Any prescribed individuals.

(6) Dual roles — Where an individual who performs work or occupies a position described in subsection (5) also performs some other work or occupies some other position and does so as an employee, nothing in subsection (5) precludes the application of this Act to that individual and his or her employer insofar as that other work or position is concerned.

2006, c. 19, Sched. D, s. 7; 2017, c. 22, Sched. 1, s. 2(1), (2)

3.1 Crown bound — This Act binds the Crown.

2017, c. 22, Sched. 1, s. 3

4. (1) Separate persons treated as one employer — Subsection (2) applies if associated or related activities or businesses are or were carried on by or through an employer and one or more other persons.

(2) Same — The employer and the other person or persons described in subsection (1) shall all be treated as one employer for the purposes of this Act.

(3) Businesses need not be carried on at same time — Subsection (2) applies even if the activities or businesses are not carried on at the same time.

(4) Exception, individuals — Subsection (2) does not apply with respect to a corporation and an individual who is a shareholder of the corporation unless the individual is a member of a partnership and the shares are held for the purposes of the partnership.

(4.1) Exception, Crown — Subsection (2) does not apply to the Crown, a Crown agency or an authority, board, commission or corporation all of whose members are appointed by the Crown.

(5) Joint and several liability — Persons who are treated as one employer under this section are jointly and severally liable for any contravention of this Act and the regulations under it and for any wages owing to an employee of any of them.

2017, c. 22, Sched. 1, s. 4

5. (1) No contracting out — Subject to subsection (2), no employer or agent of an employer and no employee or agent of an employee shall contract out of or waive an employment standard and any such contracting out or waiver is void.

(2) Greater contractual or statutory right — If one or more provisions in an employment contract or in another Act that directly relate to the same subject matter as an employment standard provide a greater benefit to an employee than the employment standard, the provision or provisions in the contract or Act apply and the employment standard does not apply.

5.1 (1) No treating as if not employee — An employer shall not treat, for the purposes of this Act, a person who is an employee of the employer as if the person were not an employee under this Act.

(2) Onus of proof — Subject to subsection 122 (4), if, during the course of an employment standards officer's investigation or inspection or in any proceeding under this Act, other than a prosecution, an employer or alleged employer claims that a person is not an employee, the burden of proof that the person is not an employee lies upon the employer or alleged employer.

2017, c. 22, Sched. 1, s. 5

6. Settlement by trade union binding — A settlement made on an employee's behalf by a trade union that represents the employee is binding on the employee.

7. Agents — An agreement or authorization that may lawfully be made or given by an employee under this Act may be made or given by his or her agent and is binding on the employee as if it had been made or given by the employee.

8. (1) Civil proceedings not affected — Subject to section 97, no civil remedy of an employee against his or her employer is affected by this Act.

(2) Notice — Where an employee commences a civil proceeding against his or her employer under this Act, notice of the proceeding shall be served on the Director on a form approved by the Director on or before the date the civil proceeding is set down for trial.

(3) Service of notice — The notice shall be served on the Director,

(a) by being delivered to the Director's office on a day and at a time when it is open;

(b) by being mailed to the Director's office using a method of mail delivery that allows delivery to be verified; or

(c) by being sent to the Director's office by fax or email.

(4) When service effective — Service under subsection (3) shall be deemed to be effected,

(a) in the case of service under clause (3)(a), on the day shown on a receipt or acknowledgment provided to the employee by the Director or his or her representative;

(b) in the case of service under clause (3)(b), on the day shown in the verification;

(c) in the case of service under clause (3)(c), on the day on which the fax or email is sent, subject to subsection (5).

(5) Same — Service shall be deemed to be effected on the next day on which the Director's office is not closed, if the fax or email is sent,

(a) on a day on which the Director's office is closed; or

(b) after 5 p.m. on any day.

2009, c. 9, s. 1

Part IV — Continuity of Employment

9. (1) Sale, etc., of business — If an employer sells a business or a part of a business and the purchaser employs an employee of the seller, the employment of the employee shall be deemed not to have been terminated or severed for the purposes of this Act and his or her employment with the seller shall be deemed to have been employment with the purchaser for the purpose of any subsequent calculation of the employee's length or period of employment.

(2) Exception — Subsection (1) does not apply if the day on which the purchaser hires the employee is more than 13 weeks after the earlier of his or her last day of employment with the seller and the day of the sale.

(3) Definitions — In this section, "sells" includes leases, transfers or disposes of in any other manner, and "sale" has a corresponding meaning.

(4) Predecessor Acts — For the purposes of subsection (1), employment with the seller includes any employment attributed to the seller under this section or a provision of a predecessor Act dealing with sales of businesses.

10. (1) New building services provider — This section applies if the building services provider for a building is replaced by a new provider and an employee of the replaced provider is employed by the new provider.

(2) No termination or severance — The employment of the employee shall be deemed not to have been terminated or severed for the purposes of this Act and his or her employment with the replaced provider shall be deemed to have been employment with the new provider for the purpose of any subsequent calculation of the employee's length or period of employment.

(3) Exception — Subsection (2) does not apply if the day on which the new provider hires the employee is more than 13 weeks after the earlier of his or her last day of employment with the replaced provider and the day on which the new provider began servicing the premises.

(4) Predecessor Acts — For the purposes of subsection (2), employment with the replaced provider includes any employment attributed to the replaced provider under this section or under a provision of a predecessor Act dealing with building services providers.

PART V — PAYMENT OF WAGES

11. (1) Payment of wages — An employer shall establish a recurring pay period and a recurring pay day and shall pay all wages earned during each pay period, other than accruing vacation pay, no later than the pay day for that period.

(2) Manner of payment — An employer shall pay an employee's wages,

> (a) by cash;

> (b) by cheque payable only to the employee;

> (c) by direct deposit in accordance with subsection (4); or

> (d) by any other prescribed method of payment.

(3) Place of payment by cash or cheque — If payment is made by cash or cheque, the employer shall ensure that the cash or cheque is given to the employee at his or her workplace or at some other place agreeable to the employee.

(4) Direct deposit — An employer may pay an employee's wages by direct deposit into an account of a financial institution if,

> (a) the account is in the employee's name;

> (b) no person other than the employee or a person authorized by the employee has access to the account; and

(c) unless the employee agrees otherwise, an office or facility of the financial institution is located within a reasonable distance from the location where the employee usually works.

(5) If employment ends — If an employee's employment ends, the employer shall pay any wages to which the employee is entitled to the employee not later than the later of,

(a) seven days after the employment ends; and

(b) the day that would have been the employee's next pay day.

2017, c. 22, Sched. 1, s. 6

12. (1) Statement re wages — On or before an employee's pay day, the employer shall give to the employee a written statement setting out,

(a) the pay period for which the wages are being paid;

(b) the wage rate, if there is one;

(c) the gross amount of wages and, unless the information is provided to the employee in some other manner, how that amount was calculated;

(d) [Repealed 2002, c. 18, Sched. J, s. 3(3).]

(e) the amount and purpose of each deduction from wages;

(f) any amount with respect to room or board that is deemed to have been paid to the employee under subsection 23(2); and

(g) the net amount of wages being paid to the employee.

(2) [Repealed 2002, c. 18, Sched. J, s. 3(4).]

(3) Electronic copies — The statement may be provided to the employee by electronic mail rather than in writing if the employee has access to a means of making a paper copy of the statement.

2001, c. 9, Sched. I, s. 1(2); 2002, c. 18, Sched. J, s. 3(3), (4)

12.1 Statement re wages on termination — On or before the day on which the employer is required to pay wages under subsection 11(5), the employer shall provide the employee with a written statement setting out,

(a) the gross amount of any termination pay or severance pay being paid to the employee;

(b) the gross amount of any vacation pay being paid to the employee;

(c) unless the information is provided to the employee in some other manner, how the amounts referred to in clauses (a) and (b) were calculated;

(d) the pay period for which any wages other than wages described in clauses (a) or (b) are being paid;

(e) the wage rate, if there is one;

(f) the gross amount of any wages referred to in clause (d) and, unless the information is provided to the employee in some other manner, how that amount was calculated;

(g) the amount and purpose of each deduction from wages;

(h) any amount with respect to room or board that is deemed to have been paid to the employee under subsection 23(2); and

(i) the net amount of wages being paid to the employee.

2002, c. 18, Sched. J, s. 3(5)

13. (1) Deductions, etc. — An employer shall not withhold wages payable to an employee, make a deduction from an employee's wages or cause the employee to return his or her wages to the employer unless authorized to do so under this section.

(2) Statute or court order — An employer may withhold or make a deduction from an employee's wages or cause the employee to return them if a statute of Ontario or Canada or a court order authorizes it.

(3) Employee authorization — An employer may withhold or make a deduction from an employee's wages or cause the employee to return them with the employee's written authorization.

(4) Exception — Subsections (2) and (3) do not apply if the statute, order or written authorization from the employee requires the employer to remit the withheld or deducted wages to a third person and the employer fails to do so.

(5) Exception — Subsection (3) does not apply if,

(a) the employee's authorization does not refer to a specific amount or provide a formula from which a specific amount may be calculated;

(b) the employee's wages were withheld, deducted or required to be returned,

(i) because of faulty work,

(ii) because the employer had a cash shortage, lost property or had property stolen and a person other than the employee had access to the cash or property, or

(iii) under any prescribed conditions; or

(c) the employee's wages were required to be returned and those wages were the subject of an order under this Act.

14. (1) Priority of claims — Despite any other Act, wages shall have priority over and be paid before the claims and rights of all other unsecured creditors of an employer, to the extent of $10,000 per employee.

(2) Exception — Subsection (1) does not apply with respect to a distribution made under the *Bankruptcy and Insolvency Act* (Canada) or other legislation enacted by the Parliament of Canada respecting bankruptcy or insolvency.

2001, c. 9, Sched. I, s. 1(3)

PART V.1 — EMPLOYEE TIPS AND OTHER GRATUITIES

[Heading added 2015, c. 32, s. 1.]

14.1 [Repealed 2017, c. 22, Sched. 1, s. 7.]

14.2 (1) Prohibition re tips or other gratuities — An employer shall not withhold tips or other gratuities from an employee, make a deduction from an employee's tips or other gratuities or cause the employee to return or give his or her tips or other gratuities to the employer unless authorized to do so under this Part.

(2) Enforcement — If an employer contravenes subsection (1), the amount withheld, deducted, returned or given is a debt owing to the employee and is enforceable under this Act as if it were wages owing to the employee.

2015, c. 32, s. 1

14.3 (1) Statute or court order — An employer may withhold or make a deduction from an employee's tips or other gratuities or cause the employee to return or give them to the employer if a statute of Ontario or Canada or a court order authorizes it.

(2) Exception — Subsection (1) does not apply if the statute or order requires the employer to remit the withheld, deducted, returned or given tips or other gratuities to a third person and the employer fails to do so.

2015, c. 32, s. 1

14.4 (1) Pooling of tips or other gratuities — An employer may withhold or make a deduction from an employee's tips or other gratuities or cause the employee to return or give them to the employer if the employer collects and redistributes tips or other gratuities among some or all of the employer's employees.

(2) Exception — An employer shall not redistribute tips or other gratuities under subsection (1) to such employees as may be prescribed.

(3) Employer, etc. not to share in tips or other gratuities — Subject to subsections (4) and (5), an employer or a director or shareholder of an employer may not share in tips or other gratuities redistributed under subsection (1).

(4) Exception — sole proprietor, partner — An employer who is a sole proprietor or a partner in a partnership may share in tips or other gratuities redistributed under subsection (1) if he or she regularly performs to a substantial degree the same work performed by,

(a) some or all of the employees who share in the redistribution; or

(b) employees of other employers in the same industry who commonly receive or share tips or other gratuities.

(5) Exception — director, shareholder — A director or shareholder of an employer may share in tips or other gratuities redistributed under subsection (1) if he or she regularly performs to a substantial degree the same work performed by,

(a) some or all of the employees who share in the redistribution; or

(b) employees of other employers in the same industry who commonly receive or share tips or other gratuities.

2015, c. 32, s. 1

14.5 (1) Transition — collective agreements — If a collective agreement that is in effect on the day section 1 of the *Protecting Employees' Tips Act, 2015* comes into force contains a provision that addresses the treatment of employee tips or other gratuities and there is a conflict between the provision of the collective agreement and this Part, the provision of the collective agreement prevails.

(2) Same — expiry of agreement — Following the expiry of a collective agreement described in subsection (1), if the provision that addresses the treatment of employee tips or other gratuities remains in effect, subsection (1) continues to apply to that provision, with necessary modifications, until a new or renewal agreement comes into effect.

(3) Same — renewed or new agreement — Subsection (1) does not apply to a collective agreement that is made or renewed on or after the day section 1 of the *Protecting Employees' Tips Act, 2015* comes into force.

2015, c. 32, s. 1

PART VI — RECORDS

15. (1) Records — An employer shall record the following information with respect to each employee, including an employee who is a homeworker:

1. The employee's name and address.

2. The employee's date of birth, if the employee is a student and under 18 years of age.

3. The date on which the employee began his or her employment.

3.1 The dates and times that the employee worked.

3.2 If the employee has two or more regular rates of pay for work performed for the employer and, in a work week, the employee performed work for the employer in excess of the overtime threshold, the dates and times that the employee worked in excess of the overtime threshold at each rate of pay.

Proposed Addition — 15(1) paras. 3.3, 3.4

3.3 The dates and times that the employee was scheduled to work or to be on call for work, and any changes made to the on call schedule.

3.4 Any cancellations of a scheduled day of work or scheduled on call period of the employee, as described in subsection 21.6 (2), and the date and time of the cancellation.

2017, c. 22, Sched. 1, s. 8(2) [To come into force January 1, 2019.]

4. The number of hours the employee worked in each day and each week.

5. The information contained in each written statement given to the employee under subsection 12(1), section 12.1,

subsections 27 (2.1), 28 (2.1), 29 (1.1) and 30 (2.1) and clause 36(3)(b).

6. [Repealed 2002, c. 18, Sched. J, s. 3(7).]

(2) Homeworkers — In addition to the record described in subsection (1), the employer shall maintain a register of any homeworkers the employer employs showing the following information:

1. The employee's name and address.

2. The information that is contained in all statements required to be provided to the employee described in clause 12(1)(b).

3. Any prescribed information.

(3) Exception — An employer is not required to record the information described in paragraph 3.1 or 4 of subsection (1) with respect to an employee who is paid a salary if,

(a) the employer records the number of hours in excess of those in his or her regular work week and,

(i) the number of hours in excess of eight that the employee worked in each day, or

(ii) if the number of hours in the employee's regular work day is more than eight hours, the number in excess; or

(b) sections 17 to 19 and Part VIII (Overtime Pay) do not apply with respect to the employee.

(4) Meaning of salary — An employee is considered to be paid a salary for the purposes of subsection (3) if,

(a) the employee is entitled to be paid a fixed amount for each pay period; and

(b) the amount actually paid for each pay period does not vary according to the number of hours worked by the employee, unless he or she works more than 44 hours in a week.

(5) Retention of records — The employer shall retain or arrange for some other person to retain the records of the information required under this section for the following periods:

1. For information referred to in paragraph 1 or 3 of subsection (1), three years after the employee ceased to be employed by the employer.

2. For information referred to in paragraph 2 of subsection (1), the earlier of,

    i. three years after the employee's 18th birthday, or

    ii. three years after the employee ceased to be employed by the employer.

3. For information referred to in paragraph 3.1, 3.2 or 4 of subsection (1) or in subsection (3), three years after the day or week to which the information relates.

Proposed Amendment — 15(5) para. 3

3. For information referred to in paragraph 3.1, 3.2, 3.3, 3.4 or 4 of subsection (1) or in subsection (3), three years after the day or week to which the information relates.

2017, c. 22, Sched. 1, s. 8(6) [To come into force January 1, 2019.]

---

4. For information referred to in paragraph 5 of subsection (1), three years after the information was given to the employee.

5. [Repealed 2002, c. 18, Sched. J, s. 3(8).]

(6) Register of homeworkers — Information pertaining to a homeworker may be deleted from the register three years after the homeworker ceases to be employed by the employer.

(7) Retain documents re leave — An employer shall retain or arrange for some other person to retain all notices, certificates, correspondence and other documents given to or produced by the employer that relate to an employee taking pregnancy leave, parental leave, family medical leave, organ donor leave, family caregiver leave, critical illness leave, child death leave, crime-related child disappearance leave, domestic or sexual violence leave, personal emergency leave, emergency leave during a declared emergency or reservist leave for three years after the day on which the leave expired.

(8) Retention of agreements re excess hours — An employer shall retain or arrange for some other person to retain copies of every agreement that the employer has made with an employee permitting the employee to work hours in excess of the limits set out in subsection 17(1) for three years after the last day on which work was performed under the agreement.

(9) Retention of averaging agreements — An employer shall retain or arrange for some other person to retain copies of every averaging agreement that the employer has made with an employee under clause 22(2)(a) for three years after the last day on which work was performed under the agreement.

2002, c. 18, Sched. J, s. 3(6)-(8); 2004, c. 21; s. 2; 2006, c. 13; s. 3(1); 2007, c. 16, Sched. A, s. 2; 2009, c. 16, s. 1; 2014, c. 6, s. 1; 2017, c. 22, Sched. 1, s. 8(1), (3)-(5), (7), (8)

15.1 (1) Record re vacation time and vacation pay — An employer shall record information concerning an employee's entitlement to vacation time and vacation pay in accordance with this section.

(2) Content of record — The employer shall record the following information:

1. The amount of vacation time, if any, that the employee had earned since the start of employment but had not taken before the start of the vacation entitlement year.

2. The amount of vacation time that the employee earned during the vacation entitlement year.

3. The amount of vacation time, if any, taken by the employee during the vacation entitlement year.

4. The amount of vacation time, if any, that the employee had earned since the start of employment but had not taken as of the end of the vacation entitlement year.

4.1 The amount of vacation pay that the employee earned during the vacation entitlement year and how that amount was calculated.

5. The amount of vacation pay paid to the employee during the vacation entitlement year.

6. The amount of wages on which the vacation pay referred to in paragraph 5 was calculated and the period of time to which those wages relate.

(3) Additional requirement, alternative vacation entitlement year — If the employer establishes an alternative vacation entitlement year for an employee, the employer shall record the following information for the stub period:

1. The amount of vacation time that the employee earned during the stub period.

2. The amount of vacation time, if any, that the employee took during the stub period.

3. The amount of vacation time, if any, earned but not taken by the employee during the stub period.

3.1 The amount of vacation pay that the employee earned during the stub period and how that amount was calculated.

4. The amount of vacation pay paid to the employee during the stub period.

5. The amount of wages on which the vacation pay referred to in paragraph 4 was calculated and the period of time to which those wages relate.

(4) When information to be recorded — The employer shall record information under this section by a date that is not later than the later of,

(a) seven days after the start of the next vacation entitlement year or the first vacation entitlement year, as the case may be; and

(b) the first pay day of the next vacation entitlement year or of the first vacation entitlement year, as the case may be.

(5) Retention of records — The employer shall retain or arrange for some other person to retain each record required under this section for five years after it was made.

(6) Exception — Paragraphs 5 and 6 of subsection (2) and paragraphs 4 and 5 of subsection (3) do not apply with respect to an employee whose employer pays vacation pay in accordance with subsection 36(3).

(7) Transition — Subsections 15.1 (2) and (3), as they read immediately before the day section 9 of Schedule 1 to the *Fair Workplaces, Better Jobs Act, 2017* came into force, continue to apply with respect to vacation entitlement years and stub periods that began before that day.

2002, c. 18, Sched. J, s. 3(9); 2017, c. 22, Sched. 1, s. 9

16. Availability — An employer shall ensure that all of the records and documents required to be retained under sections 15 and 15.1 are readily available for inspection as required by an employment standards officer, even if the employer has arranged for another person to retain them.

2004, c. 21, s. 3

PART VII — HOURS OF WORK AND EATING PERIODS

17. (1) Limit on hours of work — Subject to subsections (2) and (3), no employer shall require or permit an employee to work more than,

    (a) eight hours in a day or, if the employer establishes a regular work day of more than eight hours for the employee, the number of hours in his or her regular work day; and

    (b) 48 hours in a work week.

(2) Exception: hours in a day — An employee's hours of work may exceed the limit set out in clause (1)(a) if the employee has made an agreement with the employer that he or she will work up to a specified number of hours in a day in excess of the limit and his or her hours of work in a day do not exceed the number specified in the agreement.

(3) Exception: hours in a work week — An employee's hours of work may exceed the limit set out in clause (1)(b) if,

(a) the employee has made an agreement with the employer that he or she will work up to a specified number of hours in a work week in excess of the limit;

(b) the employer has received an approval under section 17.1 that applies to the employee or to a class of employees that includes the employee; and

(c) the employee's hours of work in a work week do not exceed the lesser of,

(i) the number of hours specified in the agreement, and

(ii) the number of hours specified in the approval.

(4) Same, pending approval — Despite subsection (3), an employee's hours of work may exceed the limit set out in clause (1)(b) even though the employer has not received the approval described in clause (3)(b), if,

(a) the employee has made an agreement described in clause (3)(a) with the employer;

(b) the employer has served on the Director an application for an approval under section 17.1;

(c) the application is for an approval that applies to the employee or to a class of employees that includes the employee;

(d) 30 days have passed since the application was served on the Director;

(e) the employer has not received a notice that the application has been refused;

(f) the employer's most recent previous application, if any, for an approval under section 17.1 was not refused;

(g) the most recent approval, if any, received by the employer under section 17.1 was not revoked;

(h) the employer has posted and kept posted a copy of the application in at least one conspicuous place in the workplace where the employee works, so that it is likely to come to the employee's attention; and

(i) the employee's hours of work in a work week do not exceed any of,

   (i) the number of hours specified in the application,

   (ii) the number of hours specified in the agreement, and

   (iii) 60 hours.

(5) Document re employee rights — An agreement described in subsection (2) or in clause (3)(a) is not valid unless,

(a) the employer has, before the agreement is made, provided the employee with a copy of the most recent document published by the Director under section 21.1; and

(b) the agreement contains a statement in which the employee acknowledges that he or she has received a document that the employer has represented is the most recent document published by the Director under section 21.1.

(6) Revocation by employee — An employee may revoke an agreement described in subsection (2) or in clause (3)(a) two weeks after giving written notice to the employer.

(7) Revocation by employer — An employer may revoke an agreement described in subsection (2) or in clause (3)(a) after giving reasonable notice to the employee.

(8) Transition: certain agreements — For the purposes of this section,

(a) an agreement to exceed the limit on hours of work in a day set out in clause (1)(a) of this section as it read on February 28, 2005 shall be treated as if it were an agreement described in subsection (2);

(b) an agreement to exceed the limit on hours of work in a work week set out in clause (1)(b) of this section as it read on February 28, 2005 shall be treated as if it were an agreement described in clause (3)(a); and

(c) an agreement to exceed the limit on hours of work in a work week set out in clause (2)(b) of this section as it read on February 28, 2005 shall be treated as if it were an agreement described in clause (3)(a).

(9) Document re employee rights—exceptions — Subsection (5) does not apply in respect of,

(a) an agreement described in subsection (8); or

(b) an agreement described in subsection (2) or in clause (3)(a) in respect of an employee who is represented by a trade union.

(10) Transition: document re employee rights — On or before June 1, 2005, an employer who made an agreement described in subsection (8) with an employee who is not represented by a trade union shall provide the employee with a copy of the most recent document published by the Director under section 21.1.

(11) Transition: application for approval before commencement — If the employer applies for an approval under section 17.1 before March 1, 2005, the 30-day period referred to in clause (4)(d) shall be deemed to end on the later of,

(a) the last day of the 30-day period; and

(b) March 1, 2005.

2004, c. 21; s. 4

17.1 (1) Hours in work week: application for approval — An employer may apply to the Director for an approval allowing some or all of its employees to work more than 48 hours in a week.

(2) Form — The application shall be in a form provided by the Director.

(3) Service of application — The application shall be served on the Director,

(a) by being delivered to the Director's office on a day and at a time when it is open;

(b) by being mailed to the Director's office using a method of mail delivery that allows delivery to be verified; or

(c) by being sent to the Director's office by electronic transmission or by telephonic transmission of a facsimile.

(4) When service effective — Service under subsection (3) shall be deemed to be effected,

(a) in the case of service under clause (3)(a), on the day shown on a receipt or acknowledgment provided to the employer by the Director or his or her representative;

(b) in the case of service under clause (3)(b), on the day shown in the verification;

(c) in the case of service under clause (3)(c), on the day on which the electronic or telephonic transmission is made, subject to subsection (5).

(5) Same — Service shall be deemed to be effected on the next day on which the Director's office is not closed, if the electronic or telephonic transmission is made,

(a) on a day on which the Director's office is closed; or

(b) after 5 p.m. on any day.

(6) Application to be posted — An employer who makes an application under subsection (1) shall,

(a) on the day the application is served on the Director, post a copy of the application in at least one conspicuous place in every workplace of the employer where the employee or class of employees in respect of whom the application applies works, so that it is likely to come to the attention of the employee or class of employees;

(b) keep the copy or copies posted as set out in clause (a) until an approval is issued or a notice of refusal is given to the employer.

(7) Criteria — The Director may issue an approval to the employer if the Director is of the view that it would be appropriate to do so.

(8) Same — In deciding whether it is appropriate to issue an approval to the employer, the Director may take into consideration any factors that he or she considers relevant, and, without restricting the generality of the foregoing, he or she may consider,

    (a) any current or past contraventions of this Act or the regulations on the part of the employer;

    (b) the health and safety of employees; and

    (c) any prescribed factors.

(9) Employees to whom approval applies — An approval applies to the employee or class of employees specified in the approval, and applies to every employee in a specified class whether or not the employee was employed by the employer at the time the approval was issued.

(10) Same — For greater certainty, all the employees of the employer may constitute a specified class.

(11) Approval to be posted — An employer to whom an approval is issued shall,

    (a) remove the copy or copies of the application that were posted under subsection (6); and

    (b) post the approval or a copy of the approval in at least one conspicuous place in every workplace of the employer where the employee or class of employees in respect of whom the approval applies works, so that it is likely to come to the attention of the employee or class of employees.

(12) Same — The employer shall keep each approval or copy posted as set out in clause (11)(b) until the approval expires or is revoked, and shall then remove it.

(13) Expiry — An approval under this section expires on the date that is specified in the approval, which shall not be more than three years after the approval was issued.

(14) Same — Despite subsection (13), an approval under this section that would allow an employee to work more than 60 hours in a week shall specify an expiry date that is not more than one year after the approval was issued.

(15) Conditions — The Director may impose conditions on an approval.

(16) Revocation — The Director may revoke an approval on giving the employer such notice as the Director considers reasonable in the circumstances.

(17) Criteria — In deciding whether to impose conditions on or to revoke an approval, the Director may take into consideration any factors that he or she considers relevant, including but not limited to any factor that the Director could consider under subsection (8).

(18) Further applications — For greater certainty, nothing in this section prevents an employer from applying for an approval after an earlier approval expires or is revoked or after an application is refused.

(19) Refusal to approve — If the Director decides that it is inappropriate to issue an approval to the employer, the Director shall give notice to the employer that the application for approval has been refused.

(20) Notice to be posted — An employer who receives notice from the Director that an application has been refused shall,

(a) remove the copy or copies of the application that were posted under subsection (6); and

(b) for the 60-day period following the date on which the notice was issued, post and keep posted the notice or a copy of it in at least one conspicuous place in every workplace of the employer where the employee or the class of employees in respect of whom the application applied works, so that it is likely to come to the attention of that employee or class of employees.

(21) Termination of old approvals — Any approval granted by the Director under a regulation made under paragraph 8 of subsection 141(1), as that paragraph read on February 28, 2005, ceases to have effect on March 1, 2005.

(22) Time for applications — An application under subsection (1) may be made on or after the day the *Employment Standards Amendment Act (Hours of Work and Other Matters), 2004* receives Royal Assent.

2004, c. 21, s. 4

17.2 Non-application of s. 5(2) — Despite subsection 5(2), an employer shall not require or permit an employee to work more than the limit specified in clause 17(1)(b), except in accordance with subsection 17(3) or (4), even if one or more provisions in the employee's employment contract that directly relate to limits on hours of work provide a greater benefit, within the meaning of subsection 5(2), to an employee than is provided by section 17.

2004, c. 21, s. 4

17.3 (1) Delegation by Director — The Director may authorize an individual employed in the Ministry to exercise a power or to perform a duty conferred on the Director under section 17.1, either orally or in writing.

(2) Residual powers — The Director may exercise a power conferred on the Director under section 17.1 even if he or she has delegated it to a person under subsection (1).

(3) Duty re policies — An individual authorized by the Director under subsection (1) shall follow any policies established by the Director under subsection 88(2).

2004, c. 21, s. 4; 2010, c. 16, Sched. 9, s. 1(1)

18. (1) Hours free from work — An employer shall give an employee a period of at least 11 consecutive hours free from performing work in each day.

(2) Exception — Subsection (1) does not apply to an employee who is on call and called in during a period in which the employee would not otherwise be expected to perform work for his or her employer.

(3) Free from work between shifts — An employer shall give an employee a period of at least eight hours free from the performance of work between shifts unless the total time worked on successive shifts does not exceed 13 hours or unless the employer and the employee agree otherwise.

(4) Weekly or biweekly free time requirements — An employer shall give an employee a period free from the performance of work equal to,

(a) at least 24 consecutive hours in every work week; or

(b) at least 48 consecutive hours in every period of two consecutive work weeks.

2002, c. 18, Sched. J, s. 3(10)

19.   Exceptional circumstances — An employer may require an employee to work more than the maximum number of hours permitted under section 17 or to work during a period that is required to be free from performing work under section 18 only as follows, but only so far as is necessary to avoid serious interference with the ordinary working of the employer's establishment or operations:

1. To deal with an emergency.

2. If something unforeseen occurs, to ensure the continued delivery of essential public services, regardless of who delivers those services.

3. If something unforeseen occurs, to ensure that continuous processes or seasonal operations are not interrupted.

4. To carry out urgent repair work to the employer's plant or equipment.

20. (1) Eating periods — An employer shall give an employee an eating period of at least 30 minutes at intervals that will result in the employee working no more than five consecutive hours without an eating period.

(2) Exception — Subsection (1) does not apply if the employer and the employee agree, whether or not in writing, that the employee is to be given two eating periods that together total at least 30 minutes in each consecutive five-hour period.

21. Payment not required — An employer is not required to pay an employee for an eating period in which work is not being performed unless his or her employment contract requires such payment.

21.1 (1) Director to prepare document — The Director shall prepare and publish a document that describes such rights of employees and obligations of employers under this Part and Part VIII as the Director believes an employee should be made aware of in connection with an agreement referred to in subsection 17(2) or clause 17(3)(a).

(2) If document not up to date — If the Director believes that a document prepared under subsection (1) has become out of date, he or she shall prepare and publish a new document.

2004, c. 21, s. 5

Proposed Addition — 21.2 Part VII.1 — Requests for Changes to Schedule or Work Location
[Heading added 2017, c. 22, Sched. 1, s. 11. To come into force January 1, 2019.]

21.2 (1) — Request for changes to schedule or work location — An employee who has been employed by his or her employer for at least three months may submit a request, in writing, to the employer requesting changes to the employee's schedule or work location.

(2) Receipt of request — An employer who receives a request under subsection (1) shall,

(a) discuss the request with the employee; and

(b) notify the employee of the employer's decision within a reasonable time after receiving it.

(3) Grant of request — If the employer grants the request or any part of it, the notification in clause (2) (b) must specify the date that the changes will take effect and their duration.

(4) Denial of request — If the employer denies the request or any part of it, the notification in clause (2) (b) must include the reasons for the denial.

2017, c. 22, Sched. 1, s. 11 [To come into force January 1, 2019.]

Proposed Addition — 21.3-21.7

PART VII.2 — SCHEDULING

[Heading added 2017, c. 22, Sched. 1, s. 12. To come into force January 1, 2019.]

21.3 (1) Three hour rule — If an employee who regularly works more than three hours a day is required to present himself or herself for work but works less than three hours, despite being available to work longer, the employer shall pay the employee wages for three hours, equal to the greater of the following:

1. The sum of,

    i. the amount the employee earned for the time worked, and

    ii. wages equal to the employee's regular rate for the remainder of the time.

2. Wages equal to the employee's regular rate for three hours of work.

(2) Exception — Subsection (1) does not apply if the employer is unable to provide work for the employee because of fire, lightning, power failure, storms or similar causes beyond the employer's control that result in the stopping of work.

2017, c. 22, Sched. 1, s. 12 [To come into force January 1, 2019.]

21.4 (1)   Minimum pay for being on call — If an employee who is on call to work is not required to work or is required to work but works less than three hours, despite being available to work longer, the employer shall pay the employee wages for three hours, equal to the greater of the following:

1.   The sum of,

    i. the amount the employee earned for the time worked, and

    ii. wages equal to the employee's regular rate for the remainder of the time.

2.   Wages equal to the employee's regular rate for three hours of work.

(2)   Exception — Subsection (1) does not apply if,

(a) the employer required the employee to be on call for the purposes of ensuring the continued delivery of essential public services, regardless of who delivers those services; and

(b) the employee who was on call was not required to work.

(3) Limit — Subsection (1) only requires an employer to pay an employee a minimum of three hours of pay during a twenty-four hour period beginning at the start of the first time during that period that the employee is on call, even if the employee is on call multiple times during those twenty-four hours.

(4) Collective agreement prevails — If a collective agreement that is in effect on January 1, 2019 contains a provision that addresses payment for being on call and there is a conflict between the provision of the collective agreement and this section, the provision of the collective agreement prevails.

(5) Same, limit — Subsection (4) ceases to apply on the earlier of the date the collective agreement expires and January 1, 2020.

2017, c. 22, Sched. 1, s. 12 [To come into force January 1, 2019.]

21.5 (1) Right to refuse — An employee has the right to refuse an employer's request or demand to work or be on call on a day that they were not scheduled to work or be on call if the request or demand is made less than 96 hours before the time he or she would commence work or commence being on call, as applicable.

(2) Exception — Subsection (1) does not apply if the employer's request or demand to work or be on call is,

(a) to deal with an emergency;

(b) to remedy or reduce a threat to public safety;

(c) to ensure the continued delivery of essential public services, regardless of who delivers those services; or

(d) made for such other reasons as may be prescribed.

(3) Notice to be provided — I An employee who refuses an employer's request or demand to work or be on call under subsection (1) shall notify the employer of the refusal as soon as possible.

(4) Collective agreement prevails — If a collective agreement that is in effect on January 1, 2019 contains a provision that addresses an employee's ability to refuse the employer's request or demand to perform work or be on call on a day the employee is not scheduled to work or be on call and there is a conflict between the provision of the collective agreement and this section, the provision of the collective agreement prevails.

(5) Same, limit — Subsection (4) ceases to apply on the earlier of the date the collective agreement expires and January 1, 2020.

(6) Definition — In this section,

"emergency" means,

(a) a situation or an impending situation that constitutes a danger of major proportions that could result in serious harm to persons or substantial damage to property and that is caused by the forces of nature, a disease or other health risk, an accident or an act whether intentional or otherwise, or

(b) a situation in which a search and rescue operation takes place.

2017, c. 22, Sched. 1, s. 12 [To come into force January 1, 2019.]

21.6 (1) Cancellation — An employer shall pay an employee wages equal to the employee's regular rate for three hours of work if the employer cancels the employee's scheduled day of work or scheduled on call period within 48 hours before the time the employee was to commence work or commence being on call, as applicable.

(2) Meaning of cancellation — For the purposes of subsection (1), a scheduled day of work or scheduled on call period is cancelled if the entire day of work or on call period is cancelled but not if the day of work or on call period is shortened or extended.

(3) Exception — Subsection (1) does not apply if,

(a) the employer is unable to provide work for the employee because of fire, lightning, power failure, storms or similar causes beyond the employer's control that result in the stopping of work;

(b) the nature of the employee's work is weather-dependent and the employer is unable to provide work for the employee for weather-related reasons; or

(c) the employer is unable to provide work for the employee for such other reasons as may be prescribed.

(4) Collective agreement prevails — If a collective agreement that is in effect on January 1, 2019 contains a provision that addresses payment when the employer cancels the employee's scheduled day of work or on call period and there is a conflict between the provision of the collective agreement and this section, the provision of the collective agreement prevails.

(5) Same, limit — Subsection (4) ceases to apply on the earlier of the date the collective agreement expires and January 1, 2020.

2017, c. 22, Sched. 1, s. 12 [To come into force January 1, 2019.]

21.7 Limit — An employee's entitlement under this Part in respect of one scheduled day of work or scheduled on call period is limited to payment for three hours.

2017, c. 22, Sched. 1, s. 12 [To come into force January 1, 2019.]

PART VIII — OVERTIME PAY

22. (1) Overtime threshold — Subject to subsection (1.1), an employer shall pay an employee overtime pay of at least one and one-half times his or her regular rate for each hour of work in excess of 44 hours in each work week or, if another threshold is prescribed, that prescribed threshold.

(1.1) Same, two or more regular rates — If an employee has two or more regular rates for work performed for the same employer in a work week,

(a) the employee is entitled to be paid overtime pay for each hour of work performed in the week after the total number of hours performed for the employer reaches the overtime threshold; and

(b) the overtime pay for each hour referred to in clause (a) is one and one-half times the regular rate that applies to the work performed in that hour.

(2) Averaging — An employee's hours of work may be averaged over separate, non-overlapping, contiguous periods of two or more consecutive weeks for the purpose of determining the employee's entitlement, if any, to overtime pay if,

(a) the employee has made an agreement with the employer that his or her hours of work may be averaged over periods of a specified number of weeks;

(b) the employer has received an approval under section 22.1 that applies to the employee or a class of employees that includes the employee; and

(c) the averaging period does not exceed the lesser of,

(i) the number of weeks specified in the agreement, and

(ii) the number of weeks specified in the approval.

(2.1) Same, pending approval — Despite subsection (2), an employee's hours of work may be averaged for the purpose of determining the employee's entitlement, if any, to overtime pay even though the employer has not received the approval described in clause (2)(b), if,

(a) the employee has made an agreement described in clause (2)(a) with the employer;

(b) the employer has served on the Director an application for an approval under section 22.1;

(c) the application is for an approval that applies to the employee or to a class of employees that includes the employee;

(d) 30 days have passed since the application was served on the Director;

(e) the employer has not received a notice that the application has been refused;

(f) the employer's most recent previous application, if any, for an approval under section 22.1 was not refused;

(g) the most recent approval, if any, received by the employer under section 22.1 was not revoked; and

(h) the employee's hours of work, pending the approval, are averaged over separate, non-overlapping, contiguous periods of not more than two consecutive weeks.

(2.2) Transition: certain agreements — For the purposes of this section, each of the following agreements shall be treated as if it were an agreement described in clause (2)(a):

1. An agreement to average hours of work made under a predecessor to this Act.

2. An agreement to average hours of work made under this section as it read on February 28, 2005.

3. An agreement to average hours of work that complies with the conditions prescribed by the regulations made under paragraph 7 of subsection 141(1) as it read on February 28, 2005.

(3) Term of agreement — An averaging agreement is not valid unless it provides for an expiry date and, if it involves an employee who is not represented by a trade union, the expiry date shall not be more than two years after the day the agreement takes effect.

(4) Agreement may be renewed — Nothing in subsection (3) prevents an employer and employee from agreeing to renew or replace an averaging agreement.

(5) Existing agreements — An averaging agreement made before this Act comes into force that was approved by the Director under the *Employment Standards Act* is valid for the purposes of subsection (2) until,

(a) one year after the day this section comes into force; or

(b) if the employee is represented by a trade union and a collective agreement applies to the employee,

(i) the day a subsequent collective agreement that applies to the employee comes into operation, or

(ii) if no subsequent collective agreement comes into operation within one year after the existing agreement expires, at the end of that year.

(5.1) Transition: application for approval before commencement — If the employer applies for an approval under section 22.1 before March 1, 2005, the 30-day period referred to in clause (2.1)(d) shall be deemed to end on the later of,

(a) the last day of the 30-day period; and

(b) March 1, 2005.

(6) Agreement irrevocable — No averaging agreement referred to in this section may be revoked before it expires unless the employer and the employee agree to revoke it.

(7) Time off in lieu — The employee may be compensated for overtime hours by receiving one and one-half hours of paid time off work for each hour of overtime worked instead of overtime pay if,

(a) the employee and the employer agree to do so; and

(b) the paid time off work is taken within three months of the work week in which the overtime was earned or, with the employee's agreement, within 12 months of that work week.

(8) Where employment ends — If the employment of an employee ends before the paid time off is taken under subsection (7), the employer shall pay the employee overtime pay for the overtime hours that were worked in accordance with subsection 11(5).

(9) Changing work — If an employee who performs work of a particular kind or character is exempted from the application of this section by the regulations or the regulations prescribe an overtime threshold of other than 44 hours for an employee who performs such work, and the duties of an employee's position require him or her to perform both that work and work of another kind or character, this Part shall apply to the employee in respect of all work performed by him or her in a work week unless the time spent by the employee performing that other work constitutes less than half the time that the employee spent fulfilling the duties of his or her position in that work week.

2001, c. 9, Sched. I, s. 1(4); 2002, c. 18, Sched. J, s. 3(11); 2004, c. 21, s. 6; 2011, c. 1, Sched. 7, s. 1; 2017, c. 22, Sched. 1, s. 13

22.1 (1) Averaging: application for approval — An employer may apply to the Director for an approval permitting the employer to average an employee's hours of work for the purpose of determining the employee's entitlement, if any, to overtime pay.

(2) Form — The application shall be in a form provided by the Director.

(3) Service of application — The application shall be served on the Director,

(a) by being delivered to the Director's office on a day and at a time when it is open;

(b) by being mailed to the Director's office using a method of mail delivery that allows delivery to be verified; or

(c) by being sent to the Director's office by electronic transmission or by telephonic transmission of a facsimile.

(4) When service effective — Service under subsection (3) shall be deemed to be effected,

(a) in the case of service under clause (3)(a), on the day shown on a receipt or acknowledgment provided to the employer by the Director or his or her representative;

(b) in the case of service under clause (3)(b), on the day shown in the verification;

(c) in the case of service under clause (3)(c), on the day on which the electronic or telephonic transmission is made, subject to subsection (5).

(5) Same — Service shall be deemed to be effected on the next day on which the Director's office is not closed, if the electronic or telephonic transmission is made,

(a) on a day on which the Director's office is closed; or

(b) after 5 p.m. on any day.

(6) Criteria — The Director may issue an approval to the employer if the Director is of the view that it would be appropriate to do so.

(7) Same — In deciding whether it is appropriate to issue the approval to the employer, the Director may take into consideration any factors that he or she considers relevant, and, without restricting the generality of the foregoing, he or she may consider,

(a) any current or past contraventions of this Act or the regulations on the part of the employer;

(b) the health and safety of employees; and

(c) any prescribed factors.

(8) Employees to whom approval applies — An approval applies to the employee or class of employees specified in the approval, and applies to every employee in a specified class whether or not the employee was employed by the employer at the time the approval was issued.

(9) Same — For greater certainty, all the employees of the employer may constitute a specified class.

(10) Approval to be posted — An employer to whom an approval is issued shall post the approval or a copy of the approval in at least one conspicuous place in every workplace of the employer where the employee or the class of employees in respect of whom the approval applies works, so that it is likely to come to the attention of that employee or class of employees.

(11) Same — The employer shall keep each approval or copy posted as set out in subsection (10) until the approval expires or is revoked, and shall then remove it.

(12) Expiry — An approval under this section expires on the date on which the averaging agreement between the employer and the employee expires, or on the earlier date that the Director specifies in the approval.

(13) Conditions — The Director may impose conditions on an approval.

(14) Revocation — The Director may revoke an approval on giving the employer such notice as the Director considers reasonable in the circumstances.

(15) Criteria — In deciding whether to impose conditions on or to revoke an approval, the Director may take into consideration any factors that he or she considers relevant, including but not limited to any factor that the Director could consider under subsection (7).

(16) Further applications — For greater certainty, nothing in this section prevents an employer from applying for an approval after an earlier approval expires or is revoked or after an application is refused.

(17) Refusal to approve — If the Director decides that it is inappropriate to issue an approval to the employer, the Director shall give notice to the employer that the application for approval has been refused.

(18) Termination of old approvals — Any approval of an averaging agreement that is granted by the Director under a regulation made under paragraph 7 of subsection 141(1), as that paragraph read on February 28, 2005, ceases to have effect on March 1, 2005.

(19) Time for applications — An application under subsection (1) may be made on or after the day the *Employment Standards Amendment Act (Hours of Work and Other Matters), 2004* receives Royal Assent.

2004, c. 21, s. 7

22.2 (1) Delegation by Director — The Director may authorize an individual employed in the Ministry to exercise a power or to perform a duty conferred on the Director under section 22.1, either orally or in writing.

(2) Residual powers — The Director may exercise a power conferred on the Director under section 22.1 even if he or she has delegated it to a person under subsection (1).

(3) Duty re policies — An individual authorized by the Director under subsection (1) shall follow any policies established by the Director under subsection 88(2).

2004, c. 21, s. 7; 2010, c. 16, Sched. 9, s. 1(2)

PART IX — MINIMUM WAGE

23. (1) Minimum wage — An employer shall pay employees at least the minimum wage.

(2) Room or board — If an employer provides room or board to an employee, the prescribed amount with respect to room or board shall be deemed to have been paid by the employer to the employee as wages.

(3) Determining compliance — Compliance with this Part shall be determined on a pay period basis.

(4) Hourly rate — Without restricting the generality of subsection (3), if the minimum wage applicable with respect to an employee is expressed as an hourly rate, the employer shall not be considered to have complied with this Part unless,

(a) when the amount of regular wages paid to the employee in the pay period is divided by the number of hours he or she worked in the pay period, other than hours for which the employee was entitled to receive overtime pay or premium pay, the quotient is at least equal to the minimum wage; and

(b) when the amount of overtime pay and premium pay paid to the employee in the pay period is divided by the number of hours worked in the pay period for which the employee was entitled to receive overtime pay or premium pay, the quotient is at least equal to one and one half times the minimum wage.

2014, c. 10, Sched. 2, s. 2

23.0.1 Change to minimum wage during pay period — If the minimum wage rate applicable to an employee changes during a pay period, the calculations required by subsection 23 (4) shall be performed as if the pay period were two separate pay periods, the first consisting of the part falling before the day on which the change takes effect and the second consisting of the part falling on and after the day on which the change takes effect.

2017, c. 22, Sched. 1, s. 14

23.1 (1) Determination of minimum wage — The minimum wage is the following:

1. On or after January 1, 2018 but before January 1, 2019, the amount set out below for the following classes of employees:

i. For employees who are students under 18 years of age, if the student's weekly hours do not exceed 28 hours or if the student is employed during a school holiday, $13.15 per hour.

ii. For employees who, as a regular part of their employment, serve liquor directly to customers, guests, members or patrons in premises for which a licence or permit has been issued under the *Liquor Licence Act* and who regularly receive tips or other gratuities from their work, $12.20 per hour.

iii. For the services of hunting and fishing guides, $70.00 for less than five consecutive hours in a day and $140 for five or more hours in a day, whether or not the hours are consecutive.

iv. For employees who are homeworkers, $15.40 per hour.

v. For any other employees not listed in subparagraphs i to iv, $14.00 per hour.

2. On or after January 1, 2019 but before October 1, 2019, the amount set out below for the following classes of employees:

i. For employees who are students under 18 years of age, if the student's weekly hours do not exceed 28 hours or if the student is employed during a school holiday, $14.10 per hour.

ii. For employees who, as a regular part of their employment, serve liquor directly to customers, guests, members or patrons in premises for which a licence or permit has been issued under the *Liquor Licence Act* and who regularly receive tips or other gratuities from their work, $13.05 per hour.

iii. For the services of hunting and fishing guides, $75.00 for less than five consecutive hours in a day and $150 for five or more hours in a day, whether or not the hours are consecutive.

iv. For employees who are homeworkers, $16.50 per hour.

v. For any other employees not listed in subparagraphs i to iv, $15.00 per hour.

3. From October 1, 2019 onwards, the amount determined under subsection (4).

(1.1) Student homeworker — If an employee falls within both subparagraphs 1 i and iv of subsection (1) or both subparagraphs 2 i and iv of subsection (1), the employer shall pay the employee not less than the minimum wage for a homeworker.

(2) Exception — If a class of employees that would otherwise be in the class described in subparagraph 1 v or 2 v of subsection (1) is prescribed and a minimum wage for the class is also prescribed,

(a) subsection (1) does not apply; and

(b) the minimum wage for the class is the minimum wage prescribed for it.

(3) Same — If a class of employees and a minimum wage for the class are prescribed under subsection (2), subsections (4) to (6) apply as if the class and the minimum wage were a class and a minimum wage under subsection (1).

(4) Annual adjustment — On October 1 of each year starting in 2019, the minimum wage that applied to a class of employees immediately before October 1 shall be adjusted as follows:

Previous wage (Index A Index B) = Adjusted wage

in which,

"Previous wage" is the minimum wage that applied immediately before October 1 of the year,

"Index A" is the Consumer Price Index for the previous calendar year,

"Index B" is the Consumer Price Index for the calendar year immediately preceding the calendar year mentioned in the description of "Index A", and

"Adjusted wage" is the new minimum wage.

(5) Rounding — If the adjustment required by subsection (4) would result in an amount that is not a multiple of 5 cents, the amount shall be rounded up or down to the nearest amount that is a multiple of 5 cents.

(6) Exception where decrease — If the adjustment otherwise required by subsection (4) would result in a decrease in the minimum wage, no adjustment shall be made.

(7) Publication of minimum wage — The Minister shall, not later than April 1 of every year after 2018, publish on a website of the Government of Ontario the minimum wages that are to apply starting on October 1 of that year.

(8) [Repealed 2017, c. 22, Sched. 1, s. 15(5).]

(9) Same — If, after the Minister publishes the minimum wages that are to apply starting on October 1 of a year, a minimum wage is prescribed under subsection (2) for a prescribed class of employees, the Minister shall promptly publish the new wage that will apply to that class starting on October 1 of the applicable year as a result of the wage having been prescribed.

(10) Review — Before October 1, 2024, and every five years thereafter, the Minister shall cause a review of the minimum wage and the process for adjusting the minimum wage to be commenced.

(11) Same — The Minister may specify a date by which a review under subsection (10) must be completed.

(12) Definition — In this section,

"Consumer Price Index" means the Consumer Price Index for Ontario (all items) published by Statistics Canada under the *Statistics Act* (Canada).

2014, c. 10, Sched. 2, s. 3; 2017, c. 22, Sched. 1, s. 15

Part X — Public Holidays

24 (1) Public holiday pay — An employee's public holiday pay for a given public holiday shall be equal to,

(a) the total amount of regular wages earned in the pay period immediately preceding the public holiday, divided by the number of days the employee worked in that period; or

(b) if some other manner of calculation is prescribed, the amount determined using that manner of calculation.

(1.1) Same, leave or vacation — If an employee is on a leave under section 50, on vacation or both for the entire pay period immediately preceding the public holiday, the calculation in clause 24 (1) (a) shall be applied to the pay period before the start of that leave or vacation.

(1.2) Same, no pay period before public holiday — If the employee was not employed during the pay period immediately preceding a public holiday, the employee's public holiday pay for the public holiday shall be equal to the amount of regular wages earned in the pay period that includes the public holiday divided by the number of days the employee worked in that period.

(2) Premium pay — An employer who is required under this Part to pay premium pay to an employee shall pay the employee at least one and one half times his or her regular rate.

2002, c. 18, Sched. J, s. 3(12); 2017, c. 22, Sched. 1, s. 16

25. (1) Two kinds of work — Subsection (2) applies with respect to an employee if,

(a) an employee performs work of a particular kind or character in a work week in which a public holiday occurs;

(b) the regulations exempt employees who perform work of that kind or character from the application of this Part; and

(c) the duties of the employee's position also require him or her to perform work of another kind or character.

(2) Same — This Part applies to the employee with respect to that public holiday unless the time spent by the employee performing the work referred to in clause (1)(b) constitutes more than half the time that the employee spent fulfilling the duties of his or her position in that work week.

26. (1) Public holiday ordinarily a working day — If a public holiday falls on a day that would ordinarily be a working day for an employee and the employee is not on vacation that day, the employer shall give the employee the day off work and pay him or her public holiday pay for that day.

(2) Exception — The employee has no entitlement under subsection (1) if he or she fails, without reasonable cause, to work all of his or her last regularly scheduled day of work before the public holiday or all of his or her first regularly scheduled day of work after the public holiday.

27. (1) Agreement to work, ordinarily a working day — An employee and employer may agree that the employee will work on a public holiday that would ordinarily be a working day for that employee, and if they do, section 26 does not apply to the employee.

(2) Employee's entitlement — Subject to subsections (3) and (4), if an employer and an employee make an agreement under subsection (1),

(a) the employer shall pay to the employee wages at his or her regular rate for the hours worked on the public holiday and substitute another day that would ordinarily be a working day for the employee to take off work and for which he or she shall be paid public holiday pay as if the substitute day were a public holiday; or

(b) if the employee and the employer agree, the employer shall pay to the employee public holiday pay for the day plus premium pay for each hour worked on that day.

(2.1) Substitute day of holiday — If a day is substituted for a public holiday under clause (2) (a), the employer shall provide the employee with a written statement, before the public holiday, that sets out,

(a) the public holiday on which the employee will work;

(b) the date of the day that is substituted for a public holiday under clause (2) (a); and

(c) the date on which the statement is provided to the employee.

(3) Restriction — A day that is substituted for a public holiday under clause (2)(a) shall be,

(a) a day that is no more than three months after the public holiday; or

(b) if the employee and the employer agree, a day that is no more than 12 months after the public holiday.

(4) Where certain work not performed — The employee's entitlement under subsection (2) is subject to the following rules:

1. If the employee, without reasonable cause, performs none of the work that he or she agreed to perform on the public holiday, the employee has no entitlement under subsection (2).

2. If the employee, with reasonable cause, performs none of the work that he or she agreed to perform on the public holiday, the employer shall give the employee a substitute day off work in accordance with clause (2)(a) or, if an agreement was made under clause (2)(b), public holiday pay for the public holiday. However, if the employee also fails, without reasonable cause, to work all of his or her last regularly scheduled day of work before the public holiday or all of his or her first regularly scheduled day of work after the public holiday, the employee has no entitlement under subsection (2).

3. If the employee performs some of the work that he or she agreed to perform on the public holiday but fails, without

reasonable cause, to perform all of it, the employer shall give the employee premium pay for each hour worked on the public holiday but the employee has no other entitlement under subsection (2).

4. If the employee performs some of the work that he or she agreed to perform on the public holiday but fails, with reasonable cause, to perform all of it, the employer shall give the employee wages at his or her regular rate for the hours worked on the public holiday and a substitute day off work in accordance with clause (2)(a) or, if an agreement was made under clause (2)(b), public holiday pay for the public holiday plus premium pay for each hour worked on the public holiday. However, if the employee also fails, without reasonable cause, to work all of his or her last regularly scheduled day of work before the public holiday or all of his or her first regularly scheduled day of work after the public holiday, the employer shall give the employee premium pay for each hour worked on the public holiday but the employee has no other entitlement under subsection (2).

5. If the employee performs all of the work that he or she agreed to perform on the public holiday but fails, without reasonable cause, to work all of his or her last regularly scheduled day of work before or all of his or her first regularly scheduled day of work after the public holiday, the employer shall give the employee premium pay for each hour worked on the public holiday but the employee has no other entitlement under subsection (2).

2002, c. 18, Sched. J, s. 3(13); 2017, c. 22, Sched. 1, s. 17

28. (1) Requirement to work on a public holiday: certain operations — If an employee is employed in a hospital, a continuous operation, or a hotel, motel, tourist resort, restaurant or tavern, the employer may require the employee to work on a public holiday that is ordinarily a working day for the employee and that is not a day on which the employee is on vacation, and if the employer does so, sections 26 and 27 do not apply to the employee.

(2) Employee's entitlement — Subject to subsections (3) and (4), if an employer requires an employee to work on a public holiday under subsection (1), the employer shall,

(a) pay to the employee wages at his or her regular rate for the hours worked on the public holiday and substitute another day that would ordinarily be a working day for the employee to take off work and for which he or she shall be paid public holiday pay as if the substitute day were a public holiday; or

(b) pay to the employee public holiday pay for the day plus premium pay for each hour worked on that day.

(2.1) Substitute day of holiday — If a day is substituted for a public holiday under clause (2) (a), the employer shall provide the employee with a written statement, before the public holiday, that sets out,

(a) the public holiday on which the employee will work;

(b) the date of the day that is substituted for a public holiday under clause (2) (a); and

(c) the date on which the statement is provided to the employee.

(3) Restriction — A day that is substituted for a public holiday under clause (2)(a) shall be,

(a) a day that is no more than three months after the public holiday; or

(b) if the employee and the employer agree, a day that is no more than 12 months after the public holiday.

(4) Where certain work not performed — The employee's entitlement under subsection (2) is subject to the following rules:

1. If the employee, without reasonable cause, performs none of the work that he or she was required to perform on the public holiday, the employee has no entitlement under subsection (2).

2. If the employee, with reasonable cause, performs none of the work that he or she was required to perform on the public

holiday, the employer shall give the employee a substitute day off work in accordance with clause (2)(a) or public holiday pay for the public holiday under clause (2)(b), as the employer chooses. However, if the employee also fails, without reasonable cause, to work all of his or her last regularly scheduled day of work before the public holiday or all of his or her first regularly scheduled day of work after the public holiday, the employee has no entitlement under subsection (2).

3. If the employee performs some of the work that he or she was required to perform on the public holiday but fails, without reasonable cause, to perform all of it, he or she is entitled to premium pay for each hour worked on the public holiday but has no other entitlement under subsection (2).

4. If the employee performs some of the work that he or she was required to perform on the public holiday but fails, with reasonable cause, to perform all of it, the employer shall give the employee wages at his or her regular rate for the hours worked on the public holiday and a substitute day off work in accordance with clause (2)(a) or public holiday pay for the public holiday plus premium pay for each hour worked on the public holiday under clause (2)(b), as the employer chooses. However, if the employee also fails, without reasonable cause, to work all of his or her last regularly scheduled day of work before the public holiday or all of his or her first regularly scheduled day of work after the public holiday, the employer shall give the employee premium pay for each hour worked on the public holiday but the employee has no other entitlement under subsection (2).

5. If the employee performs all of the work that he or she was required to perform on the public holiday but fails, without reasonable cause, to work all of his or her last regularly scheduled day of work before or all of his or her first regularly scheduled day of work after the public holiday, the employer shall give the employee premium pay for each hour worked on

the public holiday but the employee has no other entitlement under subsection (2).

2002, c. 18, Sched. J, s. 3(14); 2017, c. 22, Sched. 1, s. 18

29. (1) Public holiday not ordinarily a working day — If a public holiday falls on a day that would not ordinarily be a working day for an employee or a day on which the employee is on vacation, the employer shall substitute another day that would ordinarily be a working day for the employee to take off work and for which he or she shall be paid public holiday pay as if the substitute day were a public holiday.

(1.1) Substitute day of holiday — If a day is substituted for a public holiday under subsection (1), the employer shall provide the employee with a written statement, before the public holiday, that sets out,

(a) the public holiday that is being substituted;

(b) the date of the day that is substituted for a public holiday under subsection (1); and

(c) the date on which the statement is provided to the employee.

(2) Restriction — A day that is substituted for a public holiday under subsection (1) shall be,

(a) a day that is no more than three months after the public holiday; or

(b) if the employee and the employer agree, a day that is no more than 12 months after the public holiday.

(2.1) Employee on leave or lay-off — If a public holiday falls on a day that would not ordinarily be a working day for an employee and the employee is on a leave of absence under section 46 or 48 or on a layoff on that day, the employee is entitled to public holiday pay for the day but has no other entitlement under this Part with respect to the public holiday.

(2.2) Layoff resulting in termination — Subsection (2.1) does not apply to an employee if his or her employment has been terminated under clause 56(1)(c) and the public holiday falls on or after the day on which the lay-off first exceeded the period of a temporary lay-off.

(3) Agreement re: public holiday pay — An employer and an employee may agree that, instead of complying with subsection (1), the employer shall pay the employee public holiday pay for the public holiday, and if they do subsection (1) does not apply to the employee.

(4) Exception — The employee has no entitlement under subsection (1), (2.1) or (3) if he or she fails, without reasonable cause, to work all of his or her last regularly scheduled day of work before the public holiday or all of his or her first regularly scheduled day of work after the public holiday.

2002, c. 18, Sched. J, s. 3(15), (16); 2017, c. 22, Sched. 1, s. 19

30. (1) Agreement to work where not ordinarily a working day — An employee and employer may agree that the employee will work on a public holiday that falls on a day that would not ordinarily be a working day for that employee or on a day on which the employee is on vacation, and if they do, section 29 does not apply to the employee.

(2) Employee's entitlement — Subject to subsections (3) and (4), if an employer and an employee make an agreement under subsection (1),

(a) the employer shall pay to the employee wages at his or her regular rate for the hours worked on the public holiday and substitute another day that would ordinarily be a working day for the employee to take off work and for which he or she shall be paid public holiday pay as if the substitute day were a public holiday; or

(b) if the employer and employee agree, the employer shall pay the employee public holiday pay for the day plus premium pay for each hour worked.

(2.1) Substitute day of holiday — If a day is substituted for a public holiday under clause (2) (a), the employer shall provide the employee with a written statement, before the public holiday, that sets out,

(a) the public holiday on which the employee will work;

(b))the date of the day that is substituted for a public holiday under clause (2) (a); and

(c) the date on which the statement is provided to the employee.

(3) Restriction — A day that is substituted for a public holiday under clause (2)(a) shall be,

(a) a day that is no more than three months after the public holiday; or

(b) if the employee and the employer agree, a day that is no more than 12 months after the public holiday.

(4) Where certain work not performed — The employee's entitlement under subsection (2) is subject to the following rules:

1. If the employee, without reasonable cause, performs none of the work that he or she agreed to perform on the public holiday, the employee has no entitlement under subsection (2).

2. If the employee, with reasonable cause, performs none of the work that he or she agreed to perform on the public holiday, the employer shall give the employee a substitute day off work in accordance with clause (2)(a) or, if an agreement was made under clause (2)(b), public holiday pay for the public holiday. However, if the employee also fails, without reasonable cause, to work all of his or her last regularly scheduled day of work before the public holiday or all of his or her first regularly scheduled day of work after the public holiday, the employee has no entitlement under subsection (2).

3. If the employee performs some of the work that he or she agreed to perform on the public holiday but fails, without

reasonable cause, to perform all of it, the employer shall give the employee premium pay for each hour worked on the public holiday but the employee has no other entitlement under subsection (2).

4. If the employee performs some of the work that he or she agreed to perform on the public holiday but fails, with reasonable cause, to perform all of the work that he or she agreed to perform on the public holiday, the employer shall give the employee wages at his or her regular rate for the hours worked on the public holiday and a substitute day off work in accordance with clause (2)(a) or, if an agreement was made under clause (2)(b), public holiday pay for the public holiday plus premium pay for each hour worked on the public holiday. However, if the employee also fails, without reasonable cause, to work all of his or her last regularly scheduled day of work before the public holiday or all of his or her first regularly scheduled day of work after the public holiday, the employer shall give the employee premium pay for each hour worked on the public holiday but the employee has no other entitlement under subsection (2).

5. If the employee performs all of the work that he or she agreed to perform on the public holiday but fails, without reasonable cause, to work all of his or her last regularly scheduled day of work before or all of his or her first regularly scheduled day of work after the public holiday, the employer shall give the employee premium pay for each hour worked on the public holiday but the employee has no other entitlement under subsection (2).

2002, c. 18, Sched. J, s. 3(17); 2017, c. 22, Sched. 1, s. 20

31. Premium pay hours not overtime hours — If an employee receives premium pay for working on a public holiday, the hours worked shall not be taken into consideration in calculating overtime pay to which the employee may be entitled.

32. If employment ends — If the employment of an employee ends before a day that has been substituted for a public holiday under this Part, the employer shall pay the employee public holiday pay for that day in accordance with subsection 11(5).

PART XI — VACATION WITH PAY

33 (1) Right to vacation — An employer shall give an employee a vacation of,

(a) at least two weeks after each vacation entitlement year that the employee completes, if the employee's period of employment is less than five years; or

(b) at least three weeks after each vacation entitlement year that the employee completes, if the employee's period of employment is five years or more.

(2) Active and inactive employment — Both active employment and inactive employment shall be included for the purposes of subsection (1).

(3) Where vacation not taken in complete weeks — If an employee does not take vacation in complete weeks, the employer shall base the number of days of vacation that the employee is entitled to,

(a) on the number of days in the employee's regular work week; or

(b) if the employee does not have a regular work week, on the average number of days the employee worked per week during the most recently completed vacation entitlement year.

(4) Transition — Clause (1) (b) requires employers to provide employees with a period of employment of at least five years or more with at least three weeks of vacation after each vacation entitlement year that ends on or after December 31, 2017 but does not require them to provide additional vacation days in respect of vacation entitlement years that ended before that time.

2002, c. 18, Sched. J, s. 3(18); 2017, c. 22, Sched. 1, s. 21

34 Alternative vacation entitlement year — (1) Application —
This section applies if the employer establishes an alternative
vacation entitlement year for an employee.

(2) Vacation for stub period, less than five years of employment —
If the employee's period of employment is less than five years, the
employer shall do the following with respect to the stub period:

1. The employer shall calculate the ratio between the stub
period and 12 months.

2. If the employee has a regular work week, the employer shall
give the employee a vacation for the stub period that is equal
to two weeks multiplied by the ratio calculated under
paragraph 1.

3. If the employee does not have a regular work week, the
employer shall give the employee a vacation for the stub
period that is equal to,

2. $\times$ A $\times$ the ratio calculated under paragraph 1

where,

A = the average number of days the employee worked per
work week in the stub period.

(3) Vacation for stub period, five years or more of employment —
If the employee's period of employment is five years or more, the
employer shall do the following with respect to the stub period:

1. The employer shall calculate the ratio between the stub
period and 12 months.

2. If the employee has a regular work week, the employer shall
give the employee a vacation for the stub period that is equal
to three weeks multiplied by the ratio calculated under
paragraph 1.

3. If the employee does not have a regular work week, the
employer shall give the employee a vacation for the stub
period that is equal to,

3 $\times$ A $\times$ the ratio calculated under paragraph 1

where,

$A =$ the average number of days the employee worked per work week in the stub period.

(4) Active and inactive employment — Both active employment and inactive employment shall be included for the purposes of subsections (2) and (3).

(5) Transition — Subsection (3) requires employers to provide employees with a period of employment of at least five years or more with vacation calculated in accordance with that subsection for any stub period that ends on or after December 31, 2017 but does not require them to provide additional vacation days in respect of a stub period that ended before that time.

2002, c. 18, Sched. J, s. 3(18) ; 2017, c. 22, Sched. 1, s. 21

35 Timing of vacation — The employer shall determine when an employee shall take vacation for a vacation entitlement year, subject to the following rules:

1. The vacation must be completed no later than 10 months after the end of the vacation entitlement year for which it is given.

2. If the employee's period of employment is less than five years, the vacation must be a two-week period or two periods of one week each, unless the employee requests in writing that the vacation be taken in shorter periods and the employer agrees to that request.

3. If the employee's period of employment is five years or more, the vacation must be a three-week period or a two-week period and a one-week period or three periods of one week each, unless the employee requests in writing that the vacation be taken in shorter periods and the employer agrees to that request.

2002, c. 18, Sched. J, s. 3(18); 2017, c. 22, Sched. 1, s. 21

35.1 (1) Timing of vacation, alternative vacation entitlement year — This section applies if an employer establishes an alternative vacation entitlement year for an employee.

(2) Same — The employer shall determine when the employee shall take his or her vacation for the stub period, subject to the following rules:

1. The vacation shall be completed no later than 10 months after the start of the first alternative vacation entitlement year.

2. Subject to paragraphs 3 and 4, if the vacation entitlement is equal to two or more days, the vacation shall be taken in a period of consecutive days.

3. Subject to paragraph 4, if the vacation entitlement is equal to more than five days, at least five vacation days shall be taken in a period of consecutive days and the remaining vacation days may be taken in a separate period of consecutive days.

4. Paragraphs 2 and 3 do not apply if the employee requests in writing that the vacation be taken in shorter periods and the employer agrees to that request.

2002, c. 18, Sched. J, s. 3(18); 2017, c. 22, Sched. 1, s. 22

35.2 Vacation pay — An employer shall pay vacation pay to an employee who is entitled to vacation under section 33 or 34, equal to at least,

(a) 4 per cent of the wages, excluding vacation pay, that the employee earned during the period for which the vacation is given, if the employee's period of employment is less than five years; or

(b) 6 per cent of the wages, excluding vacation pay, that the employee earned during the period for which the vacation is given, if the employee's period of employment is five years or more.

2002, c. 18, Sched. J, s. 3(18); 2017, c. 22, Sched. 1, s. 23

36. (1) When to pay vacation pay — Subject to subsections (2) to (4), the employer shall pay vacation pay to the employee in a lump sum before the employee commences his or her vacation.

(2) Same — If the employer pays the employee his or her wages in accordance with subsection 11(4) or the employee does not take his or her vacation in complete weeks, the employer may pay the employee his or her vacation pay on or before the pay day for the period in which the vacation falls.

(3) Same — The employer may pay the employee vacation pay that accrues during a pay period on the pay day for that period if the employee agrees that it may be paid in that manner and,

(a) the statement of wages provided for that period under subsection 12(1) sets out, in addition to the information required by that subsection, the amount of vacation pay that is being paid separately from the amount of other wages that is being paid; or

(b) a separate statement setting out the amount of vacation pay that is being paid is provided to the employee at the same time that the statement of wages is provided under subsection 12(1).

(4) Same — The employer may pay the employee vacation pay at a time agreed to by the employee.

2001, c. 9, Sched. I, s. 1(5)-(7); 2002, c. 18, Sched. J, s. 3(19), (20)

37. (1) Payment during labour dispute — If the employer has scheduled vacation for an employee and subsequently the employee goes on strike or is locked out during a time for which the vacation had been scheduled, the employer shall pay to the employee the vacation pay that would have been paid to him or her with respect to that vacation.

(2) Cancellation — Subsection (1) applies despite any purported cancellation of the vacation.

38. If employment ends — If an employee's employment ends at a time when vacation pay has accrued with respect to the employee, the employer shall pay the vacation pay that has accrued to the employee in accordance with subsection 11(5).

39. Multi-employer plans — Sections 36, 37 and 38 do not apply with respect to an employee and his or her employer if,

(a) the employee is represented by a trade union; and

(b) the employer makes contributions for vacation pay to the trustees of a multi-employer vacation benefit plan.

2001, c. 9; Sched. I, s. 1(8)

40. (1) Vacation pay in trust — Every employer shall be deemed to hold vacation pay accruing due to an employee in trust for the employee whether or not the employer has kept the amount for it separate and apart.

(2) Same — An amount equal to vacation pay becomes a lien and charge upon the assets of the employer that in the ordinary course of business would be entered in books of account, even if it is not entered in the books of account.

41. (1) Approval to forego vacation — If the Director approves and an employee's employer agrees, an employee may be allowed to forego taking vacation to which he or she is entitled under this part.

(2) Vacation pay — Nothing in subsection (1) allows the employer to forego paying vacation pay.

41.1 (1) Vacation statements — An employee is entitled to receive the following statements on making a written request:

1. After the end of a vacation entitlement year, a statement in writing that sets out the information contained in the record the employer is required to keep under subsection 15.1(2).

2. After the end of a stub period, a statement in writing that sets out the information contained in the record the employer is required to keep under subsection 15.1(3).

(2) When statement to be provided — Subject to subsection (3), the statement shall be provided to the employee not later than the later of,

(a) seven days after the employee makes his or her request; and

(b) the first pay day after the employee makes his or her request.

(3) Same — If the request is made during the vacation entitlement year or stub period to which it relates, the statement shall be provided to the employee not later than the later of,

(a) seven days after the start of the next vacation entitlement year or the first vacation entitlement year, as the case may be; and

(b) the first pay day of the next vacation entitlement year or of the first vacation entitlement year, as the case may be.

(4) Restriction re frequency — The employer is not required to provide a statement to an employee more than once with respect to a vacation entitlement year or stub period.

(5) Exception — This section does not apply with respect to an employee whose employer pays vacation pay in accordance with subsection 36(3).

(6) [Repealed 2017, c. 22, Sched. 1, s. 24.]

2002, c. 18; Sched. J, s. 3(21); 2017, c. 22, Sched. 1, s. 24

PART XII — EQUAL PAY FOR EQUAL WORK

Proposed Addition — 41.2

41.2 Interpretation — In this Part,

"substantially the same" means substantially the same but not necessarily identical.

2017, c. 22, Sched. 1, s. 25 [To come into force April 1, 2018.]

42. (1) Equal pay for equal work — No employer shall pay an employee of one sex at a rate of pay less than the rate paid to an employee of the other sex when,

(a) they perform substantially the same kind of work in the same establishment;

(b) their performance requires substantially the same skill, effort and responsibility; and

(c) their work is performed under similar working conditions.

(b) a merit system;

(c) a system that measures earnings by quantity or quality of production; or

(d) any other factor other than sex.

Proposed Amendment — 42(2)(d)

(d) any other factor other than sex or employment status.
2017, c. 22, Sched. 1, s. 26(1) [To come into force April 1, 2018.]

(3) Reduction prohibited — No employer shall reduce the rate of pay of an employee in order to comply with subsection (1).

(4) Organizations — No trade union or other organization shall cause or attempt to cause an employer to contravene subsection (1).

(5) Deemed wages — If an employment standards officer finds that an employer has contravened subsection (1), the officer may determine the amount owing to an employee as a result of the contravention and that amount shall be deemed to be unpaid wages for that employee.

Proposed Addition — 42(6)

(6) Written response — An employee who believes that their rate of pay does not comply with subsection (1) may request a review of their rate of pay from the employee's employer, and the employer shall,

(a) adjust the employee's pay accordingly; or

(b) if the employer disagrees with the employee's belief, provide a written response to the employee setting out the reasons for the disagreement.
2017, c. 22, Sched. 1, s. 26(3) [To come into force April 1, 2018.]

231

Proposed Addition — 42.1

42.1 (1) Difference in employment status — No employer shall pay an employee at a rate of pay less than the rate paid to another employee of the employer because of a difference in employment status when,

(a) they perform substantially the same kind of work in the same establishment;

(b) their performance requires substantially the same skill, effort and responsibility;

and

(c) their work is performed under similar working conditions.

(2) Exception — Subsection (1) does not apply when the difference in the rate of pay is made on the basis of,

(a) ta seniority system;

(b) a merit system;

(c) a system that measures earnings by quantity or quality of production; or

(d) any other factor other than sex or employment status.

(3) Reduction prohibited — No employer shall reduce the rate of pay of an employee in order to comply with subsection (1).

(4) Organizations — No trade union or other organization shall cause or attempt to cause an employer to contravene subsection (1).

(5) Deemed wages — If an employment standards officer finds that an employer has contravened subsection (1), the officer may determine the amount owing to an employee as a result of the contravention and that amount shall be deemed to be unpaid wages for that employee.

(6) Written response — An employee who believes that their rate of pay does not comply with subsection (1) may request a review of their rate of pay from the employee's employer, and the employer shall,

(a) adjust the employee's pay accordingly; or

(b) if the employer disagrees with the employee's belief, provide a written response to the employee setting out the reasons for the disagreement.

(7) Transition, collective agreement — If a collective agreement that is in effect on April 1, 2018 contains a provision that permits differences in pay based on employment status and there is a conflict between the provision of the collective agreement and subsection (1), the provision of the collective agreement prevails.

(8) Same, limit — Subsection (7) ceases to apply on the earlier of the date the collective agreement expires and January 1, 2020.

2017, c. 22, Sched. 1, s. 27 [To come into force April 1, 2018.]

Proposed Addition — 42.2

42.2 (1)   Difference in assignment employee status — No temporary help agency shall pay an assignment employee who is assigned to perform work for a client at a rate of pay less than the rate paid to an employee of the client when,

(a) they perform substantially the same kind of work in the same establishment;

(b) their performance requires substantially the same skill, effort and responsibility; and

(c) their work is performed under similar working conditions.

(2) Exception — Subsection (1) does not apply when the difference in the rate of pay is made on the basis of any factor other than sex, employment status or assignment employee status.

(3) Reduction prohibited — No client of a temporary help agency shall reduce the rate of pay of an employee in order to assist a temporary help agency in complying with subsection (1).

(4) Organizations — No trade union or other organization shall cause or attempt to cause a temporary help agency to contravene subsection (1).

(5) Deemed wages — If an employment standards officer finds that a temporary help agency has contravened subsection (1), the officer may determine the amount owing to an assignment employee as a result of the contravention and that amount shall be deemed to be unpaid wages for that assignment employee.

(6) Written response — An assignment employee who believes that their rate of pay does not comply with subsection (1) may request a review of their rate of pay from the temporary help agency, and the temporary help agency shall,

    (a) adjust the assignment employee's pay accordingly; or

    (b) if the temporary help agency disagrees with the assignment employee's belief, provide a written response to the assignment employee setting out the reasons for the disagreement.

(7) Transition, collective agreement — If a collective agreement that is in effect on April 1, 2018 contains a provision that permits differences in pay between employees of a client and an assignment employee and there is a conflict between the provision of the collective agreement and subsection (1), the provision of the collective agreement prevails.

(8) Same, limit — Subsection (7) ceases to apply on the earlier of the date the collective agreement expires and January 1, 2020.

2017, c. 22, Sched. 1, s. 28 [To come into force April 1, 2018.]

Proposed Addition — 42.3

42.3 (1) Review — Before April 1, 2021, the Minister shall cause a review of sections 42.1 and 42.2 to be commenced.

(2) Same — The Minister may specify a date by which a review under subsection (1) must be completed.

2017, c. 22, Sched. 1, s. 29 [To come into force April 1, 2018.]

PART XIII — BENEFIT PLANS

43. Definition — In this Part,

"employer" means an employer as defined in subsection 1(1), and includes a group or number of unaffiliated employers or an association of employers acting for an employer in relation to a pension plan, a life insurance plan, a disability insurance plan, a disability benefit plan, a health insurance plan or a health benefit plan.

44. (1) Differentiation prohibited — Except as prescribed, no employer or person acting directly on behalf of an employer shall provide, offer or arrange for a benefit plan that treats any of the following persons differently because of the age, sex or marital status of employees:

1. Employees.
2. Beneficiaries.
3. Survivors.
4. Dependants.

(2) Causing contravention prohibited — No organization of employers or employees and no person acting directly on behalf of such an organization shall, directly or indirectly, cause or attempt to cause an employer to contravene subsection (1).

PART XIV — LEAVES OF ABSENCE

45. Definitions — In this Part,

"parent" includes a person with whom a child is placed for adoption and a person who is in a relationship of some permanence with a parent of a child and who intends to treat the child as his or her own and "child" has a corresponding meaning;

"same-sex partner" [Repealed 2004, c. 15, s. 2(1).]

"spouse" means,

(a) a spouse as defined in section 1 of the *Family Law Act*, or

(b) either of two persons who live together in a conjugal relationship outside marriage.

2001, c. 9, Sched. I, s. 1(9); 2004, c. 15, s. 2; 2005, c. 5, s. 23

Pregnancy Leave

46. (1) Pregnancy leave — A pregnant employee is entitled to a leave of absence without pay unless her due date falls fewer than 13 weeks after she commenced employment.

(2) When leave may begin — An employee may begin her pregnancy leave no earlier than the earlier of,

(a) the day that is 17 weeks before her due date; and

(b) the day on which she gives birth.

(3) Exception — Clause (2)(b) does not apply with respect to a pregnancy that ends with a still-birth or miscarriage.

(3.1) Latest day for beginning pregnancy leave — An employee may begin her pregnancy leave no later than the earlier of,

(a) her due date; and

(b) the day on which she gives birth.

(4) Notice — An employee wishing to take pregnancy leave shall give the employer,

(a) written notice at least two weeks before the day the leave is to begin; and

(b) if the employer requests it, a certificate from a legally qualified medical practitioner stating the due date.

(5) Notice to change date — An employee who has given notice to begin pregnancy leave may begin the leave,

(a) on an earlier day than was set out in the notice, if the employee gives the employer a new written notice at least two weeks before that earlier day; or

(b) on a later day than was set out in the notice, if the employee gives the employer a new written notice at least two weeks before the day set out in the original notice.

(6) Same, complication, etc. — If an employee stops working because of a complication caused by her pregnancy or because of a birth, still-birth or miscarriage that occurs earlier than the due date, subsection (4) does not apply and the employee shall, within two weeks after stopping work, give the employer,

(a) written notice of the day the pregnancy leave began or is to begin; and

(b) if the employer requests it, a certificate from a legally qualified medical practitioner stating,

(i) in the case of an employee who stops working because of a complication caused by her pregnancy, that she is unable to perform the duties of her position because of the complication and stating her due date;

(ii) in any other case, the due date and the actual date of the birth, still-birth or miscarriage.

2001, c. 9, Sched. I, s. 1(10)

46.1 Definition — In section 46,

"legally qualified medical practitioner" means,

(a) a person who is qualified to practice as a physician,

(b) a person who is qualified to practice as a midwife,

(c) a registered nurse who holds an extended certificate of registration under the *Nursing Act, 1991*, or

(d) in the prescribed circumstances, a member of a prescribed class of medical practitioners.

2017, c. 22, Sched. 1, s. 30

47. (1) End of pregnancy leave — An employee's pregnancy leave ends,

(a) if she is entitled to parental leave, 17 weeks after the pregnancy leave began;

(b) if she is not entitled to parental leave, on the day that is the later of,

(i) 17 weeks after the pregnancy leave began, and

(ii) 12 weeks after the birth, still-birth or miscarriage.

(1.1) Transition — Despite clause (1) (b), if an employee who is not entitled to parental leave began her pregnancy leave before January 1, 2018, her pregnancy leave ends on the day that is the later of,

(a) 17 weeks after the pregnancy leave began; and

(b) six weeks after the birth, still-birth or miscarriage.

(2) Ending leave early — An employee may end her leave earlier than the day set out in subsection (1) by giving her employer written notice at least four weeks before the day she wishes to end her leave.

(3) Changing end date — An employee who has given notice under subsection (2) to end her pregnancy leave may end the leave,

(a) on an earlier day than was set out in the notice, if the employee gives the employer a new written notice at least four weeks before the earlier day; or

(b) on a later day than was set out in the notice, if the employee gives the employer a new written notice at least four weeks before the day indicated in the original notice.

(4) Employee not returning — An employee who takes pregnancy leave shall not terminate her employment before the leave expires or when it expires without giving the employer at least four weeks' written notice of the termination.

(5) Exception — Subsection (4) does not apply if the employer constructively dismisses the employee.

2017, c. 22, Sched. 1, s. 31

Parental Leave

48. (1) Parental leave — An employee who has been employed by his or her employer for at least 13 weeks and who is the parent of a child is entitled to a leave of absence without pay following the birth of the child or the coming of the child into the employee's custody, care and control for the first time.

(2) When leave may begin — An employee may begin parental leave no later than 78 weeks after the day the child is born or comes into the employee's custody, care and control for the first time.

(2.1) Transition — Despite subsection (2), an employee may begin parental leave no later than 52 weeks after the day the child is born or comes into the employee's custody, care and control for the first time if that day was before the day subsection 32 (2) of Schedule 1 to the *Fair Workplaces, Better Jobs Act, 2017* came into force.

(3) Restriction if pregnancy leave taken — An employee who has taken pregnancy leave must begin her parental leave when her pregnancy leave ends unless the child has not yet come into her custody, care and control for the first time.

(4) Notice — Subject to subsection (6), an employee wishing to take parental leave shall give the employer written notice at least two weeks before the day the leave is to begin.

(5) Notice to change date — An employee who has given notice to begin parental leave may begin the leave,

(a) on an earlier day than was set out in the notice, if the employee gives the employer a new written notice at least two weeks before that earlier day; or

(b) on a later day than was set out in the notice, if the employee gives the employer a new written notice at least two weeks before the day set out in the original notice.

(6) If child earlier than expected — If an employee stops working because a child comes into the employee's custody, care and control for the first time earlier than expected,

(a) the employee's parental leave begins on the day he or she stops working; and

(b) the employee must give the employer written notice that he or she is taking parental leave within two weeks after stopping work.

2017, c. 22, Sched. 1, s. 32

49. (1) End of parental leave — An employee's parental leave ends 61 weeks after it began, if the employee also took pregnancy leave and 63 weeks after it began, otherwise.

(1.1) Transition — Despite subsection (1), if the child in respect of whom the employee takes parental leave was born or came into the employee's custody, care and control for the first time before the day subsection 33 (2) of Schedule 1 to the *Fair Workplaces, Better Jobs Act, 2017* came into force, the employee's parental leave ends,

(a) 35 weeks after it began, if the employee also took pregnancy leave; and

(b) 37 weeks after it began, otherwise.

(2) Ending leave early — An employee may end his or her parental leave earlier than the day set out in subsection (1) by giving the employer written notice at least four weeks before the day he or she wishes to end the leave.

(3) Changing end date — An employee who has given notice to end his or her parental leave may end the leave,

(a) on an earlier day than was set out in the notice, if the employee gives the employer a new written notice at least four weeks before the earlier day; or

(b) on a later day than was set out in the notice, if the employee gives the employer a new written notice at least four weeks before the day indicated in the original notice.

(4) Employee not returning — An employee who takes parental leave shall not terminate his or her employment before the leave expires or when it expires without giving the employer at least four weeks' written notice of the termination.

(5) Exception — Subsection (4) does not apply if the employer constructively dismisses the employee.

2017, c. 22, Sched. 1, s. 33

Family Medical Leave

[Heading added 2004, c. 15, s. 3.]

49.1 (1) Family medical leave — In this section,

"qualified health practitioner" means,

(a) a person who is qualified to practise as a physician under the laws of the jurisdiction in which care or treatment is provided to the individual described in subsection (3),

(b) a registered nurse who holds an extended certificate of registration under the Nursing Act, 1991 or an individual who has an equivalent qualification under the laws of the jurisdiction in which care or treatment is provided to the individual described in subsection (3), or

(c) in the prescribed circumstances, a member of a prescribed class of health practitioners;

"week" means a period of seven consecutive days beginning on Sunday and ending on Saturday.

(2)   Entitlement to leave — An employee is entitled to a leave of absence without pay of up to 28 weeks to provide care or support to an individual described in subsection (3) if a qualified health practitioner issues a certificate stating that the individual has a serious medical condition with a significant risk of death occurring within a period of 26 weeks or such shorter period as may be prescribed.

(3) Application of subs. (2) — Subsection (2) applies in respect of the following individuals:

1. The employee's spouse.

2. A parent, step-parent or foster parent of the employee or the employee's spouse.

3. A child, step-child or foster child of the employee or the employee's spouse.

4. A child who is under legal guardianship of the employee or the employee's spouse.

5. A brother, step-brother, sister or step-sister of the employee.

6. A grandparent, step-grandparent, grandchild or step-grandchild of the employee or the employee's spouse.

7. A brother-in-law, step-brother-in-law, sister-in-law or step-sister-in-law of the employee.

8. A son-in-law or daughter-in-law of the employee or the employee's spouse.

9. An uncle or aunt of the employee or the employee's spouse.

10. A nephew or niece of the employee or the employee's spouse.

11. The spouse of the employee's grandchild, uncle, aunt, nephew or niece.

12. A person who considers the employee to be like a family member, provided the prescribed conditions, if any, are met.

13. Any individual prescribed as a family member for the purposes of this section.

(4) Earliest date leave can begin — The employee may begin a leave under this section no earlier than the first day of the week in which the period referred to in subsection (2) begins.

(5) Latest date employee can remain on leave — The employee may not remain on a leave under this section after the earlier of the following dates:

1. The last day of the week in which the individual described in subsection (3) dies.

2. The last day of the 52-week period starting on the first day of the week in which the period referred to in subsection (2) begins.

(5.1) Same — For greater certainty, but subject to subsection (5), if the amount of leave that has been taken is less than 28 weeks it is not necessary for a qualified health practitioner to issue an additional certificate under subsection (2) in order for leave to be taken under this section after the end of the period referred to in subsection (2).

(6) Two or more employees — If two or more employees take leaves under this section in respect of a particular individual, the total of the leaves taken by all the employees shall not exceed 28 weeks during the 52-week period referred to in paragraph 2 of subsection (5) that applies to the first certificate issued for the purpose of this section.

(7) Full-week periods — An employee may take a leave under this section only in periods of entire weeks.

(8) Advising employer — An employee who wishes to take leave under this section shall advise his or her employer in writing that he or she will be doing so.

(9) Same — If the employee must begin the leave before advising the employer, the employee shall advise the employer of the leave in writing as soon as possible after beginning it.

(10) Copy of certificate — If requested by the employer, the employee shall provide the employer with a copy of the certificate referred to in subsection (2) as soon as possible.

(11) Further leave — If an employee takes a leave under this section and the individual referred to in subsection (3) does not die within the 52-week period referred to in paragraph 2 of subsection (5), the employee may, in accordance with this section, take another leave and, for that purpose, the reference in subsection (6) to "the first certificate" shall be deemed to be a reference to the first certificate issued after the end of that period.

(12) Leave under ss. 49.3, 49.4, 49.5, 49.6, 49.7 and 50 — An employee's entitlement to leave under this section is in addition to any entitlement to leave under sections 49.3, 49.4, 49.5, 49.6, 49.7 and 50.

(13) Transition — If a certificate described in subsection (2) was issued before January 1, 2018, then this section, as it read immediately before January 1, 2018, applies.

2004, c. 15, s. 3; 2014, c. 6, s. 2(2); 2017, c. 22, Sched. 1, s. 34

Organ Donor Leave

[Heading added 2009, c. 16, s. 2.]

49.2 Organ donor leave — (1) Definitions — In this section,

"legally qualified medical practitioner" means,

(a) in the case of surgery for the purpose of organ donation that takes place in Ontario, a member of the College of Physicians and Surgeons of Ontario, and

(b) in the case of surgery for the purpose of organ donation that takes place outside Ontario, a person who is qualified to practise medicine under the laws of that jurisdiction;

"organ" means kidney, liver, lung, pancreas, small bowel or any other organ that is prescribed for the purpose of this section;

"organ donation" means the donation of all or part of an organ to a person;

"prescribed" means prescribed by a regulation made under this section.

(2) Application to prescribed tissue — References to organs in this section also apply to tissue that is prescribed for the purpose of this section.

(3) Entitlement to leave — An employee who has been employed by his or her employer for at least 13 weeks and undergoes surgery for the purpose of organ donation is entitled to a leave of absence without pay.

(4) Certificate — The employer may require an employee who takes leave under this section to provide a certificate issued by a legally qualified medical practitioner confirming that the employee has undergone or will undergo surgery for the purpose of organ donation.

(5) Length of leave — The employee is entitled to take leave for the prescribed period or, if no period is prescribed, for up to 13 weeks.

(6) Extended leave — When the leave described in subsection (5) ends, if a legally qualified medical practitioner issues a certificate stating that the employee is not yet able to perform the duties of his or her position because of the organ donation and will not be able to do so for a specified time, the employee is entitled to extend the leave for the specified time, subject to subsection (7).

(7) Same — The leave may be extended more than once, but the total extension period shall not exceed 13 weeks.

(8) When leave begins — The employee may begin a leave described in subsection (5) on the day that he or she undergoes surgery for the purpose of organ donation, or on the earlier day specified in a certificate issued by a legally qualified medical practitioner.

(9) When leave ends — Subject to subsections (10) and (11), a leave under this section ends when the prescribed period has expired or, if no period is prescribed, 13 weeks after the leave began.

(10) Same — If the employee extends the leave in accordance with subsection (6), the leave ends on the earlier of,

    (a) the day specified in the most recent certificate under subsection (6); or

    (b) the day that is,

        (i) if no period is prescribed for the purposes of subsection (5), 26 weeks after the leave began, or

        (ii) if a period is prescribed for the purposes of subsection (5), 13 weeks after the end of the prescribed period.

(11) Ending leave early — The employee may end the leave earlier than provided in subsection (9) or (10) by giving the employer written notice at least two weeks before the day the employee wishes to end the leave.

(12) Advising employer — An employee who wishes to take leave under this section or to extend a leave under this section shall give the employer written notice, at least two weeks before beginning or extending the leave, if possible.

(13) Same — If the employee must begin or extend the leave before advising the employer, the employee shall advise the employer of the matter in writing as soon as possible after beginning or extending the leave.

(14) Duty to provide certificate — When the employer requires a certificate under subsection (4), (6) or (8), the employee shall provide it as soon as possible.

(15) Leave under s. 50 — An employee's entitlement to leave under this section is in addition to any entitlement to leave under section 50.

2009, c. 16, s. 2

Family Caregiver Leave

[Heading added 2014, c. 6, s. 3.]

49.3 Family caregiver leave — (1) Definitions — In this section,

"qualified health practitioner" means,

(a) a person who is qualified to practise as a physician, a registered nurse or a psychologist under the laws of the jurisdiction in which care or treatment is provided to the individual described in subsection (5), or

(b) in the prescribed circumstances, a member of a prescribed class of health practitioners;

"week" means a period of seven consecutive days beginning on Sunday and ending on Saturday.

(2) Entitlement to leave — An employee is entitled to a leave of absence without pay to provide care or support to an individual described in subsection (5) if a qualified health practitioner issues a certificate stating that the individual has a serious medical condition.

(3) Serious medical condition — For greater certainty, a serious medical condition referred to in subsection (2) may include a condition that is chronic or episodic.

(4) Same — An employee is entitled to take up to eight weeks leave under this section for each individual described in subsection (5) in each calendar year.

(5) Application of subs. (2) — Subsection (2) applies in respect of the following individuals:

1. The employee's spouse.

2. A parent, step-parent or foster parent of the employee or the employee's spouse.

3. A child, step-child or foster child of the employee or the employee's spouse.

4. A grandparent, step-grandparent, grandchild or step-grandchild of the employee or the employee's spouse.

5. The spouse of a child of the employee.

6. The employee's brother or sister.

7. A relative of the employee who is dependent on the employee for care or assistance.

8. Any individual prescribed as a family member for the purpose of this section.

(6) Advising employer — An employee who wishes to take a leave under this section shall advise his or her employer in writing that he or she will be doing so.

(7) Same — If the employee must begin the leave before advising the employer, the employee shall advise the employer of the leave in writing as soon as possible after beginning it.

(7.1) Leave deemed to be taken in entire weeks — For the purposes of an employee's entitlement under subsection (4), if an employee takes any part of a week as leave, the employer may deem the employee to have taken one week of leave.

(8) Copy of certificate — If requested by the employer, the employee shall provide the employer with a copy of the certificate referred to in subsection (2) as soon as possible.

(9) Leave under ss. 49.1, 49.4, 49.5, 49.6, 49.7 and 50 — An employee's entitlement to leave under this section is in addition to any entitlement to leave under sections 49.1, 49.4, 49.5, 49.6, 49.7 and 50.

2014, c. 6, s. 3; 2017, c. 22, Sched. 1, s. 35

Critical Illness Leave

[Heading added 2014, c. 6, s. 3; Heading amended 2017, c. 22, Sched. 1, s. 36.]

49.4 Critical illness leave — (1) Definitions — In this section,

"adult" means an individual who is 18 years or older;

"critically ill", with respect to a minor child or adult, means a minor child or adult whose baseline state of health has significantly changed and whose life is at risk as a result of an illness or injury;

"family member", with respect to an employee, means the following:

1. The employee's spouse.

2. A parent, step-parent or foster parent of the employee or the employee's spouse.

3. A child, step-child or foster child of the employee or the employee's spouse.

4. A child who is under legal guardianship of the employee or the employee's spouse.

5. A brother, step-brother, sister or step-sister of the employee.

6. A grandparent, step-grandparent, grandchild or step-grandchild of the employee or the employee's spouse.

7. A brother-in-law, step-brother-in-law, sister-in-law or step-sister-in-law of the employee.

8. A son-in-law or daughter-in-law of the employee or the employee's spouse.

9. An uncle or aunt of the employee or the employee's spouse.

10. A nephew or niece of the employee or the employee's spouse.

11. The spouse of the employee's grandchild, uncle, aunt, nephew or niece.

12. A person who considers the employee to be like a family member, provided the prescribed conditions, if any, are met.

13. Any individual prescribed as a family member for the purpose of this definition;

"minor child" means an individual who is under 18 years of age;

"qualified health practitioner" means,

(a) a person who is qualified to practise as a physician, a registered nurse or a psychologist under the laws of the jurisdiction in which care or treatment is provided to the individual described in subsection (2) or (5), or

(b) in the prescribed circumstances, a member of a prescribed class of health practitioners;

"week" means a period of seven consecutive days beginning on Sunday and ending on Saturday.

(2) Entitlement to leave — critically ill minor child — An employee who has been employed by his or her employer for at least six consecutive months is entitled to a leave of absence without pay to provide care or support to a critically ill minor child who is a family member of the employee if a qualified health practitioner issues a certificate that,

(a) states that the minor child is a critically ill minor child who requires the care or support of one or more family members; and

(b) sets out the period during which the minor child requires the care or support.

(3) Same — Subject to subsection (4), an employee is entitled to take up to 37 weeks of leave under this section to provide care or support to a critically ill minor child.

(4) Same —- period less than 37 weeks — If the certificate described in subsection (2) sets out a period of less than 37 weeks, the employee is entitled to take a leave only for the number of weeks in the period specified in the certificate.

(5) Entitlement to leave — critically ill adult — An employee who has been employed by his or her employer for at least six consecutive months is entitled to a leave of absence without pay to provide care or support to a critically ill adult who is a family member of the employee if a qualified health practitioner issues a certificate that,

(a) states that the adult is a critically ill adult who requires the care or support of one or more family members; and

(b) sets out the period during which the adult requires the care or support.

(6) Same — Subject to subsection (7), an employee is entitled to take up to 17 weeks of leave under this section to provide care or support to a critically ill adult.

(7) Same - period less than 17 weeks — If the certificate described in subsection (5) sets out a period of less than 17 weeks, the employee is entitled to take a leave only for the number of weeks in the period specified in the certificate.

(8) When leave must end — Subject to subsection (9), a leave under this section ends no later than the last day of the period specified in the certificate described in subsection (2) or (5).

(9) Limitation period — If the period specified in the certificate described in subsection (2) or (5) is 52 weeks or longer, the leave ends no later than the last day of the 52-week period that begins on the earlier of,

(a) the first day of the week in which the certificate is issued; and

(b) the first day of the week in which the minor child or adult in respect of whom the certificate was issued became critically ill.

(10) Death of minor child or adult — If a critically ill minor child or adult dies while an employee is on a leave under this section, the employee's entitlement to be on leave under this section ends on the last day of the week in which the minor child or adult dies.

(11) Total amount of leave — critically ill minor child — The total amount of leave that may be taken by one or more employees under this section in respect of the same critically ill minor child is 37 weeks.

(12) Total amount of leave - critically ill adult — The total amount of leave that may be taken by one or more employees under this section in respect of the same critically ill adult is 17 weeks.

(13) Limitation where child turns 18 — If an employee takes leave in respect of a critically ill minor child under subsection (2), the employee may not take leave in respect of the same individual under subsection (5) before the 52-week period described in subsection (9) expires.

(14) Further leave - critically ill minor child — If a minor child in respect of whom an employee has taken a leave under this section remains critically ill while the employee is on leave or after the employee returns to work, but before the 52-week period described in subsection (9) expires, the employee is entitled to take an extension of the leave or a new leave if,

(a) a qualified health practitioner issues an additional certificate described in subsection (2) for the minor child that sets out a different period during which the minor child requires care or support;

(b) the amount of leave that has been taken and the amount of leave the employee takes under this subsection does not exceed 37 weeks in total; and

(c) the leave ends no later than the last day of the 52-week period described in subsection (9).

(15) Further leave — critically ill adult — If an adult in respect of whom an employee has taken a leave under this section remains critically ill while the employee is on leave or after the employee returns to work, but before the 52-week period described in subsection (9) expires, the employee is entitled to take an extension of the leave or a new leave if,

(a) a qualified health practitioner issues an additional certificate described in subsection (5) for the adult that sets out a different period during which the adult requires care or support;

(b) the amount of leave that has been taken and the amount of leave the employee takes under this subsection does not exceed 17 weeks in total; and

(c) the leave ends no later than the last day of the 52-week period described in subsection (9).

(16) Additional leaves — If a minor child or adult in respect of whom an employee has taken a leave under this section remains critically ill after the 52-week period described in subsection (9) expires, the employee is entitled to take another leave and the requirements of this section apply to the new leave.

(17) Advising employer — An employee who wishes to take a leave under this section shall advise his or her employer in writing that he or she will be doing so and shall provide the employer with a written plan that indicates the weeks in which he or she will take the leave.

(18) Same — If an employee must begin a leave under this section before advising the employer, the employee shall advise the employer of the leave in writing as soon as possible after beginning it and shall provide the employer with a written plan that indicates the weeks in which he or she will take the leave.

(19) Same — An employee may take a leave at a time other than that indicated in the plan provided under subsection (17) or (18) if the change to the time of the leave meets the requirements of this section and,

(a) the employee requests permission from the employer to do so in writing and the employer grants permission in writing; or

(b) the employee provides the employer with such written notice of the change as is reasonable in the circumstances.

(20) Copy of certificate — If requested by the employer, the employee shall provide the employer with a copy of the certificate referred to in subsection (2) or (5) or clause (14) (a) or (15) (a) as soon as possible.

(21) Leave under ss. 49.1, 49.3, 49.5, 49.6, 49.7 and 50 — An employee's entitlement to leave under this section is in addition to any entitlement to leave under sections 49.1, 49.3, 49.5, 49.6, 49.7 and 50.

(22) Transition — If a certificate mentioned in subsection (2) or (12), as those subsections read immediately before the day section 36 of Schedule 1 to the *Fair Workplaces, Better Jobs Act, 2017* came into force, was issued before that day, then this section, as it read immediately before that day, applies. 2014, c. 6, s. 3; 2017, c. 22, Sched. 1, s. 36

Child Death Leave

[Heading added 2014, c. 6, s. 3; Heading amended 2017, c. 22, Sched. 1, s. 37..]

49.5 Child death leave — (1) Definitions — In this section,

"**child**" means a child, step-child, foster child or child who is under legal guardianship, and who is under 18 years of age;

"**crime**" means an offence under the *Criminal Code* (Canada), other than an offence prescribed by the regulations made under paragraph 209.4 (f) of the *Canada Labour Code* (Canada);

"**week**" means a period of seven consecutive days beginning on Sunday and ending on Saturday.

(2) Entitlement to leave — An employee who has been employed by an employer for at least six consecutive months is entitled to a leave of absence without pay of up to 104 weeks if a child of the employee dies.

(3) Exception — An employee is not entitled to a leave of absence under this section if the employee is charged with a crime in relation to the death of the child or if it is probable, considering the circumstances, that the child was a party to a crime in relation to his or her death.

(4) Single period — An employee may take a leave under this section only in a single period.

(5) Limitation period — An employee may take a leave under this section only during the 105-week period that begins in the week the child dies.

(6) Total amount of leave — The total amount of leave that may be taken by one or more employees under this section in respect of a death, or deaths that are the result of the same event, is 104 weeks.

(7) Advising employer — An employee who wishes to take a leave under this section shall advise the employer in writing and shall provide the employer with a written plan that indicates the weeks in which the employee will take the leave.

(8) Same — If an employee must begin a leave under this section before advising the employer, the employee shall advise the employer of the leave in writing as soon as possible after beginning it and shall provide the employer with a written plan that indicates the weeks in which the employee will take the leave.

(9) Same — change in employee's plan — An employee may take a leave at a time other than that indicated in the plan provided under subsection (7) or (8) if the change to the time of the leave meets the requirements of this section and,

> (a) the employee requests permission from the employer to do so in writing and the employer grants permission in writing; or

> (b) the employee provides the employer with four weeks written notice before the change is to take place.

(10) Evidence — An employer may require an employee who takes a leave under this section to provide evidence reasonable in the circumstances of the employee's entitlement to the leave.

(11) Leave under ss. 49.1, 49.3, 49.4, 49.6, 49.7 and 50 — An employee's entitlement to leave under this section is in addition to any entitlement to leave under sections 49.1, 49.3, 49.4, 49.6, 49.7 and 50.

(12) Transition — If, on December 31, 2017, an employee was on a crime-related child death or disappearance leave under this section, as it read on that date, then the employee's entitlement to the leave continues in accordance with this section as it read on that date.

2014, c. 6, s. 3; 2017, c. 22, Sched. 1, s. 38

Crime-Related Child Disappearance Leave

[Heading added 2017, c. 22, Sched. 1, s. 38.]

49.6 Crime-related child disappearance leave — (1) Definitions — In this section,

"child" means a child, step-child, foster child or child who is under legal guardianship, and who is under 18 years of age;

"crime" means an offence under the *Criminal Code* (Canada), other than an offence prescribed by the regulations made under paragraph 209.4 (f) of the *Canada Labour Code* (Canada);

"week" means a period of seven consecutive days beginning on Sunday and ending on Saturday.

(2) Entitlement to leave — An employee who has been employed by an employer for at least six consecutive months is entitled to a leave of absence without pay of up to 104 weeks if a child of the employee disappears and it is probable, considering the circumstances, that the child disappeared as a result of a crime.

(3) Transition — Despite subsection (2), if the disappearance occurred before January 1, 2018, the employee is entitled to a leave of absence without pay in accordance with section 49.5 as it read on December 31, 2017.

(4) Exception — An employee is not entitled to a leave of absence under this section if the employee is charged with the crime or if it is probable, considering the circumstances, that the child was a party to the crime.

(5) Change in circumstance — If an employee takes a leave of absence under this section and the circumstances that made it probable that the child of the employee disappeared as a result of a crime change and it no longer seems probable that the child disappeared as a result of a crime, the employee's entitlement to leave ends on the day on which it no longer seems probable.

(6) Child found — The following rules apply if an employee takes a leave of absence under this section and the child is found within the 104-week period that begins in the week the child disappears:

1. If the child is found alive, the employee is entitled to remain on leave under this section for 14 days after the child is found.

2. If the child is found dead, the employee's entitlement to be on leave under this section ends at the end of the week in which the child is found.

(7) Same — For greater certainty, nothing in paragraph 2 of subsection (6) affects the employee's eligibility for child death leave under section 49.5.

(8) Single period — An employee may take a leave under this section only in a single period.

(9) Limitation period — Except as otherwise provided for in subsection (8), an employee may take a leave under this section only during the 105-week period that begins in the week the child disappears.

(10) Total amount of leave — The total amount of leave that may be taken by one or more employees under this section in respect of a disappearance, or disappearances that are the result of the same event, is 104 weeks.

(11) Advising employer — An employee who wishes to take a leave under this section shall advise the employer in writing and shall provide the employer with a written plan that indicates the weeks in which the employee will take the leave.

(12) Same — If an employee must begin a leave under this section before advising the employer, the employee shall advise the employer of the leave in writing as soon as possible after beginning it and shall provide the employer with a written plan that indicates the weeks in which the employee will take the leave.

(13) Same — change in employee's plan — An employee may take a leave at a time other than that indicated in the plan provided under subsection (11) or (12) if the change to the time of the leave meets the requirements of this section and,

> (a) the employee requests permission from the employer to do so in writing and the employer grants permission in writing; or

> (b) the employee provides the employer with four weeks written notice before the change is to take place.

(14) Evidence — An employer may require an employee who takes a leave under this section to provide evidence reasonable in the circumstances of the employee's entitlement to the leave.

(15) Leave under ss. 49.1, 49.3, 49.4, 49.5, 49.7 and 50 — An employee's entitlement to leave under this section is in addition to any entitlement to leave under sections 49.1, 49.3, 49.4, 49.5, 49.7 and 50. 2017, c. 22, Sched. 1, s. 38

Domestic or Sexual Violence Leave

[Heading added 2017, c. 22, Sched. 1, s. 38.]

49.7 Domestic or sexual violence leave — (1) Definitions — In this section,

"child" means a child, step-child, foster child or child who is under legal guardianship, and who is under 18 years of age;

"week" means a period of seven consecutive days beginning on Sunday and ending on Saturday.

(2) Entitlement to leave — An employee who has been employed by an employer for at least 13 consecutive weeks is entitled to a leave of absence if the employee or a child of the employee experiences domestic or sexual violence, or the threat of domestic or sexual violence, and the leave of absence is taken for any of the following purposes:

1. To seek medical attention for the employee or the child of the employee in respect of a physical or psychological injury or disability caused by the domestic or sexual violence.

2. To obtain services from a victim services organization for the employee or the child of the employee.

3. To obtain psychological or other professional counselling for the employee or the child of the employee.

4. To relocate temporarily or permanently.

5. To seek legal or law enforcement assistance, including preparing for or participating in any civil or criminal legal proceeding related to or resulting from the domestic or sexual violence.

6. Such other purposes as may be prescribed.

(3) Exception — Subsection (2) does not apply if the domestic or sexual violence is committed by the employee.

(4) Length of leave — An employee is entitled to take, in each calendar year,

(a) up to 10 days of leave under this section; and

(b) up to 15 weeks of leave under this section.

(5) Entitlement to paid leave — If an employee takes a leave under this section, the employee is entitled to take the first five such days as paid days of leave in each calendar year and the balance of his or her entitlement under this section as unpaid leave.

(6) Domestic or sexual violence leave pay — Subject to subsections (7) and (8), if an employee takes a paid day of leave under this section, the employer shall pay the employee,

(a) either,

(i) the wages the employee would have earned had they not taken the leave, or

(ii) if the employee receives performance-related wages, including commissions or a piece work rate, the greater of the employee's hourly rate, if any, and the minimum wage that would have applied to the employee for the number of hours the employee would have worked had they not taken the leave; or

(b) if some other manner of calculation is prescribed, the amount determined using that manner of calculation.

(7) Domestic or sexual violence leave where higher rate of wages — If a paid day of leave under this section falls on a day or at a time of day when overtime pay, a shift premium, or both would be payable by the employer,

(a) the employee is not entitled to more than his or her regular rate for any leave taken under this section; and

(b) the employee is not entitled to the shift premium for any leave taken under this section.

(8) Domestic or sexual violence leave on public holiday — If a paid day of leave under this section falls on a public holiday, the employee is not entitled to premium pay for any leave taken under this section.

(9) Leave deemed to be taken in entire days — For the purposes of an employee's entitlement under clause (4) (a), if an employee takes any part of a day as leave, the employer may deem the employee to have taken one day of leave on that day.

(10) Advising employer — An employee who wishes to take leave under clause (4) (a) shall advise the employer that the employee will be doing so.

(11) Same — If an employee must begin a leave under clause (4) (a) before advising the employer, the employee shall advise the employer of the leave as soon as possible after beginning it.

(12) Leave deemed to be taken in entire weeks — For the purposes of an employee's entitlement under clause (4) (b), if an employee takes any part of a week as leave, the employer may deem the employee to have taken one week of leave.

(13) Advising employer — An employee who wishes to take a leave under clause (4) (b) shall advise the employer in writing that the employee will be doing so.

(14) Same — If an employee must begin a leave under clause (4) (b) before advising the employer, the employee shall advise the employer of the leave in writing as soon as possible after beginning it.

(15) Evidence — An employer may require an employee who takes a leave under this section to provide evidence reasonable in the circumstances of the employee's entitlement to the leave.

(16) Leave under ss. 49.1, 49.3, 49.4, 49.5, 49.6 and 50 — An employee's entitlement to leave under this section is in addition to any entitlement to leave under sections 49.1, 49.3, 49.4, 49.5, 49.6 and 50.

(17) Confidentiality — An employer shall ensure that mechanisms are in place to protect the confidentiality of records given to or produced by the employer that relate to an employee taking a leave under this section.

(18) Disclosure permitted — Nothing in subsection (17) prevents an employer from disclosing a record where,

(a) the employee has consented to the disclosure of the record;

(b) disclosure is made to an officer, employee, consultant or agent of the employer who needs the record in the performance of their duties;

(c) the disclosure is authorized or required by law; or

(d) the disclosure is prescribed as a permitted disclosure.

2017, c. 22, Sched. 1, s. 38

Personal Emergency Leave

[Heading added 2006, c. 13, s. 3(2).]

50. (0.1) Definition — In this section,

"qualified health practitioner" means,

(a) a person who is qualified to practise as a physician, a registered nurse or a psychologist under the laws of the jurisdiction in which care or treatment is provided to the employee or to an individual described in subsection (2), or

(b) in the prescribed circumstances, a member of a prescribed class of health practitioners.

(1) Personal emergency leave — An employee is entitled to a leave of absence because of any of the following:

1. A personal illness, injury or medical emergency.

2. The death, illness, injury or medical emergency of an individual described in subsection (2).

3. An urgent matter that concerns an individual described in subsection (2).

(2) Same — Paragraphs 2 and 3 of subsection (1) apply with respect to the following individuals:

1. The employee's spouse.

2. A parent, step-parent or foster parent of the employee or the employee's spouse.

3. A child, step-child or foster child of the employee or the employee's spouse.

4. A grandparent, step-grandparent, grandchild or step-grandchild of the employee or of the employee's spouse.

5. The spouse of a child of the employee.

6. The employee's brother or sister.

7. A relative of the employee who is dependent on the employee for care or assistance.

(3) Advising employer — An employee who wishes to take leave under this section shall advise his or her employer that he or she will be doing so.

(4) Same — If the employee must begin the leave before advising the employer, the employee shall advise the employer of the leave as soon as possible after beginning it.

(5) Limit — Subject to subsection (6), an employee is entitled to take a total of two days of paid leave and eight days of unpaid leave under this section in each calendar year.

(6) Same, entitlement to paid leave — If an employee has been employed by an employer for less than one week, the following rules apply:

1. The employee is not entitled to paid days of leave under this section.

2. Once the employee has been employed by the employer for one week or longer, the employee is entitled to paid days of leave under subsection (5), and any unpaid days of leave that the employee has already taken in the calendar year shall be counted against the employee's entitlement under that subsection.

3. Subsection (8) does not apply until the employee has been employed by the employer for one week or longer.

(7) Leave deemed to be taken in entire days — If an employee takes any part of a day as paid or unpaid leave under this section, the employer may deem the employee to have taken one day of paid or unpaid leave on that day, as applicable, for the purposes of subsection (5) or (6).

(8) Paid days first — The two paid days must be taken first in a calendar year before any of the unpaid days can be taken under this section.

(9) Personal emergency leave pay — Subject to subsections (10) and (11), if an employee takes a paid day of leave under this section, the employer shall pay the employee,

(a) either,

(i) the wages the employee would have earned had they not taken the leave, or

(ii) if the employee receives performance-related wages, including commissions or a piece work rate, the greater of the employee's hourly rate, if any, and the minimum wage that would have applied to the employee for the number of hours the employee would have worked had they not taken the leave; or

(b) if some other manner of calculation is prescribed, the amount determined using that manner of calculation.

(10) Personal emergency leave where higher rate of wages — If a paid day of leave under this section falls on a day or at a time of day when overtime pay, a shift premium or both would be payable by the employer,

(a) the employee is not entitled to more than his or her regular rate for any leave taken under this section; and

(b) the employee is not entitled to the shift premium for any leave taken under this section.

(11) Personal emergency leave on public holiday — If a paid day of leave under this section falls on a public holiday, the employee is not entitled to premium pay for any leave taken under this section.

(12) Evidence — Subject to subsection (13), an employer may require an employee who takes leave under this section to provide evidence reasonable in the circumstances that the employee is entitled to the leave.

(13) Same — An employer shall not require an employee to provide a certificate from a qualified health practitioner as evidence under subsection (12).

2004, c. 15, s. 4; 2004, c. 21, s. 8; 2017, c. 22, Sched. 1, s. 39.

Emergency Leave, Declared Emergencies

[Heading added 2006, c. 13, s. 3(3).]

50.1 (1) Emergency leave, declared emergencies — An employee is entitled to a leave of absence without pay if the employee will not be performing the duties of his or her position because of an emergency declared under section 7.0.1 of the *Emergency Management and Civil Protection Act* and,

(a) because of an order that applies to him or her made under section 7.0.2 of the *Emergency Management and Civil Protection Act*;

(b) because of an order that applies to him or her made under the *Health Protection and Promotion Act*;

(c) because he or she is needed to provide care or assistance to an individual referred to in subsection (8); or

(d) because of such other reasons as may be prescribed.

(2) Advising employer — An employee who takes leave under this section shall advise his or her employer that he or she will be doing so.

(3) Same — If the employee begins the leave before advising the employer, the employee shall advise the employer of the leave as soon as possible after beginning it.

(4) Evidence of entitlement — An employer may require an employee who takes leave under this section to provide evidence reasonable in the circumstances at a time that is reasonable in the circumstances that the employee is entitled to the leave.

(5) Limit — An employee is entitled to take a leave under this section for as long as he or she is not performing the duties of his or her position because of an emergency declared under section 7.0.1 of the *Emergency Management and Civil Protection Act* and a reason referred to in clause (1)(a), (b), (c) or (d), but, subject to subsection (6), the entitlement ends on the day the emergency is terminated or disallowed.

(6) Same — If an employee took leave because he or she was not performing the duties of his or her position because of an emergency that has been terminated or disallowed and because of an order made under subsection 7.0.2(4) of the *Emergency Management and Civil Protection Act* and the order is extended under subsection 7.0.8(4) of that Act, the employee's entitlement to leave continues during the period of the extension if he or she is not performing the duties of his or her position because of the order.

(7) Additional to entitlement under s. 50 — The entitlement to leave under this section is in addition to the entitlement to leave under section 50.

(8) Care or assistance, specified individuals — Clause (1)(c) applies with respect to the following individuals:

1. The employee's spouse.

2. A parent, step-parent or foster parent of the employee or the employee's spouse.

3. A child, step-child or foster child of the employee or the employee's spouse.

4. A grandparent, step-grandparent, grandchild or step-grandchild of the employee or of the employee's spouse.

5. The spouse of a child of the employee.

6. The employee's brother or sister.

7. A relative of the employee who is dependent on the employee for care or assistance.

(9) Definitions — The definitions of "parent" and "spouse" in section 45 apply for the purpose of subsection (8).

(10) Retroactive order — If an order made under section 7.0.2 of the *Emergency Management and Civil Protection Act* is made retroactive pursuant to subsection 7.2(1) of that Act,

(a) an employee who does not perform the duties of his or her position because of the declared emergency and the order is deemed to have been on leave beginning on the first day the employee did not perform the duties of his or her position on or after the date to which the order was made retroactive; and

(b) clause 74(1)(a) applies with necessary modifications in relation to the deemed leave described in clause (a).

2006, c. 13, s. 3(3)

Reservist Leave

[Heading added 2007, c. 16, Sched. A, s. 3.]

50.2 (1) Reservist leave — An employee is entitled to a leave of absence without pay if the employee is a reservist and will not be performing the duties of his or her position because,

(a) the employee is deployed to a Canadian Forces operation outside Canada;

(b) the employee is deployed to a Canadian Forces operation inside Canada that is or will be providing assistance in dealing with an emergency or with its aftermath; or

(c) the prescribed circumstances apply.

(2) Activities included in deployment outside Canada — Participation, whether inside or outside Canada, in pre-deployment or post-deployment activities that are required by the Canadian Forces in connection with an operation described in clause (1)(a) is considered deployment to the operation for the purposes of that clause.

(3) Restriction — An employee is not entitled to begin a leave under this section unless he or she has been employed by the employer for at least the prescribed period or, if no period is prescribed, for at least six consecutive months.

(4) Length of leave — An employee is entitled to take leave under this section for the prescribed period or, if no period is prescribed, for as long as clause (1)(a) or (b) or the circumstances set out in a regulation made under clause (1)(c) apply to him or her.

(5) Advising employer re start of leave — An employee who intends to take a leave under this section shall give his or her employer the prescribed period of notice of the day on which he or she will begin the leave or, if no notice period is prescribed, reasonable notice.

(6) Same — Despite subsection (5), if the employee must begin the leave before advising the employer, the employee shall advise the employer of the leave as soon as possible after beginning it.

(7) Evidence of entitlement — An employer may require an employee who takes a leave under this section to provide evidence that the employee is entitled to the leave.

(8) Same — When evidence is required under subsection (7), the employee shall,

（a) provide the prescribed evidence, or evidence reasonable in the circumstances if no evidence is prescribed; and

（b) provide the evidence at the prescribed time, or at a time reasonable in the circumstances if no time is prescribed.

(9) Advising employer re end of leave — An employee who intends to end a leave taken under this section shall give his or her employer the prescribed period of notice of the day on which he or she intends to end the leave or, if no notice period is prescribed, reasonable notice.

(10) Written notice — Notice under subsection (5), (6) or (9) shall be given in writing.

(11) Definition, emergency — In clause (1)(b),

"emergency" means,

(a) a situation or an impending situation that constitutes a danger of major proportions that could result in serious harm to persons or substantial damage to property and that is caused by the forces of nature, a disease or other health risk, an accident or an act whether intentional or otherwise, or

(b) a situation in which a search and rescue operation takes place.

(12) Transition — This section applies only if,

(a) the deployment described in subsection (1) begins on or after the day the *Fairness for Military Families Act (Employment Standards and Health Insurance), 2007* receives Royal Assent; and

(b) notice under subsection (5) or (6) is given on or after the day described in clause (a).

2007, c. 16, Sched. A, s. 3

General Provisions Concerning Leaves

51. (1) Rights during leave — During any leave under this Part, an employee continues to participate in each type of benefit plan described in subsection (2) that is related to his or her employment unless he or she elects in writing not to do so.

(2) Benefit plans — Subsection (1) applies with respect to pension plans, life insurance plans, accidental death plans, extended health plans, dental plans and any prescribed type of benefit plan.

(3) Employer contributions — During an employee's leave under this Part, the employer shall continue to make the employer's contributions for any plan described in subsection (2) unless the employee gives the employer a written notice that the employee does not intend to pay the employee's contributions, if any.

(4) Reservist leave — Subsections (1), (2) and (3) do not apply in respect of an employee during a leave under section 50.2, unless otherwise prescribed.

(5) Exception — Despite subsection (4), subsections (1), (2) and (3) apply in respect of an employee during a period of postponement under subsection 53(1.1), unless otherwise prescribed.

2007, c. 16, Sched. A, s. 4

51.1 (1) Leave and vacation conflict — An employee who is on leave under this Part may defer taking vacation until the leave expires or, if the employer and employee agree to a later date, until that later date if,

(a) under the terms of the employee's employment contract, the employee may not defer taking vacation that would otherwise be forfeited or the employee's ability to do so is restricted; and

(b) as a result, in order to exercise his or her right to leave under this Part, the employee would have to,

(i) forfeit vacation or vacation pay, or

(ii) take less than his or her full leave entitlement.

(2) Leave and completion of vacation conflict — If an employee is on leave under this Part on the day by which his or her vacation must be completed under paragraph 1 of section 35 or paragraph 1 of subsection 35.1(2), the uncompleted part of the vacation shall be completed immediately after the leave expires or, if the employer and employee agree to a later date, beginning on that later date.

(3) Alternative right, vacation pay — An employee to whom this section applies may forego vacation and receive vacation pay in accordance with section 41 rather than completing his or her vacation under this section.

2001, c. 9, Sched. I, s. 1(11); 2002, c. 18, Sched. J, s. 3(22)

52. (1) Length of employment — The period of an employee's leave under this Part shall be included in calculating any of the following for the purpose of determining his or her rights under an employment contract:

    1. The length of his or her of employment, whether or not it is active employment.

    2. The length of the employee's service whether or not that service is active.

    3. The employee's seniority.

(2) Exception — The period of an employee's leave shall not be included in determining whether he or she has completed a probationary period under an employment contract.

52.1 (1) Leave taken in entire weeks — If a provision in this Part requires that an employee who takes a leave to provide care or support to a person take the leave in periods of entire weeks and, during a week of leave, an employee ceases to provide care or support,

    (a) the employee's entitlement to leave continues until the end of the week; and

    (b) the employee may return to work during the week only if the employer agrees, whether in writing or not.

(2) Same — If an employee returns to work under clause (1)(b), the week counts as an entire week for the purposes of any provision in this Part that limits the employee's entitlement to leave to a certain number of weeks.

2014, c. 6, s. 4

53. (1) Reinstatement — Upon the conclusion of an employee's leave under this Part, the employer shall reinstate the employee to the position the employee most recently held with the employer, if it still exists, or to a comparable position, if it does not.

(1.1) Reservist leave — Despite subsection (1), the employer of an employee who has been on leave under section 50.2 may postpone the employee's reinstatement until,

(a) a prescribed day; or

(b) if no day is prescribed, the later of,

(i) the day that is two weeks after the day on which the leave ends, and

(ii) the first pay day that falls after the day on which the leave ends.

(1.2) Same — During the period of postponement, the employee is deemed to continue to be on leave under section 50.2 for the purposes of sections 51.1 and 52.

(2) Exception — Subsection (1) does not apply if the employment of the employee is ended solely for reasons unrelated to the leave.

(3) Wage rate — The employer shall pay a reinstated employee at a rate that is equal to the greater of,

(a) the rate that the employee most recently earned with the employer; and

(b) the rate that the employee would be earning had he or she worked throughout the leave.

2007, c. 16, Sched. A, s. 5

PART XV — TERMINATION AND SEVERANCE OF EMPLOYMENT

Termination of Employment

54.   No termination without notice — No employer shall terminate the employment of an employee who has been continuously employed for three months or more unless the employer,

(a) has given to the employee written notice of termination in accordance with section 57 or 58 and the notice has expired; or

(b) has complied with section 61.

55.   Prescribed employees not entitled — Prescribed employees are not entitled to notice of termination or termination pay under this Part.

56. (1) What constitutes termination — An employer terminates the employment of an employee for purposes of section 54 if,

(a) the employer dismisses the employee or otherwise refuses or is unable to continue employing him or her;

(b) the employer constructively dismisses the employee and the employee resigns from his or her employment in response to that within a reasonable period; or

(c) the employer lays the employee off for a period longer than the period of a temporary lay-off.

(2) Temporary lay-off — For the purpose of clause (1)(c), a temporary layoff is,

(a) a lay-off of not more than 13 weeks in any period of 20 consecutive weeks;

(b) a lay-off of more than 13 weeks in any period of 20 consecutive weeks, if the lay-off is less than 35 weeks in any period of 52 consecutive weeks and,

(i) the employee continues to receive substantial payments from the employer,

273

(ii) the employer continues to make payments for the benefit of the employee under a legitimate retirement or pension plan or a legitimate group or employee insurance plan,

(iii) the employee receives supplementary unemployment benefits,

(iv) the employee is employed elsewhere during the lay-off and would be entitled to receive supplementary unemployment benefits if that were not so,

(v) the employer recalls the employee within the time approved by the Director, or

(vi) in the case of an employee who is not represented by a trade union, the employer recalls the employee within the time set out in an agreement between the employer and the employee; or

(c) in the case of an employee represented by a trade union, a lay-off longer than a lay-off described in clause (b) where the employer recalls the employee within the time set out in an agreement between the employer and the trade union.

(3) Definition — In subsections (3.1) to (3.6),

"excluded week" means a week during which, for one or more days, the employee is not able to work, is not available for work, is subject to a disciplinary suspension or is not provided with work because of a strike or lock-out occurring at his or her place of employment or elsewhere.

(3.1) Lay-off, regular work week — For the purpose of subsection (2), an employee who has a regular work week is laid off for a week if,

(a) in that week, the employee earns less than one-half the amount he or she would earn at his or her regular rate in a regular work week; and

(b) the week is not an excluded week.

(3.2) Effect of excluded week — For the purpose of clauses (2)(a) and (b), an excluded week shall be counted as part of the periods of 20 and 52 weeks.

(3.3) Lay-off, no regular work week — For the purposes of clauses (1)(c) and (2)(a), an employee who does not have a regular work week is laid off for a period longer than the period of a temporary lay-off if for more than 13 weeks in any period of 20 consecutive weeks he or she earns less than one-half the average amount he or she earned per week in the period of 12 consecutive weeks that preceded the 20-week period.

(3.4) Effect of excluded week — For the purposes of subsection (3.3),

    (a) an excluded week shall not be counted as part of the 13 or more weeks but shall be counted as part of the 20-week period; and

    (b) if the 12-week period contains an excluded week, the average amount earned shall be calculated based on the earnings in weeks that were not excluded weeks and the number of weeks that were not excluded.

(3.5) Lay-off, no regular work week — For the purposes of clauses (1)(c) and (2)(b), an employee who does not have a regular work week is laid off for a period longer than the period of a temporary lay-off if for 35 or more weeks in any period of 52 consecutive weeks he or she earns less than one-half the average amount he or she earned per week in the period of 12 consecutive weeks that preceded the 52-week period.

(3.6) Effect of excluded week — For the purposes of subsection (3.5),

    (a) an excluded week shall not be counted as part of the 35 or more weeks but shall be counted as part of the 52-week period; and

    (b) if the 12-week period contains an excluded week, the average amount earned shall be calculated based on the earnings in weeks that were not excluded weeks and the number of weeks that were not excluded.

(4) Temporary lay-off not termination — An employer who lays an employee off without specifying a recall date shall not be considered to terminate the employment of the employee, unless the period of the lay-off exceeds that of a temporary lay-off.

(5) Deemed termination date — If an employer terminates the employment of an employee under clause (1)(c), the employment shall be deemed to be terminated on the first day of the lay-off.

2001, c. 9, Sched. I, s. 1(12); 2002, c. 18, Sched. J, s. 3(23)

57. Employer notice period — The notice of termination under section 54 shall be given,

(a) at least one week before the termination, if the employee's period of employment is less than one year;

(b) at least two weeks before the termination, if the employee's period of employment is one year or more and fewer than three years;

(c) at least three weeks before the termination, if the employee's period of employment is three years or more and fewer than four years;

(d) at least four weeks before the termination, if the employee's period of employment is four years or more and fewer than five years;

(e) at least five weeks before the termination, if the employee's period of employment is five years or more and fewer than six years;

(f) at least six weeks before the termination, if the employee's period of employment is six years or more and fewer than seven years;

(g) at least seven weeks before the termination, if the employee's period of employment is seven years or more and fewer than eight years; or

(h) at least eight weeks before the termination, if the employee's period of employment is eight years or more.

58. (1) Notice, 50 or more employees — Despite section 57, the employer shall give notice of termination in the prescribed manner and for the prescribed period if the employer terminates the employment of 50 or more employees at the employer's establishment in the same four-week period.

(2) Information — An employer who is required to give notice under this section,

(a) shall provide to the Director the prescribed information in a form approved by the Director; and

(b) shall, on the first day of the notice period, post in the employer's establishment the prescribed information in a form approved by the Director.

(3) Content — The information required under subsection (2) may include,

(a) the economic circumstances surrounding the terminations;

(b) any consultations that have been or are proposed to take place with communities in which the terminations will take place or with the affected employees or their agent in connection with the terminations;

(c) any proposed adjustment measures and the number of employees expected to benefit from each; and

(d) a statistical profile of the affected employees.

(4) When notice effective — The notice required under subsection (1) shall be deemed not to have been given until the Director receives the information required under clause (2)(a).

(5) Posting — The employer shall post the information required under clause (2)(b) in at least one conspicuous place in the employer's establishment where it is likely to come to the attention of the affected employees and the employer shall keep that information posted throughout the notice period required under this section.

(6) Employee notice — An employee to whom notice has been given under this section shall not terminate his or her employment without first giving the employer written notice,

(a) at least one week before doing so, if his or her period of employment is less than two years; or

(b) at least two weeks before doing so, if his or her period of employment is two years or more.

(7) Exception — Subsection (6) does not apply if the employer constructively dismisses the employee or breaches a term of the employment contract, whether or not such a breach would constitute a constructive dismissal.

59. (1) Period of employment: included, excluded time — Time spent by an employee on leave or other inactive employment is included in determining his or her period of employment.

(2) Exception — Despite subsection (1), if an employee's employment was terminated as a result of a lay-off, no part of the lay-off period after the deemed termination date shall be included in determining his or her period of employment.

60. (1) Requirements during notice period — During a notice period under section 57 or 58, the employer,

(a) shall not reduce the employee's wage rate or alter any other term or condition of employment;

(b) shall in each week pay the employee the wages the employee is entitled to receive, which in no case shall be less than his or her regular wages for a regular work week; and

(c) shall continue to make whatever benefit plan contributions would be required to be made in order to maintain the employee's benefits under the plan until the end of the notice period.

(2) No regular work week — For the purposes of clause (1)(b), if the employee does not have a regular work week or if the employee is paid on a basis other than time, the employer shall pay the employee an amount equal to the average amount of regular wages earned by the employee per week for the weeks in which the employee worked in the period of 12 weeks immediately preceding the day on which notice was given.

(3) Benefit plan contributions — If an employer fails to contribute to a benefit plan contrary to clause (1)(c), an amount equal to the amount the employer should have contributed shall be deemed to be unpaid wages for the purpose of section 103.

(4) Same — Nothing in subsection (3) precludes the employee from an entitlement that he or she may have under a benefit plan.

2001, c. 9, Sched. I, s. 1(13)

61. (1) Pay instead of notice — An employer may terminate the employment of an employee without notice or with less notice than is required under section 57 or 58 if the employer,

(a) pays to the employee termination pay in a lump sum equal to the amount the employee would have been entitled to receive under section 60 had notice been given in accordance with that section; and

(b) continues to make whatever benefit plan contributions would be required to be made in order to maintain the benefits to which the employee would have been entitled had he or she continued to be employed during the period of notice that he or she would otherwise have been entitled to receive.

(1.1) No regular work week — For the purposes of clause (1)(a), if the employee does not have a regular work week or is paid on a basis other than time, the amount the employee would have been entitled to receive under section 60 shall be calculated as if the period of 12 weeks referred to in subsection 60(2) were the 12-week period immediately preceding the day of termination.

(2) Information to Director — An employer who terminates the employment of employees under this section and would otherwise be required to provide notices of termination under section 58 shall comply with clause 58(2)(a).

2001, c. 9, Sched. I, s. 1(14), (15)

62. (1) Deemed active employment — If an employer terminates the employment of employees without giving them part or all of the period of notice required under this Part, the employees shall be deemed to have been actively employed during the period for which there should have been notice for the purposes of any benefit plan under which entitlement to benefits might be lost or affected if the employees cease to be actively employed.

(2) Benefit plan contributions — If an employer fails to contribute to a benefit plan contrary to clause 61(1)(b), an amount equal to the amount the employer should have contributed shall be deemed to be unpaid wages for the purpose of section 103.

(3) Same — Nothing in subsection (2) precludes the employee from an entitlement he or she may have under a benefit plan.

Severance of Employment

63. (1) What constitutes severance — An employer severs the employment of an employee if,

(a) the employer dismisses the employee or otherwise refuses or is unable to continue employing the employee;

(b) the employer constructively dismisses the employee and the employee resigns from his or her employment in response within a reasonable period;

(c) the employer lays the employee off for 35 weeks or more in any period of 52 consecutive weeks;

(d) the employer lays the employee off because of a permanent discontinuance of all of the employer's business at an establishment; or

(e) the employer gives the employee notice of termination in accordance with section 57 or 58, the employee gives the employer written notice at least two weeks before resigning and the employee's notice of resignation is to take effect during the statutory notice period.

(2) Definition — In subsections (2.1) to (2.4),

"excluded week" means a week during which, for one or more days, the employee is not able to work, is not available for work, is subject to a disciplinary suspension or is not provided with work because of a strike or lock-out occurring at his or her place of employment or elsewhere.

(2.1) Lay-off, regular work week — For the purpose of clause (1)(c), an employee who has a regular work week is laid off for a week if,

> (a) in that week, the employee earns less than one-quarter the amount he or she would earn at his or her regular rate in a regular work week; and

> (b) the week is not an excluded week.

(2.2) Effect of excluded week — For the purposes of clause (1)(c), an excluded week shall be counted as part of the period of 52 weeks.

(2.3) Lay-off, no regular work week — For the purpose of clause (1)(c), an employee who does not have a regular work week is laid off for 35 or more weeks in any period of 52 consecutive weeks if for 35 or more weeks in any period of 52 consecutive weeks he or she earns less than one-quarter the average amount he or she earned per week in the period of 12 consecutive weeks that preceded the 52-week period.

(2.4) Effect of excluded week — For the purposes of subsection (2.3),

> (a) an excluded week shall not be counted as part of the 35 or more weeks, but shall be counted as part of the 52-week period; and

> (b) if the 12-week period contains an excluded week, the average amount earned shall be calculated based on the earnings in weeks that were not excluded weeks and the number of weeks that were not excluded.

(3) Resignation — An employee's employment that is severed under clause (1)(e) shall be deemed to have been severed on the day the employer's notice of termination would have taken effect if the employee had not resigned.

2002, c. 18, Sched. J, s. 3(24), (25)

64. (1) Entitlement to severance pay — An employer who severs an employment relationship with an employee shall pay severance pay to the employee if the employee was employed by the employer for five years or more and,

(a) the severance occurred because of a permanent discontinuance of all or part of the employer's business at an establishment and the employee is one of 50 or more employees who have their employment relationship severed within a six-month period as a result; or

(b) the employer has a payroll of $2.5 million or more.

(2) Payroll — For the purposes of subsection (1), an employer shall be considered to have a payroll of $2.5 million or more if,

(a) the total wages earned by all of the employer's employees, in the four weeks that ended with the last day of the last pay period completed prior to the severance of an employee's employment, when multiplied by 13, was $2.5 million or more; or

(b) the total wages earned by all of the employer's employees, in the last or second-last fiscal year of the employer prior to the severance of an employee's employment was $2.5 million or more.

(3) Exceptions — Prescribed employees are not entitled to severance pay under this section.

(4) Location deemed an establishment — A location shall be deemed to be an establishment under subsection (1) if,

(a) there is a permanent discontinuance of all or part of an employer's business at the location;

(b) the location is part of an establishment consisting of two or more locations; and

(c) the employer severs the employment relationship of 50 or more employees within a six-month period as a result.

2001, c. 9, Sched. I, s. 1(16)

65. (1) Calculating severance pay — Severance pay under this section shall be calculated by multiplying the employee's regular wages for a regular work week by the sum of,

(a) the number of years of employment the employee has completed; and

(b) the number of months of employment not included in clause (a) that the employee has completed, divided by 12.

(2) Non-continuous employment — All time spent by the employee in the employer's employ, whether or not continuous and whether or not active, shall be included in determining whether he or she is eligible for severance pay under subsection 64(1) and in calculating his or her severance pay under subsection (1).

(2.1) Exception — Despite subsection (2), when an employee in receipt of an actuarially unreduced pension benefit has his or her employment severed by an employer on or after November 6, 2009, time spent in the employer's employ for which the employee received service credits in the calculation of that benefit shall not be included in determining whether he or she is eligible for severance pay under subsection 64(1) and in calculating his or her severance pay under subsection (1).

(3) Where employee resigns — If an employee's employment is severed under clause 63(1)(e), the period between the day the employee's notice of resignation took effect and the day the employer's notice of termination would have taken effect shall not be considered in calculating the amount of severance pay to which the employee is entitled.

(4) Termination without notice — If an employer terminates the employment of an employee without providing the notice, if any, required under section 57 or 58, the amount of severance pay to which the employee is entitled shall be calculated as if the employee continued to be employed for a period equal to the period of notice that should have been given and was not.

(5) Limit — An employee's severance pay entitlement under this section shall not exceed an amount equal to the employee's regular wages for a regular work week for 26 weeks.

(6) Where no regular work week — For the purposes of subsections (1) and (5), if the employee does not have a regular work week or if the employee is paid on a basis other than time, the employee's regular wages for a regular work week shall be deemed to be the average amount of regular wages earned by the employee for the weeks in which the employee worked in the period of 12 weeks preceding the date on which,

(a) the employee's employment was severed; or

(b) if the employee's employment was severed under clause 63(1)(c) or (d), the date on which the lay-off began.

(7) In addition to other amounts — Subject to subsection (8), severance pay under this section is in addition to any other amount to which an employee is entitled under this Act or his or her employment contract.

(8) Set-off, deduction — Only the following set-offs and deductions may be made in calculating severance pay under this section:

1. Supplementary unemployment benefits the employee receives after his or her employment is severed and before the severance pay becomes payable to the employee.

2. An amount paid to an employee for loss of employment under a provision of the employment contract if it is based upon length of employment, length of service or seniority.

3. Severance pay that was previously paid to the employee under this Act, a predecessor of this Act or a contractual provision described in paragraph 2.

2002, c. 18, Sched. J, s. 3(26); 2009, c. 33, Sched. 20, s. 1(1)

66. (1) Instalments — An employer may pay severance pay to an employee who is entitled to it in instalments with the agreement of the employee or the approval of the Director.

(2) Restriction — The period over which instalments can be paid must not exceed three years.

(3) Default — If the employer fails to make an instalment payment, all severance pay not previously paid shall become payable immediately.

2001, c. 9, Sched. I, s. 1(17)

Election re Recall rights

67. (1) Where election may be made — This section applies if an employee who has a right to be recalled for employment under his or her employment contract is entitled to,

(a) termination pay under section 61 because of a lay-off of 35 weeks or more; or

(b) severance pay.

(2) Exception — Clause (1)(b) does not apply if the employer and employee have agreed that the severance pay shall be paid in instalments under section 66.

(3) Nature of election — The employee may elect to be paid the termination pay or severance pay forthwith or to retain the right to be recalled.

(4) Consistency — An employee who is entitled to both termination pay and severance pay shall make the same election in respect of each.

(5) Deemed abandonment — An employee who elects to be paid shall be deemed to have abandoned the right to be recalled.

(6) Employee not represented by trade union — If an employee who is not represented by a trade union elects to retain the right to be recalled or fails to make an election, the employer shall pay the termination pay and severance pay to which the employee is entitled to the Director in trust.

(7) Employee represented by trade union — If an employee who is represented by a trade union elects to retain the right to be recalled or fails to make an election,

(a) the employer and the trade union shall attempt to negotiate an arrangement for holding the money in trust, and, if the negotiations are successful, the money shall be held in trust in accordance with the arrangement agreed upon; and

(b) if the trade union advises the Director and the employer in writing that efforts to negotiate such an arrangement have been unsuccessful, the employer shall pay the termination pay and severance pay to which the employee is entitled to the Director in trust.

(8) Where employee accepts recall — If the employee accepts employment made available under the right of recall, the amount held in trust shall be paid out of trust to the employer and the employee shall be deemed to have abandoned the right to termination pay and severance pay paid into trust.

(9) Recall rights expired or renounced — If the employee renounces the right to be recalled or the right expires, the amount held in trust shall be paid to the employee and, if the right to be recalled had not expired, the employee shall be deemed to have abandoned the right.

PART XVI — LIE DETECTORS

68. Definitions — In this Part, and for purposes of Part XVIII (Reprisal), section 74.12, Part XXI (Who Enforces this Act and What They Can Do), Part XXII (Complaints and Enforcement), Part XXIII (Reviews by the Board), Part XXIV (Collection), Part XXV (Offences and Prosecutions), Part XXVI (Miscellaneous

Evidentiary Provisions), Part XXVII (Regulations) and Part XXVIII (Transition, Amendment, Repeals, Commencement and Short Title), insofar as matters concerning this Part are concerned,

"employee" means an employee as defined in subsection 1(1) and includes an applicant for employment, a police officer and a person who is an applicant to be a police officer;

"employer" means an employer as defined in subsection 1(1) and includes a prospective employer and a police governing body;

"lie detector test" means an analysis, examination, interrogation or test that is taken or performed,

(a) by means of or in conjunction with a device, instrument or machine, and

(b) for the purpose of assessing or purporting to assess the credibility of a person.

2009, c. 9, s. 2

69. Right to refuse test — Subject to section 71, an employee has a right not to,

(a) take a lie detector test;

(b) be asked to take a lie detector test; or

(c) be required to take a lie detector test.

70. (1) Prohibition: testing — Subject to section 71, no person shall, directly or indirectly, require, request, enable or influence an employee to take a lie detector test.

(2) Prohibition: disclosure — No person shall disclose to an employer that an employee has taken a lie detector test or disclose to an employer the results of a lie detector test taken by an employee.

71. Consent to test by police — This Part shall not be interpreted to prevent a person from being asked by a police officer to take, consenting to take and taking a lie detector test administered on behalf of a police force in Ontario or by a member of a police force in Ontario in the course of the investigation of an offence.

PART XVII — RETAIL BUSINESS ESTABLISHMENTS

72. (1) Application — This Part applies with respect to,

(a) retail business establishments as defined in subsection 1(1) of the *Retail Business Holidays Act*;

(b) employees employed to work in those establishments; and

(c) employers of those employees.

(2) Exception — This Part does not apply with respect to retail business establishments in which the primary retail business is one that,

(a) sells prepared meals;

(b) rents living accommodations;

(c) is open to the public for educational, recreational or amusement purposes; or

(d) sells goods or services incidental to a business described in clause (a), (b) or (c) and is located in the same premises as that business.

73. (1) Right to refuse work — An employee may refuse to work on a public holiday or a day declared by proclamation of the Lieutenant Governor to be a holiday for the purposes of the *Retail Business Holidays Act*.

(2) Same — An employee may refuse to work on a Sunday.

(3) Notice of refusal — An employee who agrees to work on a day referred to in subsection (1) or (2) may then decline to work on that day, but only if he or she gives the employer notice that he or she declines at least 48 hours before he or she was to commence work on that day.

PART XVIII — REPRISAL

74. (1) Prohibition — No employer or person acting on behalf of an employer shall intimidate, dismiss or otherwise penalize an employee or threaten to do so,

(a) because the employee,

(i) asks the employer to comply with this Act and the regulations,

(ii) makes inquiries about his or her rights under this Act,

(iii) files a complaint with the Ministry under this Act,

(iv) exercises or attempts to exercise a right under this Act,

(v) gives information to an employment standards officer,

Proposed Addition — 74(1)(a)(v.1), (v.2)

(v.1) makes inquiries about the rate paid to another employee for the purpose of determining or assisting another person in determining whether an employer is complying with Part XII (Equal Pay for Equal Work),

(v.2) discloses the employee's rate of pay to another employee for the purpose of determining or assisting another person in determining whether an employer is complying with Part XII (Equal Pay for Equal Work),

2017, c. 22, Sched. 1, s. 41 [To come into force April 1, 2018.]

(vi) testifies or is required to testify or otherwise participates or is going to participate in a proceeding under this Act,

(vii) participates in proceedings respecting a by-law or proposed by-law under section 4 of the *Retail Business Holidays Act*,

(viii) is or will become eligible to take a leave, intends to take a leave or takes a leave under Part XIV; or

(b) because the employer is or may be required, because of a court order or garnishment, to pay to a third party an amount owing by the employer to the employee.

(2) Onus of proof — Subject to subsection 122(4), in any proceeding under this Act, the burden of proof that an employer did not contravene a provision set out in this section lies upon the employer.

PART XVIII.1 — TEMPORARY HELP AGENCIES

[Heading added 2009, c. 9, s. 3.]

Interpretation and Application

[Heading added 2009, c. 9, s. 3.]

74.1 [Repealed 2017, c. 22, Sched. 1, s. 42.]

74.2 [Repealed 2016, c. 30, s. 36(2).]

74.2.1 Assignment employees — This Part does not apply in relation to an individual who is an assignment employee assigned to provide professional services, personal support services or homemaking services as defined in the *Home Care and Community Services Act, 1994* if the assignment is made under a contract between,

(a) the individual and a local health integration network within the meaning of the *Local Health System Integration Act, 2006*; or

(b) an employer of the individual and a local health integration network within the meaning of the *Local Health System Integration Act, 2006*.

2016, c. 30, s. 36(3)

74.3 Employment relationship — Where a temporary help agency and a person agree, whether or not in writing, that the agency will assign or attempt to assign the person to perform work on a temporary basis for clients or potential clients of the agency,

(a) the temporary help agency is the person's employer;

(b) the person is an employee of the temporary help agency.

2009, c. 9, s. 3

74.4 (1) Work assignment — An assignment employee of a temporary help agency is assigned to perform work for a client if the agency arranges for the employee to perform work for a client on a temporary basis and the employee performs such work for the client.

(2) Same — Where an assignment employee is assigned by a temporary help agency to perform work for a client of the agency, the assignment begins on the first day on which the assignment employee performs work under the assignment and ends at the end of the term of the assignment or when the assignment is ended by the agency, the employee or the client.

(3) Same — An assignment employee of a temporary help agency does not cease to be the agency's assignment employee because,

(a) he or she is assigned by the agency to perform work for a client on a temporary basis; or

(b) he or she is not assigned by the agency to perform work for a client on a temporary basis.

(4) Same — An assignment employee of a temporary help agency is not assigned to perform work for a client because the agency has,

(a) provided the client with the employee's resume;

(b) arranged for the client to interview the employee; or

(c) otherwise introduced the employee to the client.

2009, c. 9, s. 3

Obligations and Prohibitions

[Heading added 2010, c. 23, s. 83.]

74.4.1 (1) Agency to keep records re: work for client, termination — In addition to the information that an employer is required to record under Part VI, a temporary help agency shall,

(a) record the number of hours worked by each assignment employee for each client of the agency in each day and each week; and

(b) retain a copy of any written notice provided to an assignment employee under subsection 74.10.1 (1).

(2) Retention of records — The temporary help agency shall retain or arrange for some other person to retain the records required under subsection (1) for three years after the day or week to which the information relates.

(3) Availability — The temporary help agency shall ensure that the records required to be retained under this section are readily available for inspection as required by an employment standards officer, even if the agency has arranged for another person to retain them.

2014, c. 10, Sched. 2, s. 4; 2017, c. 22, Sched. 1, s. 43

74.4.2 (1) Client to keep records re: work for client — A client of a temporary help agency shall record the number of hours worked by each assignment employee assigned to perform work for the client in each day and each week.

(2) Retention of records — The client shall retain or arrange for some other person to retain the records required under subsection (1) for three years after the day or week to which the information relates.

(3) Availability — The client shall ensure that the records required to be retained under this section are readily available for inspection as required by an employment standards officer, even if the client has arranged for another person to retain them.

2014, c. 10, Sched. 2, s. 4

74.5 (1) Information re agency — As soon as possible after a person becomes an assignment employee of a temporary help agency, the agency shall provide the following information, in writing, to the employee:

1. The legal name of the agency, as well as any operating or business name of the agency if different from the legal name.

2. Contact information for the agency, including address, telephone number and one or more contact names.

(2) Transition — Where a person is an assignment employee of a temporary help agency on the day this section comes into force, the agency shall, as soon as possible after that day, provide the information required by subsection (1), in writing, to the employee.

2009, c. 9, s. 3

74.6 (1) Information re assignment — A temporary help agency shall provide the following information when offering a work assignment with a client to an assignment employee:

1. The legal name of the client, as well as any operating or business name of the client if different from the legal name.

2. Contact information for the client, including address, telephone number and one or more contact names.

3. The hourly or other wage rate or commission, as applicable, and benefits associated with the assignment.

4. The hours of work associated with the assignment.

5. A general description of the work to be performed on the assignment.

6. The pay period and pay day established by the agency in accordance with subsection 11(1).

7. The estimated term of the assignment, if the information is available at the time of the offer.

(2) Same — If information required by subsection (1) is provided orally to the assignment employee, the temporary help agency shall also provide the information to the assignment employee in writing, as soon as possible after offering the work assignment.

(3) Transition — Where an assignment employee is on a work assignment with a client of a temporary help agency or has been offered such an assignment on the day this section comes into force, the agency shall, as soon as possible after that day, provide the information required by subsection (1), in writing, to the employee.

2009, c. 9, s. 3

74.7 (1) Information, rights under this Act — The Director shall prepare and publish a document providing such information about the rights and obligations of assignment employees, temporary help agencies and clients under this Part as the Director considers appropriate.

(2) Same — If the Director believes that a document prepared under subsection (1) has become out of date, the Director shall prepare and publish a new document.

(3) Same — As soon as possible after a person becomes an assignment employee of a temporary help agency, the agency shall provide a copy of the most recent document published by the Director under this section to the employee.

(4) Same — If the language of an assignment employee is a language other than English, the temporary help agency shall make enquiries as to whether the Director has prepared a translation of the document into that language and, if the Director has done so, the agency shall also provide a copy of the translation to the employee.

(5) Transition — Where a person is an assignment employee of a temporary help agency on the day this section comes into force, the agency shall, as soon as possible after that day, provide the document required by subsection (3) and, where applicable, by subsection (4), to the employee.

2009, c. 9, s. 3

74.8 (1) Prohibitions — A temporary help agency is prohibited from doing any of the following:

1. Charging a fee to an assignment employee in connection with him or her becoming an assignment employee of the agency.

2. Charging a fee to an assignment employee in connection with the agency assigning or attempting to assign him or her to perform work on a temporary basis for clients or potential clients of the agency.

3. Charging a fee to an assignment employee of the agency in connection with assisting or instructing him or her on preparing resumes or preparing for job interviews.

4. Restricting an assignment employee of the agency from entering into an employment relationship with a client.

5. Charging a fee to an assignment employee of the agency in connection with a client of the agency entering into an employment relationship with him or her.

6. Restricting a client from providing references in respect of an assignment employee of the agency.

7. Restricting a client from entering into an employment relationship with an assignment employee.

8. Charging a fee to a client in connection with the client entering into an employment relationship with an assignment employee, except as permitted by subsection (2).

9. Charging a fee that is prescribed as prohibited.

10. Imposing a restriction that is prescribed as prohibited.

(2) Exception, par. 8 of subs. (1) — Where an assignment employee has been assigned by a temporary help agency to perform work on a temporary basis for a client and the employee has begun to perform the work, the agency may charge a fee to the client in the event that the client enters into an employment relationship with the employee, but only during the six-month period beginning on the day on which the employee first began to perform work for the client of the agency.

(3) Same — For the purposes of subsection (2), the six-month period runs regardless of the duration of the assignment or assignments by the agency of the assignment employee to work for the client and regardless of the amount or timing of work performed by the assignment employee.

(4) Interpretation — In this section, "assignment employee" includes a prospective assignment employee.

2009, c. 9, s. 3

74.9 (1) Void provisions — A provision in an agreement between a temporary help agency and an assignment employee of the agency that is inconsistent with section 74.8 is void.

(2) Same — A provision in an agreement between a temporary help agency and a client that is inconsistent with section 74.8 is void.

(3) Transition — Subsections (1) and (2) apply to provisions regardless of whether the agreement was entered into before or after the date on which section 74.8 comes into force.

(4) Interpretation — In this section, **"assignment employee"** includes a prospective assignment employee.

2009, c. 9, s. 3

74.10 (1) Public holiday pay — For the purposes of determining entitlement to public holiday pay under subsection 29(2.1), an assignment employee of a temporary help agency is on a layoff on a public holiday if the public holiday falls on a day on which the employee is not assigned by the agency to perform work for a client of the agency.

(2) Same — For the purposes of subsection 29(2.2), the period of a temporary lay-off of an assignment employee by a temporary help agency shall be determined in accordance with section 56 as modified by section 74.11 for the purposes of Part XV.

2009, c. 9, s. 3

74.10.1 (1) Termination of assignment — A temporary help agency shall provide an assignment employee with one week's written notice or pay in lieu of notice if,

(a) the assignment employee is assigned to perform work for a client;

(b) the assignment had an estimated term of three months or more at the time it was offered to the employee; and

(c) the assignment is terminated before the end of its estimated term.

(2) Amount of pay in lieu — For the purposes of subsection (1), the amount of the pay in lieu of notice shall be equal to the wages the assignment employee would have been entitled to receive had one week's notice been given in accordance with that subsection.

(3) Exception — Subsection (1) does not apply if the temporary help agency offers the assignment employee a work assignment with a client during the notice period that is reasonable in the circumstances and that has an estimated term of one week or more.

(4) Same — Subsection (1) does not apply if,

(a) the assignment employee has been guilty of wilful misconduct, disobedience or wilful neglect of duty that is not trivial and has not been condoned by the temporary help agency or the client;

(b) the assignment has become impossible to perform or has been frustrated by a fortuitous or unforeseeable event or circumstance; or

(c) the assignment is terminated during or as a result of a strike or lock-out at the location of the assignment.

2017, c. 22, Sched. 1, s. 44

74.11 Termination and severance — For the purposes of the application of Part XV to temporary help agencies and their assignment employees, the following modifications apply:

1. A temporary help agency lays off an assignment employee for a week if the employee is not assigned by the agency to perform work for a client of the agency during the week.

2. For the purposes of paragraphs 3 and 10, **"excluded week"** means a week during which, for one or more days, the assignment employee is not able to work, is not available for work, refuses an offer by the agency that would not constitute constructive dismissal of the employee by the agency, is subject to a disciplinary suspension or is not assigned to perform work for a client of the agency because of a strike or lock-out occurring at the agency.

3. An excluded week shall not be counted as part of the 13 or 35 weeks referred to in subsection 56(2) but shall be counted as part of the 20 or 52 consecutive week periods referred to in subsection 56(2).

4. Subsections 56(3) to (3.6) do not apply to temporary help agencies and their assignment employees.

4.1 On and after November 6, 2009, subsection 58(1) does not apply to a temporary help agency in respect of its assignment employees.

4.2 On and after November 6, 2009, a temporary help agency shall give notice of termination to its assignment employees in accordance with paragraph 4.3 rather than in accordance with section 57 if,

    i. 50 or more assignment employees of the agency who were assigned to perform work for the same client of the agency at the same establishment of that client were terminated in the same four-week period, and

    ii. the terminations resulted from the term of assignments ending or from the assignments being ended by the agency or by the client.

4.3 In the circumstances described in paragraph 4.2, notice of termination shall be given for the prescribed period or, if no applicable periods are prescribed,

i. at least eight weeks before termination, if the number of assignment employees whose employment is terminated is 50 or more but fewer than 200,

ii. at least 12 weeks before termination, if the number of assignment employees whose employment is terminated is 200 or more but fewer than 500, or

iii. at least 16 weeks before termination, if the number of assignment employees whose employment is terminated is 500 or more.

5. A temporary help agency shall, in addition to meeting the posting requirements set out in clause 58(2)(b) and subsection 58(5), provide the information required to be provided to the Director under clause 58(2)(a) to each employee to whom it is required to give notice in accordance with paragraph 4.3 on the first day of the notice period or as soon after that as is reasonably possible.

6. Clauses 60(1)(a) and (b) and subsection 60(2) do not apply to temporary help agencies and their assignment employees.

7. A temporary help agency that gives notice of termination to an assignment employee in accordance with section 57 or paragraph 4.3 of this section shall, during each week of the notice period, pay the assignment employee the wages he or she is entitled to receive, which in no case shall be less than,

i. in the case of any termination other than under clause 56(1)(c), the total amount of the wages earned by the assignment employee for work performed for clients of the agency during the 12-week period ending on the last day on which the employee performed work for a client of the agency, divided by 12, or

ii. in the case of a termination under clause 56(1)(c), the total amount of wages earned by the assignment employee for work performed for clients of the agency during the 12-week period immediately preceding the deemed termination date, divided by 12.

8. The lump sum that an assignment employee is entitled to be paid under clause 61(1)(a) is a lump sum equal to the amount the employee would have been entitled to receive under paragraph 7 had notice been given in accordance with section 57 or paragraph 4.3 of this section.

9. Subsection 61(1.1) does not apply to temporary help agencies and their assignment employees.

9.1 For purposes of the application of clause 63(1)(e) to an assignment employee, the reference to section 58 in that clause shall be read as a reference to paragraph 4.3 of this section.

10. An excluded week shall not be counted as part of the 35 weeks referred to in clause 63(1)(c) but shall be counted as part of the 52 consecutive week period referred to in clause 63(1)(c).

11. Subsections 63(2) to (2.4) do not apply to temporary help agencies and their assignment employees.

12. Subsections 65(1), (5) and (6) do not apply to temporary help agencies and their assignment employees.

12.1 For purposes of the application of subsection 65(4) to an assignment employee, the reference to section 58 in that subsection shall be read as a reference to paragraph 4.3 of this section.

13. If a temporary help agency severs the employment of an assignment employee under clause 63(1)(a), (b), (d) or (e), severance pay shall be calculated by,

i. dividing the total amount of wages earned by the assignment employee for work performed for clients of the agency during the 12-week period ending on the last day on which the employee performed work for a client of the agency by 12, and

ii. multiplying the result obtained under subparagraph i by the lesser of 26 and the sum of,

A. the number of years of employment the employee has completed, and

B. the number of months of employment not included in sub-subparagraph A that the employee has completed, divided by 12.

14. If a temporary help agency severs the employment of an assignment employee under clause 63(1)(c), severance pay shall be calculated by,

i. dividing the total amount of wages earned by the assignment employee for work performed for clients of the agency during the 12-week period immediately preceding the first day of the lay-off by 12, and

ii. multiplying the result obtained under subparagraph i by the lesser of 26 and the sum of,

A. the number of years of employment the employee has completed, and

B. the number of months of employment not included in sub-subparagraph A that the employee has completed, divided by 12.

2009, c. 9, s. 3; 2009, c. 33, Sched. 20, s. 1(2)-(6)

74.11.1 Transition — A temporary help agency that fails to meet the notice requirements of paragraph 4.3 of section 74.11 during the period beginning on November 6, 2009 and ending on the day before the *Good Government Act, 2009* receives Royal Assent has the obligations that the agency would have had if the failure had occurred on or after the day the *Good Government Act, 2009* receives Royal Assent.

2009, c. 33, Sched. 20, s. 1(7)

Reprisal by Client

[Heading added 2009, c. 9, s. 3.]

74.12 (1) Reprisal by client prohibited — No client of a temporary help agency or person acting on behalf of a client of a temporary help agency shall intimidate an assignment employee, refuse to have an assignment employee perform work for the client, terminate the assignment of an assignment employee, or otherwise penalize an assignment employee or threaten to do so,

(a) because the assignment employee,

> (i) asks the client or the temporary help agency to comply with their respective obligations under this Act and the regulations,

> (ii) makes inquiries about his or her rights under this Act,

> (iii) files a complaint with the Ministry under this Act,

> (iv) exercises or attempts to exercise a right under this Act,

> (v) gives information to an employment standards officer,

Proposed Addition — 74.12(1)(a)(v.1)-(v.3)

(v.1) makes inquiries about the rate paid to an employee of the client for the purpose of determining or assisting another person in determining whether a temporary help agency is complying with Part XII (Equal Pay for Equal Work),

(v.2) discloses the assignment employee's rate of pay to an employee of the client for the purpose of determining or assisting another person in determining whether a temporary help agency is complying with Part XII (Equal Pay for Equal Work),

(v.3) discloses the rate paid to an employee of the client to the assignment employee's temporary help agency for the purposes of determining or assisting another person in determining whether a temporary help agency is complying with Part XII (Equal Pay for Equal Work),

2017, c. 22, Sched. 1, s. 45 [To come into force April 1, 2018.]

> (vi) testifies or is required to testify or otherwise participates or is going to participate in a proceeding under this Act,

(vii) participates in proceedings respecting a by-law or proposed by-law under section 4 of the *Retail Business Holidays Act*,

(viii) is or will become eligible to take a leave, intends to take a leave or takes a leave under Part XIV; or

(b) because the client or temporary help agency is or may be required, because of a court order or garnishment, to pay to a third party an amount owing to the assignment employee.

(2) Onus of proof — Subject to subsection 122(4), in any proceeding under this Act, the burden of proof that a client did not contravene a provision set out in this section lies upon the client.

2009, c. 9, s. 3

Enforcement

[Heading added 2009, c. 9, s. 3.]

74.12.1 [Repealed 2017, c. 22, Sched. 1, s. 46.]

74.13 (1) Meeting under s. 102 — For the purposes of the application of section 102 in respect of this Part, the following modifications apply:

1. In addition to the circumstances set out in subsection 102(1), the following are circumstances in which an employment standards officer may require persons to attend a meeting under that subsection:

    i. The officer is investigating a complaint against a client.

    ii. The officer, while inspecting a place under section 91 or 92, comes to have reasonable grounds to believe that a client has contravened this Act or the regulations with respect to an assignment employee.

    iii. The officer acquires information that suggests to him or her the possibility that a client may have contravened this Act or the regulations with respect to an assignment employee or prospective assignment employee.

iv. The officer wishes to determine whether a client, in whose residence an assignment employee or prospective assignment employee resides, is complying with this Act.

2. In addition to the persons referred to in subsection 102(2), the following persons may be required to attend the meeting:

i. The client.

ii. If the client is a corporation, a director or employee of the corporation.

iii. An assignment employee or prospective assignment employee.

3. If a person who was served with a notice under section 102 and who failed to comply with the notice is a client, a reference to an employer in paragraphs 1 and 2 of subsection 102(10) is a reference to the client.

4. If a person who was served with a notice under section 102 and who failed to comply with the notice is an assignment employee or prospective assignment employee, a reference to an employee in paragraphs 1 and 2 of subsection 102(10) is a reference to an assignment employee or prospective assignment employee, as the case requires.

(2) Interpretation, corporation — For the purposes of paragraph 3 of subsection (1), if a client is a corporation, a reference to the client includes a director or employee who was served with a notice requiring him or her to attend the meeting or to bring or make available any records or other documents.

2009, c. 9, s. 3; 2010, c. 16, Sched. 9, s. 1(4)-(6)

74.13.1 (1) Time for response — For the purposes of the application of section 102.1 in respect of this Part, the following modifications apply:

1. In addition to the circumstances set out in subsection 102.1(1), the following are circumstances in which an employment standards officer may, after giving written notice, require persons to provide evidence or submissions

to the officer within the period of time that he or she specifies in the notice:

   i. The officer is investigating a complaint against a client.

   ii. The officer, while inspecting a place under section 91 or 92, comes to have reasonable grounds to believe that a client has contravened this Act or the regulations with respect to an assignment employee or prospective assignment employee.

   iii. The officer acquires information that suggests to him or her the possibility that a client may have contravened this Act or the regulations with respect to an assignment employee or prospective assignment employee.

   iv. The officer wishes to determine whether a client in whose residence an assignment employee or prospective assignment employee resides is complying with this Act.

2. If a person who was served with a notice under section 102.1 and who failed to comply with the notice is a client, a reference to an employer in paragraphs 1 and 2 of subsection 102.1(1) is a reference to a client.

3. If a person who was served with a notice under section 102.1 and who failed to comply with the notice is an assignment employee or prospective assignment employee, a reference to an employee in paragraphs 1 and 2 of subsection 102.1(3) is a reference to an assignment employee or prospective assignment employee as the case requires.

(2) Interpretation, corporations — For the purposes of subsection (1), if a client is a corporation, a reference to the client or person includes a director or employee who was served with a notice requiring him or her to attend the meeting or to bring or make available any records or other documents.

2010, c. 16, Sched. 9, s. 1(7)

74.14 (1) Order to recover fees — If an employment standards officer finds that a temporary help agency charged a fee to an assignment employee or prospective assignment employee in contravention of paragraph 1, 2, 3, 5 or 9 of subsection 74.8(1), the officer may,

    (a) arrange with the agency that it repay the amount of the fee directly to the assignment employee or prospective assignment employee; or

    (a.1) order the agency to repay the amount of the fee to the assignment employee or prospective assignment employee; or

    (b) order the agency to pay the amount of the fee to the Director in trust.

(2) Administrative costs — An order issued under clause (1)(b) shall also require the temporary help agency to pay to the Director in trust an amount for administrative costs equal to the greater of $100 and 10 per cent of the amount owing.

(3) Contents of order — The order shall state the paragraph of subsection 74.8(1) that was contravened and the amount to be paid.

(4) Application of s. 103(3) and (6) to (9) — Subsections 103(3) and (6) to (9) apply with respect to an order issued under this section with necessary modifications and for the purpose, without limiting the generality of the foregoing, a reference to an employee is a reference to an assignment employee or prospective assignment employee.

(5) Application of s. 105 — Section 105 applies with respect to repayment of fees by a temporary help agency to an assignment employee or prospective assignment employee with necessary modifications, including but not limited to the following:

    1. The reference to clause 103(1)(a) in subsection 105(1) is a reference to clause (1)(a) of this section.

    2. A reference to an employee is a reference to an assignment employee or prospective assignment employee to whom a fee is to be paid.

2009, c. 9, s. 3; 2017, c. 22, Sched. 1, s. 47

74.15 Recovery of prohibited fees by client — If a temporary help agency charges a fee to a client in contravention of paragraph 8 or 9 of subsection 74.8(1), the client may recover the amount of the fee in a court of competent jurisdiction.

2009, c. 9, s. 3

74.16 (1) Order for compensation, temporary help agency — If an employment standards officer finds that a temporary help agency has contravened paragraph 4, 6, 7 or 10 of subsection 74.8(1), the officer may order that the assignment employee or prospective assignment employee be compensated for any loss he or she incurred as a result of the contravention.

(2) Terms of orders — If an order issued under this section requires a temporary help agency to compensate an assignment employee or prospective assignment employee, it shall also require the agency to,

(a) pay to the Director in trust,

(i) the amount of the compensation, and

(ii) an amount for administration costs equal to the greater of $100 and 10 per cent of the amount of compensation; or

(b) pay the amount of the compensation to the assignment employee or prospective assignment employee.

(3) Contents of order — The order shall state the paragraph of subsection 74.8(1) that was contravened and the amount to be paid.

(4) Application of s. 103(3) and (6) to (9) — Subsections 103(3) and (6) to (9) apply with respect to orders issued under this section with necessary modifications and for the purpose, without limiting the generality of the foregoing, a reference to an employee is a reference to an assignment employee or prospective assignment employee.

2009, c. 9, s. 3; 2017, c. 22, Sched. 1, s. 48

74.17 (1) Order re client reprisal — If an employment standards officer finds that section 74.12 has been contravened with respect to an assignment employee, the officer may order that the employee be compensated for any loss he or she incurred as a result of the contravention or that he or she be reinstated in the assignment or that he or she be both compensated and reinstated.

(2) Terms of orders — If an order issued under this section requires the client to compensate an assignment employee, it shall also require the client to,

    (a) pay to the Director in trust,

        (i) the amount of the compensation, and

        (ii) an amount for administration costs equal to the greater of \$100 and 10 per cent of the amount of compensation; or

    (b) pay the amount of the compensation to the assignment employee.

(3) Application of s. 103(3) and (5) to (9) — Subsections 103(3) and (5) to (9) apply with respect to orders issued under this section with necessary modifications, including but not limited to the following:

    1. A reference to an employer is a reference to a client.

    2. A reference to an employee is a reference to an assignment employee.

(4) Agency obligation — If an order is issued under this section requiring a client to reinstate an assignment employee in the assignment, the temporary help agency shall do whatever it can reasonably do in order to enable compliance by the client with the order.

2009, c. 9, s. 3; 2017, c. 22, Sched. 1, s. 49

74.18 (1) Agency and client jointly and severally liable — Subject to subsection (2), if an assignment employee was assigned to perform work for a client of a temporary help agency during a pay period, and the agency fails to pay the employee some or all of the wages described in subsection (3) that are owing to the employee for that pay period, the agency and the client are jointly and severally liable for the wages.

(2) Same, more than one client — If an assignment employee was assigned to perform work for more than one client of a temporary help agency during a pay period, and the agency fails to pay the employee some or all of the wages described in subsection (3) that are owing to the employee for that pay period, each client is jointly and severally liable with the agency for a share of the total wages owed to the employee that is in proportion to the number of hours the employee worked for that client during the pay period relative to the total number of hours the employee worked for all clients during the pay period.

(3) Wages for which client may be liable — A client of a temporary help agency may be jointly and severally liable under this section for the following wages:

　1. Regular wages that were earned during the relevant pay period.

　2. Overtime pay that was earned during the relevant pay period.

　3. Public holiday pay that was earned during the relevant pay period.

　4. Premium pay that was earned during the relevant pay period.

(4) Agency primarily responsible — Despite subsections (1) and (2), the temporary help agency is primarily responsible for an assignment employee's wages, but proceedings against the agency under this Act do not have to be exhausted before proceedings may be commenced to collect wages from the client of the agency.

(5) Enforcement — client deemed to be employer — For the purposes of enforcing the liability of a client of a temporary help agency under this section, the client is deemed to be an employer of the assignment employee.

(6) Same — orders — Without restricting the generality of subsection (5), an order issued by an employment standards officer against a client of a temporary help agency to enforce a liability under this section shall be treated as if it were an order against an employer for the purposes of this Act.

2014, c. 10, Sched. 2, s. 5

PART XIX — BUILDING SERVICES PROVIDERS

75. (1) New provider — This Part applies if a building services provider for a building is replaced by a new provider.

(2) Termination and severance pay — The new provider shall comply with Part XV (Termination and Severance of Employment) with respect to every employee of the replaced provider who is engaged in providing services at the premises and whom the new provider does not employ as if the new provider had terminated and severed the employee's employment.

(3) Same — The new provider shall be deemed to have been the employee's employer for the purpose of subsection (2).

(4) Exception — The new provider is not required to comply with subsection (2) with respect to,

(a) an employee who is retained by the replaced provider; or

(b) any prescribed employees.

76. (1) Vacation pay — A provider who ceases to provide services at a premises and who ceases to employ an employee shall pay to the employee the amount of any accrued vacation pay.

(2) Same — A payment under subsection (1) shall be made within the later of,

(a) seven days after the day the employee's employment with the provider ceases; or

(b) the day that would have been the employee's next regular pay day.

77. (1) Information request, possible new provider — Where a person is seeking to become the new provider at a premises, the owner or manager of the premises shall upon request give to that person the prescribed information about the employees who on the date of the request are engaged in providing services at the premises.

(2) Same, new provider — Where a person becomes the new provider at a premises, the owner or manager of the premises shall upon request give to that person the prescribed information about the employees who on the date of the request are engaged in providing services for the premises.

(3) Request by owner or manager — If an owner or manager requests a provider or former provider to provide information to the owner or manager so that the owner or manager can fulfil a request made under subsection (1) or (2), the provider or former provider shall provide the information.

78. (1) Use of information — A person who receives information under this Part shall use that information only for the purpose of complying with this Part or determining the person's obligations or potential obligations under this Part.

(2) Confidentiality — A person who receives information under section 77 shall not disclose it, except as authorized under this Part.

PART XX — LIABILITY OF DIRECTORS

79. Definition — In this Part,

"director" means a director of a corporation and includes a shareholder who is a party to a unanimous shareholder agreement.

80. (1) Application of Part — This Part applies with respect to shareholders described in section 79 only to the extent that the directors are relieved, under subsection 108(5) of the *Business Corporations Act* or subsection 146(5) of the *Canada Business Corporations Act*, of their liability to pay wages to the employees of the corporation.

(2) Non-application — This Part does not apply with respect to directors of corporations to which Part III of the *Corporations Act* applies or to which the *Co-operative Corporations Act* applies.

Proposed Amendment 80(2)

(2) Non-application — This Part does not apply with respect to directors of corporations to which the *Not-for-Profit Corporations Act, 2010* applies or to which the *Co-operative Corporations Act* applies.

2010, c. 15, s. 224 [Not in force at date of publication.]

---

(3) Same — This Part does not apply with respect to directors, or persons who perform functions similar to those of a director, of a college of a health profession or a group of health professions that is established or continued under an Act of the Legislature.

(4) Same — This Part does not apply with respect to directors of corporations,

(a) that have been incorporated in another jurisdiction;

(b) that have objects that are similar to the objects of corporations to which Part III of the *Corporations Act* applies or to which the *Co-operative Corporations Act* applies; and

---

Proposed Amendment 80(4)(b)

(b) that have objects that are similar to the objects of corporations to which the *Not-for-Profit Corporations Act, 2010* applies or to which the *Co-operative Corporations Act* applies; and

2010, c. 15, s. 224 [Not in force at date of publication.]

(c) that are carried on without the purpose of gain.

81. (1) Directors' liability for wages — The directors of an employer are jointly and severally liable for wages as provided in this Part if,

(a) the employer is insolvent, the employee has caused a claim for unpaid wages to be filed with the receiver appointed by a court with respect to the employer or with the employer's trustee in bankruptcy and the claim has not been paid;

(b) an employment standards officer has made an order that the employer is liable for wages, unless the amount set out in the order has been paid or the employer has applied to have it reviewed;

(c) an employment standards officer has made an order that a director is liable for wages, unless the amount set out in the order has been paid or the employer or the director has applied to have it reviewed; or

(d) the Board has issued, amended or affirmed an order under section 119, the order, as issued, amended or affirmed, requires the employer or the directors to pay wages and the amount set out in the order has not been paid.

(2) Employer primarily responsible — Despite subsection (1), the employer is primarily responsible for an employee's wages but proceedings against the employer under this Act do not have to be exhausted before proceedings may be commenced to collect wages from directors under this Part.

(3) Wages — The wages that directors are liable for under this Part are wages, not including termination pay and severance pay as they are provided for under this Act or an employment contract and not including amounts that are deemed to be wages under this Act.

(4) Vacation pay — The vacation pay that directors are liable for is the greater of the minimum vacation pay provided in Part XI (Vacation With Pay) and the amount contractually agreed to by the employer and the employee.

(5) Holiday pay — The amount of holiday pay that directors are liable for is the greater of the amount payable for holidays at the rate as determined under this Act and the regulations and the amount for the holidays at the rate as contractually agreed to by the employer and the employee.

(6) Overtime wages — The overtime wages that directors are liable for are the greater of the amount of overtime pay provided in Part VIII (Overtime Pay) and the amount contractually agreed to by the employer and the employee.

(7) Directors' maximum liability — The directors of an employer corporation are jointly and severally liable to the employees of the corporation for all debts not exceeding six months' wages, as described in subsection (3), that become payable while they are directors for services performed for the corporation and for the vacation pay accrued while they are directors for not more than 12 months under this Act and the regulations made under it or under any collective agreement made by the corporation.

(8) [Repealed 2017, c. 22, Sched. 1, s. 50.]

(9) Contribution from other directors — A director who has satisfied a claim for wages is entitled to contribution in relation to the wages from other directors who are liable for the claim.

(10) Limitation periods — A limitation period set out in section 114 prevails over a limitation period in any other Act, unless the other Act states that it is to prevail over this Act.

2017, c. 22, Sched. 1, s. 50

82. (1) No relief by contract, etc. — No provision in a contract, in the articles of incorporation or the by-laws of a corporation or in a resolution of a corporation relieves a director from the duty to act according to this Act or relieves him or her from liability for breach of it.

(2) Indemnification of directors — An employer may indemnify a director, a former director and the heirs or legal representatives of a director or former director against all costs, charges and expenses, including an amount paid to satisfy an order under this Act, including an order which is the subject of a filing under section 126, reasonably incurred by the director with respect to any civil or administrative action or proceeding to which he or she is a party by reason of being or having been a director of the employer if,

(a) he or she has acted honestly and in good faith with a view to the best interests of the employer; and

(b) in the case of a proceeding or action that is enforced by a monetary penalty, he or she had reasonable grounds for believing that his or her conduct was lawful.

83. Civil remedies protected — No civil remedy that a person may have against a director or that a director may have against a person is suspended or affected by this Part.

PART XXI — WHO ENFORCES THIS ACT AND WHAT THEY CAN DO

84. Minister responsible — The Minister is responsible for the administration of this Act.

85. (1) Director — The Minister shall appoint a person to be the Director of Employment Standards to administer this Act and the regulations.

(2) Acting Director — The Director's powers may be exercised and the Director's duties may be performed by an employee of the Ministry appointed as Acting Director if,

(a) the Director is absent or unable to act; or

(b) an individual who was appointed Director has ceased to be the Director and no new Director has been appointed.

(3) Same — An Acting Director shall be appointed by the Director or, in the Director's absence, the Deputy Minister of Labour.

86. (1) Employment standards officers — Such persons as are considered necessary to enforce this Act and the regulations may be appointed under Part III of the *Public Service of Ontario Act, 2006* as employment standards officers.

(2) Certificate of appointment — The Deputy Minister of Labour shall issue a certificate of appointment bearing his or her signature or a facsimile of it to every employment standards officer.

2006, c. 35, Sched. C, s. 33

87. (1) Delegation — The Minister may, in writing, delegate to any person any of the Minister's powers or duties under this Act, subject to the limitations or conditions set out in the delegation.

(2) Same: residual powers — The Minister may exercise a power or perform a duty under this Act even if he or she has delegated it to a person under this section.

88. (1) Powers and duties of Director — The Director may exercise the powers conferred upon the Director under this Act and shall perform the duties imposed upon the Director under this Act.

(2) Policies — The Director may establish policies respecting the interpretation, administration and enforcement of this Act.

(3) Authorization — The Director may authorize an employment standards officer to exercise a power or to perform a duty conferred upon the Director under this Act, either orally or in writing.

(4) Same: residual powers — The Director may exercise a power conferred upon the Director under this Act even if he or she has delegated it to a person under subsection (3).

(5) Interest — The Director may, with the approval of the Minister, determine the rates of interest and the manner of calculating interest for,

> (a) amounts owing under different provisions of this Act or the regulations, and

(b) money held by the Director in trust.

(6) Determinations not regulations — A determination under subsection (5) is not a regulation within the meaning of Part III (Regulations) of the *Legislation Act, 2006*.

(7) Other circumstances — Where money has been paid to the Director in trust and no provision is made for paying it out elsewhere in this Act, it shall be paid out to the person entitled to receive it together with interest at the rate and calculated in the manner determined by the Director under subsection (5).

(8) Surplus interest — If the interest earned on money held by the Director in trust exceeds the interest paid to the person entitled to receive the money, the Director may use the difference to pay any service charges for the management of the money levied by the financial institution with which the money was deposited.

(9) Hearing not required — The Director is not required to hold a hearing in exercising any power or making any decision under this Act.

2006, c. 21, Sched. F, s. 136(1), Table 1; 2017, c. 22, Sched. 1, s. 51

88.1 (1) Director may reassign an investigation — The Director may terminate the assignment of an employment standards officer to the investigation of a complaint and may assign the investigation to another employment standards officer.

(2) Same — If the Director terminates the assignment of an employment standards officer to the investigation of a complaint,

(a) the officer whose assignment is terminated shall no longer have any powers or duties with respect to the investigation of the complaint or the discovery during the investigation of any similar potential entitlement of another employee of the employer related to the complaint; and

(b) the new employment standards officer assigned to the investigation may rely on evidence collected by the first officer and any findings of fact made by that officer.

(3) Inspections — This section applies with necessary modifications to inspections of employers by employment standards officers.

2006, c. 19, Sched. M, s. 1(1)

88.2 (1) Recognition of employers — The Director may give recognition to an employer, upon the employer's application, if the employer satisfies the Director that it meets the prescribed criteria.

(2) Classes of employers — For greater certainty, the criteria under subsection (1) may be prescribed for different classes of employers.

(3) Information re recognitions — The Director may require any employer who is seeking recognition under subsection (1), or who is the subject of a recognition, to provide the Director with whatever information, records or accounts he or she may require pertaining to the recognition and the Director may make such inquiries and examinations as he or she considers necessary.

(4) Publication — The Director may publish or otherwise make available to the public information relating to employers given recognition under subsection (1), including the names of employers.

(5) Validity of recognitions — A recognition given under subsection (1) is valid for the period that the Director specifies in the recognition.

(6) Revocation, etc., of recognitions — The Director may revoke or amend a recognition.

2017, c. 22, Sched. 1, s. 52

88.3 (1) Delegation of powers under s. 88.2 — The Director may authorize an individual employed in the Ministry to exercise a power conferred on the Director under section 88.2, either orally or in writing.

(2) Residual powers — The Director may exercise a power conferred on the Director under section 88.2 even if he or she has delegated it to an individual under subsection (1).

(3) Duty re policies — An individual authorized by the Director under subsection (1) shall follow any policies established by the Director under subsection 88 (2). 2017, c. 22, Sched. 1, s. 52

89. (1) Powers and duties of officers — An employment standards officer may exercise the powers conferred upon employment standards officers under this Act and shall perform the duties imposed upon employment standards officers under this Act.

(2) Officers to follow policies — An employment standards officer shall follow any policies established by the Director under subsection 88(2).

(3) Hearing not required — An employment standards officer is not required to hold a hearing in exercising any power or making any decision under this Act.

90. (1) Officers not compellable — An employment standards officer is not a competent or compellable witness in a civil proceeding respecting any information given or obtained, statements made or received, or records or other things produced or received under this Act except for the purpose of carrying out his or her duties under it.

(2) Records — An employment standards officer shall not be compelled in a civil proceeding to produce any record or other thing he or she has made or received under this Act except for the purpose of carrying out his or her duties under this Act.

91. (1) Investigation and inspection powers — An employment standards officer may, without a warrant, enter and inspect any place in order to investigate a possible contravention of this Act or to perform an inspection to ensure that this Act is being complied with.

(2) Time of entry — The power to enter and inspect a place without a warrant may be exercised only during the place's regular business hours or, if it does not have regular business hours, during daylight hours.

(3) Dwellings — The power to enter and inspect a place without a warrant shall not be exercised to enter and inspect a part of the place that is used as a dwelling unless the occupier of the dwelling consents or a warrant has been issued under section 92.

(4) Use of force — An employment standards officer is not entitled to use force to enter and inspect a place.

(5) Identification — An employment standards officer shall produce, on request, evidence of his or her appointment.

(6) Powers of officer — An employment standards officer conducting an investigation or inspection may,

(a) examine a record or other thing that the officer thinks may be relevant to the investigation or inspection;

(b) require the production of a record or other thing that the officer thinks may be relevant to the investigation or inspection;

(c) remove for review and copying a record or other thing that the officer thinks may be relevant to the investigation or inspection;

(d) in order to produce a record in readable form, use data storage, information processing or retrieval devices or systems that are normally used in carrying on business in the place; and

(e) question any person on matters the officer thinks may be relevant to the investigation or inspection.

(7) Written demand — A demand that a record or other thing be produced must be in writing and must include a statement of the nature of the record or thing required.

(8) Obligation to produce and assist — If an employment standards officer demands that a record or other thing be produced, the person who has custody of the record or thing shall produce it and, in the case of a record, shall on request provide any assistance that is reasonably necessary to interpret the record or to produce it in a readable form.

(9) Records and things removed from place — An employment standards officer who removes a record or other thing under clause (6)(c) shall provide a receipt and return the record or thing to the person within a reasonable time.

(10) Copy admissible in evidence — A copy of a record that purports to be certified by an employment standards officer as being a true copy of the original is admissible in evidence to the same extent as the original, and has the same evidentiary value.

(11) Obstruction — No person shall hinder, obstruct or interfere with or attempt to hinder, obstruct or interfere with an employment standards officer conducting an investigation or inspection.

(12) Same — No person shall,

(a) refuse to answer questions on matters that an employment standards officer thinks may be relevant to an investigation or inspection; or

(b) provide an employment standards officer with information on matters the officer thinks may be relevant to an investigation or inspection that the person knows to be false or misleading.

(13) Separate inquiries — No person shall prevent or attempt to prevent an employment standards officer from making inquiries of any person separate and apart from another person under clause (6)(e).

2006, c. 19, Sched. M, s. 1(2)

91.1 (1) Self-audit — An employment standards officer may, by giving written notice, require an employer to conduct an examination of the employer's records, practices or both to determine whether the employer is in compliance with one or more provisions of this Act or the regulations.

(2) Examination and report — If an employer is required to conduct an examination under subsection (1), the employer shall conduct the examination and report the results of the examination to the employment standards officer in accordance with the notice and the requirements of this section.

(3) Notice — A notice given under subsection (1) shall specify,

  (a) the period to be covered by the examination;

  (b) the provision or provisions of this Act or the regulations to be covered by the examination; and

  (c) the date by which the employer must provide a report of the results of the examination to the employment standards officer.

(4) Same — A notice given under subsection (1) may specify,

  (a) the method to be used in carrying out the examination;

  (b) the format of the report; and

  (c) such information to be included in the employer's report as the employment standards officer considers appropriate.

(5) Same — A notice given under subsection (1) may,

  (a) require the employer to include in the report to the employment standards officer an assessment of whether the employer has complied with this Act or the regulations;

  (b) require the employer to include in the report to the employment standards officer an assessment of whether one or more employees are owed wages if, pursuant to clause (a), the employer has included an assessment that the employer has not complied with this Act or the regulations; and

(c) require the employer to pay wages owed if, pursuant to clause (b), the employer assesses that one or more employees are owed wages.

(6) Report — unpaid wages — If the employer's report includes an assessment that one or more employees are owed wages, the employer shall include the following in the report to the employment standards officer:

1. The name of every employee who is owed wages and the amount of wages owed to the employee.

2. An explanation of how the amount of wages owed to the employee was determined.

3. If the notice under subsection (1) requires payment, proof of payment of the amount owed to the employee.

(7) Same — other non-compliance — If the employer's report includes an assessment that the employer has not complied with this Act or the regulations but no employees are owed wages as a result of the failure to comply, the employer shall include in the report a description of the measures that the employer has taken or will take to ensure that this Act or the regulations will be complied with.

(8) Orders — If an employer's report includes an assessment that the employer owes wages to one or more employees, or that the employer has otherwise not complied with this Act or the regulations, and the employment standards officer determines that the employer's assessment is correct, the officer may issue an order under section 103 or 108, as the officer determines is appropriate.

(9) Inspection, investigation, enforcement not precluded — Nothing in this section precludes an employment standards officer from conducting an investigation or inspection, and from taking such enforcement action under this Act as the officer considers appropriate.

(10) Same — Without restricting the generality of subsection (9), an employment standards officer may,

(a) conduct an investigation or inspection that covers a period or part of a period specified in the notice under subsection (1); and

(b) take such enforcement action under this Act as the officer considers appropriate, including issuing an order under section 103 or 108, if, despite the employer's report indicating that the employer did comply, the officer determines that the employer did not comply with this Act or the regulations during a period or part of a period specified in the notice under subsection (1).

(11) False information — No employer shall provide a report required under this section that contains information that the employer knows to be false or misleading.

2014, c. 10, Sched. 2, s. 6

92. (1) Warrant — A justice of the peace may issue a warrant authorizing an employment standards officer named in the warrant to enter premises specified in the warrant and to exercise any of the powers mentioned in subsection 91(6), if the justice of the peace is satisfied on information under oath that,

(a) the officer has been prevented from exercising a right of entry to the premises under subsection 91(1) or has been prevented from exercising a power under subsection 91(6);

(b) there are reasonable grounds to believe that the officer will be prevented from exercising a right of entry to the premises under subsection 91(1) or will be prevented from exercising a power under subsection 91(6); or

(c) there are reasonable grounds to believe that an offence under this Act or the regulations has been or is being committed and that information or other evidence will be obtained through the exercise of a power mentioned in subsection 91(6).

(2) Expiry of warrant — A warrant issued under this section shall name a date on which it expires, which date shall not be later than 30 days after the warrant is issued.

(3) Extension of time — Upon application without notice by the employment standards officer named in a warrant issued under this section, a justice of the peace may extend the date on which the warrant expires for an additional period of no more than 30 days.

(4) Use of force — An employment standards officer named in a warrant issued under this section may call upon a police officer for assistance in executing the warrant.

(5) Time of execution — A warrant issued under this section may be executed only between 8 a.m. and 8 p.m., unless the warrant specifies otherwise.

(6) Other matters — Subsections 91(4) to (13) apply with necessary modifications to an officer executing a warrant issued under this section.

(7) Same — Without restricting the generality of subsection (6), if a warrant is issued under this section, the matters on which an officer executing the warrant may question a person under clause 91(6)(e) are not limited to those that aid in the effective execution of the warrant but extend to any matters that the officer thinks may be relevant to the investigation or inspection.

2002, c. 18, Sched. J, s. 3(27); 2009, c. 32, s. 51(1), (2)

93. Posting of notices — An employment standards officer may require an employer to post and to keep posted in or upon the employer's premises in a conspicuous place or places where it is likely to come to the attention of the employer's employees,

(a) any notice relating to the administration or enforcement of this Act or the regulations that the officer considers appropriate; or

(b) a copy of a report or part of a report made by the officer concerning the results of an investigation or inspection.

94. Powers under the — *Canada Labour Code* If a regulation is made under the *Canada Labour Code* incorporating by reference all or part of this Act or a regulation under it, the Board and any person having powers under this Act may exercise the powers conferred under the *Canada Labour Code* regulation.

95. (1) Service of documents — Except as otherwise provided in sections 8, 17.1 and 22.1, where service of a document on a person is required or permitted under this Act, it may be served,

(a) in the case of service on an individual, personally, by leaving a copy of the document with the individual;

(b) in the case of service on a corporation, personally, by leaving a copy of the document with an officer, director or agent of the corporation, or with an individual at any place of business of the corporation who appears to be in control or management of the place of business;

(c) by mail addressed to the person's last known business or residential address using any method of mail delivery that permits the delivery to be verified;

(d) by fax or email if the person is equipped to receive the fax or email;

(e) by a courier service;

(f) by leaving the document, in a sealed envelope addressed to the person, with an individual who appears to be at least 16 years of age at the person's last known business or residential address; or

(g) in a manner ordered by the Board under subsection (8).

(2) Same — Service of a document by means described in clause (1)(a), (b) or (f) is effective when it is left with the individual.

(3) Same — Subject to subsection (6), service of a document by mail is effective five days after the document is mailed.

(4) Same — Subject to subsection (6), service of a document by a fax or email sent on a Saturday, Sunday or a public holiday or on any other day after 5 p.m. is effective on the next day that is not a Saturday, Sunday or public holiday.

(5) Same — Subject to subsection (6), service of a document by courier is effective two days after the courier takes the document.

(6) Same — Subsections (3), (4) and (5) do not apply if the person establishes that the service was not effective at the time specified in those subsections because of an absence, accident, illness or cause beyond the person's control.

(7) Same — If the Director considers that a manner of service other than one described in clauses (1)(a) to (f) is appropriate in the circumstances, the Director may direct the Board to consider the manner of service.

(8) Same — If the Board is directed to consider the manner of service, it may order that service be effected in the manner that the Board considers appropriate in the circumstances.

(9) Same — In an order for service, the Board shall specify when service in accordance with the order is effective.

(10) Proof of issuance and service — A certificate of service made by the employment standards officer who issued an order or notice under this Act is evidence of the issuance of the order or notice, the service of the order or notice on the person and its receipt by the person if, in the certificate, the officer,

    (a) certifies that the copy of the order or notice is a true copy of it;

    (b) certifies that the order or notice was served on the person; and

    (c) sets out in it the method of service used.

(11) Proof of service — A certificate of service made by the person who served a document under this Act is evidence of the service of the document on the person served and its receipt by that person if, in the certificate, the person who served the document,

(a) certifies that the copy of the document is a true copy of it;

(b) certifies that the document was served on the person; and

(c) sets out in it the method of service used.

2009, c. 9, s. 4

PART XXII — COMPLAINTS AND ENFORCEMENT

Complaints

96. (1) Complaints — A person alleging that this Act has been or is being contravened may file a complaint with the Ministry in a written or electronic form approved by the Director.

(2) Effect of failure to use form — A complaint that is not filed in a form approved by the Director shall be deemed not to have been filed.

(3) Limitation — A complaint regarding a contravention that occurred more than two years before the day on which the complaint was filed shall be deemed not to have been filed.

2001, c. 9, Sched. I, s. 1(18)

96.1 (1) [Repealed 2017, c. 22, Sched. 1, s. 53.]

97. (1) When civil proceeding not permitted — An employee who files a complaint under this Act with respect to an alleged failure to pay wages or comply with Part XIII (Benefit Plans) may not commence a civil proceeding with respect to the same matter.

(2) Same, wrongful dismissal — An employee who files a complaint under this Act alleging an entitlement to termination pay or severance pay may not commence a civil proceeding for wrongful dismissal if the complaint and the proceeding would relate to the same termination or severance of employment.

(3) Amount in excess of order — Subsections (1) and (2) apply even if,

(a) the amount alleged to be owing to the employee is greater than the amount for which an order can be issued under this Act; or

(b) in the civil proceeding, the employee is claiming only that part of the amount alleged to be owing that is in excess of the amount for which an order can be issued under this Act.

(4) Withdrawal of complaint — Despite subsections (1) and (2), an employee who has filed a complaint may commence a civil proceeding with respect to a matter described in those subsections if he or she withdraws the complaint within two weeks after it is filed.

98. (1) When complaint not permitted — An employee who commences a civil proceeding with respect to an alleged failure to pay wages or to comply with Part XIII (Benefit Plans) may not file a complaint with respect to the same matter or have such a complaint investigated.

(2) Same, wrongful dismissal — An employee who commences a civil proceeding for wrongful dismissal may not file a complaint alleging an entitlement to termination pay or severance pay or have such a complaint investigated if the proceeding and the complaint relate to the same termination or severance of employment.

Enforcement under Collective Agreement

99. (1) When collective agreement applies — If an employer is or has been bound by a collective agreement, this Act is enforceable against the employer as if it were part of the collective agreement with respect to an alleged contravention of this Act that occurs,

(a) when the collective agreement is or was in force;

(b) when its operation is or was continued under subsection 58(2) of the *Labour Relations Act, 1995*; or

(c) during the period that the parties to the collective agreement are or were prohibited by subsection 86(1) of the

Labour Relations Act, 1995 from unilaterally changing the terms and conditions of employment.

(2) Complaint not permitted — An employee who is represented by a trade union that is or was a party to a collective agreement may not file a complaint alleging a contravention of this Act that is enforceable under subsection (1) or have such a complaint investigated.

(3) Employee bound — An employee who is represented by a trade union that is or was a party to a collective agreement is bound by any decision of the trade union with respect to the enforcement of this Act under the collective agreement, including a decision not to seek that enforcement.

(4) Membership status irrelevant — Subsections (2) and (3) apply even if the employee is not a member of the trade union.

(5) Unfair representation — Nothing in subsection (3) or (4) prevents an employee from filing a complaint with the Board alleging that a decision of the trade union with respect to the enforcement of this Act contravenes section 74 of the *Labour Relations Act, 1995*.

(6) Exception — Despite subsection (2), the Director may permit an employee to file a complaint and may direct an employment standards officer to investigate it if the Director considers it appropriate in the circumstances.

100. (1) If arbitrator finds contravention — If an arbitrator finds that an employer has contravened this Act, the arbitrator may make any order against the employer that an employment standards officer could have made with respect to that contravention but the arbitrator may not issue a notice of contravention.

(2) Same: Part XIII — If an arbitrator finds that an employer has contravened Part XIII (Benefit Plans), the arbitrator may make any order that the Board could make under section 121.

(3) Directors and collective agreement — An arbitrator shall not require a director to pay an amount, take an action or refrain from taking an action under a collective agreement that the director could not be ordered to pay, take or refrain from taking in the absence of the collective agreement.

(4) Conditions respecting orders under this section — The following conditions apply with respect to an arbitrator's order under this section:

1. In an order requiring the payment of wages or compensation, the arbitrator may require that the amount of the wages or compensation be paid,

i. to the trade union that represents the employee or employees concerned, or

ii. directly to the employee or employees.

2. If the order requires the payment of wages, the order may be made for an amount greater than is permitted under subsection 103(4).

3. The order is not subject to review under section 116.

(5) Copy of decision to Director — When an arbitrator makes a decision with respect to an alleged contravention of this Act, the arbitrator shall provide a copy of it to the Director.

101. (1) Arbitration and s. 4 — This section applies if, during a proceeding before an arbitrator, other than the Board, concerning an alleged contravention of this Act, an issue is raised concerning whether the employer to whom the collective agreement applies or applied and another person are to be treated as one employer under section 4.

(2) Restriction — The arbitrator shall not decide the question of whether the employer and the other person are to be treated as one employer under section 4.

(3) Reference to Board — If the arbitrator finds it is necessary to make a finding concerning the application of section 4, the arbitrator shall refer that question to the Board by giving written notice to the Board.

(4) Content of notice — The notice to the Board shall,

(a) state that an issue has arisen in an arbitration proceeding with respect to whether the employer and another person are to be treated as one employer under section 4; and

(b) set out the decisions made by the arbitrator on the other matters in dispute.

(5) Decision by Board — The Board shall decide whether the employer and the other person are one employer under section 4, but shall not vary any decision of the arbitrator concerning the other matters in dispute.

(6) Order — Subject to subsection (7), the Board may make an order against the employer and, if it finds that the employer and the other person are one employer under section 4, it may make an order against the other person.

(7) Exception — The Board shall not require the other person to pay an amount or take or refrain from taking an action under a collective agreement that the other person could not be ordered to pay, take or refrain from taking in the absence of the collective agreement.

(8) Application — Section 100 applies, with necessary modifications, with respect to an order under this section.

Enforcement by Employment Standards Officer

101.1 (1) Settlement by employment standards officer — An employment standards officer assigned to investigate a complaint may attempt to effect a settlement.

(2) Effect of settlement — If the employer and employee agree to a settlement under this section and do what they agreed to do under it,

(a) the settlement is binding on them;

(b) the complaint is deemed to have been withdrawn;

(c) the investigation is terminated; and

(d) any proceeding respecting the contravention alleged in the complaint, other than a prosecution, is terminated.

(3) Application of s. 112(4), (5), (7) and (9) — Subsections 112(4), (5), (7) and (9) apply, with necessary modifications, in respect of a settlement under this section.

(4) Application to void settlement — If, upon application to the Board, the employee or employer demonstrates that he, she or it entered into a settlement under this section as a result of fraud or coercion,

(a) the settlement is void;

(b) the complaint is deemed never to have been withdrawn;

(c) the investigation of the complaint is resumed; and

(d) any proceeding respecting the contravention alleged in the complaint that was terminated is resumed.

2010, c. 16, Sched. 9, s. 1(9)

101.2 Settlement by labour relations officer, etc. — (1) Attempt to effect settlement — Where a complaint has been assigned for investigation, a labour relations officer or an individual who is employed in the Ministry and who reports to the Director of Dispute Resolution Services may, on the Director's request, attempt to effect a settlement.

(2) Application of s. 101.1(2) to (4) — Subsections 101.1(2) to (4) apply, with necessary modifications, in respect of a settlement under this section.

(3) Labour relations officers, etc., not compellable — A person referred to in subsection (1) is not a competent or compellable witness in a civil proceeding or a proceeding under this Act respecting any information given or obtained, statements made or received, or records or other things produced or received under this Act.

(4) Records — A person referred to in subsection (1) shall not be compelled in a civil proceeding or a proceeding under this Act to produce any record or other things he or she has made or received under this Act.

(5) Confidentiality — A person who attempts to effect a settlement under this section shall not disclose to any person any information received in the course of doing so, except for a report as to whether a settlement was effected or not.

(6) Definition — In this section,

"Director of Dispute Resolution Services" has the meaning assigned by subsection 1(1) of the *Labour Relations Act, 1995*.

(7) Repeal — This section is repealed on the second anniversary of the day subsection 1(9) of Schedule 9 to the *Open for Business Act, 2010* comes into force.

2010, c. 16, Sched. 9, s. 1(9)

102. (1) Meeting may be required — An employment standards officer may, after giving at least 15 days written notice, require any of the persons referred to in subsection (2) to attend a meeting with the officer in the following circumstances:

1. The officer is investigating a complaint against an employer.

2. The officer, while inspecting a place under section 91 or 92, comes to have reasonable grounds to believe that an employer has contravened this Act or the regulations with respect to an employee.

3. The officer acquires information that suggests to him or her the possibility that an employer may have contravened this Act or the regulations with respect to an employee.

4. The officer wishes to determine whether the employer of an employee who resides in the employer's residence is complying with this Act.

(2) Attendees — Any of the following persons may be required to attend the meeting:

1. The employee.

2. The employer.

3. If the employer is a corporation, a director or employee of the corporation.

(3) Notice — The notice referred to in subsection (1) shall specify the time and place at which the person is to attend and shall be served on the person in accordance with section 95.

(4) Documents — The employment standards officer may require the person to bring to the meeting or make available for the meeting any records or other documents specified in the notice.

(5) Same — The employment standards officer may give directions on how to make records or other documents available for the meeting.

(6) Compliance — A person who receives a notice under this section shall comply with it.

(7) Use of technology — The employment standards officer may direct that a meeting under this section be held using technology, including but not limited to teleconference and videoconference technology, that allows the persons participating in the meeting to participate concurrently.

(8) Same — Where an employment standards officer gives directions under subsection (7) respecting a meeting, he or she shall include in the notice referred to in subsection (1) such information additional to that required by subsection (3) as the officer considers appropriate.

(9) Same — Participation in a meeting by means described in subsection (7) is attendance at the meeting for the purposes of this section.

(10) Determination if person fails to attend, etc. — If a person served with a notice under this section fails to attend the meeting or fails to bring or make available any records or other documents as required by the notice, the officer may determine whether an employer has contravened or is contravening this Act on the basis of the following factors:

1. If the employer failed to comply with the notice,

    i. any evidence or submissions provided by or on behalf of the employer before the meeting, and

    ii. any evidence or submissions provided by or on behalf of the employee before or during the meeting.

2. If the employee failed to comply with the notice,

    i. any evidence or submissions provided by or on behalf of the employee before the meeting, and

    ii. any evidence or submissions provided by or on behalf of the employer before or during the meeting.

3. Any other factors that the officer considers relevant.

(11) Employer includes representative — For the purposes of subsection (10), if the employer is a corporation, a reference to an employer includes a director or employee who was served with a notice requiring him or her to attend the meeting or to bring or make available any records or other documents.

2009, c. 9, s. 5; 2009, c. 32, s. 51(3); 2010, c. 16, Sched. 9, s. 1(10)

102.1 (1) Time for response — An employment standards officer may, in any of the following circumstances and after giving notice, require an employee or an employer to provide evidence or submissions to the officer within the time that he or she specifies in the notice:

1. The officer is investigating a complaint against an employer.

2. The officer, while inspecting a place under section 91 or 92, comes to have reasonable grounds to believe that an employer has contravened this Act or the regulations with respect to an employee.

3. The officer acquires information that suggests to him or her the possibility that an employer may have contravened this Act or the regulations with respect to an employee.

4. The officer wishes to determine whether the employer of an employee who resides in the employer's residence is complying with this Act.

(2) Service of notice — The notice shall be served on the employer or employee in accordance with section 95.

(3) Determination if person fails to respond — If a person served with a notice under this section fails to provide evidence or submissions as required by the notice, the officer may determine whether the employer has contravened or is contravening this Act on the basis of the following factors:

1. Any evidence or submissions provided by or on behalf of the employer or the employee before the notice was served.

2. Any evidence or submissions provided by or on behalf of the employer or the employee in response to and within the time specified in the notice.

3. Any other factors that the officer considers relevant.

2010, c. 16, Sched. 9, s. 1(11)

103. (1) Order to pay wages — If an employment standards officer finds that an employer owes wages to an employee, the officer may,

(a) arrange with the employer that the employer pay the wages directly to the employee;

(a.1) order the employer to pay wages to the employee; or

(b) order the employer to pay the amount of wages to the Director in trust.

(2) Administrative costs — An order issued under clause (1)(b) shall also require the employer to pay to the Director in trust an amount for administrative costs equal to the greater of $100 and 10 per cent of the wages owing.

(3) If more than one employee — A single order may be issued with respect to wages owing to more than one employee.

(4) [Repealed 2014, c. 10, Sched. 2, s. 7(2).]

(4.1) [Repealed 2014, c. 10, Sched. 2, s. 7(2).]

(5) Contents of order — The order shall contain information setting out the nature of the amount found to be owing to the employee or be accompanied by that information.

(6) Service of order — The order shall be served on the employer in accordance with section 95.

(7) Notice to employee — An employment standards officer who issues an order with respect to an employee under this section shall advise the employee of its issuance by serving a letter, in accordance with section 95, on the employee.

(7.1) [Repealed 2009, c. 9, s. 6.]

(7.2) [Repealed 2009, c. 9, s. 6.]

(8) Compliance — Every employer against whom an order is issued under this section shall comply with it according to its terms.

(9) Effect of order — If an employer fails to apply under section 116 for a review of an order issued under this section within the time allowed for applying for that review, the order becomes final and binding against the employer.

(10) Same — Subsection (9) applies even if a review hearing is held under this Act to determine another person's liability for the wages that are the subject of the order.

2001, c. 9, Sched. I, s. 1(20); 2009, c. 9, s. 6; 2014, c. 10, Sched. 2, s. 7; 2017, c. 22, Sched. 1, s. 54

104. (1) Orders for compensation or reinstatement — If an employment standards officer finds a contravention of any of the following Parts with respect to an employee, the officer may order that the employee be compensated for any loss he or she incurred as a result of the contravention or that he or she be reinstated or that he or she be both compensated and reinstated:

1. Part XIV (Leaves of Absence).

2. Part XVI (Lie Detectors).

3. Part XVII (Retail Business Establishments).

4. Part XVIII (Reprisal).

(2) Order to hire — An employment standards officer who finds a contravention of Part XVI may order that an applicant for employment or an applicant to be a police officer be hired by an employer as defined in that Part or may order that he or she be compensated by an employer as defined in that Part or that he or she be both hired and compensated.

(3) Terms of orders — If an order made under this section requires a person to compensate an employee, it shall also require the person to,

(a) pay to the Director in trust,

(i) the amount of the compensation, and

(ii) an amount for administration costs equal to the greater of $100 and 10 per cent of the amount of compensation; or

(b) pay the amount of the compensation to the employee.

(4) How orders apply — Subsections 103(3) and (5) to (9) apply, with necessary modifications, with respect to orders issued under this section.

2009, c. 9, s. 7; 2017, c. 22, Sched. 1, s. 55

105. (1) Employee cannot be found — If an employment standards officer has arranged with an employer or ordered an employer to pay wages under clause 103 (1) (a) or (a.1) to the employee and the employer is unable to locate the employee despite having made reasonable efforts to do so, the employer shall pay the wages to the Director in trust.

(2) Settlements — If an employment standards officer has received money for an employee under a settlement but the employee cannot be located, the money shall be paid to the Director in trust.

(3) When money vests in Crown — Money paid to or held by the Director in trust under this section vests in the Crown but may, without interest, be paid out to the employee, the employee's estate or such other person as the Director considers is entitled to it.

2017, c. 22, Sched. 1, s. 56

106. (1) Order against director, Part XX — If an employment standards officer makes an order against an employer that wages be paid, he or she may make an order to pay wages for which directors are liable under Part XX against some or all of the directors of the employer and may serve a copy of the order in accordance with section 95 on them together with a copy of the order to pay against the employer.

(2) Effect of order — If the directors do not comply with the order or do not apply to have it reviewed, the order becomes final and binding against those directors even though a review hearing is held to determine another person's liability under this Act.

(3) Orders, insolvent employer — If an employer is insolvent and the employee has caused a claim for unpaid wages to be filed with the receiver appointed by a court with respect to the employer or with the employer's trustee in bankruptcy, and the claim has not been paid, the employment standards officer may issue an order to pay wages for which directors are liable under Part XX against some or all of the directors and shall serve it on them in accordance with section 95.

(4) Procedure — Subsection (2) applies with necessary modifications to an order made under subsection (3).

(5) Maximum liability — Nothing in this section increases the maximum liability of a director beyond the amounts set out in section 81.

(6) Payment to Director — At the discretion of the Director, a director who is subject to an order under this section may be ordered to pay the wages in trust to the Director.

(7) [Repealed 2009, c. 9, s. 8(3).]

(8) [Repealed 2009, c. 9, s. 8(3).]

(9) [Repealed 2009, c. 9, s. 8(3).]

2001, c. 9, Sched. I, s. 1(21); 2009, c. 9, s. 8

107. (1) Further order, Part XX — An employment standards officer may make an order to pay wages for which directors are liable under Part XX against some or all of the directors of an employer who were not the subject of an order under section 106, and may serve it on them in accordance with section 95,

(a) after an employment standards officer has made an order against the employer under section 103 that wages be paid and they have not been paid and the employer has not applied to have the order reviewed;

(b) after an employment standards officer has made an order against directors under subsection 106(1) or (3) and the amount has not been paid and the employer or the directors have not applied to have it reviewed;

(c) after the Board has issued, amended or affirmed an order under section 119 if the order, as issued, amended or affirmed, requires the employer or the directors to pay wages and the amount set out in the order has not been paid.

(2) Payment to Director — At the discretion of the Director, a director who is subject to an order under this section may be ordered to pay the wages in trust to the Director.

(3) [Repealed 2009, c. 9, s. 9(2).]

2009, c. 9, s. 9

108. (1) Compliance order — If an employment standards officer finds that a person has contravened a provision of this Act or the regulations, the officer may,

(a) order that the person cease contravening the provision;

(b) order what action the person shall take or refrain from taking in order to comply with the provision; and

(c) specify a date by which the person must do so.

(2) Payment may not be required — No order under this section shall require the payment of wages, fees or compensation.

(3) Other means not a bar — Nothing in subsection (2) precludes an employment standards officer from issuing an order under section 74.14, 74.16, 74.17, 103, 104, 106 or 107 and an order under this section in respect of the same contravention.

(4) Application of s. 103(6) to (9) — Subsections 103(6) to (9) apply with respect to orders issued under this section with necessary modifications, including but not limited to the following:

1. A reference to an employer includes a reference to a client of a temporary help agency.

2. A reference to an employee includes a reference to an assignment employee or prospective assignment employee.

(5) Injunction proceeding — At the instance of the Director, the contravention of an order made under subsection (1) may be restrained upon an application, made without notice, to a judge of the Superior Court of Justice.

(6) Same — Subsection (5) applies with respect to a contravention of an order in addition to any other remedy or penalty for its contravention.

2009, c. 9, s. 10; 2017, c. 22, Sched. 1, s. 57

109. (1) Money paid when no review — Money paid to the Director under an order under section 74.14, 74.16, 74.17, 103, 104, 106 or 107 shall be paid to the person with respect to whom the order was issued unless an application for review is made under section 116 within the period required under that section.

(2) Money distributed rateably — If the money paid to the Director under one of those orders is not enough to pay all of the persons entitled to it under the order the full amount to which they are entitled, the Director shall distribute that money, including money received with respect to administrative costs, to the persons in proportion to their entitlement.

(3) No proceeding against Director — No proceeding shall be instituted against the Director for acting in compliance with this section.

2009, c. 9, s. 11

110. (1) Refusal to issue order — If, after a person files a complaint alleging a contravention of this Act in respect of which an order could be issued under section 74.14, 74.16, 74.17, 103, 104 or 108, an employment standards officer assigned to investigate the complaint refuses to issue such an order, the officer shall, in accordance with section 95, serve a letter on the person advising the person of the refusal.

(2) Deemed refusal — If no order is issued with respect to a complaint described in subsection (1) within two years after it was filed, an employment standards officer shall be deemed to have refused to issue an order and to have served a letter on the person advising the person of the refusal on the last day of the second year.

2009, c. 9, s. 12

111. (1) Time limit on recovery, employee's complaint — If an employee files a complaint alleging a contravention of this Act or the regulations, the employment standards officer investigating the complaint may not issue an order for wages that became due to the employee under the provision that was the subject of the complaint or any other provision of this Act or the regulations if the wages became due more than two years before the complaint was filed.

(2) Same, another employee's complaint — If, in the course of investigating a complaint, an employment standards officer finds that an employer has contravened this Act or the regulations with respect to an employee who did not file a complaint, the officer may not issue an order for wages that became due to that employee as a result of that contravention if the wages became due more than two years before the complaint was filed.

(3) Same, inspection — If an employment standards officer finds during an inspection that an employer has contravened this Act or the regulations with respect to an employee, the officer may not issue an order for wages that became due to the employee more than two years before the officer commenced the inspection.

(3.1) [Repealed 2014, c. 10, Sched. 2, s. 8(6).]

(3.2) [Repealed 2014, c. 10, Sched. 2, s. 8(6).]

(4) [Repealed 2014, c. 10, Sched. 2, s. 8(6).]

(5) [Repealed 2014, c. 10, Sched. 2, s. 8(6).]

(6) [Repealed 2014, c. 10, Sched. 2, s. 8(6).]

(7) [Repealed 2014, c. 10, Sched. 2, s. 8(6).]

(8) [Repealed 2014, c. 10, Sched. 2, s. 8(6).]

2001, c. 9, Sched. I, s. 1(22); 2002, c. 18, Sched. J, s. 3(28); 2014, c. 10, Sched. 2, s. 8

Settlements

112. (1) Settlement — Subject to subsection (8), if an employee and an employer who have agreed to a settlement respecting a contravention or alleged contravention of this Act inform an employment standards officer in writing of the terms of the settlement and do what they agreed to do under it,

(a) the settlement is binding on the parties;

(b) any complaint filed by the employee respecting the contravention or alleged contravention is deemed to have been withdrawn;

(c) any order made in respect of the contravention or alleged contravention is void; and

(d) any proceeding, other than a prosecution, respecting the contravention or alleged contravention is terminated.

(2) Compliance orders — Clause (1)(c) does not apply with respect to an order issued under section 108.

(3) Notices of contravention — This section does not apply with respect to a notice of contravention.

(4) Payment by officer — If an employment standards officer receives money for an employee under this section, the officer may pay it directly to the employee or to the Director in trust.

(5) Same — If money is paid in trust to the Director under subsection (4), the Director shall pay it to the employee.

(6) Administrative costs and collector fees — If the settlement concerns an order to pay, the Director is, despite clause (1) (c), entitled to be paid,

(a) that proportion of the administrative costs that were ordered to be paid that is the same as the proportion of the amount of wages, fees or compensation ordered to be paid that the employee is entitled to receive under the settlement; and

(b) that proportion of the collector's fees and disbursements that were added to the amount of the order under subsection 128 (2) that is the same as the proportion of the amount of wages, fees or compensation ordered to be paid that the employee is entitled to receive under the settlement.

(7) Restrictions on settlements — No person shall enter into a settlement which would permit or require that person or any other person to engage in future contraventions of this Act.

(8) Application to void settlement — If, upon application to the Board, the employee demonstrates that he or she entered into the settlement as a result of fraud or coercion,

(a) the settlement is void;

(b) the complaint is deemed never to have been withdrawn;

(c) any order made in respect of the contravention or alleged contravention is reinstated;

(d) any proceedings respecting the contravention or alleged contravention that were terminated shall be resumed.

(9) Application to Part XVIII.1 — For the purposes of the application of this section in respect of Part XVIII.1, the following modifications apply:

1. A reference to an employer includes a reference to a client of a temporary help agency.

2. A reference to an employee includes a reference to an assignment employee or prospective assignment employee.

2009, c. 9, s. 13; 2017, c. 22, Sched. 1, s. 58

Notices of Contravention

113. (1) Notice of contravention — If an employment standards officer believes that a person has contravened a provision of this Act, the officer may issue a notice to the person setting out the officer's belief and specifying the amount of the penalty for the contravention.

(1.1) Amount of penalty — The amount of the penalty shall be determined in accordance with the regulations.

(1.2) Penalty within range — If a range has been prescribed as the penalty for a contravention, the employment standards officer shall determine the amount of the penalty in accordance with the prescribed criteria, if any.

(2) Information — The notice shall contain or be accompanied by information setting out the nature of the contravention.

(3) Service — A notice issued under this section shall be served on the person in accordance with section 95.

(4) [Repealed 2009, c. 9, s. 14(1).]

(5) Deemed contravention — The person shall be deemed to have contravened the provision set out in the notice if,

(a) the person fails to apply to the Board for a review of the notice within the period set out in subsection 122(1); or

(b) the person applies to the Board for a review of the notice and the Board finds that the person contravened the provision set out in the notice.

(6) Penalty — A person who is deemed to have contravened this Act shall pay to the Minister of Finance the penalty for the deemed contravention and the amount of any collector's fees and disbursements added to the amount under subsection 128(2).

(6.1) Same — The payment under subsection (6) shall be made within 30 days after the day the notice of contravention was served or, if the notice of contravention is appealed, within 30 days after the Board finds that there was a contravention.

(6.2) Publication re notice of contraventions — If a person, including an individual, is deemed under subsection (5) to have contravened this Act after being issued a notice of contravention, the Director may publish or otherwise make available to the general public the name of the person, a description of the deemed contravention, the date of the deemed contravention and the penalty for the deemed contravention.

(6.3) Internet publication — Authority to publish under subsection (6.2) includes authority to publish on the Internet.

(6.4) Disclosure — Any disclosure made under subsection (6.2) shall be deemed to be in compliance with clause 42 (1) (e) of the *Freedom of Information and Protection of Privacy Act.*

(7) Other means not a bar — An employment standards officer may issue a notice to a person under this section even though an order has been or may be issued against the person under section 74.14, 74.16, 74.17, 103, 104 or 108 or the person has been or may be prosecuted for or convicted of an offence with respect to the same contravention.

(8) Trade union — This section does not apply with respect to a contravention of this Act with respect to an employee who is represented by a trade union.

(9) Director — This section does not apply with respect to a contravention of this Act by a director or officer of an employer that is a corporation.

2001, c. 9, Sched. I, s. 1(23); 2002, c. 18, Sched. J, s. 3(29); 2009, c. 9, s. 14; 2017, c. 22, Sched. 1, s. 59

Limitation Period

114. (1) Limitation period re orders and notices — An employment standards officer shall not issue an order to pay wages, fees or compensation or a notice of contravention with respect to a contravention of this Act concerning an employee,

(a) if the employee filed a complaint about the contravention, more than two years after the complaint was filed;

(b) if the employee did not file a complaint but another employee of the same employer did file a complaint, more than two years after the other employee filed his or her complaint if the officer discovered the contravention with respect to the employee while investigating the complaint; or

(c) if the employee did not file a complaint and clause (b) does not apply, more than two years after an employment standards officer commenced an inspection with respect to the employee's employer for the purpose of determining whether a contravention occurred.

(2) Complaints from different employees — If an employee files a complaint about a contravention of this Act by his or her employer and another employee of the same employer has previously filed a complaint about substantially the same contravention, subsection (1) shall be applied as if the employee who filed the subsequent complaint did not file a complaint.

(3) Exception — Subsection (2) does not apply if, prior to the day on which the subsequent complaint was filed, an employment standards officer had, with respect to the earlier complaint, already issued an order or advised the complainant that he or she was refusing to issue an order.

(4) Restriction on rescission or amendment — An employment standards officer shall not amend or rescind an order to pay wages, fees or compensation after the last day on which he or she could have issued that order under subsection (1) unless the employer against whom the order was issued and the employee with respect to whom it was issued consent to the rescission or amendment.

(5) Same — An employment standards officer shall not amend or rescind a notice of contravention after the last day on which he or she could have issued that notice under subsection (1) unless the employer against whom the notice was issued consents to the rescission or amendment.

(6) Application to Part XVIII.1 — For the purposes of the application of this section in respect of Part XVIII.1, the following modifications apply:

1. A reference to an employer includes a reference to a client of a temporary help agency.

2. A reference to an employee includes a reference to an assignment employee or prospective assignment employee.

2001, c. 9, Sched. I, s. 1(24); 2009, c. 9, s. 15; 2017, c. 22, Sched. 1, s. 60

115. (1) Meaning of "substantially the same" — For the purposes of section 114, contraventions with respect to two employees are substantially the same if both employees became entitled to recover money under this Act as a result of the employer's failure to comply with the same provision of this Act or the regulations or with identical or virtually identical provisions of their employment contracts.

(1.1) Application to Part XVIII.1 — For the purposes of the application of subsection (1) in respect of Part XVIII.1, the following modifications apply:

1. A reference to an employer includes a reference to a client of a temporary help agency.

2. A reference to an employee includes a reference to an assignment employee or prospective assignment employee.

(2) Exception, payment of wages, deductions — Despite subsection (1), contraventions with respect to two employees are not substantially the same merely because both employees became entitled to recover money under this Act as a result of a contravention of section 11 or 13 if the contravention of the section was with respect to wages due under different provisions of this Act or the regulations or under provisions of their employment contracts which are not identical or virtually identical.

2009, c. 9, s. 16; 2017, c. 22, Sched. 1, s. 61

PART XXIII — REVIEWS BY THE BOARD

Reviews of Orders

115.1 Interpretation — In this Part, a reference to an employee includes a reference to an assignment employee or a prospective assignment employee.

2009, c. 9, s. 17; 2017, c. 22, Sched. 1, s. 62

116. (1) Review — A person against whom an order has been issued under section 74.14, 74.16, 74.17, 103, 104, 106, 107 or 108 is entitled to a review of the order by the Board if, within the period set out in subsection (4), the person,

(a) applies to the Board in writing for a review;

(b) in the case of an order under section 74.14 or 103, pays the amount owing under the order to the Director in trust or provides the Director with an irrevocable letter of credit acceptable to the Director in that amount; and

(c) in the case of an order under section 74.16, 74.17 or 104, pays the lesser of the amount owing under the order and $10,000 to the Director in trust or provides the Director with an irrevocable letter of credit acceptable to the Director in that amount.

(2) Employee seeks review of order — If an order has been issued under section 74.14, 74.16, 74.17, 103 or 104 with respect to an employee, the employee is entitled to a review of the order by the Board if, within the period set out in subsection (4), the employee applies to the Board in writing for a review.

(3) Employee seeks review of refusal — If an employee has filed a complaint alleging a contravention of this Act or the regulations and an order could be issued under section 74.14, 74.16, 74.17, 103, 104 or 108 with respect to such a contravention, the employee is entitled to a review of an employment standards officer's refusal to issue such an order if, within the period set out in subsection (4), the employee applies to the Board in writing for such a review.

(4) Period for applying for review — An application for a review under subsection (1), (2) or (3) shall be made within 30 days after the day on which the order, letter advising of the order or letter advising of the refusal to issue an order, as the case may be, is served.

(5) Extension of time — The Board may extend the time for applying for a review under this section if it considers it appropriate in the circumstances to do so and, in the case of an application under subsection (1),

    (a) the Board has enquired of the Director whether the Director has paid to the employee the wages, fees or compensation that were the subject of the order and is satisfied that the Director has not done so; and

    (b) the Board has enquired of the Director whether a collector's fees or disbursements have been added to the amount of the order under subsection 128(2) and, if so, the Board is satisfied that fees and disbursements were paid by the person against whom the order was issued.

(6) Hearing — Subject to subsection 118(2), the Board shall hold a hearing for the purposes of the review.

(7) Parties — The following are parties to the review:

1. The applicant for the review of an order.

2. If the person against whom an order was issued applies for the review, the employee with respect to whom the order was issued.

3. If the employee applies for the review of an order, the person against whom the order was issued.

4. If the employee applies for a review of a refusal to issue an order under section 74.14, 74.16, 74.17, 103, 104 or 108, the person against whom such an order could be issued.

5. If a director of a corporation applies for the review, the applicant and each director, other than the applicant, on whom the order was served.

6. The Director.

7. Any other persons specified by the Board.

(8) Parties given full opportunity — The Board shall give the parties full opportunity to present their evidence and make their submissions.

(9) Practice and procedure for review — The Board shall determine its own practice and procedure with respect to a review under this section.

2001, c. 9, Sched. I, s. 1(25), (26); 2009, c. 9, s. 18

117. (1) Money held in trust pending review — This section applies if money with respect to an order to pay wages, fees or compensation is paid to the Director in trust and the person against whom the order was issued applies to the Board for a review of the order.

(2) Interest-bearing account — The money held in trust shall be held in an interest-bearing account while the application for review is pending.

(3) If settlement — If the matter is settled under section 112 or 120, the amount held in trust shall, subject to subsection 112(6) or 120(6), be paid out in accordance with the settlement, with interest, calculated at the rate and in the manner determined by the Director under subsection 88(5).

(4) If no settlement — If the matter is not settled under section 112 or 120, the amount paid into trust shall be paid out in accordance with the Board's decision together with interest calculated at the rate and in the manner determined by the Director under subsection 88(5).

2009, c. 9, s. 19

118. (1) Rules of practice — The chair of the Board may make rules,

    (a) governing the Board's practice and procedure and the exercise of its powers; and

    (b) providing for forms and their use.

(2) Expedited decisions — The chair of the Board may make rules to expedite decisions about the Board's jurisdiction, and those rules,

    (a) may provide that the Board is not required to hold a hearing; and

    (b) despite subsection 116(8), may limit the extent to which the Board is required to give full opportunity to the parties to present their evidence and to make their submissions.

(3) Effective date of rules under subs. (2) — A rule made under subsection (2) comes into force on the day determined by order of the Lieutenant Governor in Council.

(4) Conflict with *Statutory Powers Procedure Act* — If there is a conflict between the rules made under this section and the *Statutory Powers Procedure Act,* the rules under this section prevail.

(5) Rules not regulations — Rules made under this section are not regulations within the meaning of Part III (Regulations) of the *Legislation Act, 2006*.

2001, c. 9, Sched. I, s. 1(27); 2006, c. 19, Sched. M, s. 1(3); 2006, c. 21, Sched. F, s. 136(1), Table 1

119. (1) Powers of Board — This section sets out the Board's powers in a review under section 116.

(2) Persons to represent groups — If a group of parties have the same interest or substantially the same interest, the Board may designate one or more of the parties in the group to represent the group.

(3) Quorum — The chair or a vice-chair of the Board constitutes a quorum for the purposes of this section and is sufficient for the exercise of the jurisdiction and powers of the Board under it.

(4) Posting of notices — The Board may require a person to post and to keep posted any notices that the Board considers appropriate even if the person is not a party to the review.

(5) Same — If the Board requires a person to post and keep posted notices, the person shall post the notices and keep them posted in a conspicuous place or places in or upon the person's premises where it is likely to come to the attention of other persons having an interest in the review.

(6) Powers of Board — The Board may, with necessary modifications, exercise the powers conferred on an employment standards officer under this Act and may substitute its findings for those of the officer who issued the order or refused to issue the order.

(7) Dealing with order — Without restricting the generality of subsection (6),

(a) on a review of an order, the Board may amend, rescind or affirm the order or issue a new order; and

(b) on a review of a refusal to issue an order, the Board may issue an order or affirm the refusal.

(8) Labour relations officers — Any time after an application for review is made, the Board may direct a labour relations officer to examine any records or other documents and make any inquiries it considers appropriate, but it shall not direct an employment standards officer to do so.

(9) Powers of labour relations officers — Sections 91 and 92 apply with necessary modifications with respect to a labour relations officer acting under subsection (8).

(10) Wages, fees or compensation owing — Subsection (11) applies if, during a review of an order requiring the payment of wages, fees or compensation or a review of a refusal to issue such an order,

(a) the Board finds that a specified amount of wages, fees or compensation is owing; or

(b) there is no dispute that a specified amount of wages, fees or compensation is owing.

(11) Interim order — The Board shall affirm the order to the extent of the specified amount or issue an order to the extent of that amount, even though the review is not yet completed.

(12) Interest — If the Board issues, amends or affirms an order or issues a new order requiring the payment of wages, fees or compensation, the Board may order the person against whom the order was issued to pay interest at the rate and calculated in the manner determined by the Director under subsection 88(5).

(13) Decision final — A decision of the Board is final and binding upon the parties to the review and any other parties as the Board may specify.

(14) Judicial review — Nothing in subsection (13) prevents a court from reviewing a decision of the Board under this section, but a decision of the Board concerning the interpretation of this Act shall not be overturned unless the decision is unreasonable.

2009, c. 9, s. 20

120. (1) Settlement through labour relations officer — The Board may authorize a labour relations officer to attempt to effect a settlement of the matters raised in an application for review under section 116.

(2) Certain matters not bar to settlement — A settlement may be effected under this section even if,

(a) the employment standards officer who issued the order or refused to issue the order does not participate in the settlement discussions or is not advised of the discussions or settlement; or

(b) the review under section 116 has started.

(3) Compliance orders — A settlement respecting a compliance order shall not be made if the Director has not approved the terms of the settlement.

(4) Effect of settlement — If the parties to a settlement under this section do what they agreed to do under the settlement,

(a) the settlement is binding on the parties;

(b) if the review concerns an order, the order is void; and

(c) the review is terminated.

(5) Application to void settlement — If, upon application to the Board, the employee demonstrates that he or she entered into the settlement as a result of fraud or coercion,

(a) the settlement is void;

(b) if the review concerned an order, the order is reinstated; and

(c) the review shall be resumed.

(6) Distribution — If the order that was the subject of the application required the payment of money to the Director in trust, the Director,

(a) shall distribute the amount held in trust with respect to wages, fees or compensation in accordance with the settlement; and

(b) despite clause (4) (b), is entitled to be paid,

(i) that proportion of the administrative costs that were ordered to be paid that is the same as the proportion of the amount of wages, fees or compensation ordered to be paid that the employee is entitled to receive under the settlement, and

(ii) that proportion of the collector's fees and disbursements that were added to the amount of the order under subsection 128 (2) that is the same as the proportion of the amount of wages, fees or compensation ordered to be paid that the employee is entitled to receive under the settlement.

2009, c. 9, s. 21; 2017, c. 22, Sched. 1, s. 63

Referral of Matter under Part XIII

121. (1) Referral — If, as a result of a complaint or otherwise, the Director comes to believe that an employer, an organization of employers, an organization of employees or a person acting directly on behalf of any of them may have contravened Part XIII (Benefit Plans), the Director may refer the matter to the Board.

(2) Hearing — If a matter is referred to the Board under subsection (1), the Board shall hold a hearing and determine whether the employer, organization or person contravened Part XIII.

(3) Powers of Board — If the Board determines that the employer, organization or person acting directly on behalf of an employer or organization contravened Part XIII, the Board may order the employer, organization or person,

(a) to cease contravening that Part and to take whatever action the Board considers necessary to that end; and

(b) to compensate any person or persons who may have suffered loss or been disadvantaged as a result of the contravention.

(4) Certain review provisions applicable — Subsections 116(8) and (9), 118(1) and (3) to (5), 119(1) to (5), (8), (9), (13) and (14) and 120(1), (4) and (5) apply, with necessary modifications, with respect to a proceeding under this section.

Review of Notice of Contravention

122. (1) Review of notice of contravention — A person against whom a notice of contravention has been issued under section 113 may dispute the notice if the person makes a written application to the Board for a review,

(a) within 30 days after the date of service of the notice; or

(b) if the Board considers it appropriate in the circumstances to extend the time for applying, within the period specified by the Board.

(2) Hearing — The Board shall hold a hearing for the purposes of the review.

(3) Parties — The parties to the review are the person against whom the notice was issued and the Director.

(4) Onus — On a review under this section, the onus is on the Director to establish, on a balance of probabilities, that the person against whom the notice of contravention was issued contravened the provision of this Act indicated in the notice.

(5) Decision — The Board may,

(a) find that the person did not contravene the provision and rescind the notice;

(b) find that the person did contravene the provision and affirm the notice; or

(c) find that the person did contravene the provision but amend the notice by reducing the penalty.

(6) Collector's fees and disbursements — If the Board finds that the person contravened the provision and if it extended the time for applying for a review under clause (1)(b),

(a) before issuing its decision, it shall enquire of the Director whether a collector's fees and disbursements have been added to the amount set out in the notice under subsection 128(2); and

(b) if they have been added to that amount, the Board shall advise the person of that fact and of the total amount, including the collector's fees and disbursements, when it issues its decision.

(7) Certain provisions applicable — Subsections 116(8) and (9), 118(1), (3), (4) and (5) and 119(3), (4), (5), (13) and (14) apply, with necessary modifications, to a review under this section.

2001, c. 9, Sched. I, s. 1(28)

General Provisions Respecting the Board

123. (1) Persons from Board not compellable — Except with the consent of the Board, none of the following persons may be compelled to give evidence in a civil proceeding or in a proceeding before the Board or another board or tribunal with respect to information obtained while exercising his or her powers or performing his or her duties under this Act:

1. A Board member.

2. The registrar of the Board.

3. An employee of the Board.

(2) Non-disclosure — A labour relations officer who receives information or material under this Act shall not disclose it to any person or body other than the Board unless the Board authorizes the disclosure.

124. (1) When no decision after six months — This section applies if the Board has commenced a hearing to review an order, refusal to issue an order or notice of contravention, six months or more have passed since the last day of hearing and a decision has not been made.

(2) Termination of proceeding — On the application of a party in the proceeding, the chair may terminate the proceeding.

(3) Re-institution of proceeding — If a proceeding is terminated according to subsection (2), the chair shall re-institute the proceeding upon such terms and conditions as the chair considers appropriate.

PART XXIV — COLLECTION

125. (1) Third party demand — If an employer, director or other person is liable to make a payment under this Act and the Director believes or suspects that a person owes money to or is holding money for, or will within 365 days owe money to or hold money for the employer, director or other person, the Director may demand that the person pay all or part of the money that would otherwise be payable to the employer, director or other person to the Director in trust on account of the liability under this Act.

(1.1) Same, duration — A demand made under subsection (1) remains in force for 365 days from the date the notice of the demand is served.

(2) Client of temporary help agency — Without limiting the generality of subsection (1), that subsection applies where a client of a temporary help agency, owes money to or is holding money for a temporary help agency.

(3) Service — The Director shall, in accordance with section 95, serve notice of the demand on the person to whom the demand is made.

(4) Discharge — A person who pays money to the Director in accordance with a demand under this section is relieved from liability for the amount owed to or held for the employer, director or other person who is liable to make a payment under this Act, to the extent of the payment.

(5) Liability — If a person who receives a demand under this section makes a payment to the employer, director or other person with respect to whom the demand was made without complying with the demand, the person shall pay to the Director an amount equal to the lesser of,

(a) the amount paid to the employer, director or other person; and

(b) the amount of the demand.

2009, c. 9, s. 22; 2015, c. 27, Sched. 4, s. 1; 2017, c. 22, Sched. 1, s. 64

125.1 Security for amounts owing — If the Director considers it advisable to do so, the Director may accept security for the payment of any amounts owing under this Act in any form that the Director considers satisfactory.

2017, c. 22, Sched. 1, s. 65

125.2 Warrant — If an order to pay money has been made under this Act, the Director may issue a warrant, directed to the sheriff for an area in which any property of the employer, director or other person liable to make a payment under this Act is located, to enforce payment of the following amounts, and the warrant has the same force and effect as a writ of execution issued out of the Superior Court of Justice:

1. The amount the order requires the person to pay, including any applicable interest.

2. The costs and expenses of the sheriff.

2017, c. 22, Sched. 1, s. 65

125.3 (1) Lien on real property — If an order to pay money has been made under this Act, the amount the order requires the person to pay, including any applicable interest is, upon registration by the Director in the proper land registry office of a notice claiming a lien and charge conferred by this section, a lien and charge on any interest the employer, director or other person has in the real property described in the notice.

(2) Lien on personal property — If an order to pay money has been made under this Act, the amount the order requires the person to pay, including any applicable interest is, upon registration by the Director with the registrar under the *Personal Property Security Act* of a notice claiming a lien and charge under this section, a lien and charge on any interest in personal property in Ontario owned or held at the time of registration or acquired afterwards by the employer, director or other person liable to make a payment.

(3) Amounts included and priority — The lien and charge conferred by subsection (1) or (2) is in respect of all amounts the order requires the person to pay, including any applicable interest at the time of registration of the notice or any renewal of it and all amounts for which the person afterwards becomes liable while the notice remains registered and, upon registration of a notice of lien and charge, the lien and charge has priority over,

(a) any perfected security interest registered after the notice is registered;

(b) any security interest perfected by possession after the notice is registered; and

(c) any encumbrance or other claim that is registered against or that otherwise arises and affects the employer, director or other person's property after the notice is registered.

(4) Exception — For the purposes of subsection (3), a notice of lien and charge under subsection (2) does not have priority over a perfected purchase money security interest in collateral or its proceeds and is deemed to be a security interest perfected by registration for the purpose of the priority rules under section 30 of the *Personal Property Security Act*.

(5) Lien effective — A notice of lien and charge under subsection (2) is effective from the time assigned to its registration by the registrar and expires on the fifth anniversary of its registration unless a renewal notice of lien and charge is registered under this section before the end of the five-year period, in which case the lien and charge remains in effect for a further five-year period from the date the renewal notice is registered.

(6) Same — If an amount payable under this Act remains outstanding and unpaid at the end of the period, or its renewal, referred to in subsection (5), the Director may register a renewal notice of lien and charge; the lien and charge remains in effect for a five-year period from the date the renewal notice is registered until the amount is fully paid, and is deemed to be continuously registered since the initial notice of lien and charge was registered under subsection (2).

(7) Where person not registered owner — Where an employer, director or other person liable to make a payment has an interest in real property but is not shown as its registered owner in the proper land registry office,

(a) the notice to be registered under subsection (1) shall recite the interest of the employer, director or other person liable to make a payment in the real property; and

(b) a copy of the notice shall be sent to the registered owner at the owner's address to which the latest notice of assessment under the *Assessment Act* has been sent.

(8) Secured party — In addition to any other rights and remedies, if amounts owed by an employer, director or other person liable to make a payment remain outstanding and unpaid, the Director has, in respect of a lien and charge under subsection (2),

(a) all the rights, remedies and duties of a secured party under sections 17, 59, 61, 62, 63 and 64, subsections 65 (4), (5), (6), (6.1) and (7) and section 66 of the *Personal Property Security Act*;

(b) a security interest in the collateral for the purpose of clause 63 (4) (c) of that Act; and

(c) a security interest in the personal property for the purposes of sections 15 and 16 of the *Repair and Storage Liens Act*, if it is an article as defined in that Act.

(9) Registration of documents — A notice of lien and charge under subsection (2) or any renewal of it shall be in the form of a financing statement or a financing change statement as prescribed under the *Personal Property Security Act* and may be tendered for registration under Part IV of that Act, or by mail addressed to an address prescribed under that Act.

(10) Errors in documents — A notice of lien and charge or any renewal thereof is not invalidated nor is its effect impaired by reason only of an error or omission in the notice or in its execution or registration, unless a reasonable person is likely to be materially misled by the error or omission.

(11) Bankruptcy and Insolvency Act (Canada) unaffected — Subject to Crown rights provided under section 87 of that Act, nothing in this section affects or purports to affect the rights and obligations of any person under the *Bankruptcy and Insolvency Act* (Canada)

(12) Definitions In this section,

"real property" includes fixtures and any interest of a person as lessee of real property.

2017, c. 22, Sched. 1, s. 65

126. (1) Filing of order — If an order to pay money has been made under this Act, the Director may cause a copy of the order, certified by the Director to be a true copy, to be filed in a court of competent jurisdiction.

(2) Advice to person against whom order was made — If the Director files a copy of the order, he or she shall serve a letter in accordance with section 95 upon the person against whom the order was issued advising the person of the filing.

(3) Certificate enforceable — The Director may enforce an order filed under subsection (1) in the same manner as a judgment or order of the court.

(4) Notices of contravention — Subsections (1), (2) and (3) apply, with necessary modifications, to a notice of contravention.

Collectors

127. (1) Director may authorize collector — The Director may authorize a collector to exercise those powers that the Director specifies in the authorization to collect amounts owing under this Act or under an order made by a reciprocating state to which section 130 applies.

(2) Same — The Director may specify his or her powers under sections 125, 125.1, 125.2, 125.3, 126, 130 and the Board's powers under section 19 of the *Statutory Powers Procedure Act* in an authorization under subsection (1).

(3) Costs of collection — Despite clause 22(a) of the *Collection and Debt Settlement Services Act*, the Director may also authorize the collector to collect a reasonable fee or reasonable disbursements or both from each person from whom the collector seeks to collect amounts owing under this Act.

(4) Same — The Director may impose conditions on an authorization under subsection (3) and may determine what constitutes a reasonable fee or reasonable disbursements for the purposes of that subsection.

(5) Exception re disbursements — The Director shall not authorize a collector who is required to be registered under the *Collection and Debt Settlement Services Act* to collect disbursements.

(6) Disclosure — The Director may disclose, or allow to be disclosed, information collected under the authority of this Act or the regulations to a collector for the purpose of collecting an amount payable under this Act.

(7) Same — Any disclosure of personal information made under subsection (6) shall be deemed to be in compliance with clause 42 (1) (d) of the *Freedom of Information and Protection of Privacy Act.*

2013, c. 13, Sched. 1, s. 12; 2017, c. 22, Sched. 1, s. 66

128. (1) Collector's powers — A collector may exercise any of the powers specified in an authorization of the Director under section 127.

(2) Fees and disbursements part of order — If a collector is seeking to collect an amount owing under an order or notice of contravention, any fees and disbursements authorized under subsection 127(3) shall be deemed to be owing under and shall be deemed to be added to the amount of the order or notice of contravention.

(3) Distribution of money collected re wages or compensation — Subject to subsection (4), a collector,

(a) shall pay any amount collected with respect to wages, fees or compensation,

(i) to the Director in trust, or

(ii) with the written consent of the Director, to the person entitled to the wages, fees or compensation;

(b) shall pay any amount collected with respect to administrative costs to the Director;

(c) shall pay any amount collected with respect to a notice of contravention to the Minister of Finance; and

(d) may retain any amount collected with respect to the fees and disbursements.

(4) Apportionment — If the money collected is less than the full amount owing to all persons, including the Director and the collector, the money shall be apportioned among those to whom it is owing in the proportion each is owed and paid to them.

(5) Disclosure by collector — A collector may disclose to the Director or allow to be disclosed to the Director any information that was collected under the authority of this Act or the regulations for the purpose of collecting an amount payable under this Act.

(6) Same — Any disclosure of personal information made under subsection (5) shall be deemed to be in compliance with clause 42 (1) (d) of the *Freedom of Information and Protection of Privacy Act*.

2009, c. 9, s. 23; 2017, c. 22, Sched. 1, s. 67

129. (1) Settlement by collector — A collector may agree to a settlement with the person from whom he or she seeks to collect money, but only with the written agreement of,

(a) the person to whom the money is owed; or

(b) in the case of a notice of contravention, the Director.

(2) Restriction — A collector shall not agree to a settlement under clause (1)(a) without the Director's written approval if the person to whom the money is owed would receive less than,

(a) 75 per cent of the money to which he or she was entitled; or

(b) if another percentage is prescribed, the prescribed percentage of the money to which her or she was entitled.

(3) Orders void where settlement — If an order to pay has been made under section 74.14, 74.16, 74.17, 103, 104, 106 or 107 and a settlement respecting the money that was found to be owing is made under this section, the order is void and the settlement is binding if the person against whom the order was issued does what the person agreed to do under the settlement unless, on application to the Board, the individual to whom the money was ordered to be paid demonstrates that the settlement was entered into as a result of fraud or coercion.

(4) Notice of contravention — If a settlement respecting money that is owing under a notice of contravention is made under this section, the notice is void if the person against whom the notice was issued does what the person agreed to do under the settlement.

(5) Payment — The person who owes money under a settlement shall pay the amount agreed upon to the collector, who shall pay it out in accordance with section 128.

2009, c. 9, s. 24(1)

Reciprocal Enforcement of Orders

130. (1) Definitions — In this section,

"order" includes a judgment and, in the case of a state whose employment standards legislation contains a provision substantially similar to subsection 126(1), includes a certificate of an order for the payment of money owing under that legislation;

"state" includes another province or territory of Canada, a foreign state and a political subdivision of a state.

(2) Reciprocating states — The prescribed states are reciprocating states for the purposes of this section and the prescribed authorities with respect to those states are the authorities who may make applications under this section.

(3) Application for enforcement — The designated authority of a reciprocating state may apply to the Director for enforcement of an order for the payment of money issued under the employment standards legislation of that state.

(4) Copy of order — The application shall be accompanied by a copy of the order, certified as a true copy,

(a) by the court in which the order was filed, if the employment standards legislation of the reciprocating state provides for the filing of the order in a court; or

(b) by the designated authority, if the employment standards legislation of the reciprocating state does not provide for the filing of the order in a court.

(5) Enforcement — The Director may file a copy of the order in a court of competent jurisdiction and, upon its filing, the order is enforceable as a judgment or order of the court,

(a) at the instance and in favour of the Director; or

(b) at the instance and in favour of the designated authority.

(6) Costs — The Director or the designated authority, as the case may be,

(a) is entitled to the costs of enforcing the order as if it were an order of the court in which the copy of it was filed; and

(b) may recover those costs in the same manner as sums payable under such an order may be recovered.

PART XXV — OFFENCES AND PROSECUTIONS

Offences

131. (1) Offence to keep false records — No person shall make, keep or produce false records or other documents that are required to be kept under this Act or participate or acquiesce in the making, keeping or production of false records or other documents that are required to be kept under this Act.

(2) False or misleading information — No person shall provide false or misleading information under this Act.

132. General offence — A person who contravenes this Act or the regulations or fails to comply with an order, direction or other requirement under this Act or the regulations is guilty of an offence and on conviction is liable,

(a) if the person is an individual, to a fine of not more than $50,000 or to imprisonment for a term of not more than 12 months or to both;

(b) subject to clause (c), if the person is a corporation, to a fine of not more than $100,000; and

(c) if the person is a corporation that has previously been convicted of an offence under this Act or a predecessor to it,

(i) if the person has one previous conviction, to a fine of not more than $250,000, and

(ii) if the person has more than one previous conviction, to a fine of not more than $500,000.

133. (1) Additional orders — If an employer is convicted under section 132 of contravening section 74 or paragraph 4, 6, 7 or 10 of subsection 74.8(1) or if a client, is convicted under section 132 of contravening section 74.12, the court shall, in addition to any fine or term of imprisonment that is imposed, order that the employer or client, as the case may be, take specific action or refrain from taking specific action to remedy the contravention.

(2) Same — Without restricting the generality of subsection (1), the order made by the court may require one or more of the following:

1. A person be paid any wages that are owing to him or her.

2. In the case of a conviction under section 132 of contravening section 74 or 74.12, a person be reinstated.

3. A person be compensated for any loss incurred by him or her as a result of the contravention.

(3) Part XVI — If the contravention of section 74 was in relation to Part XVI (Lie Detectors) and the contravention affected an applicant for employment or an applicant to be a police officer, the court may require that the employer hire the applicant or compensate him or her or both hire and compensate him or her.

2009, c. 9, s. 25; 2017, c. 22, Sched. 1, s. 68

134. Offence re order for reinstatement — A person who fails to comply with an order issued under section 133 is guilty of an offence and on conviction is liable,

(a) if the person is an individual, to a fine of not more than $2,000 for each day during which the failure to comply continues or to imprisonment for a term of not more than six months or to both; and

(b) if the person is a corporation, to a fine of not more than $4,000 for each day during which the failure to comply continues.

2009, c. 9, s. 26

135. (1) Additional orders re other contraventions — If an employer is convicted under section 132 of contravening a provision of this Act other than section 74 or paragraph 4, 6, 7 or 10 of subsection 74.8(1), the court shall, in addition to any fine or term of imprisonment that is imposed, assess any amount owing to an employee affected by the contravention and order the employer to pay the amount assessed to the Director.

(2) Collection by Director — The Director shall attempt to collect the amount ordered to be paid under subsection (1) and if he or she is successful shall distribute it to the employee.

(3) Enforcement of order — An order under subsection (1) may be filed by the Director in a court of competent jurisdiction and upon filing shall be deemed to be an order of that court for the purposes of enforcement.

2009, c. 9, s. 27

136. (1) Offence re directors' liability — A director of a corporation is guilty of an offence if the director,

(a) fails to comply with an order of an employment standards officer under section 106 or 107 and has not applied for a review of that order; or

(b) fails to comply with an order issued under section 106 or 107 that has been amended or affirmed by the Board on a review of the order under section 116 or with a new order issued by the Board on such a review.

(2)   Penalty — A director convicted of an offence under subsection (1) is liable to a fine of not more than $50,000.

137. (1) Offence re permitting offence by corporation — If a corporation contravenes this Act or the regulations, an officer, director or agent of the corporation or a person acting or claiming to act in that capacity who authorizes or permits the contravention or acquiesces in it is a party to and guilty of the offence and is liable on conviction to the fine or imprisonment provided for the offence.

(2) Same — Subsection (1) applies whether or not the corporation has been prosecuted or convicted of the offence.

(3) Onus of proof — In a trial of an individual who is prosecuted under subsection (1), the onus is on the individual to prove that he or she did not authorize, permit or acquiesce in the contravention.

(4) Additional penalty — If an individual is convicted under this section, the court may, in addition to any other fine or term of imprisonment that is imposed, assess any amount owing to an employee affected by the contravention and order the individual to pay the amount assessed to the Director.

(5) Collection by Director — The Director shall attempt to collect the amount ordered to be paid under subsection (4) and if he or she is successful shall distribute it to the employee.

(6) No prosecution without consent — No prosecution shall be commenced under this section without the consent of the Director.

(7) Proof of consent — The production of a document that appears to show that the Director has consented to a prosecution under this section is admissible as evidence of the Director's consent.

137.1(1) Prosecution of employment standards officer — No prosecution of an employment standards officer shall be commenced with respect to an alleged contravention of subsection 89(2) without the consent of the Deputy Attorney General.

(2) Proof of consent — The production of a document that appears to show that the Deputy Attorney General has consented to a prosecution of an employment standards officer is admissible as evidence of his or her consent.

2001, c. 9, Sched. I, s. 1(29)

138. (1) Where prosecution may be heard — Despite section 29 of the *Provincial Offences Act*, the prosecution of an offence under this Act may be heard and determined by the Ontario Court of Justice sitting in the area where the accused is resident or carries on business, if the prosecutor so elects.

(2) Election to have judge preside — The Attorney General or an agent for the Attorney General may by notice to the clerk of the court require that a judge of the court hear and determine the prosecution.

138.1 (1) Publication re convictions — If a person, including an individual, is convicted of an offence under this Act, the Director may publish or otherwise make available to the general public the name of the person, a description of the offence, the date of the conviction and the person's sentence.

(2) Internet publication — Authority to publish under subsection (1) includes authority to publish on the Internet.

(3) Disclosure — Any disclosure made under subsection (1) shall be deemed to be in compliance with clause 42(1)(e) of the *Freedom of Information and Protection of Privacy Act.*

2004, c. 21, s. 9; 2006, c. 34, Sched. C, s. 23

139. Limitation period — No prosecution shall be commenced under this Act more than two years after the date on which the offence was committed or alleged to have been committed.

PART XXVI — MISCELLANEOUS EVIDENTIARY PROVISIONS

140. (1) Copy constitutes evidence — In a prosecution or other proceeding under this Act, a copy of an order or notice of contravention that appears to be made under this Act or the regulations and signed by an employment standards officer or the

Board is evidence of the order or notice and of the facts appearing in it without proof of the signature or office of the person appearing to have signed the order or notice.

(2) Same — In a prosecution or other proceeding under this Act, a copy of a record or other document or an extract from a record or other document that appears to be certified as a true copy or accurate extract by an employment standards officer is evidence of the record or document or the extracted part of the record or document and of the facts appearing in the record, document or extract without proof of the signature or office of the person appearing to have certified the copy or extract or any other proof.

(3) Certificate of Director constitutes evidence — In a prosecution or other proceeding under this Act, a certificate that appears to be signed by the Director setting out that the records of the ministry indicate that a person has failed to make the payment required by an order or a notice of contravention issued under this Act is evidence of the failure to make that payment without further proof.

(4) Same, collector — In a prosecution or other proceeding under this Act, a certificate shown by a collector that appears to be signed by the Director setting out any of the following facts is evidence of the fact without further proof:

1. The Director has authorized the collector to collect amounts owing under this Act.

2. The Director has authorized the collector to collect a reasonable fee or reasonable disbursements or both.

3. The Director has, or has not, imposed conditions on an authorization described in paragraph 2 and has, or has not, determined what constitutes a reasonable fee or reasonable disbursements.

4. Any conditions imposed by the Director on an authorization described in paragraph 2.

5. The Director has approved a settlement under subsection 129(2).

(5) Same, date of complaint — In a prosecution or other proceeding under this Act, a certificate that appears to be signed by the Director setting out the date on which the records of the ministry indicate that a complaint was filed is evidence of that date without further proof.

2009, c. 9, s. 28

PART XXVII — REGULATIONS

141. (1) Regulations — The Lieutenant Governor in Council may make regulations for carrying out the purposes of this Act and, without restricting the generality of the foregoing, may make the following regulations:

1. Prescribing anything for the purposes of any provision of this Act that makes reference to a thing that is prescribed.

1.1 Prescribing a method of payment for the purposes of clause 11 (2) (d) and establishing any terms, conditions or limitations on its use.

2. Establishing rules respecting the application of the minimum wage provisions of this Act and the regulations.

2.0.1 Prescribing a class of employees that would otherwise be in the class described in subparagraph 1 v or 2 v of subsection 23.1(1) and prescribing the minimum wage that applies to the class for the purposes of subsection 23.1(2).

2.0.2 Requiring an employer to pay at least the amount prescribed where an employee who regularly works more than three hours a day is required to present himself or herself for work on a day on which he or she works fewer than three hours.

Proposed Repeal — 141(1) para. 2.0.2

2.0.2 [Repealed 2017, c. 22, Sched. 1, s. 69(3).]

2017, c. 22, Sched. 1, s. 69(3) [To come into force January 1, 2019.]

2.1 Establishing a maximum pay period, a maximum period within which payments made to an employee shall be reconciled with wages earned by the employee or both.

3. Exempting any class of employees or employers from the application of this Act or any Part, section or other provision of it.

4. Prescribing what constitutes the performance of work.

5. Prescribing what information concerning the terms of an employment contract should be provided to an employee in writing.

6. Defining an industry and prescribing for that industry one or more terms or conditions of employment that apply to employers and employees in the industry or one or more requirements or prohibitions that apply to employers and employees in the industry.

7. Providing that any term, condition, requirement or prohibition prescribed under paragraph 6 applies in place of or in addition to one or more provisions of this Act or the regulations.

8. Providing that a regulation made under paragraph 6 or 7 applies only in respect of workplaces in the defined industry that have characteristics specified in the regulation, including but not limited to characteristics related to location.

9. Providing that an agreement under subsection 17(2) to work hours in excess of those referred to in clause 17(1)(a) that was made at the time of the employee's hiring and that has been approved by the Director is, despite subsection 17(6), irrevocable unless both the employer and the employee agree to its revocation.

10. Providing a formula for the determination of an employee's regular rate that applies instead of the formula that would otherwise be applicable under the definition of "regular rate" in section 1 in such circumstances as are set out in the regulation.

11. Providing for the establishment of committees to advise the Minister on any matters relating to the application or administration of this Act.

11.1 Providing, for the purposes of subsection 51(4), that subsections 51(1), (2) and (3) apply in respect of an employee during a leave under section 50.2.

11.2 Providing, for the purposes of subsection 51(5), that subsections 51(1), (2) and (3) do not apply in respect of an employee during a period of postponement under subsection 53(1.1).

12. Prescribing the manner and form in which notice of termination must or may be given and the content of such notice.

13. Prescribing what constitutes a constructive dismissal.

14. Providing that the common law doctrine of frustration does not apply to an employment contract and that an employer is not relieved of any obligation under Part XV because of the occurrence of an event that would frustrate an employment contract at common law except as prescribed.

14.1 Providing that payments to an employee by way of pension benefits, insurance benefits, workplace safety and insurance benefits, bonus, employment insurance benefits, supplementary employment insurance benefits or similar arrangements shall or shall not be taken into account in determining the amount that an employer is required to pay to an employee under clause 60(1)(b), section 61 or section 64.

15. Providing for and governing the consolidation of hearings under this Act.

16. Prescribing the minimum number of hours in a day or week for which an employee is entitled to be paid the minimum wage or a contractual wage rate and imposing conditions in respect of that entitlement.

16.1 Governing penalties for contraventions for the purposes of subsection 113 (1).

17. Defining any word or expression used in this Act that is not defined in it.

18. Prescribing the manner in which the information required by subsection 58(2) shall be given to the Director.

19. Respecting any matter necessary or advisable to carry out effectively the intent and purpose of this Act.

(1.1) Restricted application — A regulation made under paragraph 11.1 or 11.2 of subsection (1) may be restricted in its application to one or more of the following:

1. Specified benefit plans.

2. Employees who are members of prescribed classes.

3. Employers who are members of prescribed classes.

4. Part of a leave under section 50.2.

(2) Regulations re Part XIII — The Lieutenant Governor in Council may make regulations respecting any matter or thing necessary or advisable to carry out the intent and purpose of Part XIII (Benefit Plans), and without restricting the generality of the foregoing, may make regulations,

(a) exempting a benefit plan, part of a benefit plan or the benefits under such a plan or part from the application of Part XIII;

(b) permitting a differentiation in a benefit plan between employees or their beneficiaries, survivors or dependants because of the age, sex or marital status of the employees;

(c) suspending the application of Part XIII to a benefit plan, part of a benefit plan or benefits under such a plan or part for the periods of time specified in the regulation;

(d) prohibiting a reduction in benefits to an employee in order to comply with Part XIII; and

(e) providing the terms under which an employee may be entitled or disentitled to benefits under a benefit plan.

(2.0.1) Regulations re organ donor leave — The Lieutenant Governor in Council may make regulations,

(a) prescribing other organs for the purpose of section 49.2;

(b) prescribing tissue for the purpose of section 49.2;

(c) prescribing one or more periods for the purpose of subsection 49.2(5).

(2.0.2) Same — A regulation made under clause (2.0.1)(c) may prescribe different periods with respect to the donation of different organs and prescribed tissue.

(2.0.3) Transitional regulations — The Lieutenant Governor in Council may make regulations providing for any transitional matter that the Lieutenant Governor in Council considers necessary or advisable in connection with the implementation of the amendments made by the *Fair Workplaces, Better Jobs Act, 2017*.

(2.0.4) Conflict with transitional regulations — In the event of a conflict between this Act or the regulations and a regulation made under subsection (2.0.3), the regulation made under subsection (2.0.3) prevails.

(2.1) Regulations re emergency leaves, declared emergencies — If a regulation is made prescribing a reason for the purposes of clause 50.1(1)(d), the regulation may,

(a) provide that it has effect as of the date specified in the regulation;

(b) provide that an employee who does not perform the duties of his or her position because of the declared emergency and the prescribed reason is deemed to have taken leave beginning on the first day the employee does not perform the duties of his or her position on or after the date specified in the regulation; and

(c) provide that clause 74(1)(a) applies, with necessary modifications, in relation to the deemed leave described in clause (b).

(2.2) Retroactive regulation — A date specified in a regulation made under subsection (2.1) may be a date that is earlier than the day on which the regulation is made.

(2.3) Regulation extending leave — The Lieutenant Governor in Council may make a regulation providing that the entitlement of an employee to take leave under section 50.1 is extended beyond the day on which the entitlement would otherwise end under subsection 50.1(5) or (6), if the employee is still not performing the duties of his or her position because of the effects of the emergency and because of a reason referred to in clause 50.1(1)(a), (b), (c) or (d).

(2.4) Same — A regulation made under subsection (2.3) may limit the duration of the extended leave and may set conditions that must be met in order for the employee to be entitled to the extended leave.

(3) Regulations re Part XIX — The Lieutenant Governor in Council may make regulations prescribing information for the purposes of section 77.

(3.1) Regulations re Part XXII — A regulation made under paragraph 16.1 of subsection (1) may,

    (a) establish different penalties or ranges of penalties for different types of contraventions or the method of determining those penalties or ranges;

    (b) specify that different penalties, ranges or methods of determining a penalty or range apply to contraveners who are individuals and to contraveners that are corporations; or

    (c) prescribe criteria an employment standards officer is required or permitted to consider when imposing a penalty.

(4) Regulations re Part XXV — If the Lieutenant Governor in Council is satisfied that laws are or will be in effect in the state for the enforcement of orders made under this Act on a basis substantially similar to that set out in section 126, the Lieutenant Governor in Council may by regulation,

    (a) declare a state to be a reciprocating state for the purposes of section 130; and

(b) designate an authority of that state as the authority who may make applications under section 130.

(5) Classes — A regulation made under this section may be restricted in its application to any class of employee or employer and may treat different classes of employee or employer in different ways.

(5.1) Regulations may be conditional — A regulation made under this section may provide that it applies only if one or more conditions specified in it are met.

(6) Terms and conditions of employment for an industry — Without restricting the generality of paragraphs 6 and 7 of subsection (1), a regulation made under paragraph 6 or 7 may establish requirements for the industry respecting such matters as a minimum wage, the scheduling of work, maximum hours of work, eating periods and other breaks from work, posting of work schedules, conditions under which the maximum hours of work set out in the regulation may be exceeded, overtime thresholds and overtime pay, vacations, vacation pay, working on public holidays and public holiday pay and treating some public holidays differently than others for those purposes.

(7) [Repealed 2004, c. 21, s. 10(5).]

(8) Conditions, revocability of approval — A regulation made under paragraph 9 of subsection (1) may authorize the Director to impose conditions in granting an approval and may authorize the Director to rescind an approval.

(9) Restriction where excess hours agreements approved — An employer may not require an employee who has made an agreement approved by the Director under a regulation made under paragraph 9 of subsection (1) to work more than 10 hours in a day, except in the circumstances described in section 19.

(10) Revocability of part of approved excess hours agreement — If an employee has agreed to work hours in excess of those referred to in clause 17(1)(a) and hours in excess of those referred to in clause 17(1)(b), the fact that the Director has approved the agreement in accordance with a regulation made under paragraph 9 of subsection (1) does not prevent the employee from revoking, in accordance with subsection 17(6), that part of the agreement dealing with the hours in excess of those referred to in clause 17(1)(b).

2001, c. 9, Sched. I, s. 1(30), (31); 2002, c. 18, Sched. J, s. 3(30); 2004, c. 15, s. 5; 2004, c. 21, s. 10; 2006, c. 13, s. 3(4); 2007, c. 16, Sched. A, s. 6; 2009, c. 16, s. 3; 2014, c. 6, s. 5; 2014, c. 10, Sched. 2, s. 9; 2017, c. 22, Sched. 1, s. 69(1), (2), (4)-(6)

PART XXVIII — TRANSITION, AMENDMENT, REPEALS, COMMENCEMENT AND SHORT TITLE

142. (1) Transition — Part XIV.1 of the *Employment Standards Act*, as it read immediately before its repeal by this Act, continues to apply only with respect to wages that became due and owing before the Employee Wage Protection Program was discontinued and only if the employee to whom the wages were owed provided a certificate of claim, on a form prepared by the Ministry, to the Program Administrator before the day on which this section comes into force.

(2) [Repealed 2009, c. 9, s. 29.]

(3) [Repealed 2001, c. 9, Sched. I, s. 1(32).]

(4) [Repealed 2001, c. 9, Sched. I, s. 1(32).]

(5) [Repealed 2001, c. 9, Sched. I, s. 1(32).]

2001, c. 9, Sched. I, s. 1(32); 2009, c. 9, s. 29

143. [Repealed 2001, c. 41, s. 144(1).]

144. (1) Repeals — The *Employment Standards Act* and section 143 of this Act are repealed.

(2) Same — The *One Day's Rest in Seven Act* is repealed.

(3) Same — The *Government Contracts Hours and Wages Act* is repealed.

(4) Same — The *Employment Agencies Act* is repealed.

(5) Same — The *Industrial Standards Act* is repealed.

145. Commencement — This Act comes into force on a day to be named by proclamation of the Lieutenant Governor.

146. Short title — The short title of this Act is the *Employment Standards Act, 2000.*

ONT. REG. 286/01 — BENEFIT PLANS

made under the *Employment Standards Act, 2000*

O. Reg. 286/01, as am. O. Reg. 335/05; 526/05 (Fr.); CTR 12 MR 10 - 2

1. Definitions — For the purposes of Part XIII of the Act and this Regulation,

"actuarial basis" means the assumptions and methods generally accepted and used by fellows of the Canadian Institute of Actuaries to establish, in relation to the contingencies of human life such as death, accident, sickness and disease, the costs of pension benefits, life insurance, disability insurance, health insurance and other similar benefits, including their actuarial equivalents;

"age" means any age of 18 years or more and less than 65 years;

"benefits" includes,

(a) an aggregate, annual, monthly or other periodic amount or the accrual of such an amount to which an employee, or the employee's beneficiaries, survivors or dependants is, are or will become entitled under a benefit plan provided on superannuation, retirement, disability, accident or sickness,

(b) any medical, hospital, nursing, drug or dental expenses or other similar amounts or expenses paid under a benefit plan, and

(c) any amounts under a benefit plan to which an employee is entitled on termination of employment or to which any person is entitled upon the death of an employee;

"dependant" means a dependant as defined in the relevant benefit plan, and "dependent child" and "dependent spouse" have corresponding meanings;

"disability benefit plan" means a benefit plan that provides benefits to an employee for loss of income because of sickness, accident or disability;

"former Act" means the *Employment Standards Act*, R.S.O. 1990, c. E.14;

"health benefit plan" means a benefit plan that provides benefits to an employee, a spouse or a dependant of an employee or deceased employee for medical, hospital, nursing, drug or dental expenses or other similar expenses;

"life insurance plan" means a benefit plan that, on the employee's death, provides a lump sum or periodic payments to the employee's beneficiary, survivor or dependant, and includes accidental death and dismemberment insurance;

"long-term disability benefit plan" means a disability benefit plan under which the payments or benefits to an employee are payable for a period of not less than 52 weeks or until recovery, retirement or death, whichever period is shorter;

"marital status" includes,

(a) the condition of being an unmarried person who is supporting, in whole or in part, a dependent child or children, and

(b) common law status as defined in the relevant benefit plan;

"normal pensionable date" means the date specified in a pension plan at which an employee can retire from his or her employment and receive the regular pension benefit provided by the pension plan, whether the date is the day on which the employee attains a given age or the day on which he or she has completed a given period of employment;

"pension plan" means a benefit plan that provides benefits to a participating employee or to his or her spouse or dependant, on the employee's retirement or termination of employment, out of contributions made by the employer or the employee or both and the investment income, gains, losses and expenses on or from those contributions, and includes,

(a) a unit-benefit pension plan, under which the benefits are determined with reference to a percentage of salary or wages and length of employment or a specified period of employment,

(b) a defined benefit pension plan, under which the benefits are determined as a fixed amount and with reference to length of employment or a specified period of employment,

(c) a money purchase pension plan, under which the benefits are determined with reference to the accumulated amount of the contributions paid by or for the credit of an employee, and the investment income, gains, losses and expenses on or from those contributions,

(d) a profit sharing pension plan, under which payments or contributions by an employer are determined by reference to profits or out of profits from the employer's business, and the benefits are determined with reference to the accumulated amount of contributions paid by or for the credit of an employee and the investment income, gains, losses and expenses on or from those contributions, and

(e) a composite pension plan, which is any combination of the pension plans described in clauses (a) to (d);

"same-sex partner" [Repealed O. Reg. 335/05, s. 1(5).]

"same-sex partnership status" [Repealed O. Reg. 335/05, s. 1(5).]

"sex" includes,

(a) a distinction between employees that excludes an employee from a benefit under a benefit plan or gives an employee a preference to a benefit under a benefit plan because the employee is or is not a head of household, principal or primary wage earner or other similar condition, and

(b) a distinction between employees in a benefit plan because of the pregnancy of a female employee;

"short-term disability benefit plan" means a disability benefit plan other than a long-term disability benefit plan;

"spouse" means a spouse as defined in the relevant benefit plan;

"voluntary additional contribution" means an additional contribution by an employee under a pension plan, except a contribution whose payment, under the terms of the plan, obliges the employer to make a concurrent additional contribution.

O. Reg. 335/05, s. 1

2. Pension plans, permitted differentiation re employee's sex — **(1)** The prohibition in subsection 44(1) of the Act does not apply in respect of a differentiation in the rates of contribution by an employer to a pension plan if the differentiation is made on an actuarial basis because of an employee's sex and in order to provide equal benefits under the plan.

(2) The prohibition in subsection 44(1) of the Act does not apply in respect of a differentiation made under a pension plan if,

(a) the *Pension Benefits Act* applies to the pension plan; and

(b) the differentiation is made,

(i) because of an employee's sex, and

(ii) in respect of employment before January 1, 1987, other than employment that is described in clause 52(3)(b) or (c) of the *Pension Benefits Act*.

(3) The prohibition in subsection 44(1) of the Act does not apply in respect of a differentiation made under a pension plan if,

(a) the *Pension Benefits Act* does not apply to the pension plan; and

(b) the differentiation is made,

(i) because of an employee's sex, and

(ii) in respect of employment before July 12, 1988.

(4) In subsections (2) and (3),

"differentiation" means a type of differentiation to which the prohibition in the predecessor of subsection 33(2) of the former Act did not apply on December 31, 1987.

3. Pension plans, permitted differentiation re marital status — (1) The prohibition in subsection 44(1) of the Act does not apply to,

(a) an increase in benefits payable to an employee under a pension plan that provides for the increased benefits because the employee has a dependent spouse;

(b) a differentiation under a pension plan because of marital status, if the differentiation is made for the purpose of providing benefits that are payable periodically during the joint lives of an employee who is entitled to the pension and the employee's spouse, and thereafter during the life of the survivor of them, as provided in the pension plan; and

(c) a differentiation in the rates of contribution of an employer to a defined benefit or a unit-benefit pension plan that provides an increase in benefits to an employee because of marital status, if the rates of contribution of the employer differentiate between employees because of marital status.

(2) For the purposes of clause (1)(b), benefits are deemed to be payable periodically despite the fact that they are commuted, if the amount of the annual benefit payable to the employee at the normal pensionable date is not more than 2 per cent of the Year's Maximum Pensionable Earnings, as defined in the *Canada Pension Plan* in the year that the employee terminated the employment.

(3) Clause (1)(b) does not apply if the *Pension Benefits Act* applies to the pension plan and the plan contravenes the provisions of that Act respecting joint and survivor pensions.

O. Reg. 335/05, s. 2

4. Pension plans, permitted differentiation re employee's age —
(1) The prohibition in subsection 44(1) of the Act does not apply
in respect of a differentiation that is made on an actuarial basis
because of an employee's age and that relates to,

    (a) the rates of voluntary additional contributions to a
pension plan;

    (b) the rates of contributions that an employee is required to
make to a money purchase or profit sharing pension plan;

    (c) the rates of contributions by an employer to a unit-benefit
or defined benefit pension plan, unless the *Pension Benefits
Act* applies to the plan and the plan contravenes the
provisions of that Act respecting age differentiation;

    (d) the rates of contributions by an employer to a money
purchase or profit sharing pension plan,

        (i) when the employer transfers the assets from a unit-
benefit or defined benefit pension plan to the money
purchase or profit sharing pension plan, and

        (ii) if the differentiation is made in order to protect
employees' pension benefits from being adversely affected
by the transfer; or

    (e) benefits payable to employees, if the *Pension Benefits Act*,

        (i) permits the differentiation, or

        (ii) does not apply to the pension plan.

(2) Despite subsection (1), the requirement that a differentiation
be determined on an actuarial basis does not apply to a
differentiation described in clause (1)(a), (b) or (e) that is made
in respect of the employment of a person before July 12, 1988.

(3) The prohibition in subsection 44(1) of the Act does not apply
with respect to a provision in a pension plan that makes a
differentiation because of age in establishing a normal
pensionable date for voluntary retirees or an early voluntary
retirement date or age, unless,

    (a) the *Pension Benefits Act* applies to the plan; and

(b) the plan contravenes the provisions of that Act respecting normal retirement dates and early retirement pensions.

5. Life insurance plans, permitted differentiation re employee's sex — The prohibition in subsection 44(1) of the Act does not apply to,

(a) a differentiation in the contributions of an employee to a voluntary employee-pay-all life insurance plan that is made on an actuarial basis because of sex; and

(b) a differentiation in the contributions of an employer to a life insurance plan that is made on an actuarial basis because of an employee's sex and in order to provide equal benefits under the plan.

6. Life insurance plans, permitted differentiation re marital status — (1) The prohibition in subsection 44(1) of the Act does not apply to,

(a) benefits under a life insurance plan that are payable periodically to the surviving spouse of a deceased employee for the life of the surviving spouse or until the surviving spouse becomes a spouse of another person;

(b) a benefit under a life insurance plan that is payable to an employee on the death of his or her spouse; and

(c) a differentiation in the contributions of an employee or an employer to a life insurance plan, if,

(i) the differentiation is made because of marital status, and

(ii) the life insurance plan provides benefits that are payable periodically to an employee's surviving spouse.

(2) Clause (1)(a) also applies to benefits of less than $25 a month that have been commuted to a lump sum payment.

O. Reg. 335/05, s. 3

7. Life insurance plans, permitted differentiation re age — The prohibition in subsection 44(1) of the Act does not apply to,

(a) a differentiation, made on an actuarial basis because of an employee's age, in benefits or contributions under a voluntary employee-pay-all life insurance plan; and

(b) a differentiation, made on an actuarial basis because of an employee's age and in order to provide equal benefits under the plan, in an employer's contributions to a life insurance plan.

8. Disability benefit plans, permitted differentiation re age, sex or leave of absence — The prohibition in subsection 44(1) of the Act does not apply to,

(a) a differentiation, made on an actuarial basis because of an employee's age or sex, in the rate of contributions of an employee to a voluntary employee-pay-all short or long-term disability benefit plan; and

(b) a differentiation, made on an actuarial basis because of an employee's age or sex and in order to provide equal benefits under the plan, in the rate of contributions of an employer to a short or long-term disability benefit plan.

9. Health benefit plans, permitted differentiation re sex or marital status — The prohibition in subsection 44(1) of the Act does not apply to,

(a) a differentiation, made on an actuarial basis because of sex, in the rate of contributions of an employee to a voluntary employee-pay-all health benefit plan;

(b) a differentiation, made on an actuarial basis because of an employee's sex and in order to provide equal benefits under the plan, in the rate of contributions of an employer to a health benefit plan;

(c) a differentiation in an employee's benefits or contributions under a health benefit plan because of marital status, if the differentiation is made in order to provide benefits for the employee's spouse or dependent child; and

(d) a differentiation in the rate of contributions of an employer to a health benefit plan, where there are specified premium rates and where that differentiation for employees having marital status and for employees without marital status is on the same proportional basis.

O. Reg. 335/05, s. 4

10. Participation in benefit plan during leave of absence — (1) A benefit plan to which Part XIII of the Act applies shall not disentitle an employee who is on a leave of absence described in subsection (2) from continuing to participate in the benefit plan during the leave of absence, if the benefit plan entitles an employee who is on a leave of absence other than one described in subsection (2) to continue to participate.

(2) This section applies to,

(a) a leave of absence under Part XIV of the Act; and

(b) any longer leave of absence that the employee has applied for under a provision in the contract of employment that prevails under subsection 5(2) of the Act.

CTR 12 MR 10 - 2

11. Former exclusion from certain benefit plans — If an employee was excluded from participating in a benefit plan or in a benefit under a benefit plan before November 1, 1975 and ceased to be so excluded on that date, the employee is entitled to participate as of that date.

12. Compliance not to be achieved by reductions — No employer shall reduce the employer's contributions to or the benefits under a health benefit plan in causing the plan to comply with Part XIII of the Act and this Regulation, or with Part X of the former Act or a predecessor of that Part and the related regulations.

13. Change to normal pensionable date under certain plans — Despite the application of Part X of the former Act or a predecessor of that Part to a pension plan that was in existence on November 1, 1975, if the normal pensionable date of a class of employees was increased in order to have the plan comply with that Part, an employee who is a member of that class is entitled to pension benefits on the normal pensionable date as provided by the pension plan before it was increased.

14. Revocation — Regulation 321 of the Revised Regulations of Ontario, 1990 and Ontario Regulation 70/00 are revoked.

15. Commencement — This Regulation comes into force on the day Part XIII of the *Employment Standards Act, 2000* comes into force.

ONT. REG. 287/01 — BUILDING SERVICES PROVIDERS

made under the *Employment Standards Act, 2000*

O. Reg. 287/01, as am. O. Reg. 533/05 (Fr.)

1. Prescribed services for a building — The following are prescribed as services for a building for the purposes of the definition of "building services" in subsection 1(1) of the Act:

    1. Services that are intended to relate only to the building and its occupants and visitors with respect to,

        i. a parking garage or parking lot, and

        ii. a concession stand.

    2. Property management services that are intended to relate only to the building.

2. Prescribed employees — **(1)** The following are prescribed for the purposes of clause 75(4)(b) of the Act as employees with respect to whom a new provider is not required to comply with Part XV (Termination and Severance of Employment) of the Act:

    1. An employee whose work, before the changeover date, included providing building services at the premises, but who did not perform his or her job duties primarily at those premises during the 13 weeks before the changeover date.

    2. An employee whose work included providing building services at the premises, but who,

        i. was not actively at work immediately before the changeover date, and

ii. did not perform his or her job duties primarily at the premises during the most recent 13 weeks of active employment.

3. An employee who did not perform his or her job duties at the premises for at least 13 weeks during the 26-week period before the changeover date.

4. An employee who refuses an offer of employment with the new provider that is reasonable in the circumstances.

(2) For the purposes of paragraph 4 of subsection (1), if the new provider requested information under subsection 77(1) of the Act, the terms and conditions of the employee's employment with the replaced provider on the date of the request are one of the circumstances that shall be taken into account in determining whether the offer is reasonable.

(3) The 26-week period referred to in paragraph 3 of subsection (1) shall be calculated without including any period during which the provision of building services at the premises was temporarily discontinued.

(4) With respect to an employee's services at the premises, the 26-week period referred to in paragraph 3 of subsection (1) shall be calculated without including any period during which the employee was on a leave of absence under Part XIV of the Act.

(5) In this section,

"changeover date" means the day the new provider begins to provide services at the premises.

3. Information about employees — (1) The following is the information about each employee that the owner or manager of premises shall give for the purposes of subsection 77(1) of the Act:

1. The employee's job classification or job description.

2. The wage rate actually paid to the employee.

3. A description of any benefits provided to the employee, including the cost of each benefit and the benefit period to which the cost relates.

4. The number of hours that the employee works in a regular work day and in a regular work week.

5. The date on which the provider hired the employee.

6. Any period of employment attributed to the provider under section 10 of the Act.

7. The number of weeks that the employee worked at the premises during the 26 weeks before the request date.

8. A statement indicating whether either of the following subparagraphs applies to the employee:

   i. The employee's work, before the request date, included providing building services at the premises, but the employee did not perform his or her job duties primarily at those premises during the 13 weeks before the request date.

   ii. The employee's work included providing building services at the premises, but the employee was not actively at work immediately before the request date, and did not perform his or her job duties primarily at the premises during the most recent 13 weeks of active employment.

(2) The following is the information about each employee that the owner or manager of the premises shall give for the purposes of subsection 77(2) of the Act:

1. The information listed in paragraphs 1 to 8 of subsection (1).

2. The employee's name, residential address and telephone number.

(3) If the employee's hours of work vary from week to week, paragraph 4 of subsection (1) does not apply and the owner or manager shall, instead, provide the number of the employee's non-overtime hours for each week that the employee worked during the 13 weeks before the request date.

(4) The 26-week period referred to in paragraph 7 of subsection (1) shall be calculated without including any period during which the provision of building services at the premises was temporarily discontinued.

(5) The 26-week period referred to in paragraph 7 of subsection (1) shall be calculated without including any period during which the employee was on a leave of absence under Part XIV of the Act.

(6) In this section,

"request date" means the date on which information is requested under subsection 77(1) or (2) of the Act, as the case may be.

4. Revocation — Ontario Regulation 138/96 is revoked.

5. Commencement — This Regulation comes into force on the day Parts IV and XIX of the *Employment Standards Act, 2000* come into force.

Ont. Reg. 285/01— Exemptions, Special Rules and Establishment of Minimum Wage

made under the *Employment Standards Act, 2000*

O. Reg. 285/01, as am. O. Reg. 361/01; 401/03; 50/05; 525/05 (Fr.); 552/ 05; 18/06; 92/06; 294/07; 444/07; 547/07; 586/07; 432/08 [Repealed O. Reg. 443/08, s. 4.]; 443/08; 31/14.

1. Definitions — In this Regulation, "construction employee" means,

(a) an employee employed at the site in any of the activities described in the definition of "construction industry", or

(b) an employee who is engaged in off-site work, in whole or in part, but is commonly associated in work or collective bargaining with an employee described in clause (a);

"construction industry" means the businesses that are engaged in constructing, altering, decorating, repairing or demolishing buildings, structures, roads, sewers, water or gas mains, pipe lines, tunnels, bridges, canals or other works at the site;

"domestic worker" means a person who is employed by a householder to perform services in the household or to provide care, supervision or personal assistance to children, senior or disabled members of the household, but does not include a sitter who provides care, supervision or personal assistance to children on an occasional, short-term basis;

"hotel, motel, tourist resort, restaurant and tavern" means an establishment that provides accommodation, lodging, meals or beverages for payment, and includes hotels, motels, motor hotels, tourist homes, tourist camps, tourist cabins and cottages, tourist inns, catering establishments and all other establishments of a similar nature;

"information technology professional" means an employee who is primarily engaged in the investigation, analysis, design, development, implementation, operation or management of information systems based on computer and related technologies through the objective application of specialized knowledge and professional judgment;

"recorded visual and audio-visual entertainment production industry" means the industry of producing visual or audio-visual recorded entertainment that is intended to be replayed in cinemas or on the Internet, as part of a television broadcast, or on a VCR or DVD player or a similar device, but does not include the industry of producing commercials (other than trailers), video games or educational material;

"residential care worker" means a person who is employed to supervise and care for children or developmentally handicapped persons in a family-type residential dwelling or cottage and who resides in the dwelling or cottage during work periods, but does not include a foster parent;

"road building" means the preparation, construction, reconstruction, repair, alteration, remodelling, renovation, demolition, finishing and maintenance of streets, highways or parking lots, including structures such as bridges, tunnels or retaining walls in connection with streets or highways, and all foundations, installation of equipment, appurtenances and work incidental thereto;

"seasonal employee" means an employee who works not more than 16 weeks in a calendar year for an employer;

"taxi cab" means a vehicle, with seating accommodation for not more than nine persons exclusive of the driver, used to carry persons for hire;

"wage rate" means, where an employee is paid for piecework, the rate paid per piece and if there is more than one piece rate, each of the piece rates, and the number of pieces paid at each rate.

O. Reg. 552/05, s. 1

1.1 Family Day a public holiday — Family Day, being the third Monday in February, is prescribed as a public holiday for the purpose of the definition of "public holiday" in section 1 of the Act.

O. Reg. 547/07, s. 1

Exemptions Re Various Parts of Act

2. Exemptions from Parts VII to XI of Act — (1) Parts VII, VIII, IX, X and XI of the Act do not apply to a person employed,

(a) as a duly qualified practitioner of,

(i) architecture,

(ii) law,

(iii) professional engineering,

(iv) public accounting,

(v) surveying, or

(vi) veterinary science;

(b) as a duly registered practitioner of,

(i) chiropody,

(ii) chiropractic,

(iii) dentistry,

(iv) massage therapy,

(v) medicine,

(vi) optometry,

(vii) pharmacy,

(viii) physiotherapy, or

(ix) psychology;

(c) as a duly registered practitioner under the *Drugless Practitioners Act*;

(d) as a teacher as defined in the *Teaching Profession Act*;

(e) as a student in training for an occupation mentioned in clause (a), (b), (c) or (d);

(f) in commercial fishing;

(g) as a salesperson or broker, as those terms are defined in the *Real Estate and Business Brokers Act, 2002*; or

(h) as a salesperson, other than a route salesperson, who is entitled to receive all or any part of his or her remuneration as commissions in respect of offers to purchase or sales that,

(i) relate to goods or services, and

(ii) are normally made away from the employer's place of business.

(2) Subject to sections 24, 25, 26 and 27 of this Regulation, Parts VII, VIII, IX, X and XI of the Act do not apply to a person employed on a farm whose employment is directly related to the primary production of eggs, milk, grain, seeds, fruit, vegetables, maple products, honey, tobacco, herbs, pigs, cattle, sheep, goats, poultry, deer, elk, ratites, bison, rabbits, game birds, wild boar and cultured fish.

O. Reg. 92/06, s. 1

Special Rule Re Emergency Leave

3. Special rule re emergency leave — Section 50 of the Act does not apply to any of the following persons in circumstances in which the exercise of the entitlement would constitute an act of professional misconduct or a dereliction of professional duty:

1. A person described in clause 2(1)(a), (c), (d) or (e).

2. A person employed as a registered practitioner of a health profession set out in Schedule 1 to the *Regulated Health Professions Act, 1991*, including a person described in clause 2(1)(b).

Exemption re Certain Deductions, Etc.

[Heading added O. Reg. 444/07, s. 1.]

3.1 Fees, s. 28 of — ***Ontario Municipal Employees Retirement System Act, 2006*** **(1)** An employer is exempted from the application of section 13 of the Act if the employer participates in an OMERS pension plan under the *Ontario Municipal Employees Retirement System Act, 2006*, but only with respect to fees that a by-law made under section 28 of that Act requires employees to pay.

(2) Subsection (1) applies only if the employer remits the fees in accordance with the by-law.

O. Reg. 444/07, s. 1

Exemptions Re Hours of Work and Eating Periods

4. Exemptions from Part VII of Act — **(1)** Sections 17, 18 and 19 of the Act do not apply to,

(a) a person employed as a firefighter as defined in section 1 of the *Fire Protection and Prevention Act, 1997*;

(b) a person whose work is supervisory or managerial in character and who may perform non-supervisory or non-managerial tasks on an irregular or exceptional basis;

(c) a person employed as a fishing or hunting guide;

(d) a construction employee;

(e) a person who is employed as the superintendent, janitor or caretaker of a residential building and resides in the building; or

(f) a person employed as an embalmer or funeral director.

(2) Sections 17 and 19 of the Act do not apply to a person employed,

(a) as a landscape gardener; or

(b) to install and maintain swimming pools.

(3) Part VII of the Act does not apply to,

(a) a person whose employment is directly related to,

(i) the growing of mushrooms,

(ii) the growing of flowers for the retail and wholesale trade,

(iii) the growing, transporting and laying of sod,

(iv) the growing of trees and shrubs for the wholesale and retail trade,

(v) the breeding and boarding of horses on a farm, or

(vi) the keeping of furbearing mammals, as defined in the *Fish and Wildlife Conservation Act, 1997*, for propagation or the production of pelts for commercial purposes;

(b) an information technology professional; or

(c) a person employed in the recorded visual and audio-visual entertainment production industry.

O. Reg. 552/05, s. 2

Establishment of Minimum Wage

5. Minimum wage — (1) From June 1, 2014 onwards, the minimum wage is as follows:

1. For an employee who is a student under 18 years of age, if the weekly hours of the student are not in excess of 28 hours

or if the student is employed during a school holiday, $10.30 an hour.

2. For an employee who, as a regular part of his or her employment, serves liquor directly to customers, guests, members or patrons in premises for which a licence or permit has been issued under the *Liquor Licence Act*, $9.55 an hour.

3. For the services of a hunting or fishing guide, $55.00 for less than five consecutive hours in a day and $110.00 for five or more hours in a day whether or not the hours are consecutive.

4. For an employee who is a homeworker, $12.10 an hour.

5. For any other employee, $11.00 an hour.

(1.1) [Repealed O. Reg. 31/14, s. 1(2).]

(1.2) [Repealed O. Reg. 31/14, s. 1(2).]

(1.3) [Repealed O. Reg. 31/14, s. 1(2).]

(1.4) [Repealed O. Reg. 294/07, s. 1(1).]

(2) [Repealed O. Reg. 31/14, s. 1(2).]

(3) If an employee falls within both paragraphs 1 and 4 of subsection (1), the employer shall pay the employee not less than the minimum wage for a homeworker.

(4) If an employer provides room or board to an employee, the following are the amounts that shall be deemed to have been paid as wages for the purposes of determining whether the minimum wage has been paid:

1. For room, $31.70 a week if the room is private and $15.85 a week if the room is not private.

2. For board, $2.55 a meal and not more than $53.55 a week.

3. For both room and board, $85.25 a week if the room is private and $69.40 a week if the room is not private.

(5) The amount provided in subsection (4) in respect of a room shall be deemed to have been paid as wages only if the room is,

(a) reasonably furnished and reasonably fit for human habitation;

(b) supplied with clean bed linen and towels; and

(c) reasonably accessible to proper toilet and wash-basin facilities.

(6) Room or board shall not be deemed to have been paid by the employer to an employee as wages unless the employee has received the meals or occupied the room.

(7) For the purpose of determining whether an employee other than a student has been paid the minimum wage, the employee shall be deemed to have worked for three hours if he or she,

(a) regularly works more than three hours a day;

(b) is required to present himself or herself for work; and

(c) works less than three hours.

(8) Subsection (7) does not apply if the employer is unable to provide work for the employee because of fire, lightning, power failure, storms or similar causes beyond the employer's control that result in the stopping of work.

O. Reg. 401/03, s. 1; 294/07, s. 1; 31/14, s. 1

5.1 Change to minimum wage during pay period — If the minimum wage rate applicable to an employee changes during a pay period, the calculations required by subsection 23(4) of the Act shall be performed as if the pay period were two separate pay periods, the first consisting of the part falling before the day on which the change takes effect and the second consisting of the part falling on and after the day on which the change takes effect.

O. Reg. 401/03, s. 2; 294/07, s. 2; 31/14, s. 2

6. When work deemed to be performed — (1) Subject to subsection (2), work shall be deemed to be performed by an employee for the employer,

(a) where work is,

(i) permitted or suffered to be done by the employer, or

(ii) in fact performed by an employee although a term of the contract of employment expressly forbids or limits hours of work or requires the employer to authorize hours of work in advance;

(b) where the employee is not performing work and is required to remain at the place of employment,

(i) waiting or holding himself or herself ready for call to work, or

(ii) on a rest or break-time other than an eating period.

(2) Work shall not be deemed to be performed for an employer during the time the employee,

(a) is entitled to,

(i) take time off work for an eating period,

(ii) take at least six hours or such longer period as is established by contract, custom or practice for sleeping and the employer furnishes sleeping facilities, or

(iii) take time off work in order to engage in the employee's own private affairs or pursuits as is established by contract, custom or practice;

(b) is not at the place of employment and is waiting or holding himself or herself ready for call to work.

Exemptions Re Minimum Wage

7. Exemptions from Part IX of Act — Part IX of the Act does not apply to,

(a) a person who is employed as a student in a recreational program operated by a charitable organization registered under Part I of the *Income Tax Act* (Canada) and whose work or duties are directly connected with the recreational program;

(b) a person employed as a student to instruct or supervise children;

(c) a person employed as a student at a camp for children;

(d) a person who is employed as the superintendent, janitor or caretaker of a residential building and resides in the building.

Exemptions Re Overtime Pay

8. Exemptions from Part VIII of Act — Part VIII of the Act does not apply to,

(a) a person employed as a firefighter as defined in section 1 of the *Fire Protection and Prevention Act, 1997*;

(b) a person whose work is supervisory or managerial in character and who may perform non-supervisory or non-managerial tasks on an irregular or exceptional basis;

(c) a person employed as a fishing or hunting guide;

(d) a person employed,

    (i) as a landscape gardener, or

    (ii) to install and maintain swimming pools;

(e) a person whose employment is directly related to,

    (i) the growing of mushrooms,

    (ii) the growing of flowers for the retail and wholesale trade,

    (iii) the growing, transporting and laying of sod,

    (iv) the growing of trees and shrubs for the retail and wholesale trade,

    (v) the breeding and boarding of horses on a farm, or

    (vi) the keeping of furbearing mammals, as defined in the *Fish and Wildlife Conservation Act, 1997*, for propagation or the production of pelts for commercial purposes;

(f) a person employed as a student to instruct or supervise children;

(g) a person employed as a student at a camp for children;

(h) a person who is employed as a student in a recreational program operated by a charitable organization registered under Part I of the *Income Tax Act* (Canada) and whose work or duties are directly connected with the recreational program;

(i) a person who is employed as the superintendent, janitor or caretaker of a residential building and resides in the building;

(j) a person employed as a taxi cab driver;

(k) a person employed as an ambulance driver, ambulance driver's helper or first-aid attendant on an ambulance; or

(l) an information technology professional.

Exemptions Re Public Holidays

9. Exemptions from Part X of Act — (1) Part X of the Act does not apply to,

(a) a person employed as a firefighter as defined in section 1 of the *Fire Protection and Prevention Act, 1997*;

(b) a person employed as a fishing or hunting guide;

(c) a person employed,

    (i) as a landscape gardener, or

    (ii) to install and maintain swimming pools;

(d) a person whose employment is directly related to,

    (i) mushroom growing,

    (ii) the growing of flowers for the retail and wholesale trade,

    (iii) the growing, transporting and laying of sod,

    (iv) the growing of trees and shrubs for the retail and wholesale trade,

    (v) the breeding and boarding of horses on a farm, or

    (vi) the keeping of furbearing mammals, as defined in the *Fish and Wildlife Conservation Act, 1997*, for propagation or the production of pelts for commercial purposes;

(e) a person employed as a student to instruct or supervise children;

(f) a person employed as a student at a camp for children;

(g) a person who is employed as a student in a recreational program operated by a charitable organization registered under Part I of the *Income Tax Act* (Canada) and whose work or duties are directly connected with the recreational program;

(h) a person who is employed as the superintendent, janitor or caretaker of a residential building and resides in the building;

(i) a person employed as a taxi cab driver;

(j) a person who is employed as a seasonal employee in a hotel, motel, tourist resort, restaurant or tavern and provided with room and board; or

(k) [Repealed O. Reg. 443/08, s. 1.]

(2) Part X of the Act does not apply to a construction employee who works in the construction industry and receives 7.7 per cent or more of his or her hourly rate or wages for vacation pay or holiday pay.

O. Reg. 586/07, s. 1; 443/08, s. 1

Exemption Re Retail Business Establishments

10. Application of s. 73 of Act — (1) Despite section 73 of the Act, an employee in a retail business establishment shall not refuse to work on a Sunday if he or she agreed, at the time of being hired, to work on Sundays.

(2) Subsection (1) does not apply to an employee who declines to work on a Sunday for reasons of religious belief or religious observance.

(3) The employer shall not make an employee's agreement to work on Sundays a condition of being hired if the condition would be contrary to section 11 of the *Human Rights Code.*

Special Rules Re Homemakers

11. Homemakers — (1) In this section,

"homemaker" means a person who is employed,

(a) to perform homemaking services for a householder or member of a household in the householder's private residence, and

(b) by a person other than the householder.

(2) Despite section 6, the hours of work in respect of which a homemaker is to be paid at least the minimum wage shall be not more than 12 hours in a day.

(3) Parts VII (Hours of Work and Eating Periods) and VIII (Overtime Pay) and paragraph 4 of subsection 15(1) (record of hours worked) of the Act do not apply to a homemaker who is paid in accordance with subsection (2).

Special Rules Re Homeworkers

12. Homeworkers — (1) The employer of a homeworker shall advise the homeworker in writing of the type of work that he or she is being employed to perform and,

(a) if the homeworker is to be paid according to the number of hours worked, of the amount to be paid for an hour of work in a regular work week;

(b) if the homeworker is to be paid according to the number of articles or things manufactured, of the amount to be paid for each article or thing manufactured in a regular work week; or

(c) if the homeworker is to be paid on some other basis, the basis on which he or she is to be paid.

(2) If the employer of a homeworker who is paid according to the number of articles or things manufactured requires the manufacture of a certain number of articles or things to be completed by a certain date or time, the employer shall advise the homeworker of those requirements in writing.

(3) In this section,

"manufacture" includes preparation, improvement, repair, alteration, assembly or completion.

Special Rules and Exemptions Re Overtime Pay

13. Road building — (1) Despite Part VIII of the Act, in the case of an employee engaged at the site of road building in relation to streets, highways or parking lots,

(a) subject to clause (b), the employer shall pay overtime pay for each hour worked in excess of 55 hours in a work week, at an amount not less than one and one-half times the employee's regular rate; and

(b) if the employee works less than 55 hours in a work week, the difference between 55 hours and the number of hours actually worked, up to an amount not exceeding 22 hours, may be added to the maximum set out in clause (a) for the purpose of determining the employee's overtime pay for the next work week.

(2) Despite Part VIII of the Act, in the case of an employee engaged at the site of road building in relation to structures such as bridges, tunnels or retaining walls in connection with streets or highways,

(a) subject to clause (b), the employer shall pay overtime pay for each hour worked in excess of 50 hours in a work week, at an amount not less than one and one-half times the employee's regular rate; and

(b) if the employee works less than 50 hours in a work week, the difference between 50 hours and the number of hours actually worked, up to an amount not exceeding 22 hours, may be added to the maximum set out in clause (a) for the purpose of determining the employee's overtime pay for the next work week.

14. Hotels, motels, tourist resorts, restaurants and taverns — Despite Part VIII of the Act, the employer shall pay an employee who works for the owner or operator of a hotel, motel, tourist resort, restaurant or tavern for 24 weeks or less in a calendar year and who is provided with room and board overtime pay for each hour worked in excess of 50 hours in a work week, at an amount not less than one and one-half times the employee's regular rate.

15. Fresh fruit and vegetable processing — Despite Part VIII of the Act, the employer shall pay a seasonal employee whose employment is directly related to the canning, processing and packing of fresh fruits or vegetables or their distribution by the canner, processor or packer overtime pay for each hour worked in excess of 50 hours in a work week, at an amount not less than one and one-half times the employee's regular rate.

16. Sewer and watermain construction — Despite Part VIII of the Act, the employer shall pay an employee who is employed in laying, altering, repairing or maintaining sewers and watermain and in work incidental thereto, or in guarding the site during the laying, altering, repairing or maintaining of sewers and watermain, overtime pay for each hour worked in excess of 50 hours in a work week, at an amount not less than one and one-half times the employee's regular rate.

17. Local cartage — **(1)** Despite Part VIII of the Act, the employer shall pay an employee who is a driver of a vehicle or a driver's helper overtime pay for each hour worked in excess of 50 hours in a work week, at an amount not less than one and one-half times the employee's regular rate.

(2) Subsection (1) applies to employees who are,

(a) drivers of vehicles used in the business of carrying goods for hire within a municipality or to any point not more than five kilometres beyond the municipality's limits; or

(b) drivers' helpers on such vehicles.

18. Highway transport — **(1)** Despite Part VIII of the Act, the employer shall pay an employee to whom this subsection applies overtime pay for each hour worked in excess of 60 hours in a work week, at an amount not less than one and one-half times the employee's regular rate.

(2) Subsection (1) applies to an employee who is the driver of any of the following:

1. A truck whose operator held an operating licence under the former Act on December 31, 2005.

2. A truck whose operator held a certificate of intercorporate exemption under the former Act on December 31, 2005, if after that date the truck is operated to carry, for compensation, goods of another person who is not an affiliated corporation under the former Act, such that the operator would be required to hold an operating licence under the former Act if it were still in force.

3. A truck that is operated to carry goods of another person for compensation, if the operator,

    i. did not hold an operating licence or a certificate of intercorporate exemption under the former Act on December 31, 2005, and

    ii. would be required to hold an operating licence under the former Act if it were still in force.

(3) For the purposes of paragraph 2 of subsection (2), subsection 3(6) of the former Act does not apply.

(4) For the purposes of subparagraph 3 ii of subsection (2), subsections 3(5) and (6) of the former Act do not apply.

(5) Subsection (1) does not apply to an employee to whom section 17 applies.

(6) For the purposes of this section, in computing the number of hours worked by an employee in a week, only the hours during which he or she is directly responsible for the truck shall be included.

(7) In this section,

"commercial motor vehicle" has the same meaning as in the former Act;

"former Act" means the *Truck Transportation Act*;

"**operate**" has the same meaning as in the former Act, and "**operator**" has a corresponding meaning;

"**truck**" means a commercial motor vehicle or the combination of a commercial motor vehicle and trailer or trailers drawn by it.

O. Reg. 18/06, s. 1

Special Rules Re Domestic Workers

19. Domestic workers — (1) A householder shall provide the domestic worker with written particulars of employment respecting,

(a) the regular hours of work, including the starting and finishing times; and

(b) the hourly rate of pay.

(2) If the householder provides room or board to the domestic worker, the following are the amounts that shall be deemed to have been paid as wages for the purposes of determining whether the minimum wage has been paid:

1. For a private room, $31.70 a week.

2. For a non-private room, $0.00.

3. For board, $2.55 a meal and not more than $53.55 a week.

4. For both room and board, $85.25 a week if the room is private and $53.55 a week if the room is not private.

(3) The amount provided in subsection (2) in respect of a room shall be deemed to have been paid as wages only if the room is,

(a) reasonably furnished and reasonably fit for human habitation;

(b) supplied with clean bed linen and towels; and

(c) reasonably accessible to proper toilet and wash-basin facilities.

(4) Room or board shall not be deemed to have been paid by the householder to the domestic worker as wages unless the employee has received the meals or occupied the room.

O. Reg. 401/03, s. 3; 294/07, s. 3; 31/14, s. 3

411

Special Rules Re Residential Care Workers

20. Residential care workers — (1) In this section,

"day" means the 24-hour period between 12:00 midnight on a day and 12:00 midnight on the next day.

(2) Despite section 6 and subject to subsection (3), the employer shall pay to a residential care worker for each day of work wages in a minimum amount, not less than an amount calculated by multiplying 12 hours by the worker's regular rate, which shall not be less than the minimum wage.

(3) If a residential care worker, by arrangement with the employer, is free from the performance of normal and regular duties in a day and as a result works less than 12 hours, the worker shall be paid wages not less than an amount calculated by multiplying the number of hours actually worked by the worker's regular rate as mentioned in subsection (2).

(4) In addition to the wage payable under subsection (2), the employer shall pay to a residential care worker not less than the worker's regular rate for not more than three additional hours worked in excess of 12 hours of work in a day, if the worker,

    (a) makes and keeps an accurate daily record of the number of hours worked in the day; and

    (b) provides the record to the employer on or before the first pay day after the pay day for the pay period in which the work is performed.

21. Free time — (1) Despite section 18 of the Act, every employer shall give to a residential care worker not less than 36 hours in each work week, either consecutive or as may be arranged with the consent of the worker, free from the performance of any duties for the employer.

(2) If the residential care worker consents, at the employer's request, to do work during a free hour mentioned in subsection (1),

(a) that hour shall be added to one of the next eight 36-hour periods of free time; or

(b) the employer shall pay the residential care worker at least one and one-half times the worker's regular rate for the time spent doing work during a free hour.

22. When work deemed not to be performed — Despite section 6, work shall be deemed not to be performed during any time that satisfies the following conditions:

1. The residential care worker spends the time at the dwelling or cottage,

    i. attending to private affairs or pursuits, or

    ii. resting, sleeping or eating.

2. The time is, by agreement with the employer, free from the performance of any duties.

23. Exemptions — Parts VII (Hours of Work and Eating Periods) and VIII (Overtime Pay) and paragraph 4 of subsection 15(1) (record of hours worked) of the Act do not apply to or in respect of a residential care worker.

Special Rules Re Fruit, Vegetable and Tobacco Harvesters

24. Application — Sections 25, 26 and 27 apply to an employee who is employed on a farm to harvest fruit, vegetables or tobacco for marketing or storage.

25. Minimum wage — (1) For each pay period, the employer shall pay to each employee an amount that is at least equal to the amount the employee would have earned at the minimum wage.

(2) The employer shall be deemed to comply with subsection (1) if employees are paid a piece work rate that is customarily and generally recognized in the area as having been set so that an employee exercising reasonable effort would, if paid such a rate, earn at least the minimum wage.

(3) Subsection (2) does not apply in respect of an employee described in paragraph 1 of subsection 5(1).

(4) For the purposes of this section, "piece work rate" means a rate of pay calculated on the basis of a unit of work performed.

(5) If an employer provides room or board to an employee, the following are the amounts which shall be deemed to have been paid by the employer to the employee as wages for the purposes of determining whether the minimum wage has been paid:

1. For serviced housing accommodation, $99.35 a week.

2. For housing accommodation, $73.30 a week.

3. For room, $31.70 a week if the room is private and $15.85 a week if the room is not private.

4. For board, $2.55 a meal and not more than $53.55 a week.

5. For both room and board, $85.25 a week if the room is private and $69.40 a week if the room is not private.

(6) The amount provided in subsection (5) in respect of housing accommodation shall be deemed to have been paid as wages only if the accommodation,

(a) is reasonably fit for human habitation;

(b) includes a kitchen with cooking facilities;

(c) includes at least two bedrooms or a bedroom and a living room; and

(d) has its own private toilet and washing facilities.

(7) The amount provided in subsection (5) in respect of serviced housing accommodation shall be deemed to have been paid as wages only if,

(a) the accommodation complies with clauses (6)(a) to (d); and

(b) light, heat, fuel, water, gas or electricity are provided at the employer's expense.

(8) The amount provided in subsection (5) in respect of a room shall be deemed to have been paid as wages only if the room is,

(a) reasonably furnished and reasonably fit for human habitation;

(b) supplied with clean bed linen and towels; and

(c) reasonably accessible to proper toilet and wash-basin facilities.

(9) Room or board shall not be deemed to have been paid by the employer to an employee as wages unless the employee has received the meals or occupied the room.

O. Reg. 401/03, s. 4; 294/07, s. 4; 31/14, s. 4

26. Vacation or vacation pay — (1) If an employee has been employed by the employer for 13 weeks or more, the employer shall, in accordance with Part XI of the Act,

(a) give the employee a vacation with pay; or

(b) pay the employee vacation pay.

(2) An employee entitled to vacation pay under subsection (1) earns vacation pay from the commencement of his or her employment.

(3) Section 41 of the Act does not apply to the employee.

27. Public holidays — (1) Part X of the Act applies to an employee who has been employed by an employer for a period of 13 weeks or more.

(2) For the purposes of this section, an employee shall be deemed to be employed in a continuous operation.

(3) [Repealed O. Reg. 443/08, s. 2.]

O. Reg. 443/08, s. 2

SPECIAL RULES RE COMMISSION AUTOMOBILE SALES SECTOR

28. Commission automobile sales sector — (1) This section applies with respect to employees who sell automobiles partially or exclusively on a commission basis.

(2) For each pay period, the employer shall pay to each employee an amount that is at least equal to the amount the employee would have earned at the minimum wage.

(3) A pay period shall not exceed one month.

(4) Payments made to an employee shall be reconciled with wages earned by the employee for each reconciliation period.

(5) No balance shall be carried forward past any reconciliation period.

(6) The reconciliation of payments made to an employee and wages earned by an employee shall not result in any employee receiving less than the minimum wage for any pay period.

(7) For each year, the reconciliation periods shall be:

1. January 1-March 31.

2. April 1-June 30.

3. July 1-September 30.

4. October 1-December 31.

(8) If an employee's employment terminates before the end of a reconciliation period, payments made to the employee shall be reconciled with wages earned by him or her, and subsection (6) applies.

O. Reg. 401/03, s. 5; 294/07, s. 5; 31/14, s. 5

SPECIAL RULE RE EMPLOYEES WHO MAY ELECT TO WORK OR NOT

29. [Repealed O. Reg. 443/08, s. 3.]

DIRECTOR'S APPROVALS

30. [Repealed O. Reg. 50/05, s. 1.]

31. [Repealed O. Reg. 50/05, s. 1.]

32. Certain approved agreements irrevocable — (1) Despite subsection 17(6) of the Act, an agreement under subsection 17(2) of the Act that was made at the time of the employee's hiring and that has been approved by the Director is irrevocable unless both the employer and the employee agree to its revocation.

(2) The Director may impose conditions in granting an approval.

O. Reg. 50/05, s. 2

Exemption Re Certain Existing Arrangements

32.1 Existing arrangements for long shifts — (1)
Clause 17(1)(a) of the Act does not apply with respect to the class of employees each of whom,

> (a) has an arrangement described in subsection (2) with an employer to whom a permit was issued under section 18 of the *Employment Standards Act*; and

> (b) is not required by the employer to work more than 10 hours a day.

(2) The arrangement,

> (a) provides that the employee is willing to work, at the employer's request, more hours per day than the number of hours in his or her regular work day;

> (b) was made at or before the time of the employee's hiring and before September 4, 2001; and

> (c) has not been revoked by the mutual consent of the employer and employee.

(3) The terms of the arrangement need not be reduced to writing.

O. Reg. 361/01, s. 1

33. Commencement — This Regulation comes into force on the day Parts VII to XI of the *Employment Standards Act, 2000* come into force.

Ont. Reg. 289/01— Enforcement

made under the *Employment Standards Act, 2000*

O. Reg. 289/01 [Corrected Ont. Gaz. 18/08/01 Vol. 134:33.], as am. O. Reg. 142/03; 532/05 (Fr.); 475/06; 295/11; 315/17.

1. Prescribed penalties re notices of contravention — The
following penalties are prescribed for the purposes of subsection
113(1) of the Act:

Item	Contravention	Penalty
1.	If the notice relates to a contravention of section 2, 15, 15.1 or 16 of the Act	$250
2.	If the notice relates to the second contravention of section 2, 15, 15.1 or 16 of the Act in a three-year period	$500
3.	If the notice relates to the third or subsequent contravention of section 2, 15, 15.1 or 16 of the Act in a three-year period	$1,000
4.	If the notice relates to a contravention of a provision of the Act other than section 2, 15, 15.1 or 16	$250
5.	If the notice relates to the second contravention of a provision of the Act other than section 2, 15, 15.1 or 16 in a three-year period	$500
6.	If the notice relates to the third or subsequent contravention of a provision of the Act other than section 2, 15, 15.1 or 16 in a three-year period	$1,000
7.	If the notice relates to a contravention of a provision of the Act other than section 2, 15, 15.1 or 16 and the contravention affects more than one employee	$250, multiplied by the number of employees affected
8.	If the notice relates to the second contravention of a provision of the Act other than section 2, 15, 15.1 or 16 in a three-year period and the contravention affects more than one employee	$500, multiplied by the number of employees affected
9.	If the notice relates to the third or subsequent contravention of a provision of the Act other than section 2, 15, 15.1 or 16 in a three-year period and the contravention affects more than one employee	$1,000, multiplied by the number of employees affected

O. Reg. 142/03, s. 1; 315/17, s. 1

2. Reciprocal enforcement of orders — (1) Each state listed in Column 1 of the Table to this section is prescribed as a reciprocating state for the purposes of section 130 of the Act.

(2) Each authority listed in Column 2 of the Table to this section is prescribed as the designated authority for the state listed opposite it in Column 1.

COLUMN 1	COLUMN 2
Alberta	Director of Employment Standards for Alberta
British Columbia	Director of Employment Standards for British Columbia
Manitoba	Director of Employment Standards for Manitoba
New Brunswick	Director of Employment Standards for New Brunswick
Newfoundland and Labrador	Director of Labour Standards for Newfoundland and Labrador
Northwest Territories	Labour Standards Board of the Northwest Territories
Nova Scotia	Director of Employment Standards for Nova Scotia
Nunavut	Nunavut Labour Standards Board
Prince Edward Island	Inspector of Labour Standards for Prince Edward Island
Quebec	Commission des normes du travail
Saskatchewan	Director of Labour Standards for Saskatchewan
Yukon	Director of Employment Standards for the Yukon

Corrected Ont. Gaz. 18/08/01 Vol. 134:33; O. Reg. 475/06, s. 1; 295/11, s. 1

3. Commencement — This Regulation comes into force on the day Parts XXII, XXIII and XXIV of the *Employment Standards Act, 2000* come into force.

ONT. REG. 476/06 — FAMILY MEDICAL LEAVE — PRESCRIBED INDIVIDUALS

made under the *Employment Standards Act, 2000*

O. Reg. 476/06

1. Individuals prescribed as family members — (1) The following individuals are prescribed as family members for the purpose of section 49.1 of the Act:

1. A brother or sister of the employee.

2. A grandparent of the employee or of the employee's spouse.

3. A grandchild of the employee or of the employee's spouse.

4. The father-in-law or mother-in-law of the employee.

5. A brother-in-law or sister-in-law of the employee.

6. A son-in-law or daughter-in-law of the employee or of the employee's spouse.

7. An uncle or aunt of the employee or of the employee's spouse.

8. The nephew or niece of the employee or of the employee's spouse.

9. The spouse of the employee's grandchild, uncle, aunt, nephew or niece.

10. A foster parent of the employee's spouse.

11. A person who considers the employee to be like a family member.

(2) In paragraphs 1 to 5 of subsection (1), a reference to a relationship includes the corresponding "step" relationship.

(3) An example of the effect of subsection (2) is that paragraph 2 of subsection (1) includes a step-grandparent of the employee or of the employee's spouse.

2. Condition — This Regulation applies to an employee who takes leave under section 49.1 of the Act to provide care or support to a person described in paragraph 11 of subsection 1(1) only if the employee, on the employer's request, provides the employer with a copy of the document provided to an agency or department of the Government of Canada for the purpose of claiming compassionate care benefits under the *Employment Insurance Act* (Canada) in which it is stated that the employee is considered to be like a family member.

ONT. REG. 316/04 — POSTING OF INFORMATION CONCERNING RIGHTS AND OBLIGATIONS

made under the *Employment Standards Act, 2000*

O. Reg. 316/04, as am. O. Reg. 524/05 (Fr.).

1. Material to be posted — The material that is prescribed for the purposes of subsection 2(1) of the Act is the poster prepared by the Ministry, identified as version 2.0 and entitled "What You Should Know About The *Ontario Employment Standards Act*", whether printed in colour or in black and white.

2. Revocation — Ontario Regulation 290/01 is revoked.

ONT. REG. 288/01 — TERMINATION AND SEVERANCE OF EMPLOYMENT

made under the *Employment Standards Act, 2000*

O. Reg. 288/01, as am. O. Reg. 531/05 (Fr.); 549/05; 492/06; 397/09; 95/10.

1. Definitions — In this Regulation,

"construction employee" has the same meaning as in Ontario Regulation 285/01 (*Exemptions, Special Rules and Establishment of Minimum Wage*);

"disability benefit plan" [Repealed O. Reg. 492/06, s. 1.]

O. Reg. 492/06, s. 1

TERMINATION OF EMPLOYMENT

2. (1) Employees not entitled to notice of termination or termination pay — The following employees are prescribed for the purposes of section 55 of the Act as employees who are not entitled to notice of termination or termination pay under Part XV of the Act:

1. Subject to subsection (2), an employee who is hired on the basis that his or her employment is to terminate on the expiry of a definite term or the completion of a specific task.

2. An employee on a temporary lay-off.

3. An employee who has been guilty of wilful misconduct, disobedience or wilful neglect of duty that is not trivial and has not been condoned by the employer.

4. An employee whose contract of employment has become impossible to perform or has been frustrated by a fortuitous or unforeseeable event or circumstance.

5. An employee whose employment is terminated after refusing an offer of reasonable alternative employment with the employer.

6. An employee whose employment is terminated after refusing alternative employment made available through a seniority system.

7. An employee who is on a temporary lay-off and does not return to work within a reasonable time after having been requested by his or her employer to do so.

8. An employee whose employment is terminated during or as a result of a strike or lock-out at the place of employment.

9. A construction employee.

10. [Repealed O. Reg. 397/09, s. 4.]

11. An employee whose employment is terminated when he or she reaches the age of retirement in accordance with the employer's established practice, but only if the termination would not contravene the *Human Rights Code*.

12. An employee,

    i. whose employer is engaged in the building, alteration or repair of a ship or vessel with a gross tonnage of over ten tons designed for or used in commercial navigation,

    ii. to whom a legitimate supplementary unemployment benefit plan agreed on by the employee or his or her agent applies, and

    iii. who agrees or whose agent agrees to the application of this exemption.

(2) Paragraph 1 of subsection (1) does not apply if,

    (a) the employment terminates before the expiry of the term or the completion of the task;

    (b) the term expires or the task is not yet completed more than 12 months after the employment commences; or

    (c) the employment continues for three months or more after the expiry of the term or the completion of the task.

(3) Paragraph 4 of subsection (1) does not apply if the impossibility or frustration is the result of an illness or injury suffered by the employee.

    O. Reg. 549/05, s. 1; 492/06, s. 2; 397/09, ss. 1, 4; 95/10, s. 1

3. (1) Notice, 50 or more employees — The following periods are prescribed for the purposes of subsection 58(1) of the Act:

1. Notice shall be given at least eight weeks before termination if the number of employees whose employment is terminated is 50 or more but fewer than 200.

2. Notice shall be given at least 12 weeks before termination if the number of employees whose employment is terminated is 200 or more but fewer than 500.

3. Notice shall be given at least 16 weeks before termination, if the number of employees whose employment is terminated is 500 or more.

(2) The following information is prescribed as the information to be provided to the Director under clause 58(2)(a) of the Act and to be posted under clause 58(2)(b) of the Act:

1. The employer's name and mailing address.

2. The location or locations where the employees whose employment is being terminated work.

3. The number of employees working at each location who are paid,

    i. on an hourly basis,

    ii. on a salaried basis, and

    iii. on some other basis.

4. The number of employees whose employment is being terminated at each location who are paid,

    i. on an hourly basis,

    ii. on a salaried basis, and

    iii. on some other basis.

5. The date or dates on which it is anticipated that the employment of the employees referred to in paragraph 4 will be terminated.

6. The name of any trade union local representing any of the employees whose employment is being terminated.

7. The economic circumstances surrounding the terminations.

8. The name, title and telephone number of the individual who completed the form on behalf of the employer.

(3) The employer shall provide the information referred to in subsection (2) to the Director by setting it out in the form approved by the Director under clause 58(2)(a) of the Act and delivering the form to the Employment Practices Branch of the Ministry of Labour between 9 a.m. and 5 p.m. on any day other than a Saturday, Sunday or other day on which the offices of the Branch are closed.

(4) Section 58 of the Act does not apply to the employer and employees if,

(a) the number of employees whose employment is terminated at the establishment is not more than 10 per cent of the number of employees who have been employed there for at least three months; and

(b) the terminations were not caused by the permanent discontinuance of part of the employer's business at the establishment.

4. Manner of giving notice — (1) Subject to section 5, a notice of termination shall be,

(a) given in writing;

(b) addressed to the employee whose employment is to be terminated; and

(c) served on the employee in accordance with section 95 of the Act.

(2) If an employer bound by a collective agreement is or will be laying off an employee for a period that will or may be longer than a temporary lay-off and the employer would be or might be in breach of the collective agreement if the employer advised the employee that his or her employment was to be terminated, the employer may provide the employee with a written notice of indefinite lay-off and the employer shall be deemed as of the date on which that notice was given to have provided the employee with a notice of termination.

O. Reg. 397/09, s. 2

5. Notice of termination where seniority rights apply — (1) This section applies with respect to employees whose employment contracts provide seniority rights by which an employee who is to be laid off or whose employment is to be terminated may displace another employee.

(2) If an employer who proposes to terminate the employment of an employee described in subsection (1) posts a notice in a conspicuous part of the workplace setting out the name, seniority, job classification and proposed lay-off or termination date of the employee, the notice shall constitute notice of termination as of the day of posting to any employee whom the employee named in the notice displaces.

(3) Clause 60(1)(a) of the Act does not apply to an employee who displaces another employee in the circumstances described in this section.

6. Temporary work, 13-week period — (1) An employer who has given an employee notice of termination in accordance with the Act and the regulations may provide temporary work to the employee without providing a further notice of termination in respect of the day on which the employee's employment is finally terminated if that day occurs not later than 13 weeks after the termination date specified in the original notice.

(2) The provision of temporary work to an employee in the circumstances described in subsection (1) does not affect the termination date as specified in the notice or the employee's period of employment.

7. Inclusion of vacation time in notice period — The period of a notice of termination given to an employee shall not include any vacation time unless the employee, after receiving the notice, agrees to the inclusion of the vacation time in the notice period of the notice.

8. Period of employment — (1) For the purposes of this Regulation and sections 54 to 62 of the Act, an employee's period of employment is the period beginning on the day he or she most recently commenced employment and ending on,

(a) if notice of termination is given in accordance with Part XV of the Act, the day it is given; and

(b) if notice of termination is not given in accordance with Part XV of the Act, the day the employee's employment is terminated.

(2) For the purposes of subsection (1), two successive periods of employment that are not more than 13 weeks apart shall be added together and treated as one period of employment.

SEVERANCE OF EMPLOYMENT

9. Employees not entitled to severance pay — (1) The following employees are prescribed for the purposes of subsection 64(3) of the Act as employees who are not entitled to severance pay under section 64 of the Act:

1. An employee whose employment is severed as a result of a permanent discontinuance of all or part of the employer's business that the employer establishes was caused by the economic consequences of a strike.

2. Subject to subsection (2), an employee whose contract of employment has become impossible to perform or has been frustrated.

3. An employee who, on having his or her employment severed, retires and receives an actuarially unreduced pension benefit that reflects any service credits which the employee, had the employment not been severed, would have been expected to have earned in the normal course of events for purposes of the pension plan.

4. An employee whose employment is severed after refusing an offer of reasonable alternative employment with the employer.

5. An employee whose employment is severed after refusing reasonable alternative employment made available through a seniority system.

6. An employee who has been guilty of wilful misconduct, disobedience or wilful neglect of duty that is not trivial and has not been condoned by the employer.

7. A construction employee.

8. An employee engaged in the on-site maintenance of buildings, structures, roads, sewers, pipelines, mains, tunnels or other works.

9. [Repealed O. Reg. 397/09, s. 5.]

(2) Paragraph 2 of subsection (1) does not apply if,

(a) the impossibility or frustration is the result of,

(i) a permanent discontinuance of all or part of the employer's business because of a fortuitous or unforeseen event,

(ii) the employer's death, or

(iii) the employee's death, if the employee received a notice of termination before his or her death; or

(b) the impossibility or frustration is the result of an illness or injury suffered by the employee.

O. Reg. 549/05, s. 2; 492/06, s. 3; 397/09, ss. 3, 5; 95/10, s. 2

10. Revocation — Regulation 327 of the Revised Regulations of Ontario, 1990 and Ontario Regulations 691/92, 169/95 and 382/95 are revoked.

11. Commencement — This Regulation comes into force on the day Part XV of the *Employment Standards Act, 2000* comes into force.

ONT. REG. 291/01 — TERMS AND CONDITIONS OF EMPLOYMENT IN DEFINED INDUSTRIES — WOMEN'S COAT AND SUIT INDUSTRY AND WOMEN'S DRESS AND SPORTSWEAR INDUSTRY

made under the *Employment Standards Act, 2000*

O. Reg. 291/01, as am. O. Reg. 530/05 (Fr.); 585/07.

1. Definitions — In this Regulation,

"defined industries" means the women's coat and suit industry and the women's dress and sportswear industry;

"fur industry" means all work done in the manufacture, repair or remodelling, in whole or in part, of coats, jackets, similar garments, neck-pieces, cuffs and other pieces made of fur (not including imitation or simulated fur), except work done on the employer's premises by only one person;

"industry holiday" means,

(a) New Year's Day,

(a.1) Family Day, being the third Monday in February,

(b) Good Friday,

(c) Victoria Day,

(d) Canada Day,

(e) Labour Day,

(f) Thanksgiving Day,

(g) Christmas Day, and

(h) Boxing Day, being December 26 or the Monday next following when Christmas falls on a Saturday;

"piece-work basis" in relation to how an employee is paid, means payment based on the number of articles or things that are manufactured, prepared, improved, repaired, altered, assembled or completed;

"special rate work" means,

(a) in relation to an employee who is not a homeworker, work described in clause 11(1)(a), and

(b) in relation to a homeworker, work described in clause 11(1)(b);

"women's coat and suit industry" means all work done in the manufacture anywhere in Ontario, in whole or in part, of cloaks, coats, suits, wraps, wind-breakers, skirts manufactured for use as part of a suit, jackets or blazers, manufactured from any material including suede, leather, simulated, synthetic, pile and fur fabrics, of any description, for female persons of all ages, but does not include work done in,

(a) the manufacture of,

    (i) ski-suits or skating suits, in whole or in part,

    (ii) athletic uniforms, in whole or in part,

    (iii) riding-coats, or

    (iv) lounging-robes, bathrobes, kimonos, pyjamas or beach wraps,

(b) the making of cloaks, coats, suits, wraps, wind-breakers, skirts manufactured for use as part of a suit, jackets or blazers, manufactured from any material including suede, leather, simulated, synthetic, pile and fur fabrics, of any description, for female persons of all ages by a custom tailor, who,

    (i) makes cloaks, coats, suits, wraps, wind-breakers, skirts manufactured for use as part of a suit, jackets or blazers individually for a retail customer, according to the measurements and specifications of the retail customer, and

    (ii) does not employ more than four persons in making cloaks, coats, suits, wraps, wind-breakers, skirts manufactured for use as part of a suit, jackets or blazers, or

(c) the receiving, warehousing, shipping or distributing of raw materials or manufactured products or in sales, design or administrative operations;

"women's dress and sportswear industry" means all work done in the manufacture in whole or in part of all types, kinds and styles of garments worn by female persons and includes, without limiting the generality of the foregoing, garments commonly known as dresses, gowns, sportswear, play clothes, skirts, trousers, pants, slacks, blouses, tops, vestees, at-home wear, pantsuits and jumpsuits, but does not include work done in a separate manufacturing area in,

(a) the manufacture of garments for female persons not over 14 years of age or of a size up to and including girls' Canada Standard Size 14,

(b) the making of such garments by a custom dressmaker or custom manufacturer who,

> (i) makes such garments individually for retail customers with whom the dressmaker or manufacturer deals directly according to the measurements and specifications of the retail customers, and

> (ii) does not employ more than four persons in making such garments,

(c) the manufacture of garments in the women's coat and suit industry,

(d) the manufacture of garments in the fur industry,

(e) the manufacture of undergarments and lingerie, namely, brassieres, slips, half-slips, panties, girdles and corsets,

(f) the manufacture of sleepwear, namely, garments intended to be and worn as sleeping garments, including peignoir sets consisting of an undergarment worn as a sleeping garment and an overgarment made of lightweight fabric,

(g) the manufacture of utility garments, namely, bathrobes, kimonos, housecoats, brunchcoats and terry cloth gowns, for utilitarian purposes and of a design, colour and pattern distinct from and not worn in conjunction with any other garment made by the manufacturer doing work within the designation or made by or for another manufacturer doing work within the designation or with whom such manufacturer is associated directly or indirectly in any manner whatsoever,

(h) the manufacture of cloth and fabric, including the spinning of yarn and knitting of fabric,

(i) the manufacture of such garments made from knitted material by a knitwear manufacturer who,

> (i) makes available to the Director on request, during reasonable business hours, all of the records pertaining to

431

garments and material produced, purchased and sold by the manufacturer,

(ii) manufactures such garments and the knitted material on the same premises, and

(iii) does not manufacture such garments for another manufacturer doing work within the designation or with whom such manufacturer is associated directly or indirectly in any manner whatsoever,

(j) the manufacture of blouses, defined as a woman's tailored garment of a maximum length of 26 inches measured from the middle of the collar and of design, colour and pattern distinct from and not intended to be worn in conjunction with any other garments made by or for the manufacturer or made by or for a manufacturer with whom the manufacturer is associated directly or indirectly,

(k) the manufacture of bathing suits, knitted sweaters or any style of apron, or

(l) the receiving, warehousing, shipping or distributing of raw materials or manufactured products or in sales, design or administrative operations.

O. Reg. 585/07, s. 2

2. Terms and conditions of employment — (1) This Regulation sets out the terms and conditions of employment that apply to employees and employers in the defined industries.

(2) Except as modified by this Regulation, the Act applies to employees and employees in the defined industries.

3. Minimum pay for short periods of work — (1) Despite subsection 5(7) of Ontario Regulation 285/01 (*Exemptions, Special Rules and Establishment of Minimum Wage*), if an employee is required to work for a period of less than four hours or is required to report to work but does not work any hours, the employee shall be deemed to have worked four hours and the employer shall pay the employee accordingly.

(2) This section does not apply to homeworkers.

4. Non-application of ss. 18 to 21 of Act — Sections 18 to 21 of the Act do not apply with respect to employees in the defined industries.

5. When an employee may not be required to work — **(1)** An employer shall not require or allow an employee to perform work,

  (a) on an industry holiday; or

  (b) between midnight and 6:00 a.m.

(2) Subsection (1) applies despite any agreement under subsection 17(2) of the Act.

6. Normal work day and normal work week — **(1)** An employee's normal work day shall not exceed 8 hours, including paid breaks but not including eating periods.

(2) A normal work day shall not be on a Saturday or Sunday.

(3) An employee's normal work week shall not exceed 40 hours, including paid breaks but not including eating periods.

(4) A normal work week is determined on the basis of the period from midnight on Saturday to midnight on the following Saturday.

7. Normal work day under work schedule — **(1)** If an employer establishes a work schedule in accordance with sections 8 and 9 and satisfies the requirements in those sections, an employee's normal work day is determined under the work schedule and not under section 10.

(2) This section does not apply to homeworkers.

8. Work schedule — The following apply with respect to an employer's work schedule:

  1. The work schedule shall set out the starting time of the normal work day for all employees.

  2. If the work schedule provides for a single shift, a normal work day shall not begin after 9:30 a.m.

  3. A normal work day shall not be scheduled on a Saturday or Sunday.

4. Each employee shall have a half-hour eating period midway through the employee's normal work day.

5. The employer shall file the work schedule with the Director at least seven days before it becomes effective.

6. The employer shall post the work schedule at least seven days before it becomes effective, and shall keep it posted while the work schedule is in effect. The work schedule shall be posted in a conspicuous place or places in the workplace where it is most likely to come to the attention of the employees to whom it relates.

9. Work schedule requirements, two shifts — The employer's work schedule may provide for two shifts subject to the following:

1. The employer shall file the work schedule with the Director at least 15 days before it becomes effective instead of as paragraph 5 of section 8 requires.

2. An employee shall be scheduled to work only the earlier shift or the later shift and shall not be required to change shifts unless the employee or the employee's agent agrees.

3. An employee who works on the later shift shall be paid at least 5 per cent more than the employee would be paid if the employee worked the earlier shift.

4. If immediately before the work schedule becomes effective the employer only had one shift,

   i. the work schedule shall not result in an employee who was working in that single shift working less than a normal work day or working fewer normal work days, and

   ii. an employee who was employed immediately before the work schedule became effective shall not be scheduled to work the later shift unless the employee or the employee's bargaining agent agrees.

10. Normal work day if no work schedule — (1) If section 7 does not apply, the normal work day for an employee begins at 8:00 a.m. on each of Monday to Friday, with an unpaid half-hour eating period midway through the working day and two paid 10-minute breaks, one before and one after the eating period.

(2) This section does not apply with respect to employees who are homeworkers.

11. Special rate work — (1) An employer shall not require or allow an employee who is not a homeworker to perform work,

(a) in excess of 8 hours, including paid breaks but not including eating periods, on any of Monday to Friday; or

(b) on Saturday or Sunday.

(2) An employer shall not require or allow an employee who is a homeworker to perform work in excess of 40 hours in a week, determined on the basis of the period from midnight on Saturday to midnight on the following Saturday.

(3) Subsections (1) and (2) apply instead of subsection 17(1) of the Act.

(4) Subsection 17(2) of the Act applies, but shall be read as if the words "in excess of an amount set out in subsection (1)" were struck out and "in excess of an amount set out in subsection 11(1) or (2) of Ontario Regulation 291/01 (*Terms and Conditions of Employment in Defined Industries*)" substituted.

12. Breaks relating to special rate work after normal work day — (1) Despite section 20 of the Act, before an employee performs more than two hours of special rate work after the end of a normal work day, the employer shall give the employee a paid 15minute break.

(2) The break under subsection (1) shall be paid at the special rate determined under section 14.

(3) If an employee performs more than five hours of special rate work on a Saturday or Sunday, the employer shall permit the employee a half-hour eating period so that the employee does not work more than five consecutive hours without an eating period.

(4) This section does not apply with respect to employees who are homeworkers.

13. Pay for special rate work — Despite Part VIII of the Act, the employer shall pay an employee the special rate determined under section 14 for all special rate work.

14. Special rate — **(1)** The special rate is an hourly rate for all employees, even for those employees who are not normally paid on an hourly basis.

(2) The special rate is one and one-half times the following:

1. For an employee who is not paid on a piece-work basis, the hourly average of the wages paid to him or her during the most recent pay period in which the employee worked normal work days before the pay period in which he or she performed special rate work.

2. For an employee who is paid on a piece-work basis, the hourly average of the wages paid to him or her,

   i. during the months from July to December in the previous year, in the case of special rate work performed during the months from January to June, and

   ii. during the months from January to June in the same year, in the case of special rate work performed during the months from July to December.

(3) The special rate for an employee who is a homeworker shall be determined under paragraph 2 of subsection (2) whether or not the employee is paid on a piece-work basis.

(4) The following shall not be considered in determining an employee's special rate under subsection (1):

1. Pay at the special rate.

2. Vacation pay and year-end vacation payments.

3. Industry holiday pay under subsection 18(3).

4. Termination pay and severance pay.

5. Entitlements under a provision of the employment contract that, under subsection 5(2) of the Act, prevails over Part VIII, X, XI or XV of the Act.

15. Vacation — (1) Despite Part XI of the Act, the employer shall give a vacation of two weeks to an employee upon the completion of each 12-month period of employment, whether or not the employment was active employment.

(2) The employer shall determine the period when an employee may take the vacation to which he or she is entitled under subsection (1), which may be a two-week period or two periods of one week each, but in any case the employee shall be given the vacation not later than 10 months after the end of the 12-month period for which it is given.

(3) A week of vacation is calculated on the basis of the period from midnight on Saturday to midnight on the following Saturday.

16. Vacation pay — (1) Despite Part XI of the Act, the employer shall pay an employee vacation pay for the employee's vacation.

(2) An employee's vacation pay shall be equal to 4 per cent of all wages, not including vacation pay or any year-end vacation payment, earned by the employee during the period for which the vacation is given.

17. Year-end vacation payment — (1) Despite Part XI of the Act, the employer shall pay an employee, in addition to vacation pay under section 16, a year-end vacation payment in accordance with this section.

(2) An employee who has been employed by an employer for at least three continuous months is entitled to a year-end vacation payment equal to 2 per cent of all wages, excluding vacation pay, earned during the year to which the year-end vacation payment applies.

(3) For the purpose of this section, the year to which a year-end vacation payment applies shall be,

(a) the 12-month period established for the purpose by the practice of the employer; or

(b) if the employer has not established such a year, the 12-month period beginning on December 1 in a year and ending on November 30 in the following year.

(4) Subject to subsection (5), the employer shall pay the year-end vacation payment no later than six weeks after the end of the year to which it applies.

(5) If the employment of the employee is terminated in a year, the employer shall pay the year-end vacation payment for that year no later than seven days after the termination.

18. Industry holiday pay — (1) Despite Part X of the Act, the employer shall pay an employee for each industry holiday, unless,

(a) the employee has been employed by the employer for less than three months; or

(b) the employee was scheduled to work on the first normal work day either before or after the industry holiday and the employee failed to work that day as scheduled.

(2) The amount the employer shall pay an employee for an industry holiday is,

(a) if the employee is not paid on a piece-work basis, the average of the wages paid for the days the employee works during the two-month period before the industry holiday; and

(b) if the employee is paid on a piece-work basis, the hourly average of the wages paid,

(i) for the days the employee works during the months from July to December in the previous year, in the case of an industry holiday that falls in the months from January to June, and

(ii) for the days the employee works during the months from January to June in the same year, in the case of an industry holiday that falls in the months from July to December.

(3) The industry holiday pay for an employee who is a homeworker shall be determined under clause (2)(b) whether or not the employee is paid on a piece-work basis.

(4) The following shall not be considered in determining the amount of an employee's industry holiday pay:

1. Pay at the special rate.

2. Vacation pay and year-end vacation payments.

3. Industry holiday pay under subsection (3).

4. Termination pay and severance pay.

5. Entitlements under a provision of the employment contract that, under subsection 5(2) of the Act, prevails over Part VIII, X, XI or XV of the Act.

19. Special rules for Victoria Day and Canada Day — (1) Despite Part X of the Act and section 5, an employer may require an employee to work a normal work day on Victoria Day or Canada Day if the employee or the employee's agent agrees and the holiday does not fall on a Saturday or Sunday.

(2) The normal work day that the employer may require an employee to work under subsection (1) is the normal work day that would have applied if the day were not Victoria Day or Canada Day.

(3) Subject to subsection (4), if an employee works a normal work day on Victoria Day or Canada Day, the following apply:

1. The employer shall pay the employee industry holiday pay under section 18 if the employee is entitled to industry holiday pay.

2. The employer shall pay the employee the special rate determined under section 14 for the work on the holiday.

(4) If an employee works a normal work day on Victoria Day or Canada Day, the employer may, if the employee or the employee's agent agrees, substitute a normal work day for the industry holiday and the following apply:

1. The industry holiday shall be deemed to be a normal work day.

2. The substituted normal work day shall be deemed to be the industry holiday.

3. The substituted normal work day shall be before the employee's next paid vacation day.

(5) If an employee is required to work a normal work day on Victoria Day or Canada Day but fails, without reasonable cause, to report for work, the employee is not entitled to industry holiday pay under section 18.

20. Industry review committee — (1) The Minister may establish a committee to advise the Minister on matters related to employment standards within the Ontario garment manufacturing industry.

(2) The committee shall be composed of a chair, and as many members equal in number representative of employers and employees respectively as the Minister considers proper, all of whom shall be appointed by the Minister.

(3) The members of the committee shall be appointed for a term not exceeding one year and are eligible for reappointment.

(4) The Minister may fill a vacancy in the membership of the committee by appointing a person to fill the unexpired term.

21. Revocation — The following are revoked:

1. Regulation 658 of the Revised Regulations of Ontario, 1990.

2. Regulation 659 of the Revised Regulations of Ontario, 1990 and Ontario Regulation 282/99.

3. Regulation 660 of the Revised Regulations of Ontario, 1990 and Ontario Regulation 283/99.

22. Commencement — This Regulation comes into force on the day Part XXVII and subsection 144(5) of the *Employment Standards Act, 2000* come into force.

ONT. REG. 491/06 — TERMS AND CONDITIONS OF EMPLOYMENT IN DEFINED INDUSTRIES — AMBULANCE SERVICES

made under the *Employment Standards Act, 2000*

O. Reg. 491/06

1. Definitions — In this Regulation,

"defined industry" means the industry of providing land ambulance services or air ambulance services, as defined in the *Ambulance Act*;

"emergency medical attendant" and **"paramedic"** have the same meanings as in the *Ambulance Act*.

2. Scope — This Regulation is restricted in its application to,

(a) employees in the defined industry who work as emergency medical attendants and are represented by a bargaining agent under the *Labour Relations Act, 1995*;

(b) employees in the defined industry who work as paramedics and are represented by a bargaining agent under the *Labour Relations Act, 1995*; and

(c) employers of employees described in clauses (a) and (b).

3. Terms and conditions of employment — This Regulation sets out terms and conditions of employment that apply to employees and employers described in section 2.

4. Hours free from work — (1) If an employer and the bargaining agent that represents an employee agree, subsection (2) applies to that employer and employee instead of subsection 18(1) of the Act.

(2) An employer shall give an employee a period of at least eight consecutive hours free from performing work in each day.

5. Eating periods — (1) If an employer and the bargaining agent that represents an employee agree to a term that addresses the employee's entitlement to an eating period as described in subsection (2), that term applies to that employer and employee instead of section 20 of the Act.

(2) For the purpose of subsection (1), an employer and bargaining agent may agree to any of the following terms:

1. A term that entitles an employee to one or more eating periods that are or may be shorter than or at intervals that are or may be longer than are required by section 20 of the Act, including a term that does not specify the intervals.

2. A term that entitles an employee to fewer eating periods than are required by section 20 of the Act.

3. A term that entitles an employee to eating periods or to compensation or time free from performing work if the employee does not receive an eating period.

4. A term that provides that an employee is not entitled to eating periods, but provides that the employer shall make efforts to enable the employee to receive eating periods, whether or not the term entitles the employee to compensation or time free from performing work if the employee does not receive an eating period.

5. A term that provides that an employee is not entitled to eating periods.

6. A term that entitles an employee to eating periods or provides that an employee may be given an eating period, but provides that any eating period may be interrupted or missed.

7. A term that combines elements of two or more terms described in paragraphs 1 to 6.

Ont. Reg. 502/06 — Terms and Conditions of Employment in Defined Industries — Automobile Manufacturing, Automobile Parts Manufacturing, Automobile Parts Warehousing and Automobile Marshalling

made under the *Employment Standards Act, 2000*

O. Reg. 502/06, as am. O. Reg. 370/16, ss. 1, 2 (Fr.).

1. Definitions — (1) In this Regulation,

"automobile" includes a van or truck with a gross vehicle weight rating of 14,000 pounds (6,350 kilograms) or less; "automobile manufacturing" means assembling automobiles;

"automobile marshalling" means receiving assembled automobiles from employers in the automobile manufacturing industry, storing the automobiles before delivery to purchasers or persons who sell to purchasers, organizing them for delivery and arranging for delivery;

"automobile parts manufacturing" means,

(a) producing automobile parts that are supplied directly to employers in the automobile manufacturing industry or in the automobile parts warehousing industry, and

(b) producing elements of automobile parts where those elements are supplied directly to employers who produce automobile parts as described in clause (a);

"automobile parts warehousing" means receiving automobile parts from employers in the automobile parts manufacturing industry, storing the parts before delivery to employers in the automobile manufacturing industry, organizing them for delivery, and delivering them or arranging for delivery;

"defined industries" means the automobile manufacturing industry, the automobile parts manufacturing industry, the automobile parts warehousing industry and the automobile marshalling industry;

443

"gross vehicle weight rating" means the value specified by the vehicle manufacturer as the loaded weight of a single vehicle.

(2) For the purposes of this Regulation,

(a) an employee of an employer who carries on any activity described in the definition of **"automobile marshalling"** in subsection (1) is employed in the automobile marshalling industry even if other activities constitute the majority of the employer's activities;

(b) an employee of an employer who produces any automobile parts or elements of automobile parts that are supplied as described in clauses (a) and (b) of the definition of "automobile parts manufacturing" in subsection (1) is employed in the automobile parts manufacturing industry even if the production of other things constitutes the majority of the employer's production; and

(c) an employee of an employer who carries on any activity described in the definition of "automobile parts warehousing" in subsection (1) is employed in the automobile parts warehousing industry even if other activities constitute the majority of the employer's activities.

2. Scope — This Regulation is restricted in its application to,

(a) employees employed in the defined industries,

(i) who are directly involved in any of the activities mentioned in the definition of the respective defined industry, or

(ii) whose attendance at the workplace during any of the activities mentioned in the definition of the respective defined industry is essential to that activity; and

(b) employers of the employees described in subclauses (a)(i) and (ii).

3. Hours free from work — **(1)** If an employer and an employee agree, subsections (2) and (3) apply instead of subsection 18(1) of the Act.

(2) The employer shall give the employee a period of at least 11 consecutive hours free from performing work in each day, subject to subsection (3).

(3) On one day in each work week, the period that is free from performing work may be shorter than 11 consecutive hours but shall be at least eight consecutive hours.

4. Personal emergency leave — (1) This section modifies the application of section 50 of the Act to an employee whose employer regularly employs 50 or more employees.

(2) An employee is entitled to a leave of absence without pay of a total of seven days in each calendar year because of any of the following:

1. A personal illness, injury or medical emergency.

2. The illness, injury or medical emergency of an individual described in subsection (4).

3. An urgent matter that concerns an individual described in subsection (4).

(3) An employee is entitled to a leave of absence without pay of up to three days because of the death of an individual described in subsection (4).

(4) Paragraphs 2 and 3 of subsection (2) and subsection (3) apply with respect to the following individuals:

1. The employee's spouse.

2. A parent, step-parent or foster parent of the employee or the employee's spouse.

3. A child, step-child or foster child of the employee or the employee's spouse.

4. A grandparent, step-grandparent, grandchild or step-grandchild of the employee or of the employee's spouse.

5. The spouse of a child of the employee.

6. The employee's brother or sister.

7. A relative of the employee who is dependent on the employee for care or assistance.

(5) An employee who wishes to take leave under this section shall advise his or her employer that he or she will be doing so.

(6) If the employee must begin the leave before advising the employer, the employee shall advise the employer of the leave as soon as possible after beginning it.

(7) If an employee takes any part of a day as leave under this section, the employer may deem the employee to have taken one day's leave on that day.

(8) An employer may require an employee who takes leave under this section to provide evidence reasonable in the circumstances that the employee is entitled to the leave.

O. Reg. 370/16, s. 1

ONT. REG. 160/05 — TERMS AND CONDITIONS OF EMPLOYMENT IN DEFINED INDUSTRIES — LIVE PERFORMANCES, TRADE SHOWS AND CONVENTIONS

made under the *Employment Standards Act, 2000*

O. Reg. 160/05, as am. O. Reg. 529/05 (Fr.).

1. Definitions — In this Regulation,

"defined industry" means the industry of producing,

(a) live performances of theatre, dance, comedy, musical productions, concerts and opera, and

(b) trade shows and conventions;

"technical and production support" includes stage and set construction, hair cutting and styling, preparation and fitting of wigs and costumes, preparation and application of make-up, preparation and operation of lighting, sound and stage equipment and props, and stage management.

2. Scope — This Regulation is restricted in its application to,

(a) employees in the defined industry who provide technical and production support; and

(b) employers of the employees described in clause (a).

3. Terms and conditions of employment — This Regulation sets out terms and conditions of employment that apply to employees and employers described in section 2.

4. Hours free from work — (1) If the employer and the employee agree, subsection (2) applies instead of subsection 18(1) of the Act.

(2) An employer shall give an employee a period of at least eight consecutive hours free from performing work in each day.

ONT. REG. 159/05 — TERMS AND CONDITIONS OF EMPLOYMENT IN DEFINED INDUSTRIES — MINERAL EXPLORATION AND MINING

made under the *Employment Standards Act, 2000*

O. Reg. 159/05, as am. O. Reg. 523/05 (Fr.).

1. Definitions — In this Regulation,

"defined industries" means the mineral exploration industry and the mining industry;

"mineral exploration" means prospecting, staking or exploration for minerals and any related activities, and includes,

(a) advanced exploration such as the excavation of an exploratory shaft, adit or decline, the extraction of minerals for the purpose of proving a mineral deposit, and the installation of a mill for test purposes, and

(b) site rehabilitation;

"mining" means the extraction, concentration and smelting of economic minerals from a mineral deposit for commercial purposes, and **"mine"** has a corresponding meaning.

2. Scope — (1) This Regulation is restricted in its application to,

(a) employees in the mineral exploration industry who work at sites of mineral exploration, subject to subsection (2);

(b) employees in the mining industry who,

(i) work at mines, and

(ii) during periods of consecutive days of work, do not live at their principal residences but instead live in bunkhouses, hotels or motels, or other temporary accommodation; and

(c) employers of the employees described in clauses (a) and (b).

(2) Clause (1)(a) does not apply to an employee whose employer's principal business is mining.

3. Terms and conditions of employment — This Regulation sets out terms and conditions of employment that apply to employees and employers described in section 2.

4. Days free from work — **(1)** If the employer and the employee agree, subsections (2) and (3) apply instead of subsection 18(4) of the Act.

(2) The employer shall not require or permit the employee to perform work on more than 28 consecutive days.

(3) The employer shall give the employee days free from work in accordance with the following:

1. The number of days free from work shall be equal to the number of consecutive days on which the employee worked before the period of days free from work, divided by three.

2. Despite paragraph 1, if dividing by three under that paragraph produces a mixed number, the number of days free from work shall be the next higher whole number.

3. If the employee is entitled to more than one day free from work, those days shall be consecutive, and all of them shall be given before the employee returns to work.

ONT. REG. 390/05 — TERMS AND CONDITIONS OF EMPLOYMENT IN DEFINED INDUSTRIES — PUBLIC TRANSIT SERVICES

made under the *Employment Standards Act, 2000*

O. Reg. 390/05, as am. O. Reg. 528/05 (Fr.).

1. Definition — In this Regulation,

"defined industry" means the industry of providing public transit services;

"public transit service" means any service for which a fare is charged for transporting the public by vehicles operated by or on behalf of a municipality or a local board, or under an agreement with a municipality or a local board;

"vehicle" includes transportation facilities for the physically disabled, but does not include,

(a) vehicles and marine vessels used for sightseeing tours,

(b) buses used to transport pupils, including buses owned and operated by, or operated under a contract with, a school board, private school or charitable organization,

(c) buses owned and operated by a corporation or organization solely for its own purposes without compensation for transportation,

(d) taxicabs,

(e) railway systems of railway companies incorporated under federal or provincial statutes,

(f) ferries,

(g) aviation systems, or

(h) ambulances.

2. Scope — This Regulation is restricted in its application to,

(a) employees in the defined industry who operate public transit vehicles or who work as collectors; and

(b) employers of the employees described in clause (a).

3. Terms and conditions of employment — This Regulation sets out terms and conditions of employment that apply to employees and employers described in section 2.

4. Hours free from work — **(1)** If the employer and employee agree, subsection (2) applies instead of subsection 18(1) of the Act.

(2) An employer shall give an employee a period of at least eight consecutive hours free from performing work in each day.

5. Eating periods — Section 20 of the Act does not apply to an employee who,

(a) is working a straight shift, and has chosen to work that shift;

(b) is working a split shift for which no meal break that complies with section 20 of the Act is provided, and has chosen to work that shift; or

(c) is working a straight shift, or a split shift for which no meal break that complies with section 20 of the Act is provided, and has chosen to work whatever shift the employer assigns.

ONT. REG. 398/09 — TERMS AND CONDITIONS OF EMPLOYMENT IN DEFINED INDUSTRIES — TEMPORARY HELP AGENCY INDUSTRY

made under the *Employment Standards Act, 2000*

O. Reg. 398/09

1. Definition — In this Regulation,

"defined industry" means the temporary help agency industry.

2. Scope — This Regulation is restricted in its application to temporary help agencies and their assignment employees.

3. Transitional terms and conditions of employment — This Regulation sets out transitional terms and conditions of employment that apply to employers and employees described in section 2 following the coming into force of the *Employment Standards Amendment Act (Temporary Help Agencies), 2009.*

4. Determination of temporary lay-off — For the purposes of subsection 56(2) of the Act, the following rules apply:

1. Only a period of 20 consecutive weeks or 52 consecutive weeks, as the case may be, that begins after November 5, 2009 shall be taken into account.

2. In the case of a lay-off that begins on or before November 5, 2009, only the part of the lay-off, if any, that occurs after November 5, 2009, shall be taken into account.

5. Deemed termination date — For the purposes of subsection 56(5) of the Act, if part of a lay-off is taken into account under paragraph 2 of section 4, the employment is deemed to be terminated on November 6, 2009.

6. Mass termination provisions, notice — For the purposes of the provisions of the Act that require an employer to provide notice otherwise than in accordance with section 57 of the Act if the employment of 50 or more employees is terminated in the same four-week period, only four-week periods that end before November 6, 2009 or begin after November 5, 2009 shall be taken into account.

7. Severance — **(1)** For the purposes of clause 63(1)(c) of the Act, the following rules apply:

1. Only a period of 52 consecutive weeks that begins after November 5, 2009 shall be taken into account.

2. In the case of a lay-off that begins on or before November 5, 2009, only the part of the lay-off, if any, that occurs after November 5, 2009, shall be taken into account.

(2) For the purposes of clause 63(1)(d) of the Act, only a lay-off of an employee that begins after November 5, 2009 because of a permanent discontinuance of all of a temporary help agency's business at an establishment of the agency after that date results in a severance of the employee's employment.

(3) For the purposes of clause 63(1)(e) of the Act, only a notice of termination given after November 5, 2009 shall be taken into account.

8. Length of employment — (1) Where the entitlement of an assignment employee under a provision of Part XV of the Act is dependent on or varies with how long he or she has been employed by a temporary help agency, nothing in this Regulation shall be construed to exclude time spent in the employ of the agency before November 6, 2009.

(2) Subsection (1) applies in respect of any provision of Part XV of the Act or the regulations that makes reference to length of employment, however expressed, and, without restricting the generality of the foregoing, applies in respect of,

(a) a reference to a period of employment;

(b) a reference to continuous employment;

(c) a reference to employment whether or not continuous and whether or not active; and

(d) a reference to a number of years or months of employment.

9. Commencement — This Regulation comes into force on the day it is filed.

INDEX

The commentary entries in the index are referenced to page numbers. The legislation entries in the index are referenced to the section numbers of the *Employment Standards Act, 2000* preceded by the acronym ESA.

For example, in the entry:

Organ donor leave, date on which donor leave beginning, 72; ESA 49.2(8)

72 refers to page 72 of the commentary

ESA 49.2(8) refers to section 49.2(8) of the *Employment Standards Act, 2000*

Where Ontario regulations made under the *Employment Standards Act, 2000* are reproduced and indexed, the number and title of the regulation is followed by the page number in the Quick Reference.

A

and Automobile Marshalling
, 443

B

Bill 148, *Fair Workplaces, Better Jobs Act*
- followed from Final Report of the Changing Workplaces Review, 158
- enforcement provisions amended, 159
- • monetary penalties, warrants, liens, 159
- significant changes, 158
- • increased vacation entitlements, 159
- • minimum wage increases, 159
- • personal emergency leave, 159
- • temporary help agencies changes, 159

Benefit plans
- differentiation permissible for certain exceptions, 9
- differentiation prohibited based on age, gender or marital status, 22; ESA 44
- Reg. 286/01 — Benefit Plans, 383

Building services providers
- "building services" defined, 121-122; ESA 1(1)

- "building services provider" defined, 122; ESA 1(1)
- employment not deemed to be terminated or severed where employment continued, 122; ESA 10(2)
- information to be furnished to new provider of building services, 124; ESA 77
- • specific information respecting each employee, 124
- new building services provider, 122
- • compliance with termination and severance provisions, 122; ESA 75(2)
- • • compliance not required where employee not performed duties, 123
- • • compliance not required where employee refuses offer, 123
- • • compliance not required where employee retained, 123
- • • compliance required where employment not continued, 123
- • • "prescribed" employees not entitled to termination or severance pay, 123

Q

"Quirk" Principle, 64, *See also* Emergency leave, personal

R

Record keeping
- Bill 148 changes effective January 2018 and January 2019, 17
- retention of information pertaining to employees for three years, 18-19; ESA 15(5)
- • information to be retained, 16
- • records and documents readily available for inspection, 19
- salaried employees, hours of work information not required for, 18
- • record of excess hours to be kept, 18; ESA 15(8)
- student employees, 17
- third party to retain documents relating to leaves of absence, 19; ESA 15(7)
- types of information to be recorded, 17-18; ESA 15(1)
- vacation records, 17, 94-96; ESA 15.1
- • information to be recorded, 94-95
- • vacation pay, 17

- • vacation time, 94-95
- • when to be prepared, 95-96

Reprisals
- enforcement by employment standards officer, 157
- • authority of employment standards officer if employee subject of reprisal, 157
- • compensation order, 157
- • no maximum recovery amount, 157
- • • payment of amount to Director with administration fee, 157
- four-step test to determine, 154-155
- generally, 153
- onus on employer to prove actions not reprisal, 154; ESA 74(2)
- • exception to reverse onus where employer applying for review, 154
- penalties for failure to comply with court order, additional, 158
- prohibition against intimidating, dismissing or penalizing employee, 153; ESA 74(1)
- prohibition against penalizing employee due to court

Sunday as condition of employment, 29

• • • • where adversely affecting employees of certain religious backgrounds, 29

Review application

• application form, 150

• • facts and reasons for application to be set out, 150

• • reasons why extension of time warranted, 151

• application to OLRB, 150-141; ESA 116

• • quasi-judicial administrative tribunal, 150

• application within 30 days after order or letter served, 150; ESA 116(4)

• • extension of time for applying, 150; ESA 116(5)

• compensation order, where, 150

• • payment of amount ordered to Director first, 150

• decision being final and binding on parties, 152; ESA 119(13)

• hearing before OLRB for purposes of review, 151; ESA 116(6)

• • regional center closest to workplace, 151

• judicial review of OLRB's decision, 152; ESA 119(14)

• labour relations officer, role of, 151

• • mediation process, 151

• mediation of settlement prior to hearing, 151

• • distribution of monies held in trust upon settlement being reached, 151

• order to pay wages, where, 150

• parties to, ESA 116(7)

• powers of OLRB, 150; ESA 119

• • notice of contravention rescinded, affirmed or amended, 151

• • substituting its own decision for that of officer, 151-152

• review of certain decisions of employment standards officers, 150

• • compensation order, 150

• • compliance order, 150

• • notice of contravention, 150

• • order to pay wages, 150

• • refusal to make an order, 150

• • reinstatement order, 150

S

Sale of business

- continuity of employment, 23
- employee deemed not to have employment terminated, 23; ESA 9
- length of employment with seller included in calculating vacation entitlement, 23
- transfer of vacation pay liability, 24

Salesperson Commissioned

- defined, 44-45
- exempt from hours of work, overtime, public holidays, vacation provisions, 44-45
- route salesperson not exempt, 45

"Sea Change" Principle, 65, *See also* Emergency leave

Settlements

- administrative surcharge pro rated where settlement concerning order to pay wages, 149; ESA 112(6)
- • example of pro rating, 149
- • incentive to settle, 149
- notification to employment standards officer, 148; ESA 112
- • disclosure of all terms of settlement, 148

- • joint statement of parties, 148
- settlement agreement respecting contravention, 149
- • complaint deemed withdrawn, 149
- • order respecting contravention void, 149
- • restrictions on settlements, 149; ESA 112(7)
- • • future contraventions, not permitting, 149
- • • settlement void where OLRB finding fraud or coercion, 149; ESA 112(8)

Severance of employment *See also* Termination of employment

- defined, ESA 63(1)
- payments on severance, 108-109
- recall rights, ESA 67
- severance occurring in certain circumstances, 108-109
- severance pay, 108-118
- • calculation, 112-113; ESA 65
- • • "actuarially unreduced pension benefits" standards, 113
- • • employees with regular work week, 112